Corporate Social Responsibility in Contemporary China

CORPORATIONS, GLOBALISATION AND THE LAW

Series Editor: Janet Dine, *Director, Centre for Commercial Law Studies, Queen Mary, University of London, UK*

This uniquely positioned monograph series aims to draw together high quality research work from established and younger scholars on what is an intriguing and under-researched area of the law. The books will offer insights into a variety of legal issues that concern corporations operating on the global stage, including interaction with the World Trade Organization (WTO), international financial institutions and nation states, in both developing and developed countries. While the underlying foundation of the series will be that of company law, broadly-defined, authors are encouraged to take an approach that draws on the work of other social sciences, such as politics, economics and development studies and to offer an international or comparative perspective where appropriate. Specific topics to be considered will include corporate governance, corporate responsibility, taxation and criminal liability, amongst others. The series will undoubtedly offer an important contribution to legal thinking and to the wider globalisation debate.

Titles in the series include:

Corporate Social Responsibility in Contemporary China

Jingchen Zhao

Senior Lecturer in Corporate and Commercial Law, University of Sussex, UK

CORPORATIONS, GLOBALISATION AND THE LAW

Edward Elgar

Cheltenham, UK • Northampton, MA, USA

Published by
Edward Elgar Publishing Limited
The Lypiatts
15 Lansdown Road
Cheltenham
Glos GL50 2JA
UK

Edward Elgar Publishing, Inc.
William Pratt House
9 Dewey Court
Northampton
Massachusetts 01060
USA

A catalogue record for this book
is available from the British Library

Library of Congress Control Number: 2013951843

This book is available electronically in the ElgarOnline.com Law Subject Collection, E-ISBN 978 1 78100 558 3

ISBN 978 1 78100 557 6

Typeset by Columns Design XML Ltd, Reading
Printed and bound in Great Britain by T.J. International Ltd, Padstow

Contents

Acknowledgements

I wish to thank a number of people and organizations. My grateful thanks to Sussex Law School and Salford Law School for awarding me research grants and scholarships that enabled me to go to conferences while finishing this book. Special thanks are due to Prof. Andrew Keay and Prof. David Milman for their continuing support, stimulating suggestions and encouragement in helping me to write this book. Prof. Heather Keating and Prof. Craig Barker from Sussex Law School and Prof. Mark James from Salford Law School (now at Northumbria School of Law) have also provided immense support and inspiration, for which I am hugely indebted.

I am also grateful to several publishers for allowing me to draw on material from my previously published articles. With the permission of the named publishers, I used material from the following articles: 'The Harmonious Society, Corporate Social Responsibility and Legal Responses to Ethical Norms in Chinese Company Law' (2012) 12 *Journal of Corporate Law Studies* 163 (Hart Publishing); 'Promoting Stakeholders' Interests in the Unique Chinese Corporate Governance Model: More Socially Responsible Corporations?' (2010) *International Company and Commercial Law Review* 373 (Sweet & Maxwell); 'The Regulation and Steering of Corporate Social Responsibility in China: Stories after the Enforcement of Chinese Company Law 2006' (2011) 22 *International Company and Commercial Law Review* 400 (Sweet & Maxwell).

I would also like to express my sincere gratitude to my friends and colleagues Shuangge Wen, Wangwei Lin, Verona Ni Dhrisceoil, John Tribe, Phoebe Li, Zhong Zhang, Carlo Petrucci, Andrea Gilluley, Sue Biell, Debra Morris, Donald Loftus, Qingsong Mou and Mitchell O'Grady, and to my proofreader Louise Maskill for her excellent and efficient work. Special thanks are also due to my publisher, and to all the reviewers for their helpful comments and suggestions.

Finally, as always, I am extremely thankful to my parents Guoqing Li and Gang Zhao and my brother Rongchen Zhao for their encouragement, understanding and support.

Abbreviations

ACCA	Association of Chartered Certified Accountants
CCL	Chinese Company Law
CLCL	Chinese Labour Contract Law
CLL	Chinese Labour Law
CLRSG	Company Law Review Steering Group (UK)
CPA	certified public accountant
CSR	corporate social responsibility
CSRC	Chinese Securities Regulatory Commission
ESG	environmental, social and corporate governance
ESOP	employee shareholder ownership plan
ESVP	enlightened shareholder value principle
GRI	Global Reporting Initiative
NGO	non-governmental organization
OFR	operating and financial review
SASAC	State-owned Assets Supervision and Administration Commission
SEAAR	social and ethical accounting, auditing and reporting
SEC	Securities and Exchange Commission (US)
SEPA	State Environmental Protective Administration
SOE	state-owned enterprise

Table of legislation

1. Introduction

My intention in writing this book is to critically analyse contemporary notions of corporate social responsibility (CSR) in China. A very direct question that will be applicable to the book is whether CSR can be an effective solution to irresponsible corporate behaviours and problems of human rights, climate change, food safety and environmental pollution in China, all issues in which corporations are closely involved. The book devotes itself to a critical reading of the existing scholarship on CSR in China, and uses a legal approach to discuss this contemporary topic.

Over the last three decades China has achieved unprecedented economic growth as 'a champion of a state-led growth model'.[1] China represents a novel environment for research, practice and legislation for CSR by virtue of the distinctive roles of its government and regulation, and the integration of the Chinese economy into the globalized map.[2] As such, *Corporate Social Responsibility in Contemporary China* considers the treatment of CSR in the academic literature and the inherent scepticism underpinning the reception of analyses of CSR within a legal framework. As the Chinese economy continues its rapid growth and market reform, economic aggression and corporate voracity cannot ride roughshod over the call for sustainable transition or outstrip the need to maintain the health, welfare and safety of both people and planet.[3] However, China's sustainability crisis, including environmental and social problems, is seriously hindering the movement of the Chinese economy towards a stronger and more respectable position. In terms of environmental problems, a pressing issue will be water scarcity, since 20 per cent of the world's population in China only has access to 8 per cent

---

[1]   B. van Rooij, 'The People's Regulation: Citizens and Implementation of Law in China' (2012) 25 *Columbia Journal of Asian Law* 116 at 118.
[2]   P.K. Ip, 'The Challenge of Developing a Business Ethics in China' (2008) 88 *Journal of Business Ethics* 211.
[3]   J. Kong, 'What Virtues and Formalities Can Do for Corporate Social Responsibility and the Rule of Law in China' (2012) 14 *European Journal of Law Reform* 414 at 417.

of the world's fresh water supply.[4] China's air pollution problems are also significant, with China ranked 128th out of 133 countries in 2006 with a score of 22.3 in terms of overall air quality, the worst score among all the Asia-Pacific nations.[5] Based on more recent data China was ranked 116th out of 132 countries in the Environmental Performance Index in 2012.[6] The egregious social problems also drain China's economy and threaten the political stability and confidence of China's ruling party. A controversial issue since 2012 has been the question of whether China is able to afford high speed trains at the cost of passenger safety. The rapid economic rise has brought risks to environmental food safety, construction safety, and occupational and property safety. This growth has also led to challenges that must be addressed 'to avoid weakening the nation's ability to sustain economic growth and development progress in decades to come'.[7] The role played by corporations in facing these challenges is increasingly recognised, and they are encouraged or even required to answer the call to introduce the practice of CSR.

The role of corporations in society is high on the agenda for the Chinese government. Hardly a day goes by without media reports on corporate scandals and misbehaviour towards stakeholders, or, more positively, on corporate contributions and philanthropic actions from business for the benefit of wider society in China. Monopolies, disordered markets, the gap in wealth, fake commodities, environmental pollution and the erosion of consumers' and workers' rights seem like globalised problems that arise while businesses pursue profits. In comparison with countries with better enforcement of laws that regulate CSR, such as labour protection and environmental responsibilities, the relatively low level of economic development and imperfect legal regimes

---

[4]   For more discussions on this issue, see T. Riley and H. Cai, 'Unmasking Chinese Business Enterprises: Using Information Disclosure Law to Enhance Republic Participation in Corporate Environmental Decision Making' (2009) 33 *Harvard Environmental Law Review* 177.

[5]   See Yale Centre for Environmental Law and Policy and Centre for International Earth Science Information Network, *Pilot 2006 Environmental Performance Index* (2006) p. 51.

[6]   See Yale Centre for Environmental Law and Policy and Centre for International Earth Science Information Network, *EPI 2012: Environmental Performance Index and Pilot Trend Environmental Performance Index* (2012) p. 10.

[7]   S. Zadek, M. Forstater and K. Yu, *Corporate Responsibility and Sustainable Economic Development in China: Implications for Business* (US Chamber of Commerce, National Chamber Foundation and Asia Department, 2012) p. 4, available at www.uschamber.com/.

always lead to slow development of CSR systems in developing countries like China.[8] From a negative point of view, developing countries, especially the least developed nations, are badly affected by social problems such as employees' working standards, pollution and resource exhaustion, which may be a result of low tax revenues. Therefore, research on CSR in China seems essential for corporations and various corporate stakeholders, including Chinese people, who are simultaneously customers, part of local communities and government taxpayers, in order that they might understand, critically evaluate and attempt to promote socially responsible corporations with support from law.

The scope of CSR in China has moved rapidly beyond its roots, which were limited to compliance and philanthropy. It has developed towards a global concept with strategic concern for addressing issues such as project quality, employee management, governance and human rights, with the strong and purposeful evolution of regulatory elements for building better supply chains and attracting more international talent and investment. A positive aspect of the increasing awareness of CSR in China is that the government and government agencies at different levels have embraced CSR as an instrument to address environmental and social issues. This trend towards the official endorsement of CSR standards, public policy and legislative philosophy will be important in an economy that is still greatly influenced by the state. It will be valuable to consider the law and regulations surrounding CSR at various levels, pointing out gaps and disparities between domestic and international standards and between standards in China and those in developed markets. Therefore, CSR-related legislation will be discussed not only from the point of view of international principles and standards, but also with reference to law and regulations in the United Kingdom and Europe. Positively, Chinese political leaders introduced the Harmonious Society policy in order to reduce the conflict between the drive for profits and corporations' responsibility to environment and society. However, the effectiveness of this policy in affecting managers' decisions and their development agendas is still questionable. Furthermore, it is also uncertain how much impact it has had on the Chinese government, NGOs and consumer campaigners in terms of corporate decisions and their effects on social and environmental welfare.

---

[8] S. Shen and H. Cheng, 'Economic Globalisation and the Construction of China's Corporate Social Responsibility' (2009) 51 *International Journal of Law and Management* 134 at 135.

1.1 CORPORATE SOCIAL RESPONSIBILITY AND REGULATION OF CSR

The concept of CSR, once known as *'noblessse oblige'*, has experienced a vigorous resurgence since the 1950s.[9] The term took shape and gathered momentum during the 1950s and 1960s, developing out of a time when the sole corporate motive had been to ensure business success via profits.[10] Perhaps because of its wide-ranging coverage, there is no universally accepted definition of CSR. The term is a comparatively contemporary one, referring to sustainable development with respect to environmental and social issues. The topic has been widely discussed among academics from various disciplines, including philosophy, business management, law, politics, sociology and economics, as well as pragmatically by businessmen and politically by public representatives.[11] CSR functions as a built-in, self-regulating mechanism whereby businesses monitor and ensure their adherence to law, ethical standards and international norms. Social responsibility is the obligation of managers to choose and act in ways that benefit both the interests of the organisation and those of society as a whole.

In the modernized economy, adherents of the CSR movement recognize the tripartite relationship between government, corporations and society to achieve a combination of economic, social, environmentally friendly and philanthropic goals. The dynamic nature of CSR implies that it is sometimes necessary to redefine the boundaries of what is acceptable, feasible and profitable and relate these boundaries to corporate decisions and strategies.[12] Companies are required to become more powerful and stronger with respect to their command over resources, and equally more responsible and accountable for their decisions and actions in terms of societal outcomes. Despite the fact that CSR has been traditionally regarded as a voluntary responsibility of corporations, the emphasis on corporations' attention to CSR has not been entirely

---

[9]   H. Mintzerberg, 'The Case for Corporate Social Responsibility' (1983) 4 *Journal of Business Strategy* 3.

[10]   T. Levitt, 'The Danger of Social Responsibility' (1958) 36 *Harvard Business Review* 41.

[11]   A. Elbing, 'The Value Issue of Business: The Responsibility of the Businessman' (1970) 13 *Academy of Management Journal* 79.

[12]   U. Baxi, 'Market Fundamentalisms: Business Ethics at the Altar of Human Rights' (2005) 5 *Human Rights Law Review* 1.

voluntary in practice.[13] The debate surrounding CSR is closely related to the responsibilities of boards of directors, especially their duties towards various stakeholders, including employees, customers, suppliers, creditors, the environment, government and local communities. CSR is not an isolated term; it overlaps with some policies and is synonymous with others. Discussions about CSR lie both within and beyond law.[14] Therefore, together with debates on the voluntary and mandatory nature of CSR, another question which will be examined is the regulation of CSR. Should CSR be regulated through state regulation, soft law and codes of conduct or self-regulation? While a consensus has not been reached in the general debate, the question in China provokes intense controversy and interest.

1.2 INTRODUCTION TO THE CORE TERMS IN THE BOOK

It has been observed that corporate social performance is related to the political, labour, education and cultural systems of a country.[15] The arguments in this book proceed in a logical order. Discussions flow smoothly from Chinese history and culture to corporate governance models and political policies in China and their impact on CSR. The emphasis of the whole book will be on arguments surrounding legal aspects and responses to CSR issues in the unique Chinese environment. Within the flow of this logic, debates on corporate objectives within the classical model of stakeholder theory and the shareholder primacy norm will be discussed to enhance the discussions of CSR in China. First, however, a series of core terms and related concepts, such as CSR, the stakeholder approach, the shareholder primacy norm and the different

---

[13] M.E. Porter and M.R. Kramer, 'Strategy and Society: The Link between Competition Advantage and Corporate Social Responsibility' (2006) 84 *Harvard Business Review* 78.

[14] D. Matten and J. Moon, 'A Conceptual Framework for Understanding CSR' in A. Habisch, J. Jonker, M. Wegner and R. Chidpeter (eds), *Corporate Social Responsibility Across Europe* (Heidelberg: Springer, 2005) p. 335; see also D. Matten and J. Moon, '"Implicit" and "Explicit" CSR: A Conceptual Framework for a Comparative Understanding of Corporate Social Responsibility' (2008) 33 *Academy of Management Review* 404.

[15] I. Ioannou and G. Serafeim, 'What Drives Corporate Social Performance: The Role of Nation-Level Institutions' (2012) 43 *Journal of International Business Studies* 834.

forms of Chinese corporations, will be introduced and defined in the following section in order to ensure consistency within the book.

1.2.1 Stakeholder Approach

The use of the term 'stakeholder' to refer to the various interests which participate in a business has been commonly accepted since the publication of Freeman's book *Strategic Management*[16] in 1984. The concept of stakeholders was defined as 'those groups without whose support the organisation would cease to exist'.[17] They have legitimate interests in or claims on the operations of the firm.[18] These stakeholders are inter-related, and every company has their unique stakeholder groups. However, the groups which are most frequently seen as stakeholders are employees, customers, creditors, local communities, the environment, government and society or the public at large. The stakeholder theory was defined by Clarkson who stated that 'the firm is a system of stakeholders operating within the larger system of the host society that provides the necessary legal and market infrastructure for the firm's activities. The purpose of the firm is to create wealth or value for its stakeholders by converting their stake into goods and services'.[19]

Contemporary stakeholder approach arguments have always been par-alleled by the emergence of the global CSR movement.[20] According to stakeholder theory, the directors are required to consider the interests of the company's stakeholders apart from the interests of the company

---

[16]   R.E. Freeman, *Strategic Management: A Stakeholder Approach* (Boston, MA: Pitman, 1984); for some examples demonstrating the acceptance of the term in major academic writings see A.F. Alkhafaji, *A Stakeholder Approach to Corporate Governance: Managing in a Dynamic Environment* (New York: Quorum Books, 1989); J.W. Anderson, *Corporate Social Responsibilities* (New York: Quorum Books, 1984); J.J. Brummer, *Corporate Responsibility and Legitimacy: An Interdisciplinary Analysis* (New York: Greenwood Press, 1991); S.N. Brenner and E.A. Molander, 'Is the Ethics of Business Changing'(1977) 58 *Harvard Business Review* 54.
[17]   R.E. Freeman, *Strategic Management: A Stakeholder Approach* (Boston, MA: Pitman, 1984) pp. 31–2.
[18]   A.B. Carroll, *Business and Society: Ethics and Stakeholder Management* (Cincinnati, OH: South-Western Publishing Co., 1989) p. 57.
[19]   M. Clarkson, *A Risk Based Model of Stakeholder Theory, Proceedings of the Second Toronto Conference on Stakeholder Theory* (Toronto: Centre for Corporate Social Performance and Ethics, University of Toronto, 1994).
[20]   C.A. Williams and J.M. Conley, 'An Emerging Third Way? The Erosion of the Anglo-American Shareholder Value Construct' (2005) 38 *Cornell International Law Journal* 493 at 494.

shareholders. The directors must not only manage the corporation for the betterment of the shareholders, but also in the interests of a multitude of stakeholders, clearly including the shareholders, who can affect or be affected by the actions of the company.[21] The theory is defined by the Company Law Review Steering Group (CLRSG) as the pluralist theory,[22] which views the corporation as a locus in relation to wider external stakeholders' interests besides shareholders' interests. The stakeholder theory is embraced in many continental European jurisdictions (most notably Germany) and Japan.[23]

Donaldson and Preston argued that stakeholder theory can be sub-divided into descriptive, instrumental and normative approaches.[24] The descriptive approach decides whether stakeholder interests should be taken into account, while the instrumental approach is concerned with the impact stakeholders may have in terms of corporate effectiveness. The normative approach is concerned with justifying whether corporations should take stakeholders' interests into account even in the absence of any obvious benefits to shareholders.

It is argued that a consideration of stakeholders' interests enables the creation of long-term favourable conditions for the company to be more competitive. It is useful to regard 'the company' as 'the company as a whole', a coherent body in which the various stakeholders are bound together through the business.[25] The long-term focus on creating value for various stakeholders will enable the directors to devote themselves to improving the long-term interests of the corporation, and does not exclude long-term value-enhancing strategies.[26] Taking social responsi-bilities into account in the development of corporate strategies is one of the most important and most direct impacts of adopting the stakeholder theory model. The concept of CSR implies that corporations should integrate social and environmental concerns in their operations and

---

[21]   R.E. Freeman, 'A Stakeholder Theory of the Modern Corporation' in T.L. Beauchamp and N.E. Bowie (eds), *Ethical Theory and Business*, 5th edn (Upper Saddle River, NJ: Prentice Hall, 1997) p. 69.

[22]   CLRSG, *Completing the Structure* (2000) para 3.5.

[23]   L.L. Dallas, 'Working Toward a New Paradigm' in L.E. Mitchell (ed.), *Progressive Corporate Law* (London: Kluwer, 1995) p. 35 at p. 39.

[24]   T. Donaldson and L.E. Preston 'The Stakeholder Theory of the Corpor-ation: Concept, Evidence, and Implications' (1995) 20 *Academy of Management Review* 65.

[25]   J. Parkinson, *Reforming Directors' Duties*, Policy Paper 12 (Political Economy Research Centre, University of Sheffield, 1998).

[26]   R. Aggarwal and A. Chandra, 'Stakeholder Management: Opportunities and Challenges' (1990) 40 *Business* 48 at 49.

interactions with stakeholders. 'The evolution of CSR theory provides a sort of social responsibilities and performance paradigm that is, in essence, a solid foundation for corporate social management and stakeholder engagement.'[27] Very early discussions of the CSR concept suggested that CSR is about attending to stakeholder rights and taking proactive, voluntary steps to avoid harm or wrongful consequences to stakeholders.[28] CSR theory suggests that corporations should recognize obligations beyond their shareholders, based on stakeholder theory.

1.2.2   Shareholder Primacy Norm

The shareholder primacy norm is the corporate governance model prevailing in the United States, the United Kingdom and some other common law countries with effective legal enforcement of shareholder rights. The directors' duties are exclusively owed to the company and the maximization of the wealth of the shareholder is the fundamental focus of the fiduciary duties.[29] It is constructed in terms of financing though equity, dispersed ownership, active markets for corporate control, and flexible labour markets.[30] Companies rely on stock and bond markets for their external financing. Corporate law provides relatively extensive protection for shareholders, with active enforcement of that protection in the courts.

According to the maintenance of efficiency theory, it is more efficient if directors run corporations with the aim of maximizing shareholder wealth since the least cost is expended in doing this. The directors can

---

[27]   R.T. Byerly, 'Seeking Global Solutions for the Common Good: A New World Order and Corporate Social Responsibilities' in I. Demirag, *CSR, Accountability and Governance: Global Perspectives* (Sheffield: Greenleaf Publishing, 2005) ch. 7, p. 122.

[28]   See the initial argument for CSR in H.R. Brown, *Social Responsibilities of the Businessman* (New York: Harper & Row, 1953); see also A.B. Carroll, 'The Pyramid of Social Responsibility: Towards the Moral Management of Organizational Stakeholders' (1991) 34 *Business Horizons* 39 at 39–48.

[29]   *Percival v Wright* [1902] 2 Ch. 421; *Multinational Gas and Petrochemical Co. v Multinational Gas and Petrochemical Services Ltd* [1983] Ch. 258 ('*Multinational Gas*'); *Grove v Flavel* [1986] 43 SASR 410 at 417 (Jacobs J); *Peskin v Anderson* [2000] BCC 1110 (and affirmed on appeal by the Court of Appeal (14 December 2000). Also see the comments of the Jenkins Committee, Cmnd 1749 (1962) at para. 89.

[30]   R.V. Aguilera and G. Jackson, 'The Cross-national Diversity of Corporate Governance: Dimensions and Determinants' (2003) 28 *Academy of Management Review* 447.

work more efficiently if they focus on one objective only,[31] without any unpoliced managerial discretion.[32] Besides, the contracts between the firm and its shareholders are implicit since all they amount to is a claim on the company's residual cash flow.[33] Shareholders are also vulnerable as they are unable to negotiate special terms by signing contracts with the company, and in many ways they are at the mercy of the directors because the monitoring of directors is not easily undertaken.[34] In contrast, various stakeholders have explicit contracts with the company, which will protect their legal rights.

1.2.3 Corporate Social Responsibility

So far, a consensus regarding the definition of CSR has yet to be reached, because the expectations and demands of various stakeholders in corporate practices are constantly adjusting due to rapid changes in the business world. Table 1.1 shows significant variations in definitions of CSR.

Despite the fact that the term CSR has been defined in various ways, a few common characteristics can be drawn from the definitions listed above. First of all, CSR holds that responsible behaviour on the part of corporations can help achieve corporate and wider goals, in particular the general good of society. Secondly, the scope of CSR mainly focuses on social and environmental concerns, in addition to the traditional economic goals of corporations. Most researchers suggest that CSR aims to improve quality of life and community harmonization, working towards a

---

[31] M. van der Weide, 'Against Fiduciary Duties to Corporate Stakeholders' (1996) 21 *Delaware Journal of Corporate Law* 27 at 56–7; see also J. Fisch, 'Measuring Efficiency in Corporate Law: The Role of Shareholder Primacy' (2006) *Journal of Corporation Law* 637; L.A. Stout, 'Bad and Not-So-Bad Arguments for Shareholder Primacy' (2002) 75 *South California Law Review* 1189; M.C. Jensen, 'Value Maximization, Stakeholder Theory, and the Corporate Objective Function' (2001) 14 *Journal of Applied Corporate Finance* 8; R. Daines, 'Does Delaware Law Improve Firm Value?' (2001) 62 *Journal of Financial Economics* 525; G. Subramanian, 'The Disappearing Delaware Effect' (2004) 46 *Journal of Law, Economics and Organisation* 525; L.A. Bebchuk, A. Cohen and A. Ferrell, 'Does the Evidence Favor State Competition in Corporate Law' (2002) 90 *California Law Review* 1775.
[32] A.K. Sundaram and A.C. Inkpen, 'The Corporate Objective Revisited' (2004) 15 *Organization Science* 350 at 354.
[33] *Ibid.* at 355.
[34] See L. Zingales, 'Corporate Governance' in P. Newman, *The New Palgrave Dictionary of Economics and Law* (Basingstoke: Macmillan, 1998) p. 501.

Table 1.1   Definitions of corporate social responsibility

Year	Source	Definition
1973	K. Davis, 'The Case for and against Business Assumption of Social Responsibilities' (1973) 16 *Academy of Management Journal* 312	CSR is the firm's consideration of, and response to, issues beyond the narrow economic, technical, and legal requirements of the firm ... to accomplish social benefits along with the traditional economic gains which the firm seeks.
1997	J. Elkingston, *Cannibals with Forks: The Triple Bottom Line of 21st Century Business* (Oxford: Capstone Publishing 1997)	CSR is taking care of societal, ecological and economical concerns.
1998	World Business Council for Sustainable Development	CSR is the continuing commitment by business to behave ethically and contribute to economic development while improving the quality of life of the workforce and their families as well as of the local community and society at large.
2000	A.B. Carroll and A.K. Buchholtz, *Business and Society: Ethics and Stakeholder Management,* 5th edn (Australia: Thomson South-Western, 2003)	Corporate social responsibility encompasses the economic, legal, ethical, and philanthropic expectations placed on organisations by society at a given point in time.
2001	A. McWilliams and D.S. Siegel, 'Corporate Social Responsibility: A Theory of the Firm Perspective' (2001) 26 *Academy of Management Review* 117	CSR is the situation where companies participate in public welfare issues more than is required for their interests by legal regulations.
2003	S.A. Aaronson, 'Corporate Responsibility in the Global Village: The British Role and the American Laggard' (2003) 108 *Business and Society Review* 309	The making of business decisions is connected with the moral values, observance of law bindings and care for the whole society and environment.
2003	United Nations (H.E. Ward, E. Wilson, L. Zarsky and T. Fox, 'CSR and Developing Countries: What Scope for Government Action?', United Nations Sustainable Development Innovation Briefs, Issue 1)	CSR is a directors' responsibility which aims both to examine the role of business in society, and to maximise the positive societal outcomes of business activity.*

Year	Source	Definition
2003	World Bank (D. Petkoski and B. Herman, 'Summary Report' in D. Petkoski and B. Herman (eds), *Implementing the Monterrey Consensus: Governance Roles of Public, Private and Advocacy Stakeholders* (2003))	The commitment of business to contribute to sustainable economic development, working with employees, their families, the local community, and society at large to improve their quality of life, in ways that are both good for business and good for development.**
2008	Chinese Government (State-Owned Assets Supervision and Administration Commission, *Central Corporations CSR Research Report*)	Corporations should carry out their social responsibilities by abiding by all relevant laws, regulations, and business ethics codes. While pursuing economic profits, corporations are held responsible by shareholders, employees, consumers, suppliers, communities, and other stakeholders. Moreover, corporations have responsibilities to protect the environment.
2011	M. Baker, 'Corporate Social Responsibility: What Does It Mean?'	CSR is the business administration procedure for a general good effect on society.***
2011	C. Nakajima, 'The Importance of Legally Embedding Corporate Social Reasonability' (2011) 32 *Company Lawyer* 257	CSR is a directors' responsibility that has focused on corporations' voluntary actions which are over and above legal requirements, and which contribute to sustainable economic development so that the business can address both its own competitive interests and the interests of wider society.

Notes:

*   Available at www.un.org/esa/sustdev/publications/innovationbriefs/no1.pdf.
**   Available at http://info.worldbank.org/etools/docs/library/57431/monterrey_econference.pdf.
***   Available from blog of Mallen Barker at www.mallenbaker.net/csr/definition.php.

more sustainable society at large via the performance of corporations. Thirdly, CSR plays a due role: on one hand, it deals with minimizing the impacts of corporate misconduct in the sphere in which a business operates, and on the other, it encompasses a vast array of philanthropic corporate activities which are important, especially in developing countries, to enhance corporate reputation, culture and image. Last but not least, despite the fact that many definitions emphasize the voluntary characteristics of CSR beyond enforceable legal requirements, the practice of CSR is established on the basis of the fulfilment of traditional economic and legal responsibilities, which are normally achieved via directors' duties and corporate reports on social and environmental issues.[35]

Legal awareness of the need for CSR requires us to define CSR in a manner that integrates both mandatory and voluntary behaviours.[36] CSR as a concept covers many issues, encompassing sustainability development, corporate governance development and corporate objectives, employment rights, consumer protection rights, occupational health and safety, local taxation law and socially responsible investments from shareholders, especially institutional shareholders. Most corporate governance scholars have recognized the connection between 'good behaviour towards stakeholders to whom no legal duty is owed and fulfilment of the shareholder primacy obligation required in corporate law and the role the courts have played in guiding the way'.[37]

Corporate practices are typically influenced by an array of legal domains, such as securities regulation, taxation law, contract law, employment law, environmental law, consumer protection law and insolvency law.[38] Decisions are made under the mandatory legal rules embodied by these legislative instruments. When they manage their businesses, directors will find 'their decision tree considerably trimmed

---

[35]   See W. Vandekerckhove and M.S.R. Commers, 'Beyond Voluntary/ Mandatory Juxtaposition: Towards a European Framework on CSR as Network Governance' (2005) 1 *Social Responsibility Journal* 98; M. Blowfield, 'Corporate Social Responsibility: Reinventing the Meaning of Development' (2005) 81 *International Affairs* 515; O. Aiyegbayo and C. Villers, 'The Enhanced Business Review: Has it Made Corporate Governance More Effective' (2011) *Journal of Business Law* 699; K. Campbell and D. Vick, 'Disclosures Law and the Market for Corporate Social Responsibility' in D. McBarnet, A. Voiculescu and T. Campbell, *The New Corporate Accountability: Corporate Social Responsibility and the Law* (Cambridge: Cambridge University Press, 2007) p. 241; A. Johnson, 'After the OFR: Can UK Shareholder Value Still be Enlightened?' (2006) 7 *European Business Organization Law Review* 817.

[36]   J.A. Zerk, *Multinationals and Corporate Social Responsibility: Limitations and Opportunities in International Law* (Cambridge: Cambridge University Press, 2006) 32.

[37]   I.L. Fannon, 'The Corporate Social Responsibility Movement and Law's Empire: Is there a Conflict?' (2007) 58 *Northern Ireland Legal Quarterly* 1 at 16.

[38]   OECD, *OECD Principles of Corporate Governance* (2004) p. 2, available at www.oecd.org.

and their discretion decidedly diminished by mandatory legal rules enacted in the name of protecting stakeholders'.[39] While CSR is worthy of study from multiple disciplinary perspectives, it is also fundamentally affected by how law and other forms of regulation treat it.[40] Apart from behaviours that are legally prescribed or prohibited, legal responsibility also includes what is legally permissible.[41] Therefore, the scope of legal responsibilities is not just limited to that strand of responsibility in which legal compulsion and sanctions apply towards legal outcomes.[42] The interaction between law and CSR will embrace a 'minimum position of legal compliance and harm-avoidance where the law is lacking, a mid-way position of facilitating corporate contributions to sustainable development and other forms of community investment where the business case warrants it, and a more expansive position of'[43] 'active alignment of internal business goals with externally set societal goals'.[44]

CSR is an issue of potential significance not only to governments but also to wider society in terms of both welfare and development,[45] in the sense that CSR may 'assist a government in fulfilling welfare state goals of political character or based in law as obligations'.[46] In the United States, President Obama called for a new concept of responsibility as the only proportional remedy for a crisis of infinite magnitude, the result of the US recession.[47] Under the banner of CSR, many local and international institutions seek to raise public awareness of the necessity for transnational corporations to abide by certain health, environmental and

---

[39]   A. Winkler, 'Corporate Law or the Law of Business? Stakeholders and Corporate Governance at the End of History' (2004) 67 *Law and Contemporary Problems* 109 at 111.

[40]   B. Horrigan, *Corporate Social Responsibility in the 21st Century: Debates, Models and Practices Across Government, Law and Business* (Cheltenham: Edward Elgar, 2010) p. 26.

[41]   *Ibid.*

[42]   P. Cane, *Responsibility in Law and Morality* (Oxford: Hart Publishing, 2003) p. 30.

[43]   B. Horrigan, *Corporate Social Responsibility in the 21st Century: Debates, Models and Practices Across Government, Law and Business* (Cheltenham: Edward Elgar, 2010) p. 26.

[44]   H.E. Ward, E. Wilson, L. Zarsky and T. Fox, *CSR and Developing Countries: What Scope for Government Action?*, United Nations Sustainable Development Innovation Briefs, Issue 1, available at www.un.org/esa/sustdev/publications/innovationbriefs/no1.pdf.

[45]   K. Buhmann, 'Corporate Social Responsibility: What Role for Law? Some Aspects of Law and CSR' (2006) *Corporate Governance* 188 at 189.

[46]   *Ibid.*

[47]   Barack H. Obama, President of the United States, Inaugural Address.

social standards. Companies are closely regulated by various groups of actors who may include shareholders, public authorities, inter-governmental bodies, trade unions, NGOs, insurers and consumer groups.[48] All these positive and responsible actions will in turn have a collective societal-friendly impact on the government's subsequent policies and legislative direction. CSR-related actions are always based on a good mix of social and legal norms, and legal requirements to report non-financial issues are becoming increasingly common in countries in the European Union and elsewhere.[49]

Because of various forms of manifestation of CSR-related perform-ance, the regulations governing CSR are also in a variety of forms and are drafted and enforced by regulatory bodies at different levels. At the most fundamental level, government regulations are normally formal and binding in law, or they are recommendations that have guiding effects but no legal standing. Local government bodies issue public regulations that are regional, national or supra-national,[50] based on delegated state, government or international powers[51] that are founded on the member-ship of each country.[52] Meanwhile, globalization has further increased the complexity of the legal environment by exposing corporations to international law and the laws of foreign nations.[53] Progressive advocates who are engaged in promoting more sustainable businesses, more environmentally-friendly companies and firms focused on human rights will also drive corporations to adopt more socially responsible ethical

---

[48]   J.A. Zerk, *Multinationals and Corporate Social Responsibility: Limitations and Opportunities in International Law* (Cambridge: Cambridge University Press, 2006) 41.

[49]   For example, the Business Review, in line with the minimum requirements of the EU Accounts Modernisation Directive 2003, which called for companies' annual reports to include 'both financial and, where appropriate, non-financial key performance indicators relevant to the particular business, including infor-mation relating to environmental and employee matters (when necessary)' (art. 14 amending art. 46 of the Accounts Directive); see also Companies Act 2006 s. 417(3); this is a replacement for Operating and Financial Review; for discussions on Business Review and Operating and Financial Review, see A. Johnson, 'After the OFR: Can UK Shareholder Value Still Be Enlightened?' (2006) 7 *European Business Organization Law Review* 817.

[50]   E.g. the European Union.

[51]   E.g. the OECD, United Nations, ILO or UNICEF.

[52]   K. Buhmann, 'Corporate Social Responsibility: What Role for Law? Some Aspects of Law and CSR' (2006) *Corporate Governance* 188 at 194.

[53]   J.F. Steiner and G.A. Steiner, *Business, Government, and Society: A Managerial Perspective, Text and Cases*, 13th edn (New York: McGraw-Hill, 2012) 42.

codes and guidelines for conduct, although the adoption of these codes is largely on a voluntary basis.

1.2.4 Corporate Social Responsibility in China

CSR can be directly related to the idea that corporations should engage in activities that are more than shareholder wealth maximization or 'strictly business'. Instead, companies, in addition to their economic responsibility at the bottom of the corporate responsibility pyramid, should have legal, ethical and philanthropic responsibilities.[54] Within the CSR literature corporations are suggested to provide various political and public benefits that are commonly associated with governments and public welfare.[55] The general thrust of CSR's opponents is to refute Friedman's argument that the only social responsibility of business is to increase its profit.[56] Many scholars also argue that CSR has been concerned with suggesting that those companies who promote the interests of society will tend to be financially successful, especially in the long term.[57] The mantra of business has evolved from 'profit alone' to 'profit, people and planet', to include people's issues, social issues and environmental issues. It is recognized that all these factors are no longer seen as incidental and CSR has come to the fore as a core business issue.[58] CSR is becoming a key basis on which corporations aim to build the trust and confidence of their stakeholders, which may in itself be a primary source of competitive edge.[59]

---

[54] A.B. Carroll, 'The Pyramid of Corporate Social Responsibility: Toward the Moral Management of Organizational Stakeholders' (1991) 34 *Business Horizons* 39.

[55] A. Crane, D. Matten and J. Moon, *Corporations and Citizenship* (Cambridge: Cambridge University Press, 2008).

[56] M. Friedman, 'The social reasonability', *New York Times Magazine*, 13 September 1970.

[57] M. Orlitzky, 'Corporate Social Performance and Financial Performance: A Research Synthesis' in A. Crane, A. McWilliams, D. Matten, J. Moon and D. Siegel (eds), *The Oxford Handbook of CSR* (Oxford: Oxford University Press, 2008) p. 113; see also S. Urip, *CSR Strategies: Corporate Social Responsibility for a Competitive Edge in Emerging Markets* (Chichester: John Wiley & Sons, 2010) ch. 1.

[58] S. Urip, *CSR Strategies: Corporate Social Responsibility for a Competitive Edge in Emerging Markets* (Chichester: John Wiley & Sons, 2010) p. 5.

[59] *Ibid.* at 13.

When Margolis and Walsh wrote their overview of companies' social initiatives in 2003 they declared that 'the world cries out for repair'.[60] They recognized the increasing pressure for corporations to take a responsible perspective on social and environmental problems, even as they pursue seemingly competing financial demands. This is necessary not least because, despite their limitations, in the current era of economic globalization they may be the bodies of last resort for achieving all manner of social objectives.[61] It is argued that corporate responses towards CSR have never been either strategic or operational; rather, they are cosmetic, focusing on public relationships and media campaigns, the centrepieces of which are the glossy CSR reports that showcase companies' social and environmental good deeds.[62] The sincerity of CSR and CSR-related reports has been a highly controversial issue, especially in countries with emerging markets such as China.

The embedding of CSR into Chinese corporate strategic management policies, corporate governance-related codes and regulations and corporate law is the result of external pressure from multinational corporations, in combination with internal pull factors from the modernized role of state-owned enterprises (SOEs) and a strong civil society with more demanding consumers, suppliers and local communities.[63] The adoption of CSR by the state reveals a realistic recognition that the country is not able to address the challenges brought by its rapid but uneven economic transition and the growth of corporations. It is argued that SOEs in China, as international operators or global brands, have begun to recognize that an effective CSR framework offers an efficient tool to enable corporations to move up the value chain and negotiate the complex demands of consumers and civil society in diverse environments.[64] The case for adopting CSR in China is not only to secure a domestic licence to operate, but also to help shape the global competitive environment to reward sustainability. After China was granted entry into the WTO, the

---

[60]   J.D. Margolis and J.P. Walsh, 'Misery Loves Companies: Rethinking Social Initiatives by Business' (2003) 48 *Administrative Science Quarterly* 268.

[61]   M. Blowfirled and A. Murrary, *Corporate Responsibility*, 2nd edn (Oxford: Oxford University Press, 2011) pp. 346–7.

[62]   M.E. Porter and M.R. Kramer, 'Strategy and Society: The Link between Competition Advantage and Corporate Social Responsibility' (2006) 84 *Harvard Business Review* 78 at 80.

[63]   L. Zu, *Corporate Social Responsibility, Corporate Restructuring and Firm's Performance* (Berlin: Springer-Verlag, 2009) pp. 44–50.

[64]   G. Long, S. Zadek and J. Wickerham, 'Advancing Sustainable Competitiveness of China's Transnational Corporations' *AccountAbility* (London, 2009) p. 35.

CSR criteria imposed by international joint ventures prompted the evolution of a model which has a positive influence on Chinese enterprises' participation in international competition.

In the three decades since China opened its door to the outside world, a legal system regulating the corporate and financial market has been established based heavily on Chinese Company Law. Since the Sixth Plenary Session of the Sixteenth Central Committee of the Chinese Communist Party in 2006, the emphasis on 'building a harmonized society' has been adopted as the long-term goal of Chinese socialism.[65] From the perspective of corporations, these policy statements have symbolic importance for advancing CSR in China.[66] Regulating corporate behaviour through politically legitimate measures is arguably an effective way to achieve these goals.

Since 2005, the idea of building a Harmonious Society, a 'scientific development concept'[67] that shifts China's primary focus from a model based purely on economic growth to a more balanced, Confucian-style approach aimed at maintaining growth while addressing daunting social concerns,[68] affirms the government's attention and policy support for the adoption of CSR as an important step towards the sustainable development of enterprises and the promotion of corporate competitiveness, corporate image and China's reputation globally. This shift has led to a chain reaction in Chinese corporate objectives, moving from basic economic responsibility to responsibility for improving the social and natural environments, and onwards to a position of influencing basic social values and concepts. Of course, the evolution of CSR can also be seen as a collective result of a number of different factors: developments in the regulatory environment; changes in people's understanding of value in China; the evolution of civil society to act as both watchdog and

---

[65]   *Ibid.*

[66]   L.W. Lin, 'Corporate Social Responsibility in China: Window Dressing or Structural Change' (2010) 28 *Berkeley Journal of International Law* 64 at 88.

[67]   Former President Hu Jintao, 'Scientific Outlook Development', Lecture for Yale University, 24 April 2006; in the lecture, Hu clarified that 'China will pursue a scientific outlook on development that makes economic and social development people-oriented, comprehensive, balanced and sustainable. We will work to strike a proper balance between urban and rural development, development among regions, economic and social development, development of man and nature, and domestic development and opening wider to the outside world; it is also rooted in the cultural heritages of the Chinese nation'.

[68]   J.P. Gies and B. Holt, 'Harmonious Society: Rise of the New China' (2009) *Strategic Studies Quarterly* 75.

partner to business; progress in developing basic CSR tools and frameworks for use in China; the development of a gatekeeper system involving an increasing number of professionals such as lawyers, auditors and accountants; and social phenomena, such as corruption and the status of workers.

Indeed, there are also initiatives and attempts in legislation to improve CSR within corporations and raise CSR awareness and understanding across sectors. The attempts constitute both general provisions for corporate objectives[69] and specific provisions for protecting various stakeholders in corporate law[70] or other laws that directly relate to the legitimate rights of certain stakeholders.[71] Corporations in China, which are regarded as one of the biggest suppliers of the world market, are engaged in developing philanthropic projects to promote their corporate image. However, urgent discussion is required concerning how it may be possible to establish a corporate responsibility programme which is adherent to law, codes of conduct and international standards.

The idea of CSR, which is new to China, was not conceptualized when the first Chinese Company Law (CCL) was drafted in the 1990s. The employee participation and work council[72] was more of a politically and economically path-dependent body where the employees were regarded as the masters of state-owned enterprises. Some level of awareness of CSR began in the 1990s when unethical business behaviours were rampant and the government passed the State Council's Decision Concerning Correcting and Regulating the Order of the Market Economy in April 2001. Since then, awareness has been promoted to a legislative level.[73] The process of modernizing corporate law in China started in 2004, and CSR was one of the many issues considered in the revision of the CCL. The New Chinese Company Law was passed by the National People's Congress and took effect in January 2006, wherein CSR was given explicit recognition.

---

69   CCL 2006 art. 5.
70   For example, regarding employees, see CCL 2006 arts 14 and 17.
71   For example, regarding employees, see Labour Contract Law 2008.
72   See CCL 1994 arts 16, 45, 55, 56, 68, 121, 122.
73   M.H. Jensen, *Serve the People! Corporate Social Responsibility (CSR) in China*, Copenhagen Discussion Paper 2006-6 (Asia Research Centre, 2006), available at http://openarchive.cbs.dk/bitstream/handle/10398/7405/cdp%202006-006.pdf.

Institutional failures and corporate scandals are often attributed to weak legal institutions and a lack of government transparency.[74] A common criticism is that China's 'weak legal institutions are inexplicably inexcusable since China boasts length, breadth and depth in its legal tradition'.[75] This arguably is reflected in the CSR-related legislation. The issue of CSR was explicitly stipulated in the new CCL 2006. However, even after the enforcement of this law, the world has witnessed a series of CSR-related incidents such as food and production safety incidents and unfair treatment of employees and neglect of the environment. In response, activities including interference by the government, increased accountability of corporations towards the public and requirements for sustainable development, began to emerge. The China Enterprise Confederation Global Compact Promotion Office was established in order to help Chinese enterprises to take part in the United Nations' Global Compact.

1.2.5 Different Types of Corporations in CCL 2006

With the development of the Chinese domestic and international economy, many types of companies have been introduced in China. During the period between 1949 and 1956 when the new China was being established under the leadership of the Chinese Communist Party, the Provisional Regulations on Private Enterprises 1950 and Implementing Methods for Provisional Regulations on Private Enterprises were passed in order to encourage private enterprises to continue to operate in China. According to the Regulations, there were five types of private companies in China, including: unlimited liability companies (*wu xian gong si*); limited liability companies (*yu xian ze ren gong si*); companies limited by shares (*gu fen you xian gong si*); companies formed by one or more shareholders with unlimited liability and one or more shareholders with limited liability (*liang he gong si*); and companies formed by one or more shareholders having unlimited liability and one or more shareholders having liability limited to their share contributions, with the company capital divided into equal shares (*gu fen liang he gong si*).[76]

Apart from these private enterprises, SOEs have always played a significant role in the Chinese economy. More than two-thirds of the

---

[74]   D.J. Goelz, 'China's Environmental Problems: Is a Specialised Court the Solution?' (2009) 18 *Pacific Rim Law and Policy Journal* 155 at 168.

[75]   J.W. Head, *Global Business Law, Principles and Practice of International Commerce and Investment*, 2nd edn (Durham, NC: Carolina Academic Press, 2007) pp. 58–9.

[76]   Provisional Regulations on Private Enterprises 1950 art. 3.

companies listed in the Fortune 5000 are SOEs, excluding banks and insurance companies. The largest and most important of the companies are controlled by a central holding company known as the State Owned Assets Supervision and Administration Commission, which is the world's largest controlling shareholder. Traditionally, SOEs were more than corporations wholly owned by the state as the only shareholder. They are more 'aptly seen as a division or aggregation of productive assets within the loosely organised firm of China, Inc'.[77] It is worth noting that Chinese SOEs are some of 150 or so corporations that report directly to central government, while thousands more fall into a grey area.[78] The post-Mao period saw a stage of reform through efforts to change SOEs, which were plagued by low productivity, unresponsiveness to economic signals and waste.[79] The changes also involved a re-evaluation of the roles of directors, which are closely related to the bureaucratic hierarchy and powerful political positions. Since 1980, the SOEs have gradually lost some of their primacy and advantage with the introduction of the Chinese government's policy on the separation of government functions and business operations. SOEs are converting to other forms of companies under the CCL, including companies limited by shares, limited liability companies or wholly state-owned limited liability companies.

Legally, based on article 2 of CCL 2006, Chinese Company Law only deals with two types of company, including limited liability companies (*youxian zeren gongsi*) and companies limited by shares (*gufen youxiang gongsi*). A limited liability company is a type of organization normally intended for a small and closely connected group of investors; these are recognized as 'private' or 'closed' companies. On the other hand, companies limited by shares are the equivalent of Delaware corporations or the German *Aktiengesellschaft*, and they may be traded on a stock exchange. Companies limited by shares do not have to trade their shares

[77] D.C. Clark and N.C. Howson, 'Pathway to Minority Shareholder Protection: Derivative Action in the People's Republic of China' in D. Puchniak, H. Baum and M. Ewing-Chow (eds), *The Derivative Action in Asia: A Comparative and Functional Approach* (Cambridge: Cambridge University Press, 2012) p. 243 at p. 244.

[78] J.R. Woetzel, 'Reassessing China's State-Owned Enterprises' (2008) *McKinsey Quarterly* 1.

[79] D.C. Clark and N.C. Howson, 'Pathway to Minority Shareholder Protection: Derivative Action in the People's Republic of China' in D. Puchniak, H. Baum and M. Ewing-Chow (eds), *The Derivative Action in Asia: A Comparative and Functional Approach* (Cambridge: Cambridge University Press, 2012) ch. 6, p. 2.

through a stock exchange. However, if they do, a company limited by shares will be a listed company limited by shares.

1.3 RESEARCH OBJECTIVES, ORIGINALITY AND METHODOLOGY

Over the decades, CSR has continued to grow in importance and significance and has been regarded as a subject of considerable debate, commentary, theory building and research from various disciplines.[80] CSR and its relationship with corporations' financial performance has always been one of the most heated topics in academic debate, as well as in corporate behaviour and practice. As a highly contentious topic with permeable boundaries, CSR draws from various research traditions, focusing on different issues relating to the overall topic.[81] At the heart of the debate there are questions still awaiting a comprehensive and convincing answer, especially after the financial crisis in 2008, while the lack of confidence shown by investors and the public towards corporations is becoming increasingly worrying. Can corporations do well by doing good? Can corporations make efficient profits by doing good? Is fair trade helping farmers to get better and fairer returns in developing countries? How are corporations in China not only addressing their own basic and strategic needs, but also the overall needs of society with regard to their local communities? What form of CSR interventions have been applied and carried out with the intention of promoting community development in China? What obstacles and opportunities hinder and help community and business organizations participate in economic development, community development, social service delivery and public policy dialogues?

From the point of view of corporations, what do the business community and organizations get out of CSR? How do corporations gain tangible benefits from engaging in CSR policies, corporate strategies and

---

[80]   A.B. Carroll and K.M. Shabana, 'The Business Case for Corporate Social Responsibility: A Review of Concept, Research and Practice' (2010) 12 *International Journal of Management Reviews* 85.

[81]   A. Lockett, J. Moon and W. Visser, 'Corporate Social Responsibility in Management Research: Focus, Nature, Salience and Influence' (2006) 43 *Journal of Management Studies* 115 at 117.

activities and practices as enforcement measures of these policies?[82] Do people care about CSR if it does not benefit them directly? What kind of partnerships can be developed and maintained between corporations, government, NGOs and local communities in the context of CSR? What does CSR practice in China look like? What is the future of CSR in China, with a consideration of Chinese history, politics, culture, traditions and law? Can Chinese law play an active part in promoting CSR? If the answer to this final question is 'yes', apart from the effects of soft law, how will it be possible to enforce hard law on CSR, which has voluntary roots? Furthermore, how can China build an efficient regulatory framework to promote CSR as an effective policy to benefit stakeholders?

This book is an up-to-date examination of contemporary issues such as the Harmonious Society in China, the 2008 financial crisis and its impact on the Chinese economy, and discussions of recent corporate scandals over the last few years including the Sanlu Baby Milk scandal, the Wenchuan earthquake and CSR donations, the Beijing Olympic Games and CSR, and the Fujia chemical plant, which produced a potentially toxic chemical paraxylene. It is inter-disciplinary, with a focus on discussions of the legal aspects of CSR. Just like the legal framework for corporate governance, the legal framework for CSR in China comprises four levels: basic laws, administrative regulations, regulatory provision and self-disciplinary rules.

Currently there is a shortage of similar examinations published in the English language. Regarding CCL 2006, this book takes a closer look at related provisions aiming to introduce social and environmental aspects into corporate decisions and corporate objectives through legislation. Suggestions for how to enforce these laws more effectively and efficiently will be discussed with reference to UK law, especially related provisions and legislative experiences after suggestions from the Company Law Review Steering Group and the drafting of the Companies Act 2006. The reconstruction of the Chinese corporate governance model will also be discussed as a measure for prompting Chinese corporations in a more socially responsible direction.

Three main approaches will be adopted in order to address the research questions and reach conclusions about the effectiveness of the enforcement and regulation of CSR in a Harmonious Society with a long history dominated by Confucian values. These methods include literature-based

---

[82]   A.B. Carroll and K.M. Shabana, 'The Business Case for Corporate Social Responsibility: A Review of Concept, Research and Practice' (2010) *International Journal of Management Reviews* 85.

library research, comparative research and a doctrinal analysis. CSR reports from Chinese listed companies will also be studied in order to gather industry perspectives on CSR reporting and enrich the social and public impact of the research. The primary approach adopted throughout the book will be a literature-based analysis, including qualitative reviews of modern secondary sources. The literature-based review will be supported by a doctrinal analysis of the law relating to CSR in China. This is concerned with the analysis of legal doctrine and how it has been developed in conjunction with the social economy in China.

1.4 STRUCTURE OF THE RESEARCH

This book offers a comprehensive discussion on the new conceptualization of CSR, with a focus on the legal side. The book is organized in nine chapters. Chapter 1 provides an introduction with discussions of the basic terms that will be used throughout the book, such as CSR, the shareholder primacy norm and stakeholder theory, as well as the classification and definition of companies in China as recognised by CCL 2006. Chapter 2 presents a detailed analysis of CSR in China from a historical developmental perspective. This chapter also shows how the ideology of Chinese CSR has a grounding in Chinese history, culture, traditions and corporate law. The development of CSR in China will be discussed from a historical and cultural perspective. The relationship between CSR and Confucian philosophy will be presented, together with an examination of CSR in a few important historical periods including the late *Qing* dynasty, the Republic of China, and the initial transformation period of the People's Republic of China from a strictly planned economy to a socialist market economy with Chinese characteristics.

CSR in contemporary China will be discussed in Chapter 3 as a term that is attracting increasing attention from lawyers, economists, corporate directors and government policy-makers as a result of external push factors and internal drivers. A unique Chinese corporate governance module, including a specially developed CSR policy system, will be introduced in Chapter 4 in order to find solutions for the problems of how to promote socially responsible corporations under such a corporate governance system. Focusing on the legal aspects of CSR, Chapters 5 and 6 will assess the stakeholder position in China, examining the current legal protection offered to them and making suggestions for reform. CSR challenges in China after the financial crisis will be also discussed in order to predict the development of CSR in the future.

Turning to enforcement of CSR policies in China with the development of an efficient legal system that incorporates CSR, issues surrounding mandatory information disclosure will be introduced in Chapter 7. The political policy of the Harmonious Society will be examined in Chapter 8, with a discussion proposing a linkage between CSR and the government's policy and a dialogue on the positive effects of government interference in CSR in China.

The main structure of the project can be logically expressed as shown in Figure 1.1.

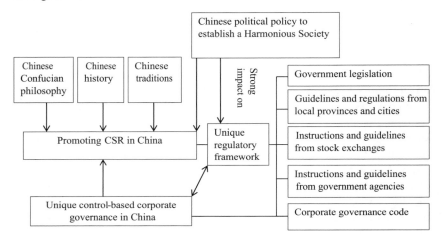

Figure 1.1   Structure of the book

2. The evolution of corporate social responsibility in China: Historical evidence

2.1 HISTORY OF CORPORATE SOCIAL RESPONSIBILITY IN A GLOBAL CONTEXT

Corporate objectives and the role and responsibility of the board of directors have been at the centre of academic debate for decades in various disciplines, including law, economics, management, politics and sociology. According to Hay and Gray, the evolution of corporate social responsibility (CSR) has travelled through three phases.[1] It is worth discussing these phases to illuminate the progression and development of CSR as a modernized concept.

Phase one was characterized by a 'profit maximizer' tendency. This was the initial understanding of corporate objectives, based on the premise that individual self-interests would prevail and the sole objective of managers is to make profit for the shareholders. Profit maximization is generally regarded as an accurate description of corporate behaviour up to the 1920s. After the First World War there was a shift in business attitudes towards a more profit-oriented view, with the United States taking the lead and modernizing its economy. In the first half of the twentieth century, America was a society characterized by economic scarcity, with economic growth and wealth accumulation as the primary national goals. Corporations and other forms of business organizations were regarded as vehicles for eliminating economic scarcity.[2] Social problems, such as working conditions, treatment of employees, child labour, environmental problems and protection of the interests of the community, were given little attention. The correlation between the

---

[1] R. Hay and E. Gray, 'Social Responsibilities of Business Management' (1974) 17 *Academy of Management Journal* 135.
[2] *Ibid.* at 136.

welfare of the economy and the welfare of society was not perceived.[3] Business ethics and social, environmental and philanthropic corporate responsibilities were relegated to subordinate concerns. The 'profit maximizer' phase of CSR complemented the Calvinistic philosophy which pervaded the nineteenth and early twentieth centuries.[4] This philosophy taught that the road to salvation was through hard work and the accumulation of wealth. It was a logical philosophy to adopt in a corporation, where a director of a company could demonstrate his or her diligence and good faith to the company through accumulating wealth by adhering to the rule that pursuing profit should be the company's sole purpose.

Phase two was characterized by 'trusteeship management', a development process that emerged in the 1920s and 1930s. Taking account of structural changes in business institutions and society, the trusteeship concept viewed corporate managers as fiduciaries, responsible for maintaining an equitable balance between shareholders and various stakeholders. The director was regarded as a trustee for the various contributor groups to the firm, rather than simply as an agent for the providers of equity.[5] The development of this structural trend was the result of increasing diffusion in terms of share ownership in US corporations,[6] as well as the development of a more pluralistic society.[7] In the area of law, a continuing and long-standing debate began during this phase, embedded in corporate law scholarship. The debate was between those who favoured the shareholder primacy norm and those who favoured stakeholder theory, who believed that corporations have a social responsibility to a wider group of constituencies, such as employees, local communities, creditors, suppliers, consumers and government.[8]

---

[3]   S. Sheikh, *Corporate Social Responsibility: Law and Practice* (Abingdon and New York: Routledge Cavendish, 1996) p. 11.

[4]   J.D. German, 'The Social Utility of Wicked Self-Love: Calvinism, Capitalism, and Public Policy in Revolutionary New England' (1995) *Journal of American History* 965.

[5]   R. Hay and E. Gray, 'Social Responsibilities of Business Management' (1974) 17 *Academy of Management Journal* 135 at 136.

[6]   By the early 1930s, the largest stockholders in corporations such as American Telephone and Telegraph, United States Steel, and the Pennsylvania Railroad owned less than 1 per cent of the total shares in these companies.

[7]   R. Hay and E. Gray, 'Social Responsibilities of Business Management' (1974) 17 *Academy of Management Journal* 135 at 136.

[8]   For a good discussion of these two models, see A. Keay, *The Corporate Objective* (Cheltenham: Edward Elgar, 2011).

In the 1930s, US corporations were evolving from an organizational form used primarily for public works (building and operating railroads, ferry services, bridges and the like) to the foundational form most suitable for private business enterprise.[9] At this time two academics, Berle and Dodd, were debating two problems, namely, how to properly characterize the developing structure of corporate law, and how corporate law should develop in the future.[10] Berle argued that the whole body of corporate law was essentially a variant of trust law, in which corporate managers owed fiduciary duties to manage the corporation in the interests of the shareholder beneficiaries.[11] He also used the term 'shareholder primacy norm' when he described how 'all powers granted to a corporation or to the management of a corporation ... are ... exercisable only for the rateable benefit of all shareholders as their interest appears'.[12] However, this descriptive claim is based on the premise that shareholders are the owners of the company and directors are the agents of the shareholders, a premise which is not without problems. Dodd suggested that if the corporation can be viewed as a separate legal entity that is separate from its shareholders, then it has citizenship responsibilities. Directors should act as trustees with citizenship responsibilities on behalf of all the company's constituencies.[13] Afterwards, Berle and Means's analysis took for granted that shareholders, as the property owners, were entitled to management's undivided loyalty. By 1932, corporate law had already endorsed the view that shareholders' financial interests should guide managerial decision-making without regard to competing claims from non-shareholders.[14]

---

[9]   J.E. Fisch, 'Robert Clark's Corporate Law: Twenty Years of Change: Measuring Efficiency in Corporate Law: The Role of Shareholder Primacy' (2006) 31 *Iowa Journal of Corporate Law* 637 at 647–8; the related trust and trustee function debate has been the subject of several articles in the *Harvard Law Review*; e.g. A.A. Berle, 'For Whom are Corporate Managers Trustees?: A Note' (1932) 45 *Harvard Law Review* 1365; E.M. Dodd, 'For Whom Corporate Managers are Trustees?' (1932) 45 *Harvard Law Review* 1145.

[10]   J.E. Fisch, 'Robert Clark's Corporate Law: Twenty Years of Change: Measuring Efficiency in Corporate Law: The Role of Shareholder Primacy' (2006) 31 *Iowa Journal of Corporate Law* 637 at 647.

[11]   A.A. Berle, 'Corporate Powers as Powers in Trust' (1931) 44 *Harvard Law Review* 1049 at 1074.

[12]   *Ibid.* at 1049.

[13]   E. Dodd, 'For Whom are Corporate Managers Trustees?' (1932) 45 *Harvard Law Review* 1145.

[14]   A.A. Berle and G.C. Means, *The Modern Corporation and Private Property* (London and New York: Macmillan Corporation, 1932).

Phase three, which was known as 'the quality of life' concept within social responsibility, became popular after the 1950s. The emergence of the concept is regarded as a significant metamorphosis in societal goals, which the nation experienced when society's principal requirement of business developed into the demand for increasing amounts of goods and services, thereby continuously raising the living standards of the American people.[15] When the basic living requirements of people have been satisfied, social problems such as air and water pollution, the health and safety of employees, the rate of employment, product safety and damage to the landscape become more prominent. As a result, the public places less trust in corporations, and national priorities shift from wealth accumulation to improvements in quality of life for the people. This phase involves a significant change in corporate objectives. The basic economic objective is starting to be seen as a component of corporate responsibility in combination with social responsibility and ethical responsibility, placing people as a central concern of corporate behaviour.

2.2 EMERGENCE OF THE SUSTAINABILITY CONCEPT IN THE GLOBALIZED ECONOMIC CLIMATE, AND THE INVOLVEMENT OF LAW

Regarding the discussion of CSR itself, the story goes back to the 1940s. In Dean Donal David's comments to the incoming MBA class at Harvard Business School in 1948, he exhorted future business executives to take heed of the responsibility that had come to rest on the shoulders of business leaders.[16] It is argued that the roots of contemporary social responsibility theories and norms can be traced back to the period between 1945 and 1960, the early years of the Cold War.[17] Bert Spector has argued that Dean David advocated an expanded notion of CSR, using the norm as a means of aligning business interests with a defence of free-market capitalism.[18]

However, the term CSR was not exported from the United States until the 1970s. For example, in the United Kingdom the concept of CSR was

---

[15] R. Hay and E. Gray, 'Social Responsibilities of Business Management' (1974) 17 *Academy of Management Journal* 135 at 137.

[16] B. Spector, 'Business Responsibility in a Divided World: The Cold War Roots of the Corporate Social Responsibility Movement' (2008) 9 *Enterprise and Society: International Journal of Business History* 314.

[17] *Ibid.*

[18] *Ibid.*

non-existent until the 1970s. This lack of CSR as a corporate strategy was due to a greater reliance on public-owned enterprises for the performance of essential tasks, and a long-standing governmental involvement in the British economy and society.[19] This state involvement in Britain before the 1970s limited companies' roles in executive CSR, and largely prevented them from putting CSR on their corporate agendas. More recently, pressure from the European Union has been a major factor influencing the United Kingdom to adopt the term. Since 1973, the United Kingdom's membership of the European Economic Community has had an impact on the recognition of CSR by both government and corporations in Britain. The experience of the United States is still regarded as a model for the development of CSR in other jurisdictions.

Figuratively speaking, CSR as an analytical concept for assessing desirable and practical relationships between corporations, shareholders and society is an 'American expert product'.[20] Formal definitions of CSR started to proliferate in the 1970s, with a strong emphasis on corporate social performance at a time when CSR was becoming the centre of debates surrounding corporate social responsiveness and corporate social performance.[21] Companies at that time were responding to social and environmental issues, rather than voluntarily discharging or assuming responsibility to society.[22]

On the CSR front, fewer definitions of CSR were produced in the 1980s with empirical studies focusing on CSR practice and discussion of alternative approaches, such as corporate public policy, business ethics, stakeholder theory and strategic management.[23] The term 'business ethics' started to be broadly accepted in the 1980s, with a focus on fostering an ethical corporate culture and an explosion in research on

---

[19] E. Epstein, 'The Social Role of Business Enterprise in Britain: An American Perspective' (1977) 14 *Journal of Management Studies* 213.

[20] *Ibid.*

[21] A.B. Carroll, 'Corporate Social Responsibility: Evolution of a Definitional Construct' (1999) 38 *Business and Society* 268; S.P. Sethi, 'Dimensions of Corporate Social Performance: An Analytic Framework' (1975) 17 *California Management Review* 58.

[22] See R. Ackerman, 'How Companies Respond to Social Demands' (1973) 51 *Harvard Business Review* 88; see also E.A. Murray, 'The Social Response Process in Commercial Banks: An Empirical Investigation' (1976) 1 *Academy of Management Review* 5.

[23] A.B. Carroll, 'Corporate Social Responsibility: Evolution of a Definitional Construct' (1999) 38 *Business and Society* 268 at 285–9.

corporate financial performance.[24] The term 'business ethics' is an oxymoron,[25] bringing two contradictory concepts together with cheerful pessimism or into a deafening silence.[26] The debate surrounding this oxymoron is increasing in intensity, along with the debates concerning CSR. Carroll and Shabana argued that for academics, the 'search for a business case for CSR began and came of age' during the 1980s.[27]

With the globalization of corporations and their products and an increasing number of multinational companies in the 1990s, the term CSR has increased its global reach, as well as its strong orientation in the United States. In Europe, CSR has been achieved through regulations, but in countries in Africa or Asia, softer institutions such as religions or tribal traditions and customs have shaped societal expectations of businesses organizations in a more implicit manner.[28] Globalized corporate citizens are required to respond to external CSR challenges by seeking solutions through dialogue with affected shareholders and with government representatives and NGOs, and by pledging compliance with global principles and codes regarding environmental impact, disclosure and transparency, human rights and financial integrity.[29] Corporations are expected to act as 'peace-makers' in a world of rising tensions.[30] As a result, the 1990s and 2000s became the era of global corporate citizenship, with corporations

---

[24]   W.C. Frederick, 'Corporate Social Responsibility: Deep Roots, Flourishing Growth, Promising Future' in A. Crane, A. McWilliams, D. Matten, J. Moon and D. Siegel (eds), *The Oxford Handbook of Corporate Social Responsibility* (Oxford: Oxford University Press, 2008) p. 522.

[25]   J.W. Collins, 'The Business Ethics an Oxymoron' (1994) *Business Horizon* 1.

[26]   A. Crane and D. Matten, *Business Ethics: Managing Corporate Citizen and Sustainability in the Age of Globalisation*, 3rd edn (Oxford: Oxford University Press 2010) p. 4.

[27]   A.B. Carroll and K.M. Shabana, 'The Business Case for Corporate Social Responsibility: A Review of Concept, Research and Practice' (2010) *International Journal of Management Reviews* 85 at 88.

[28]   D. Matten and J. Moon, 'Implicit and Explicit CSR: A Conceptual Framework for a Comparative Understanding of Corporate Social Responsibility' (2008) 33 *Academy of Management Review* 404.

[29]   M. McIntosh, R. Thomas, D. Leipziger and G. Coleman, *Living Corporate Citizenship: Strategic Routes to Socially Responsible Business* (Harlow and London: Prentice-Hall/*Financial Times*, 2003).

[30]   T.L Ford and C.A. Schipani, 'Corporate Governance, Stakeholder Accountability, and Sustainable Peace: A Symposium' (2002) 35 *Vanderbilt Journal of Transnational Law* 389.

accepting responsibility and aspiring to attain global citizenship.[31] Social responsibility is now worldwide in scope and magnitude, and businesses are increasingly being recognized as truly global corporate citizens.[32]

Since the beginning of the new century there has been a series of commercial crises, from the corporate collapse of Barings Bank to the collapse of Enron, from the financial scandal surrounding Royal Ahold to the collapse of HIH in Australia, and of course the Wall Street financial crisis that is likely to be with us for some time. Although CSR continues to offer legitimacy to businesses in considering the interests of stakeholders, the emergence of and a preoccupation with business ethics has obscured the continued growth and development of the social responsibility theme.[33] In an atmosphere of tension and anxiety it seems logical that the attention of both academics and practitioners should have turned to profit-making and profit maximization in order to reduce the negative effects of the financial crisis on domestic economies. However, does this goal necessarily have to be achieved at the expense of CSR? Environmentalists and other pluralists in the areas of corporate law and corporate governance are worried that sustainability and increased corporate responsibility towards social and philanthropic concerns are being removed from the boardroom agenda as companies tighten their belts in the face of turbulent stock markets, the 'credit crunch' and a looming economic slowdown. Also, it could be argued that CSR may be regarded by corporations as a 'fad whose time has come and gone'.[34]

CSR is an unavoidable theme affecting economic endeavours in twenty-first century society. CSR is infiltrating into corporate awareness, corporate culture and corporate strategies, which should all be consistent with the overall economic climate. Since each corporation has its own individual stakeholder groups, companies need to develop unique and customized ways of expressing and realizing their CSR strategy. While globalization has thrust corporations into societies' awareness, theories of

---

[31] W.C. Frederick, 'Corporate Social Responsibility: Deep Roots, Flourishing Growth, Promising Future' in A. Crane, A. McWilliams, D. Matten, J. Moon and D. Siegel (eds), *The Oxford Handbook of Corporate Social Responsibility* (Oxford: Oxford University Press, 2008) p. 522 at 527–8.

[32] M. McIntosh, R. Thomas, D. Leipziger and G. Coleman, *Living Corporate Citizenship: Strategic Routes to Socially Responsible Business* (Prentice-Hall/*Financial Times*, 2003).

[33] A.B. Carroll, 'A look at the future of business ethics', *Athens Banner-Herald*, 10 January 2009.

[34] T. Macalister, 'A change in the climate: credit crunch makes the bottom line the top issue', *The Guardian*, 6 March 2008.

CSR continue to develop and be practised in various ways that parallel the socio-cultural diversity of values found in corporations throughout the world.[35]

Economic responsibility and social values within the CSR remit make 'sustainability' 'a mantra for the twenty-first century'.[36] Sustainability is 'the activities demonstrating the inclusion of social and environmental aspects in the normal business operations of a company and its interaction with its stakeholders'. The concept has economic, social and environmental dimensions, a triad which is known as the triple bottom line of corporate sustainability.[37] It encourages a growth in economic, social and environmental capital based on the rejection of a simple focus on economic sustainability, and involving a consideration of the survival of the company itself and the continuing development of its financial health. In the context of sustainability, the development of CSR has shed light on discussions of the role played by law in promoting socially responsible companies. It is questionable whether law can meet the challenges brought by the requirement for sustainability when the world is experiencing an unprecedented rate of change.[38] Theoretical insights into corporations, company law and corporate governance are emerging, illuminating concerns about the assessment and implementation of CSR. The next cycle of law and policy reform regarding corporate responsibility, corporate objectives and corporate accountability, with associated discussions of directors' duties in corporate law, is likely to engage with the development of CSR in the twenty-first century. The notion of company law and related regulations must be consistent with, and keep up to date with, changes in thinking and practice in terms of law and

---

[35]   W.C. Frederick, 'Corporate Social Responsibility: Deep Roots, Flourishing Growth, Promising Future' in A. Crane, A. McWilliams, D. Matten, J. Moon and D. Siegel (eds), *The Oxford Handbook of Corporate Social Responsibility* (Oxford: Oxford University Press, 2008) p. 522 at 528–9.

[36]   T. Dyllick and K. Hockerts, 'Beyond the Business Case for Corporate Sustainability' (2002) 11 *Business Strategy and the Environment* 130; see also B. Horrigan, '21st Century Corporate Social Responsibility Trend: An Emerging Comparative Body of Law and Regulation on Corporate Responsibility, Governance and Sustainability' (2007) 4 *Macquarie Journal of Business Law* 85.

[37]   T. Dyllick and K. Hockerts, 'Beyond the Business Case for Corporate Sustainability' (2002) 11 *Business Strategy and the Environment* 130 at 131.

[38]   R.M. Bratspies, 'Sustainability: Can Law Meet the Challenge?' (2011) 34 *Suffolk Transitional Law Review* 283.

regulation generally.[39] Law attempts to constitute a corporate 'conscience'[40] by getting companies 'to want to do what they should do, not just legally compliant outputs or actions'.[41] The embedding of legal characteristics in the CSR movement will change understandings of the objectives of law and regulation, of the sources and scope of legal and regulatory standards, and of enforcement mechanisms.[42] These changes will need to be consistent with a wider framework encompassing the corporate responsiveness of systems and dynamic governance, regulations and responsibility across the global public, private and civil sectors.[43]

The development of sustainability is closely associated with the history of government policies, regulation and law.[44] In 1972, the Club of Rome published its report *The Limits to Growth*,[45] and observed that economic growth was in direct conflict with ecological sustainability. In the same year, the UN Conference on the Human Environment was held in Stockholm and the United Nations Environment Programme was established in Nairobi. Further, it is believed that environmental challenges require international cooperation from all: states, business and civil society. Awareness of the scope of international environmental law extended to create a new field defined by science, philosophy, ethics, economics and politics.[46] It is argued in the *Corporate Responsibility*

---

[39]   C. Parker, C. Scott, N. Lacey and J. Braithwaite (eds), *Regulating Law* (Oxford: Oxford University Press, 2004) pp. 3–5.

[40]   P. Selznick, *The Communitarian Persuasion* (Washington, DC: Woodrow Wilson Centre Press, 2002) pp. 4–6.

[41]   C. Parker, 'Meta-Regulation: Legal Accountability for Corporate Responsibility' in D. McBarnet, A. Voiculescu and T. Campbell (eds), *The New Corporate Accountability: Corporate Social Responsibility and the Law* (Cambridge: Cambridge University Press, 2007) p. 207 at p. 208.

[42]   B. Horrigan, '21st Century Corporate Social Responsibility Trend: An Emerging Comparative Body of Law and Regulation on Corporate Responsibility, Governance and Sustainability' (2007) 4 *Macquarie Journal of Business Law* 85 at 87.

[43]   *Ibid.*

[44]   K. Bosselmann, *The Principle of Sustainability: Transforming Law and Governance* (Aldershot: Ashgate, 2008) p. 25.

[45]   D.H. Meadows, D.L. Meadows and W. Behrens, *The Limits to Growth* (New York: Universe Books, 1972).

[46]   A. Kiss and D. Shelton, *International Environmental Law*, 2nd edn (New York: Transnational Publisher, 2000) pp. 11–25; see also P. Sands, *Principles of International Environmental Law*, 2nd edn (Cambridge: Cambridge University Press, 2003).

Report[47] generated by the UK government's Department for Business, Enterprise and Regulatory Reform (DBERR, now known as the Department for Business, Innovation and Skills, DBIS) that the vision of corporate responsibility is to satisfy everyone's basic needs and enjoy a better quality of life, but to do so without compromising the quality of life for future generations.[48] Corporate responsibility is the collective goal of individuals, groups, business and government, aiming to limit climate change and protect natural resources, stimulate cohesive and healthy communities, and promote fairness and justice in order to build a strong and stable economy.[49] The direct and indirect effects of corporate responsibility are improved efficiency, better risk management, attracting and retaining respected employees, the adoption of innovative practices and products, and ultimately attracting more shareholders, especially institutional shareholders who are willing to engage in socially responsible investment.[50]

The financial crisis of 2008 makes the ethical dimension as important as the regulatory one.[51] On 15 September 2008, 'Dark Monday' triggered a radical reconstruction of Wall Street with the bankruptcy of Lehman Brothers, the change in ownership of Merrill Lynch and US$40 million in government relief required by AIG. The question has been asked whether, in the aftermath of an era of business mistakes, ethical mistakes are also part of the crisis.[52] Recent developments in CSR theory have provided a socially responsible performance paradigm to establish a solid foundation for stakeholder-oriented strategic management policies. Recent developments in relation to CSR, such as corporate strategic policies, environmental stewardship and sustainability, can all be viewed as implementations of stakeholder theory.[53] Since 2007, unusually at a time when life for most corporations has grown decidedly tougher due to the global financial crisis, businesses 'as diverse as KPMG, the German

---

[47]   HM Government, *Corporate Responsibility Report*, available at www.bis.gov.uk/files/file50312.pdf.

[48]   *Ibid.* at 5.

[49]   *Ibid.* at 5.

[50]   *Ibid.* at 6–7.

[51]   T. Donaldson, 'Three Ethical Roots of the Economic Crisis' (2012) 106 *Journal of Business Ethics* 5.

[52]   *Ibid.*

[53]   S. Zambon and A. Del Bello, 'Towards a Stakeholder Responsible Approach: The Constructive Role of Reporting' (2005) 5 *Corporate Governance: International Journal of Business in Society* 130.

chemical giant Bayer, the tobacco multinational Reynolds, Ford, Star-bucks, BP and Shell have all issued CSR reports, reaffirming their commitment to one of the most significant causes of the twenty-first century'.[54] It is worth mentioning that the FTSE Group, an independent company jointly owned by the *Financial Times* and the London Stock Exchange and a world-leader in the creation and management of over 120,000 equity, bond and alternative asset class indices,[55] sets FTSE4Goods inclusion criteria[56] which are designed to measure the performance of companies against globally-recognized corporate responsibility standards, and to facilitate investments in those companies. Apart from working towards environmental sustainability, the FTSE Group demands that member stocks develop positive relationships with stakeholders, uphold and support universal human rights, ensure good supply chain labour standards and act to counter bribery.

Taking the United Kingdom as an example, recent responses to the financial crisis from various authorities and firms have further asserted the importance of promoting stakeholders' interests to benefit the long-term interests of the company. Many of the factors seem to be inextricably linked to a failure in corporate governance during the unfolding of this financial crisis. The disadvantages of the shareholder value principle, particularly the pursuit of immediate short-term interests and a lack of responsibility to stakeholders (primarily customers), have been suggested as the main reasons for the global financial crisis. It is argued that contemporary financial services firms acquired a habit of 'rewarding short and suffering (or succeeding) long', which is normally known as the doctrine of 'Pay for Peril'.[57] The state of the global economy since 2007, in which there has been an excessively 'narrow focus on "the business of business" in the financial sector, has almost brought the global economy to its knees'.[58]

It has been argued that one of the fundamental causes of the crisis was a lack of business ethics and integrity.[59] 'It has been both a failure of

---

[54]   S.D. Wild, 'Accountants and the Crisis: CSR – Man Overboard' (2008) *Accountancy Age*, available at www.accountancyage.com/accountancyage/features/2222355/accountants-crisis-csr-man.

[55]   See FTSE: the Index Company at www.ftse.com/About_Us/index.jsp.

[56]   See FTSE, *FTSE4Good Index Series Inclusion Criteria* (2008).

[57]   T. Donaldson, 'Three Ethical Roots of the Economic Crisis' (2012) 106 *Journal of Business Ethics* 5 at 6.

[58]   S. Carey, 'CSR and the Credit Crunch' (2009) *New Statesman* (January).

[59]   C. Pedamon, 'Corporate Social Responsibility: A New Approach to Promoting Integrity and Responsibility' (2010) 31 *Company Lawyer* 172.

governments to regulate and the failure of businesses to understand their broader ethical responsibilities and focus too narrowly on short-term profits.'[60] During the 2008 financial crisis, since which time there has been a very serious economic downturn in the global economy, there has been a temptation under the pressure of low budgets to disregard stakeholders' interests and downgrade CSR. In reviewing the sustainable landscape of the business community, it would be very easy to make an assumption that business leaders are becoming increasingly reluctant to include CSR in their business strategic agendas. However, in line with the suggestions of officials in the United Kingdom, it would be extremely dangerous for corporations to ignore stakeholders' interests and ethical concerns, particularly because this crisis was partly caused by an ethical failure in the first place.[61] Ignoring CSR in the post-crisis context would demonstrate a serious lack of understanding of the nature of business, since this ethical crisis is not unprecedented but its seriousness is.[62]

2.3   CORPORATE SOCIAL RESPONSIBILITY IN ACTION

As early as the eighteenth century, some companies acted in a socially responsible manner by building houses and schools for their employees and their children.[63] Over the last few decades, a great deal of literature has focused on incentives for corporations, as well as the nature, advantages and drawbacks of CSR. Bowen was an early scholar who claimed that businesses have an obligation to 'pursue those policies, to make those decisions or to follow those lines of action' which are desirable in terms of the objective and value of our society'.[64] Globalization has increased the awareness of business responsibility within society, and CSR is widely recognized as a worthwhile commitment to ensure sustainable benefits for both corporations and communities. It also functions as a significant basis for a business to build the trust and

---

[60]   S. Carey, 'CSR and the Credit Crunch' (2009) *New Statesman* (January).

[61]   *Ibid.*

[62]   C. Pedamon, 'Corporate Social Responsibility: A New Approach to Promoting Integrity and Responsibility' (2010) 31 *Company Lawyer* 172.

[63]   See T. Cannon, *Corporate Responsibility* (Harlow: Pearson Education, 1994) p. 16.

[64]   H. B. Bowen, *Social Responsibilities of the Businessman* (New York: Harper & Row, 1953).

confidence of stakeholders, which is a key source of competitive edge and a crucial aspect of systematic strategic management policies.[65] However, CSR has also become something of a millstone for the business community, since it has created a new raft of pressures in an increasingly complicated and sophisticated trading environment, making sustainability a buzzword for every corporation that is trying to generate support.[66] It is important, under the principles of CSR, to conduct business in a socially and environmentally responsible manner, in order to move corporate strategy in the direction of a more stakeholder-friendly model by requiring companies to 'go beyond the creation of short-term shareholder wealth in pursuit of broader objectives such as sustainable growth, equitable employment practices, and long-term social and environmental well-being'.[67]

CSR essentially involves a shift in focus in terms of corporate responsibility, moving from wealth maximization for shareholders within the obligation of the law[68] towards responsibility to a broader range of stakeholders, the combination of social, environmental and community concerns, including protection of the environment and the local community, and accountability for philanthropic, ethical and legal obligations.[69] CSR has always been a topic worthy of attention in the public agendas of governments and corporations, and it continues to be an issue of significant interest in various spheres of society.[70] In parallel, it has

---

[65] S. Urip, *CSR Strategies: Corporate Social Responsibility for a Competitive Edge in Emerging Markets* (Chichester: John Wiley & Sons, 2010) p. 13.

[66] D.E. Hawkins, *Corporate Social Responsibility: Balancing Tomorrow's Sustainability and Today's Profitability* (Basingstoke: Palgrave MacMillan, 2006) p. 1.

[67] C.A. Williams and J.M. Conley, 'An Emerging Third Way? The Erosion of the Anglo-American Shareholder Value Construct' (2005) 38 *Cornell International Law Journal* 493 at 496.

[68] M. Friedman, 'The social responsibility of business is to increase its profits', *New York Times Magazine*, 13 September 1970.

[69] D. McBarnet, 'Corporate Social Responsibility beyond Law, through Law, for Law: The New Corporate Accountability' in D. McBarnet, A. Voiculescu and T. Campbell (eds), *The New Corporate Accountability: Corporate Social Responsibility and the Law* (Cambridge: Cambridge University Press, 2007) p. 9.

[70] F. den Hond, F.G.A. de Bakker and P. Neergaard, 'Introduction to Managing Corporate Social Responsibility in Action: Talking, Doing and Measuring' in F. den Hond, F.G.A. de Bakker and P. Neergaard (eds), *Managing Corporate Social Responsibility in Action: Talking, Doing and Measuring* (Aldershot: Ashgate, 2007).

also gained a prominent position in academic work, from a multi-disciplinary perspective as well as from practice-oriented scholars, as demonstrated by the many studies on different business and society initiatives.

In spite of the voluntary nature of CSR, legal responsibilities under company law, employment law, consumer protection law, environmental law and insolvency law are playing an increasingly important role in enforcing 'voluntary' CSR policies. 'There is then increasing legal intervention in the arena of CSR, to an extent where its voluntariness must be questioned not only in terms of the social and market forces, but in terms of the legal forces driving it.'[71] Few of the commitments which companies normally sign up to in their voluntary CSR polices[72] are entirely free of legal obligations, although they are not exclusively regulated by corporate law. Legal, market and social forces always play interactive roles in corporate governance mechanisms. Commitments are routinely made by companies in their codes of conduct, in order to comply with the law and meet their legal obligations. The law is being deployed to enforce, rather than simply to encourage, commitments to corporate stakeholders in order to move towards more ethically, socially and environmentally responsible corporations. Beyond mere compliance, even CSR codes and policies that are presented as voluntary are in fact increasingly being encroached on by law. 'New legal developments are directly and indirectly fostering voluntary CSR and market pressures, while new legal tools are being evolved, and old ones used creatively, to make what businesses have perceived as voluntary, or beyond law, in fact legally enforceable.'[73]

Given the intensity of the debate about different corporate governance models in different areas, it is easy and logical to assume that systems differ markedly between Anglo-American countries and continental European countries and Japan. However, 'recent events and market forces

---

[71]   D. McBarnet, 'Corporate Social Reasonability beyond Law, through Law, for Law: The New Corporate Accountability' in D. McBarnet, A. Voiculescu and T. Campbell (eds), *The New Corporate Accountability: Corporate Social Responsibility and the Law* (Cambridge: Cambridge University Press, 2007) p. 9 at p. 43.

[72]   Addressing issues such as health and safety, discrimination, the environment and corruption.

[73]   D. McBarnet, 'Corporate Social Reasonability beyond Law, through Law, for Law: The New Corporate Accountability' in D. McBarnet, A. Voiculescu and T. Campbell (eds), *The New Corporate Accountability: Corporate Social Responsibility and the Law* (Cambridge: Cambridge University Press, 2007) p. 9 at p. 31.

are leading toward increased harmonisation of corporate governance on each side of the Atlantic'.[74] The interests of various stakeholders are widely considered by directors in the United Kingdom and the United States. The growth of large national corporations in the first decade of the twentieth century has already made it evident that directors' decisions profoundly affect corporate stakeholders, including consumers and the larger communities that are dependent on industry.[75] More recently, companies in the United States and the United Kingdom have begun recruiting the services of CSR consultants to produce CSR codes, write or verify CSR reports, train staff in CSR and market their CSR credentials.[76] In a worldwide business survey in December 2005, among 4,238 executives surveyed, 84 per cent thought that high returns had to be balanced with contributions to the broader public good, while only 6 per cent of the executives agreed with Friedman's view that the sole purpose of business was to produce high returns for the shareholder.[77]

2.4 EVOLUTION AND MORALITY IN THE HISTORY OF CSR IN CHINA

The significance of the corporate responsibility movement cannot be thoroughly discussed without reviewing its history. Business has traditionally been regarded as 'a rightly regulated instrument of social development'.[78] Nearly 40 years ago, the corporate responsibility movement was seen by Eberstadt as a historical swing to recreate the social contract of power with responsibility, which seemed likely to become an

---

[74] A. Payne, 'Corporate Governance in the USA and Europe: They are Closer than You Might Think' (2006) 6(1) *Corporate Governance: International Journal of Effective Board Performance* 69 at 70.

[75] A. Winkler, 'Corporate Law or the Law of Business? Stakeholders and Corporate Governance at the End of History' (2004) 67 *Law and Contemporary Problems* 109 at 115.

[76] D. McBarnet, 'Corporate Social Responsibility beyond Law, through Law, for Law: The New Corporate Accountability' in D. McBarnet, A. Voiculescu and T. Campbell (eds), *The New Corporate Accountability: Corporate Social Responsibility and the Law* (Cambridge: Cambridge University Press, 2007) p. 9 at p. 11.

[77] McKinsey & Co., 'The McKinsey Global Survey of Business Executives: Business and Society' (2006) 2 *McKinsey Quarterly* 33.

[78] N.N. Eberstadt, 'What History Tells Us about Corporate Responsibility' (1973) 66 *Business and Society Review* 76 at 77.

important and welcome reform.[79] Despite the generally accepted fact within academia that the term 'CSR' was first used in 1953 by Bowen,[80] the practice of and evidence for social responsibility from business organizations can be traced back to ancient Greece. The recent growth and popularity of CSR can be traced back over centuries to find evidence of the business community's concern for society.[81] The spirit of CSR and CSR-oriented corporate behaviours and actions provides evidence and support for the emergence and development of CSR as a subject, with discussion and study from various disciplines. Most of the CSR-related research began in the United States, where a sizeable body of literature has accumulated. However, Europe has also become captivated with CSR and has taken it as a serious topic for research, conferences and consultancies.[82] Countries in Asia have also begun to pay increasing amounts of attention to CSR policies and practice.[83]

Coming back to the theme of this book, no investigation of CSR in contemporary China can be complete without a discussion of the impact on CSR from historical and cultural perspectives. The history of CSR in China has many aspects, and the understanding of different dimensions of the concept is key to realizing the assorted ways in which corporations have interacted with various stakeholders in the past, as well as predicting the trend of these relationships in the future. To help appreciate the context in which Chinese CSR evolved, it is reasonable to begin with a discussion of Chinese history and the development of Chinese business organizations and related transactions, all regulated by the unique Chinese legal system.

---

[79]   *Ibid.*

[80]   H.R. Bowen, *Social Responsibilities of Businessmen* (New York: Harper & Row, 1953); see also G. Balabanis, H. Phillips and J. Lyall, 'Corporate Social Responsibility and Economic Performance in the Top British Companies: Are They Linked' (1998) 98 *European Business Review* 25; W.B. Werther and D. Chandler, *Strategic Corporate Social Responsibility: Stakeholders in a Global Environment* (London: Sage, 2006).

[81]   A.B. Carroll, 'A History of Corporate Social Responsibility: Concept and Practice' in A. Crane, A. McWilliams, D. Matten, J. Moon and D. Siegel (eds), *The Oxford Handbook of Corporate Social Responsibility* (Oxford: Oxford University Press, 2008) p. 20.

[82]   D. Matten and J. Moon, 'Corporate Social Responsibility Education in Europe' (2004) 54 *Journal of Business Ethics* 323.

[83]   A.B. Carroll, 'A History of Corporate Social Responsibility: Concept and Practice' in A. Crane, A. McWilliams, D. Matten, J. Moon and D. Siegel (eds), *The Oxford Handbook of Corporate Social Responsibility* (Oxford: Oxford University Press, 2008) p. 20 at p. 21.

In this chapter, the discussion will include the historical social responsibility values of Chinese businessmen in the context of the dominant Confucian ethical and philosophical system in China. Going beyond ancient Chinese history, attention will be given to two important periods of time in the history of business organization development and reconstruction in China. These two periods are the late *Qing* dynasty (1644–1911) since the 1860s, and the *Ming Guo* period (1912–1949). Systems featuring '*Zhuanli*' (whereby the government offers particular corporation(s) monopolist rights on certain products over a period of time and/or in a certain geographical area); '*Baoxiao*' (rendering to the government via donations or contributions from individuals or organizations to their superiors); and '*Guanli*' (official government-authorized profits and dividends for investors) will be discussed in order to analyse the late *Qing* dynasty. Furthermore, CSR initiatives known as *Sheiye Jiuguo* (rescuing China through practical enterprise), *Shehui Cishan* (social charitable service) and *Laozi Duili* (conflicts between employees and investors) will be also discussed in relation to the period of the Republic of China.

2.4.1   Value of Confucian Culture and Chinese Contemporary CSR

While speaking about 'Corporate Citizenship and Socially Responsible Investment in Hong Kong' in 2002, it was argued by Robert Davies, CEO of the Prince of Wales International Business Leader Forum, that 'business culture and the definition of corporate responsibility must always take account of the local context'.[84] Therefore, it is important to understand the culture that infuses business practice in China in order to have a good understanding of CSR in contemporary China. Business practice in China, as in most of the countries in East Asia, can be seen as deriving from a Confucian philosophy, which is often used to explain the central importance that many Asians place on bonds of family and friendship and the respect and courtesy they show for wisdom, leadership, customs and the elderly.[85]

---

[84]   R. Davies, 'Corporate Citizenship and Socially Responsible Investment: Emerging Challenges and Opportunities in Asia', paper presented at the Association for Sustainable and Responsible Investment in Asia Conference, Hong Kong, 10 January 2005.

[85]   G. Whelan, 'Corporate Social Responsibility in Asia: A Confucian Context' in S. May, G. Cheney and J. Roper, *The Debate over Corporate Social Responsibility* (Oxford: Oxford University Press, 2008) p. 105 at p. 106.

China is a nation with a history of civilization spanning more than 5,000 years, and the Chinese have been deeply influenced by Confucian philosophy for more than 2,000 years. Confucius lived from 551 to 479 BC; his influence on Asian culture is remarkable and arguably outweighs that of Aristotle in the West.[86] Confucianism has undergone an evolutionary history over thousands of years, and has become the idea most widely accepted and practised by the Chinese people as their dominant culture with an impact on values. The central notion of Confucianism is the idea that all people maintain 'a sort of familistic relationship with each other'.[87] 'Confucius made the natural love and obligations obtaining between members of the family the basis for a general morality.'[88] Confucius believed that a society structured or formed in a manner that is analogous to the arrangement of a family would normally give rise to the greatest good for the greatest number.[89] It is argued that Confucianism is organic and utilitarian in that it considers the greatest good for a given community as its fundamental ethical concern, and particularistic because one has different duties and obligations to various parties depending on one's personal relationship with them.[90] The philosophy was established to broaden the awareness of justified values to form a general morality. Furthermore, the system of thought is also closely related to the idea of benevolence and justified philanthropic corporate actions.

Confucian principles are established upon five cardinal virtues: *Ren* (Kindness, Benevolence); *Li* (Courtesy, Propriety); *Yi* (Justice, Righteousness); *Zhi* (Wisdom); and *Xin* (Trust, Fidelity).[91] Confucian philosophy rests on two primary facets: *Ren* and *Li*. *Ren* is variously described as

[86]	L. Marinoff, 'What is Business Ethics? What are its Prospects in Asia?' in F.J. Richter and P.C.M. Mar (eds), *Asia's New Crisis: Renewal through Total Ethical Management* (Singapore: John Wiley & Son, 2004) p. 16.

[87]	H.C. Tai, 'The Oriental Alternative: An Hypothesis on Culture and Economy' in H.C. Tai (ed.), *Confucianism and Economic Development: An Oriental Alternative* (Washington, DC: Washington Institute Press, 1989) p. 6 at p. 14.

[88]	D.C. Lau, 'Introduction in Confucius' in *The Analects* (London: Penguin Books, 1979) p. 18.

[89]	X. Yao, *An Introduction to Confucianism* (Cambridge: Cambridge University Press, 2007) pp. 26–7.

[90]	G. Whelan, 'Corporate Social Responsibility in Asia: A Confucian Context' in S. May, G. Cheney and J. Roper, *The Debate over Corporate Social Responsibility* (Oxford: Oxford University Press, 2008) p. 105 at p. 107.

[91]	It was Confucius who suggested '*Ren*', '*Yi*' and '*Li*', while Mencius expanded the idea by suggesting '*Zhi*' and Dong Zhongshu completed the five virtues by suggesting '*Xin*'.

benevolence, philanthropy and humaneness, while *Li* reflects the rules and norms of society that dictate acceptable behaviour.[92] Confucius' theory of virtue is fundamental for an understanding of human nature based on *Ren*, relational-centric behaviour as a result of mutual understanding.[93] Furthermore, the public relational system is based on localization, represented as *Li*. This metaphorically transcribes extensive behavioural patterns that are recognized as appropriate and authentic ways of approaching human life, and codes of conduct which are seen by Westerners as rites, rituals, observances, conducts, etiquettes, and the social and political system.[94] *Ren* and *Li* together address the nature and essence of organizations, including business organizations; they are shaped by the people in the organization, while each individual is shaped by the society. Therefore, an understanding of the people in the organization and the relationships between these individuals (the internal stakeholders of the corporation), as well as the external stakeholders of the business organization, is key for the strategic design and development of that company.[95]

Furthermore, consistent with *Ren*, *Yi* emphasizes mutual profit and the limitation of self-interests by encouraging honesty and righteousness.[96] *Zhi,* interpreted by Mencius, emphasizes wisdom to differentiate right and wrong, define value, and the ability to understand oneself and other people.[97] It is implied in Confucianism that people should be wise enough to make decisions consistent with moral commitments based on judgements and depending on their knowledge. Changes in people's knowledge and awareness of CSR will result in the modification of

---

[92]   Confucian (552–479 BC), *Lun Yu.*

[93]   R. Fan, *Reconstructionist Confucianism: Rethinking Morality after the West* (London: Springer, 2010) pp. 206–8.

[94]   R. Fan, 'Reconsidering Surrogate Decision Marking: Aristotelianism and Confucianism on Ideal Human Relations' (2002) 52 *Philosophy East and West* 346 at 353–6.

[95]   J. Roper and H. Hu, 'Modern Chinese Confucianism: A Model for Western Human Capital Development?', paper presented at the European Academy of Business in Society Annual Colloquium, Warsaw (2005) p. 5; see also J. Roper and E. Weymes, 'Reinstating the Collective: A Confucian Approach to Well-being and Social Capital Development in a Globalised Economy' (2007) 26 *Journal of Corporate Citizenship* 135.

[96]   D.C. Lau, *Confucian: The Analects* (London: Penguin Books, 1979); see also S.H. Hsu, 'A New Business Excellence Model with Business Integrity from Ancient Confucian Thinking' (2007) 18 *Total Quality Management and Business Excellence* 413.

[97]   D.C. Lau, *Confucian: The Analects* (London: Penguin Books, 1979).

people's attitudes towards CSR, and facilitate its adoption in corporate strategy. *Xin* emphasizes sincerity and honesty, which enables smooth stakeholder relationships (including a better supply chain) and better relationships between corporations, the local community and the environment. *Xin* is a deep and profound sense of moral truth with a sense of moral consistency, coherence and completeness.[98] Despite the fact that *Xin* is closely related to moral justice and comprehensiveness, it is argued that fiduciary communities or organizations with the virtue of *Xin* should be ones where the relationships between people are established based on mutual trust (*xin ren*) and creditable prestige (*xin yu*), which derives exclusively from the virtue of carrying the burden of one's commitment in maintaining one's own creditability (*xin yong*), believability, reliability or dependability (*xin lai*).[99] Applying this analysis to a corporate perspective, this mutual trust can be extended to the relationship between companies and their stakeholders, including consumers, suppliers and local communities, while creditable prestige is beneficial for corporate reputations. Creditability and reliability have a direct and positive impact on long-term sustainable development of corporations towards their eventual status as creditable corporate citizens.

If the focus is shifted to the various stakeholders, the need to protect their interests can also find its roots within Confucian philosophy. The five virtues were those criteria and values that people used in exercising and executing a self-cultivated Confucian philosophy. This people-centred concept is a reflection of the values of Confucianism, including collectivism, hierarchy, harmony, loyalty and strategic thinking, and it has had a great impact on the development of human capital in business organizations in China.[100] The relationships between employer and employee and between employees are expected to be based on trust and respect. Within corporations, employers owe loyalty to their employees who are more likely to be highly committed to their work and their employer; this mutual regard exists in order to establish a relationship which reflects

---

[98]   Z.L. Lu, 'Fiduciary Society and Confucian Theory of Xin-on Tu Wei-ming's Fiduciary Proposal' (2001) 11 *Asian Philosophy* 83 at 83–5.

[99]   *Ibid.* at 90.

[100]   M. Warner and Y. Zhu, 'Human Resource Management "with Chinese Characters": A Comparative Study of the People's Republic of China and Taiwan' (2002) 9 *Asia Pacific Business Review* 21 at 37; J. Pfeffer and J.F. Veiga, 'Putting People First for Organisational Success' (1999) 13 *Academy of Management Executive* 37; see also W. Shen and R. Price, 'Confucianism, Labour Law and the Rise of Worker Activism' (2011), available at SSRN, http://ssrn.com/abstract=1789966.

humanity and benevolence.[101] Because of the hierarchical nature of Confucian loyalty, employers will regard employees (their primary internal stakeholders) as closer 'family members' in comparison with external stakeholders. Furthermore, the Confucian hierarchy encourages the recognition of talent and virtue, which will benefit the employees' interests in the increasingly globalized new economy and the modern knowledge-based economic climate.

The scope of the impact of Confucianism on stakeholders' interests extends beyond employees to other stakeholders in society, who might be externally or internally related to corporations or corporate decisions and are expected to be treated with benevolence, honour, respect and trust. Chinese society is dependent on this hierarchical operating system and on the efficient performance of roles, with individuals and organizations abiding by the social norms of conduct. The social norms are embodied within five relationship sets, between ruler and subject, father and son, husband and wife, elder and younger brothers, and elder person and younger person. These five relationships are characterized by a specific set of reciprocal properties or customs.[102] The importance of Confucian principles for organizations extends beyond relationships within the family to encompass the relationships with the wider community, which forms the basis of the notion of *Guanxi*. Despite the fact that *Guanxi* is always pejoratively and critically discussed in terms of the relationship between Chinese culture and Chinese legal systems, corruption, social defects, and so on, it does have its positive and useful sides, and it is necessary for a complete understanding of the influence of Chinese history on Chinese culture.

The establishment of *Guanxi* normally starts from *Jiating Guanxi* (the family relationship) and develops to more sophisticated forms of *Guanxi*; for example, *Pengyou Guanxi* (friendship relationships); *Shengyi Guanxi* (business relationships); *Shangye Guanxi* (commercial relationships); *Hezuo Guanxi* (corporate relationships, including the relationship between company and government or the one between company and local community); and *Huli Guanxi* (mutually beneficial relationships). Once *Guanxi* has been established the relationship becomes individualized, personal and particularistic, and *Guanxi* may play a more important and long-term role for corporations, enabling a smoother and more

---

[101]   J. Roper and E. Weymes, 'Reinstating the Collective: A Confucian Approach to Well-being and Social Capital in a Globalised Economy' (2007) 26 *Journal of Corporate Citizenship* 135.

[102]   M. Backman, *The Asian Insider: Unconditional Wisdom for Asian Business* (Basingstoke: Palgrave Macmillan, 2004) p. 10.

efficient supply chain and a more reputable relationship with government, local community, the environment and the media. This facilitates the long-term sustainable development of the corporation as a result of trust and respect for the integrity of others. *Guanxi* makes business negotiations and transactions more effective and efficient, with a basis of trust and personal integrity which is important for countries with comparatively poor legal systems and enforcement measures. 'The successful combination of a strong Confucian tradition with commercial activities epitomises the ideal of modern Confucian entrepreneurship, bringing together traditional cultural virtues and respecting the employee's value and new business concepts bred by a market economy with an innovative and sustainable consciousness.'[103]

Confucian philosophy thinks of the 'natural and human worlds as an organism made up of multitudinous interconnected parts. Each part has its proper position and function in the order of things. If any part falls from its place or is disrupted in its function, the harmony of the whole is impaired'.[104] This deeply influences the shape of business culture and corporate decision-making in China. According to Chinese tradition, businessmen have various ties with Confucian culture, and the notion of the Confucian businessman has been regarded as a more responsible and justified businessman in Chinese society for many years. This has always influenced the management philosophy of Chinese businesses.[105] With representatives such as Confucius and Mencius, Confucianism suggests that the traditional cultural values should place emphasis on human capital, interpersonal relations and harmonious development, and the core thoughts of society should be 'humanity, righteousness, harmony, loyalty, courtesy, honesty and cleanness'.[106]

---

[103] L. Zhao and J. Roper, 'A Confucian Approach to Well-being and Social Capital Development' (2011) 30 *Journal of Management Development* 740 at 743; see also R. Lufrano, *Honourable Merchants: Commerce and Self-Cultivation in Late Imperial China* (Honolulu, University of Hawaii Press, 1997); T.S. Cheung and A.Y. King, 'Righteousness and Profitableness: The Moral Choices of Contemporary Confucian Entrepreneurs' (2004) 54 *Journal of Business Ethics* 245.

[104] W.B. Zhang, *Confucianism and Modernization: Industrialization and Democratization of the Confucian Regions* (London: Macmillan Press, 1999) p. 37.

[105] W. Zhu and Y. Yao, 'On the Value of Traditional Confucian Culture and the Value of Modern Corporate Social Responsibility' (2008) 3 *International Journal of Business and Management* 58.

[106] For discussion of the relationship between these core thoughts and CSR, see W. Zhu and Y. Yao, 'On the Value of Traditional Confucian Culture and the

One of the key issues in business ethics is to put moral precepts into business practice. At the corporate level, the historic Confucian philosophy and the dominance of the state as a shareholder have had a profound effect on the development of Chinese corporate governance. Zapalska and Edwards suggested that Confucian cultural values are a significant factor in business and economic development in China.[107] The philosophy provides a foundation to establish a sustainable environment by regarding the world as an organic whole with multitudinous interconnected parts.[108] The harmonization of these interrelated parts depends on the smooth functioning of each part. Within a corporation, pursuit of profit and shareholder wealth maximization should be constrained by responsible corporate behaviours towards other sectors within society. Confucianism, linking corporate culture with historical culture, 'places emphasis on business ethics and morality, not dissimilar to the notion of CSR in a modern business context'.[109] CSR is defined as 'actions that purport to further some social good, beyond the interests of the firm'.[110]

According to Zhang, Confucius did not provide any general rules or principles for people to follow because situations are complicated and unpredictable.[111] It is emphasized that Confucius only taught that people should consider and understand the impact of their actions, rather than memorizing fixed rules.[112] This can be interpreted to suggest that, according to Confucius, a greater emphasis should be placed on the rule of virtue than on the rule of law.[113] Therefore, it is not hard to see that

Value of Modern Corporate Social Responsibility' (2008) 3 *International Journal of Business and Management* 58.

[107]   A.M. Zapalska and W. Edwards, 'Chinese Entrepreneurship in a Cultural and Economic Perspective' (2001) 39 *Journal of Small Business Management* 286.

[108]   W.B. Zhang, *Confucianism and Modernization: Industrialization and Democratization of the Confucian Regions* (London: Macmillan Press, 1999).

[109]   L. Zhao and J. Roper, 'A Confucian Approach to Well-being and Social Capital Development' (2011) 30 *Journal of Management Development* 740 at 743.

[110]   A. McWilliams and D. Siegel, 'Corporate Social Responsibility: A Theory of the Firm Perceptive' (2001) 26 *Academy of Management Review* 117.

[111]   W.B. Zhang, *Confucianism and Modernization: Industrialization and Democratization of the Confucian Regions* (London: Macmillan Press, 1999) p. 37.

[112]   *Ibid.* at 37.

[113]   G. Whelan, 'Corporate Social Responsibility in Asia: A Confucian Context' in S. May, G. Cheney and J. Roper, *The Debate over Corporate Social Responsibility* (Oxford: Oxford University Press, 2008) p. 105 at p. 107.

Confucianism embodies rich stakeholder and CSR principles which are voluntary in nature. The rule of virtue will persuade directors to have voluntary regard for corporate stakeholder based on Confucian philosophy. Adherents to the essence of Confucianism will consider the impact of corporate actions in a more socially responsible fashion. Compared with the rule of law, the rule of virtue is more flexible, more positive and more active.[114] It is more encouraging and convincing for corporate decision-makers to adopt voluntary ethical and philanthropic responsibilities in a society which puts more emphasis on the rule of virtue.

In China, the philosophy of social responsibility comes largely from Confucianism since the idea has been rooted in the country for more than 2,000 years, and it permeates the lives of Chinese people everywhere. Ethical and moral directions from corporate law legislators and philanthropic donations from companies are the results of the Chinese Confucian value system. In comparison with the ideas dominating in the Anglo-American model, Confucian thought[115] focuses more on collectivism than individualism, more on moral rightness than profit maximization, more on long-term interests than short-term ones, and more on hierarchy rather than on equality. Confucian thought also emphasizes the importance of harmony and minimizing disharmony and conflict within the company, thereby ensuring the smoother functioning of the firm. That will lead to directors' consideration for their employees. Also, Confucian thought recommends awareness of others and the pursuit of actions which are in harmony with others and the surrounding context. This will lead to corporate strategies in favour of external stakeholders, such as local communities, the environment, their consumers and suppliers. Ultimately, CSR philosophy will result in long-term performance benefits because of commitment and trust between stakeholders and the company, and will promote the media reputation of the corporations and further strengthen the reputation of 'China' as a brand.

---

[114]   L.S. Hus, *The Political Philosophy of Confucianism: An Interpretation of the Social and Political Ideas of Confucius, His Forerunners, and His Early Disciples* (London: George Rutledge & Son, 1932) p. 192.

[115]   For more discussion of the Anglo-American corporate governance model and Confucian values, see L. Miles, 'The Application of Anglo-American Corporate Practices in Societies Influenced by Confucian Values' (2006) 111 *Business and Society Review* 305.

2.4.2 Unique CSR Framework in China and Influences from Confucian Philosophy

While it is generally believed that CSR is a Westernized invention which arose in conjunction with modern industrialization, there is evidence that CSR in developing countries, including China, draws strongly on deep-rooted indigenous cultural traditions of philanthropy, business ethics and community embeddedness.[116] There is no existing national legal institution that is perfectly consistent with the framework in another country under economic globalization.[117] Therefore, the convergence of CSR tends to be a process of increasing resemblance, rather than copying or wholesale reproduction.[118] Various traditions have placed different levels of importance on the development of corporate culture and CSR. International dimensions of CSR are subject to the differing development of various aspects within countries, including different levels of productivity growth, different GDPs, different cultural traditions and different history and challenges.

It will be recalled that historically there has been ethical condemnation of usurious business practices in developing countries that practice Hinduism, Islam, Buddhism and Christianity.[119] The Confucian philosophy is also consistent with path dependence theory in terms of elements of history, tradition and culture. This theory can justify the unique CSR framework in China. Confucian philosophy is rooted in Taoism, which introduced the idea of harmony between *Yin* and *Yang*. *Li* and *Ren* working together, in harmony with freedom of individual behaviour constrained by social norms that dictate that behaviour, will be benevolent and will not infringe the requirement to consider others in complicated societal relationships.[120] This organic and utilitarian outlook

---

[116] W. Visser, 'Corporate Social Responsibility in Developing Countries' in A. Crane, A. McWilliams, D. Matten, J. Moon and D. Siegel (eds), *The Oxford Handbook of Corporate Social Responsibility* (Oxford: Oxford University Press, 2008) p. 473 at p. 480.

[117] S. Shen and H. Cheng, 'Economic Globalisation and the Construction of China's Corporate Social Responsibility' (2009) 51 *International Journal of Law and Management* 134 at 135.

[118] *Ibid.*

[119] W. Visser and A. Macintosh, 'A Short Review of the Historical Critique of Usury' (1998) 8 *Accounting, Business and Financial History* 175.

[120] L. Zhao and J. Roper, 'A Confucian Approach to Well-being and Social Capital Development' (2011) 30 *Journal of Management Development* 740 at 742.

and pragmatic approach to benevolent action is consistent with government intervention. 'Confucius would allow the State to undertake any sort of activity so long as such an activity increases the actual welfare of the people and so long as it does not impose upon the people too much financial burden.'[121] According to Backman, different from Western countries, but similar to countries which are deeply influenced by Confucianism, the Chinese government rules by law rather than enforces the rule of law.[122] The law is adopted as a tool for the ruler's willingness, and the judiciary is an arm of the government.[123] This is consistent with social hierarchies in Confucian philosophy, emphasizing 'a pattern of orderly subordination to authority'.[124] Working within Confucian philosophy, the blueprint for CSR is different and fits into a unique practice with a strong impact from government interference.

The Confucian philosophy has helped companies achieve great success and maintain a harmonious but competitive business environment. Confucian cultural values based on a relational culture, mutual exchange, family and collective tropism have profoundly affected enterprises in Japan, South Korea, Hong Kong and Singapore. The philosophy provides a sense of certainty and direction for Confucian entrepreneurs. In China, it has facilitated the gradual transition of the Chinese economy into global markets in association with the controlling power of the government.[125]

Employee loyalty, which features in the Confucian philosophy, has a strong impact on Japanese companies, helping them to establish a managerial ideology of intensive participation and collective responsibility. This feature of Confucianism has played an important role in the efficiency of the network-oriented *keiretsu* corporate governance model, in which employees and banks are regarded as the two most important stakeholders. Also in line with Confucian thought, in Korea the business environment is dominated by conglomerates known as *chaebol* (financial houses), a term which is commonly used to refer to 'conglomerates of

---

[121]   L.S. Hus, *The Political Philosophy of Confucianism: An Interpretation of the Social and Political Ideas of Confucius, His Forerunners, and His Early Disciples* (London: George Routledge & Son, 1932) p. 106.

[122]   M. Backman, *Asian Eclipse: Exposing the Dark Side of Business in Asia* (Singapore: John Wiley & Sons, 1999) p .11.

[123]   *Ibid.* at 12.

[124]   *Ibid.* at 37.

[125]   W. Goetzmann and E. Koll, *The History of Corporate Ownership in China: State Patronage, Company Legislation, and the Issue of Control*, Working Paper, National Bureau of Economic Research, United States (2004).

many related companies, including a number of companies listed on the stock exchange, which are engaged in a broad range of industrial and services business'.[126] Despite the presence of similar traits drawn from Confucianism, the Japanese *keiretsu* model puts importance on community harmony through corporations and cross-shareholding, while the Korean framework gives significance to hierarchical order in corporations' internal structure. The Chinese government's policy for a Harmonious Society means that the Chinese model sits somewhere in between. This also demonstrates the individuality of the Chinese corporate governance framework and CSR policy.

2.4.3 CSR in the Late *Qing* Dynasty

During the nineteenth century, the Imperial *Qing* dynasty gradually began to decline as the power of Western countries surged and consolidated.[127] Based on political, economic and minatory invasions, Western powers imposed 'unequal treaties' that created foreign concessions in China's ports. Regional warlords rose as central government atrophied. During that period of time, Chinese companies grew with pressure from Western countries, competition and the Chinese Imperial government. During this critical historical period, corporations owed special social responsibilities to the public. The evolution of people's understanding of enterprises and business practices in the late *Qing* dynasty played an important role in introducing the company as a business organization into China, a fact which is reflected in the profound social transformation in modern China. The development of the enterprise system in the late *Qing* dynasty had a significant impact on the nature and scope of the renovation of the enterprise system and the effectiveness of social transformation, which still has a direct impact on modern social economic progress.[128]

More than a century ago, in 1904, the Chinese Imperial government promulgated a set of laws to tackle social needs, with the purpose of

---

[126]   B. Black, B. Metzger, T.J. O'Brien and Y.M. Shin, 'Corporate Governance in Korea at the Millennium: Enhancing International Competitiveness (Final Report and Legal Reform Recommendation to the Ministry of Justice of the Republic of Korea, 15 May 2005, with an Introduction to the Report by Bernard Black)' (2001) 26 *Journal of Corporation Law* 537 at 551.

[127]   See X. Zhang and C. Xu, 'The Late Qing Dynasty Diplomatic Transformation: Analysis from an Ideational Perspective' (2007) 1 *Chinese Journal of International Politics* 405.

[128]   Y. Yan, *History Research on Thought and Practice of Enterprise System in the Late Qing Dynasty*, Ph.D Thesis, Central China Normal University (2003).

building a framework for a modern, Westernised, limited liability company in China. This was the Company Law of the *Qing* dynasty (*Daqing Gongsilü* 1904). In this statutory instrument, for the first time in Chinese history, China recognized the concept of a 'company' or 'corporation' from a legal perspective. It was regarded as the government's response to increasing competition and stimulation from foreign business enterprise in China.[129] During the *Ming* and *Qing* dynasties before the introduction of this law and the founding of the Republic in 1911, private household businesses, many of them of substantial size and scope, were the central institutions for domestic private economic activities in Imperial China. Family businesses played a significant role in China with the successful production and distribution of commercial goods. From 1904 to 1908, 272 commercial organizations registered as companies under the Company Law of the *Qing* dynasty 1904, with registered capital of US$22 million.[130] So-called 'modern' business enterprises only came into existence in China after 1840, when the British government launched the Opium War against China with the consequence that the *Qing* dynasty was forced to open its door to foreign investment.[131] In 1913, there were 136 Western investors in China with more than US$100,000 capital invested. The total investment of these enterprises amounted to US$103 million.

It was concluded by Dou that the companies in the late *Qing* dynasty had a number of unique characteristics.[132] First, the function of companies in that period of time was to revitalize industries, in order to strengthen the power of government and with the ultimate purpose of creating more social wealth. Secondly, companies had dual functions, both raising capital and investing as shareholders. Thirdly, corporations had separate legal personalities. Fourthly, internal corporate governance structures were established, and the separation between ownership and control was recognized; the three forces of agent, principal and third

---

[129]   W. Goetzmann and E. Koll, *The History of Corporate Ownership in China: State Patronage, Company Legislation, and the Issue of Control*, Working Paper, National Bureau of Economic Research, United States (2004) p. 150.

[130]   X. Du, *Chinese National Capitalism and Old Chinese Government (Minzu Ziben Zhuyi yu Jiu Zhongguo Zhengfu) (1840–1937)* (Shanghai: Shanghai Social Science Academy Press, 1991) pp. 29–31.

[131]   M. Gu, *Understanding Chinese Company Law*, 2nd edn (Hong Kong: Hong Kong University Press, 2010).

[132]   J. Dou, *Researches on Chinese Enterprise System and Thoughts (Zhongguo Gongsi Zhi Sixiang Yanjiu) (1942–1996)* (Shanghai: Shanghai University of Finance and Economic Press, 1999).

party were visualized as standing at the points of a triangle, and law regulating companies, directors and companies' third parties were part of agency law. Finally, the government recognized the separation of the government function from the function of enterprises. These five characteristics gave corporations in the late *Qing* dynasty legal and corporate governance bases which enabled them to include CSR-related objectives in their corporate behaviours.

Financial challenges to the *Qing* government in the 1860s, which had heavy debts, made companies attractive as a new way of raising capital both for the companies themselves and for the government, balancing the merchants' capital and the government's authority to benefit the company, the government and the employees. CSR in this period of time mostly rested on enterprises' surplus distribution. However, the bargaining power of the government was far stronger than the other two participants in the relationship, with the effect that the government controlled the initial emergence of businesses in the form of corporations.

Monopolist rights and profits shared by government and the company (*Zhuanli Quan*)

The government authorizes certain corporation(s), granting them monopoly and franchise rights for a certain product during a period of time and/or in a certain geographical area. In essence, the government uses its power, offering these enterprises monopoly rights by stopping new companies in a similar area coming into business in order to generate short-term profits. Corporations are willing to share profits with government to obtain monopolies, taking into account the excessive short-term profits.[133] Enterprises with 'official supervision and merchant management' were supposed to provide funds as repayment for Imperial grace.[134] The potential attraction of making excessive profit made corporations compete to cooperate with the government, which was in many ways to the government's benefit. The government had the right to decide who would benefit from the profits as the result of the franchise. CSR features started to emerge in corporate actions based on *Zhuanli Quan*.

---

[133] See M. Friedman, 'Monopoly and the Social Responsibility of Business and Labor' in M. Friedman, *Capitalism and Freedom*, 40th anniversary edn (Chicago, IL: University of Chicago Press, 2002) p. 208; see also B.A. McDaniel, *Entrepreneurship and Innovation: An Economic Approach* (New York: M.E. Sharp, 2002).

[134] G. Wu, *Zheng Guanying: Merchant Reformer of Late Qing China and His Influence on Economics, Politics, and Society* (New York: Cambria Press, 2010) p. 51.

Profit was not purely returnable to investors; rather, it was to be shared with government, an important external political-oriented stakeholder in the corporation, even in the modern market economy of the time.

A good example is the ten-year monopoly granted by the *Qing* government in 1882 to the Shanghai Cotton Cloth Mill, which signifies the start of the machine weaving age in China. The monopoly was granted to Zheng Guanying, a leading innovator and one of the most important political thinkers of the late *Qing* period.[135] The profits from the Shanghai Cotton Cloth Mill were shared by the company and the government, and it was regarded as a measure taken by government to cultivate local machine weavers and counter the trade in imported cotton cloth. However, the *Zhuanli Zhi* did not work efficiently, and criticisms were levelled of unfair competition, inefficiency, mutual suspicion and a tense relationship between the *Qing* government and the merchants.[136] Economists admit the symbolic significance of authorizing a monopoly at this particular time in China, especially in terms of industrial developments in international competitiveness. However, there are also scholars who viewed the monopoly as a barrier, hindering potential competitors from entering the industry and thereby actually slowing down, if not curtailing, the pace of industrial development.[137]

System of rendering to government (*Baoxiao Zhi*)

Baoxiao Zhi was a special wealth distribution system for profit in enterprise during the late *Qing* dynasty. The system was a kind of arrangement by which the government divided enterprises' profits mainly based on its political power. Under *Baoxiao Zhi* the government invested in enterprises with capital, helping enterprises to start up and then benefit from their profits. In the very late period of the *Qing* dynasty, the government required a bigger percentage of the profits, relying on its unbalanced and overly influential bargaining power. The corporations'

---

[135]   *Ibid.*

[136]   X. Huang, *Corporate Social Responsibility: Theory and Practice in China (Qiye Shehui Zeren: Lilun Yu Zhongguo Shijian)* (Beijing: Social Sciences Academic Press, 2010) pp. 142–3.

[137]   S. Zhao, 'The Proposal on Patented Management by Zheng Guanying and Practice from Shanghai Machine Weaving Bureau' (2005) 4 *Journal of Shijiazhuang Teachers College* 22.

contributions and capital distributions to the corporations became arbitrary and compulsory, resulting in them taking on overly onerous and burdensome social responsibilities.[138]

System of official government-authorized profits and dividends for investors (*Guanli Zhi*)

Guanli is generally defined as the interest paid by the private capital-raising companies to capital providers, according to interest rates fixed by the government. It is also known as *Guanxi* (the official interest rate) or *Guxi* (the share rate). *Guanli* is the interest rate that is officially authorized by the government, in order to give the public confidence in relying on the rate when making investments, since their investment and return from the investment is legitimate and protected by law. The *Guanli* system was designed by the *Qing* government in order to attract more investment from public funds to capitalize enterprises with the purpose of benefiting government, enterprises and investors. This is different from the shareholders or investors who voluntarily invest in corporations, whose dividends depend on the corporations' performance and share prices. Investors under the *Guanli* system are guaranteed to receive interest accruing at fixed annual rates, regardless of the performance of the company. Therefore, the investors under this system have the dual roles of shareholders and creditors. The corporations, in this system, have enlarged responsibility towards their investors, who are also creditors, and as such they are highly important external economic power-based stakeholders.

Case study: Li Hongzhang, his corporation and CSR

The not-for-profit corporate objective was adopted when corporations were first established and accepted as an important business organization in modern China. Progressive Chinese governors and businessmen planned to start businesses by registering companies, hoping to counter competition from Western companies. At this particular historical stage, in the presence of increasing internal and external political and economic pressure, the objectives of Chinese enterprises put more emphasis on how to help China become stronger, with broader and more socially responsible objectives of a political nature.

---

[138] Y. Yan, 'An Exploratory Analysis about the Rendering Government: A Special Distribution System of Enterprises' Profits during the Late Qing Dynasty' (2005) 4 *Journal of Anhui TV University* 101.

The company established by Li Hongzhang was a good example. Li, the governor-general of the capital province of Zhili, organized his steamship company to make a profit shipping government tax grain from central China to Beijing. From 1875 to 1877, Li purchased eight gunboats from England for the Chinese navy. In 1878, a cotton cloth mill established by Li in Shanghai was given a ten-year monopoly using foreign textile machinery, in order to save the government's output in terms of importing textiles. In 1880, he requested permission to build four railway routes, followed by the establishment of the Imperial Telegraph Administration and the School of Telegraphy in Tianjin. The following year, a naval academy was also founded by Li in Tianjin, manufacturing ammunition for Remington and Krupp guns. From 1881, Li sent Chinese students to England, France and Germany for enrolment in their military academies. The example of Li Hongzhang and the corporate decisions made by him can be seen as evidence of corporate behaviours beyond a simple focus on profit. Despite the fact that these corporate responsibilities had a strong connection with the protection of the government and the growth of military strength, these corporate behaviours have CSR characteristics in terms of their increased responsibilities towards stakeholders, such as the government.

2.4.4   Corporate Social Responsibility in the Republic of China (1912–1949)

This is a historical period marked by great turbulence and changes, as well as internal and external interference, especially the two World Wars. The Republic of China was founded by Sun Yat-sen after the triumph of the Xinhai Revolution. However, the fruits of this triumph were soon dominated by Yuan Shikai and other northern warlords, who imposed dictatorial rules internally and relied on imperialist powers externally. The Chinese people suffered from poverty and misery. This situation gave corporations a particular social responsibility and mission towards the government and the public.

Shiye Jiuguo **(industrialization for the nation's salvation)**
Shiye Jiuguo was first advocated by the prominent reformer Kang Youwei in 1898, during the late *Qing* dynasty. It was regarded as an important principle during the era of the Republic of China, and it was commonly advocated that an important way for China to become a strong and prosperous country, able to resist foreign aggression, was through industrialization. In the period of the Republic of China when the country

struggled to modernize, resist imperialist invasion and become self-reliant, it was believed that industrialization through actively setting up agriculture, industry, commerce, transportation and mining was the way to revive the economy, strengthen the armed forces and save the nation.

Statistically, there was a dramatic increase in the number of enterprises set up in response to the call for *shiye jiuguo*; 2,001 and 1,219 enterprises were set up in the years 1912 and 1913, respectively.[139] From 1914 to 1920, the number of factories increased by 1,061, and corporate capital increased by 169.8 million Yuan. From 1921 to 1927, the number of factories increased by 936, with an average capital of 249,000 Yuan. From 1928 to 1934, the number of factories increased by 984, with the equivalence to an average capital of 316,000 Yuan.[140]

This period gave businessmen a unique historical responsibility requiring them to use their corporations to save their country. Making profits seemed less important in comparison with the more highly respected duty of the nation's salvation. In his speech at the China Association of Industry Welcome Conference in Shanghai, Sun Yat-sen stated that, based on his observations on the sources of wealth in strong countries, the only medicine to cure Chinese poverty was industrialization.[141] New objectives and new understanding of enterprises required corporate objectives to be modernized, and business people were regarded as corporate citizens who would contribute to their country. The corporations established in this environment undoubtedly and unavoidably carried these political and social functions.

Modernized corporate objectives and company law

From a legal perspective, the concept of the 'company' or 'corporation' did not become a legal term until the end of the *Qing* dynasty.[142] China's first company law (*Gongsilü*) was issued on 21 January 1904 by the newly-created Ministry of Commerce (*Shangbu*). The Chinese Company Law 1904 was the first modernized law, drafted by the Imperial Law

---

[139]   Z. Chen and L. Yao, *Information on Chinese Modern Industrial History* (*Zhongguo Jindai Gongye Shi Ziliao*) (Beijing: SDX Joint Publishing Company, 1957) p. 10.

[140]   C. Wu and T. Jiang, *History of Chinese Enterprises: Modern History Volume* (*Zhongguo Qiye Shi: Jindai Juan*) (Beijing: Enterprise Management Publishing House, 2004) pp. 390–1.

[141]   Y. Sun, *Complete Work of Sun Yat-sen: Volume 2* (Beijing: Zhonghua Book Company, 1982) p. 340.

[142]   M. Gu, *Understanding Chinese Company Law*, 2nd edn (Hong Kong: Hong Kong University Press, 2010) p. 6.

Codification Commission, which gave the highest priority to enacting a law governing the organization of commercial companies and using it as a tool for promoting China's industrialized development.[143] The goal of the first Chinese Company Law was to respond to the argument that the only way to make Chinese entrepreneurs competitive with their Western and Japanese counterparts was to change the legal and economic foundations of business relationships.[144] This company law was also introduced in the realm of commercial law to match the perceived Western law standards, in order to justify demands to abolish the extra-territorial system which had restricted China's sovereignty since the 1840s.[145]

The Chinese Company Law 1904 ran to 131 articles with nine commerce principles, and the draft of this statutory instrument largely relied on legislative experience from English law (Companies Act 1855 and Companies Act 1862) and Japanese law (Commercial Code 1899). The Company Law 1904 established four types of business organizations, including the partnership, the limited partnership, joint stock companies and the company limited by shares.[146] The Ordinance Concerning Commercial Associations 1914 (*Gongsi Tiaoli*), drafted by the Northern Warlords government, replaced, revised and expanded the Company Law 1904. Mainly drawing on legislative experience from German Company Law, the new law was much more detailed, with 251 articles, and was arguably clearer and more comprehensive than its predecessor.[147] The company was defined as an 'organization set up for the purpose of carrying out commercial activities'.

The nationalist regime produced many legal codes and a new Company Law in 1929. The new law revealed traces of influences from German and Japanese Company Law. At the same time, it was based on the 1914

---

[143]   C. Li, 'The *Kung-ssu-lü* of 1904 and the Modernization of Chinese Company Law' (1974) 10 *Zhengda Faxue Pinglun (Chengchi Law Review)* 171 at 173–4.

[144]   W.C. Kirby, 'China Unincorporated: Company Law and Business Enterprise in Twentieth-Century China' (1995) 54 *Journal of Asian Studies* 43.

[145]   *Ibid.* at 44; see also T. Chien, *The Government and Politics of China, 1912–1949* (Cambridge, MA: Harvard University Press, 1950) pp. 419–20.

[146]   Chinese Company Law 1904 art. 1.

[147]   Z. Yang, *A Chinese Model of Corporate Governance* (*Gongsi Zhide de Zhongguo Moshi*) (Beijing: Social Sciences Academic Press, 2009) p. 61; many German scholars also argued the similarity of the laws, see H.H. Reute, *Der Einfluβ des adbendländishen Rechtes auf die Rechtsgestaltung in Japan and China* (Bonn: Ludwig Rörschield Verlag, 1940); K. Bünger, 'Ausländische Handelsgesellschaften in China und im Chinesischen Recht' (1930) 5 *Blätter für Internationales Privatrecht* 83.

Ordinance, with 233 articles, 90 of which were revised from its predecessor. The new Company Law was promulgated by the Nanjing government of the Republic, and came into force in the Republic of China on of 1 July 1931. According to article 1 of Company Law 1929, companies were defined as 'organizations set up with a view to profits (*Yingli Wei Mudi*)'. The corporate objective, for the first time in Chinese company law history, was clearly stipulated as profit seeking. This is regarded as the greatest change in company law, as previous laws had defined the company as 'a juristic person formed for the purpose of carrying on commercial transactions'.[148] The progressive part of this provision was to enable enterprises to carry on business without the government's interference. This was progress in terms of CSR. The law made legitimate the most fundamental corporate responsibility, namely, economic responsibility, and denied *Baoxiao Zhi* and *Guanli Zhi* with their strong aspects of interference from and profit sharing with the government. This was an important step towards encouraging the establishment of businesses as corporations. 'With this change, the government exempted itself, and its future enterprises, from the limitation of Company Law.'[149]

Corporate philanthropic responsibility in the Republic of China
China suffered from a series of natural and social disasters during the Republic of China period, with continual floods, droughts, hurricanes, diseases and wars. However, many enterprises and entrepreneurs performed and implemented their philanthropic responsibility towards the public and the local community. Zhang Jian, a famous entrepreneur and politician, is a good example of these philanthropic corporate actions towards society; he contributed to various charitable causes in the areas of industrialization, education and public services. One of the most well-known was building Nantong Museum, the first museum in China.

Based on statistics from Tao regarding the Shanghai Charitable Foundation during the Northern Warlords period, donations became the most common and important sources for charitable foundations. It was reported that 27.81 per cent of the Foundation was funded by donations from enterprises, while 44.84 per cent was from donations from entrepreneurs.[150] Despite the fact that many of these philanthropic corporate

---

[148]   W.C. Kirby, 'China Unincorporated: Company Law and Business Enterprise in Twentieth-Century China' (1995) 54 *Journal of Asian Studies* 43 at 52.
[149]   *Ibid.* at 52.
[150]   S. Tao, 'Initial Studies on Sources of Shanghai Foundation in the Northern Warlords Time Period (*Beiyang Zhengfu Shiqi Shanghai Cishan Zijin Laiyuan Chutan*)' (2004) 1 *Files and History (Dang'an Yu Shixue)* 50 at 52.

actions are purely voluntary in terms of modern CSR, at that time these charitable corporate behaviours were regarded as initiatives by which corporations aimed to ease conflicts between the rich and the poor by helping and supporting their stakeholders, for example, their employees and local communities, to facilitate the smoother operation of the business in the long term. These decisions added value to the corporations in both direct and indirect ways. A better and more respectable relationship between corporations and stakeholders, as well as a more harmonious business environment, both acted to promote the success of the corporations.

This purely voluntary CSR is defined by Yang and Ge as 'altruistic' charitable actions, the result of recognition of the needs of society.[151] Altruistic charitable actions are mostly limited to remedies for people who are suffering from natural disasters or wars. On the other hand, 'mutually beneficial' charitable actions towards a company's own stakeholders are regarded as measures to balance and coordinate corporate social, political and economic power.[152] Typical 'mutually-beneficial' charitable actions might take the form of free or cheaper education for the employees' children, and free training and education for employees in the form of night school (for example, the Hang Kou Bank night school) and vocational school (for example, the Shanghai Book Company).

2.4.5   Transformation of CSR in the People's Republic of China in the Era of Traditional SOEs

After the establishment of the People's Republic of China in 1949, the initial development stage of the company and company-related policies was related to the strongly centralized planned economy during the years between 1949 and 1978. Between 1949 and 1956, the Provisional Regulation on Private Enterprise 1950 and Implementing Methods for the Provisional Regulation on Private Enterprises 1951 were passed by the new Chinese government in order to encourage private enterprises to continue carrying on their business in China as legitimated legal institutions. Companies existed in the forms of unlimited liability companies, limited liability companies, companies limited by shares, companies formed by one or more shareholders with unlimited liability and one or more shareholders with limited liability, and companies formed by one or

[151]   T. Yang and D. Ge, *Corporations and Public Welfare* (*Gongsi Yu Shehui Gongyi II*) (Beijing: Social Sciences Academic Press, 2009) pp. 26–7.
[152]   Ibid.

more shareholders having unlimited liability and one or more share-holders having liability limited to their share contributions. Also, the company capital was divided into equal shares.[153] Three years later, the Provisional Regulations on Joint Venture Enterprises by Public Owner-ship and Private Ownership were issued.[154]

Despite variations on these business organizations during the 1950s, state-owned enterprises (SOEs) and collectively owned enterprises became the predominant forms of business organization when China completed its socialist reformation in 1956. SOEs under the planned economy were always defined as traditional SOEs. Between 1957 and 1978, the only business organizations in existence in China were SOEs and collectively owned enterprises. It was required by the Working Regulation on State-Owned Industry Enterprise 1961 that all factories must establish cooperative relations if they manufactured similar products or had similar needs. A group of special companies in charge of factory collaborations was established for the purpose of administrating these roles in line with the State plan.[155] These 'companies' were not the same as the traditional understanding of the company, which normally has the goal of making profit.

During the time of planned economy, the *Danwei* (work unit) was becoming popular, referring to a place of employment and commonly used in the context of SOEs. This is a unique organizational structure which divides individuals into different groups based on their employers. Li and Zhang argued that *Danwei* owed its distinct character to the era of the planned economy in China. First, the nature of the *Danwei*, including the ownership and management structures, directly decided the identifi-cation, position and profits of the individual employees of the *Danwei*. Secondly, the employees were bound to their *Danwei* unreservedly for every aspect of life, including housing, child care, primary and high school for children, shops, services and transportation. The impact of a work unit on individual employees went far beyond work-related issues, encompassing marriage, travel, and so on.[156] Besides being paid a basic monthly salary, employees and civil servants understood that *Danwei* was

[153]   M. Gu, *Understanding Chinese Company Law*, 2nd edn (Hong Kong: Hong Kong University Press, 2010) p. 8.
[154]   *Ibid.* at 8.
[155]   J. Ping, *New Company Law Text Book (Xin Gongsi Fa Jiaocheng)* (Beijing: The Law Press, 1997) p. 16.
[156]   P. Li and Y. Zhang, *Analysis on Social Cost of State-Owned Enterprises (Guoyou Qiye Shehui Chengben Fen'xi)* (Beijing: Social Sciences Academic Press, 2000) pp. 120–35.

a system that was employee-centred, and which was used by the government for redistributing profits. Together with the interests of their relatives, the interests of employees as primary internal stakeholders were protected under the *Danwei* system.

In examining the nature of the *Danwei* system, CSR-related responsibilities can be observed in the following three areas. First, *Danwei* is able to provide employees with guaranteed lifetime employment, which was commonly known as the *Tie Fan Wan* (Iron Rice Bowl) for their employees; this largely stemmed from Chinese culture based on Confucian values. The system of *Tie Fan Wan* is in some ways similar to the employment relationship system within the Japanese *keiretsu* corporate governance system. In the *keiretsu* system, a typical insider network-oriented stakeholder model, employees have traditionally come to expect that they will have lifelong employment with the same company.[157] The system is designed to enhance the cooperation between the working class and the Chinese Communist Party, in order to carry out their political agenda and transfer their working focus from the rural to the urban areas of China. However, the *Tie Fan Wan* system discouraged employees from improving themselves and hindered them from getting information outside of their *Danwei*. The system also increased opportunities for holding-up and free-riding from the point of view of human capital holders, and decreased productivity as a result.[158]

Secondly, in the traditional planned economy period in China, the norm of 'enterprises running social activities (*qiye ban shehui*)' is regarded as strong evidence of the early stages of CSR in Chinese SOEs. The *Danwei* is the employer of the workers, and it is also the provider of the employees' social security and life security. There is strong reliance from employees on their *Danwei* as an organizational support for their needs. The unique *Baoxiao* (reimbursement) system and *Fenfang* (free housing services for employees) within the *Danwei* granted the basic needs of its employees. This system of 'enterprises running social activities' made up for deficiencies in the schemes by which the government ran social activities during the planned economy period. It was an arrangement from corporations with regard to the interests of their stakeholders.

---

[157]   C.A. Mallin, *Corporate Governance*, 3rd edn (Oxford: Oxford University Press, 2010).
[158]   X. Li, 'The Economic Character of the Enterprise Identified as a Unit (*Danweihua Qiye de Jingji Xingzhi*)' (2001) 7 *Economic Research Journal (Jingji Yanjiu)* 35 at 36–8.

Thirdly, when SOEs were running into financial difficulties or facing insolvency, the SOEs expected to be bailed out by the government. This government strategy was termed a 'soft budget constraint' by Konai and others from the 1970s onwards.[159] Konai observed 'soft budget constraints' in the Hungarian economy of the 1970s, a socialist economy experimenting with the introduction of market reform.[160] The intention was to illuminate economic behaviour in socialist economies characterized by shortages.[161] More recently, the term has also regularly been invoked in the literature on the economic transition from socialism to capitalism.[162] According to the theory, despite the fact that SOEs were vested with a moral and financial interest in maximizing their profits, the chronic loss-makers among them were not allowed to fail as they were always bailed out with financial subsidies or other instruments.[163] Paternalism is argued as a reason for bailing out an ailing enterprise, particularly if the enterprise is owned by the state and the state officials feel protective and responsible for it.[164] This paternalistic 'love' from the government towards the SOEs makes the companies' reliance on the government more mutually justifiable. A market economy seems necessary in China, whereby market forces will force SOEs with poor performance to become insolvent.

---

[159] See J. Konai, '"Hard" and "Soft" Budget Constraint' (1980) 25 *Acta Oeconomica* 231; J. Konai and A. Matits, 'Softness of the Budget Constraint: An Analysis Relying on Data of Firms' (1984) 32 *Acta Oeconomica* 223; J. Konai, 'Gomulka on the Soft Budget Constraint: A Reply' (1985) 19 *Economics of Planning* 49; J. Konai, 'The Concept of the Soft Budget Constraint Syndrome in Economic Theory' (1998) 26 *Journal of Comparative Economics* 11; J. Konai, E. Maskin and G. Roland, 'Understanding the Soft Budget Constraint' (2003) 41 *Journal of Economic Literature* 1095; for discussions on soft budget constraints and law, see J. Konai, 'Legal Obligation, Non-Compliance and Soft Budget Constraint', entry for P. Newman, *New Palgrave Dictionary of Economics and the Law* (New York: Macmillan, 1998) p. 533.

[160] J. Konai, 'Resource-Constrained Versus Demand Constrained Systems' (1979) 47 *Econometrica* 801.

[161] J. Konai, E. Maskin and G. Roland, 'Understanding the Soft Budget Constraint' (2003) 41 *Journal of Economic Literature* 1095.

[162] For example, World Bank, *From Plan to Market: World Development Report* (Oxford: Oxford University Press, 1997); World Bank (B. Pleskovic and N. Stern (eds), *Annual Bank Conference on Development Economics* (Washington, DC: World Bank, 1999)).

[163] J. Konai, E. Maskin and G. Roland, 'Understanding the Soft Budget Constraint' (2003) 41 *Journal of Economic Literature* 1095 at 1096.

[164] *Ibid.* at 1099.

From the arguments above, it can be concluded that many SOEs in modern China have been growing and changing in line with Chinese economic transformations since the time of the early traditional planned economy. Corporations, at that stage, bore responsibilities beyond the scope of corporate responsibility, but those responsibilities should have been born by the government. Close relationships between SOEs, employees and the government hindered the speed of development in China, and the development of CSR can mainly be observed from the corporations' concerns and responsibilities towards their employees and the government.

3. Corporate social responsibility in contemporary China: A growing awareness

Corporate social responsibility (CSR) has attracted a critical mass of debates and controversy in China in the last half decade. It is argued that the start of China's commitment to the connection between the ascendancy of industry and social good can be dated back to China's opening up to the world in the late 1970s, or even as far back as the Communist revolution of 1949.[1] However, the ideas and practices to which the label 'CSR' is now applied have been in evidence in Chinese society for hundreds if not thousands of years. In contrast to the commonly recognized voluntary nature of CSR in Western countries, CSR-related discussions, debates and headlines in China still focus on legal or compliance issues, with positive discourses about many corporate philanthropic actions. Considering the size of the Chinese economy and its increasingly important global position, the scope of CSR-related topics in China is very broad.

3.1 EVOLUTION OF CORPORATE SOCIAL RESPONSIBILITY IN CHINA

The evolution of CSR developed with the reform of state-owned enterprises (SOEs), since this has been regarded as the central link in the reform and restructuring of China's economy.[2] The path of CSR reform has gone through different stages, such as 'delegation of powers and interests, instituting the contract operational responsibility system and

---

[1] Z. Zhang, *Difficult Transformation: Studies on the Contemporary Chinese Corporation* (*Jiannan de Bianqian: Jindai Zhongguo Gongsi Zhidu Yanjiu*) (Shanghai: Academy of Social Science Press, 2002) p. 5.
[2] L. Zu, *Corporate Social Responsibility, Corporate Restructuring and Firm's Performance* (Berlin: Springer-Verlag, 2009) p. 2.

establishing a modern enterprise system'.[3] The reform of SOEs can be divided into the management reform stage from 1974 to 1984, the dual track system stage from 1984 to 1992, and the ownership reform stage post-1992.

In the management reform stage, management teams were given more autonomy to increase economic incentives for SOEs to ensure that they were making profits.[4] During the dual track system stage, marked by the Provisional Regulations on Expanding the Autonomy of Enterprises promulgated in May 1984, SOEs were allowed to sell products beyond the state plan at prices up to 20 per cent above the state price. This was the dual (plan and market) track system. Within this stage, market-oriented reforms were initiated with the promulgation of Regulations Concerning Deepening Enterprises Reform and Increasing Vitality of Enterprises, issued in 1986. During the latter part of this period, the reform of SOEs slowed down due to concerns about the social and economic impacts of reform measures, including more expensive living costs and increasing unemployment. The performance of SOEs during this time stayed at a low level.

In the third stage, Deng Xiaoping's famous Southern Tour marked a new developmental stage in SOE reform when he urged governments to think less about ideological correctness and more about economic development. He made the famous analogy that 'it doesn't matter if a cat is black or white, as long as it catches mice, it is a good cat'. Loss-making large and medium-sized SOEs were required to get out of debt and improve their profitability by setting up modern corporate systems between 1998 and 2000. The policy of *Tie Fan Wan* had to be abolished when the government adopted a policy of SOE restructuring by 'laying off redundant workers and downsizing employees to improve efficiency and profitability'.[5] It was the task of the government to reduce the cost of SOEs by terminating or laying off redundant workers and employees on a large scale in order to improve economic performance.[6] During this stage, SOEs restructuring with a broad scope became prevalent, and there was a rapid decline in the number of SOEs and in

---

[3]   *Ibid.* at 2.

[4]   J.L. Wu, '"Market Socialism" and Chinese Economic Reform', paper submitted to the IES's Round Table on Market and Socialism Reconsidered (2004), available at bm.ust.hk.

[5]   China News Agency, 'Decision on Major Issues Concerning the Reform and Development of SOEs', 26 September 1999.

[6]   L. Zu, *Corporate Social Responsibility, Corporate Restructuring and Firm's Performance* (Berlin: Springer-Verlag, 2009) p. 4.

employment within surviving SOEs.[7] This obviously had a profound impact on the interests of various stakeholders, such as employees, local communities and society as a whole.

Regarding the stages of CSR development in China, different classifications have been suggested according to different criteria. Zhou identified at least three phases of CSR development in China.[8] The first phase, from 1996 to 2000, was the period when the concept of CSR was first introduced in China. Chinese firms were exposed to CSR practices via auditing by multinational corporations. Many Chinese corporations were prepared to seek to comply with demanding CSR-related requirements for the benefit of their consumers. CSR, in this phase, was not regarded as an important idea or theme since profit-making was still regarded as the main objective for corporations, and the government, media and general public were not involved in CSR. Yi Xiaozhun, the Assistant Minister of Commerce in China, indicated that 'despite the impressive progress, we are by and large at the starting stage of CSR. We need to further explore relevant concepts and systems that accommodate the realities of Chinese society and conform to the law of development of human civilization'.[9]

The second phase was the so called wait-and-see years from 2000 to 2004. During this period, progressive academics, international organizations and NGOs worked systemically to introduce the concept of CSR to China. Government organizations began to adopt CSR into their policies and regulations in response to pressure from international organizations and multinational corporations. These organizations, collaborators and competitors were increasingly being recognized as important external stakeholders for Chinese companies. During this time, CSR investigation committees were created in the Ministry of Labour, the Ministry of Commerce and the Chinese Enterprise Confederation.[10]

The third phase is the most recent, from 2004 to the present, when the Chinese approach to CSR is shifting from a passive to an active and

---

[7]   See B. Naughton, *The Chinese Economy: Transitions and Growth* (Cambridge, MA: MIT Press, 2007).

[8]   W. Zhou, *Will CSR Work in China?* Business for Social Responsibility Working Paper (2006).

[9]   X. Yi, 'Improving Corporate Responsibility Competitiveness to Promote Harmonious Society', available at www.wtoguide.net/html/2005Sino-European/14_36_14_633.html.

[10]   W. Zhou, *Will CSR Work in China?* Business for Social Responsibility Working Paper (2006).

participatory one.[11] The former approach regards CSR as a way to avoid economic sanctions and trade barriers, while the latter approach requires that CSR should be considered by companies and adopted into corporate strategic polices in order to promote the long-term success of corporations and to create more social wealth in a Harmonious Society.

Huang also divided the evolution of CSR in China into three stages, but his stages were different from those described by Zhou. He argued that the development of CSR could be divided into the profit maximizer phase (1978–1995), the CSR integration phase (1995–2002) and the CSR regulatory phase (post 2002). In the first phase, making profit was the centralized theme among all businesses. The separation of ownership and control and the increasing importance of private companies made the pursuit of profit the only purpose of most enterprises. Ignorance of social and environmental responsibilities made corporations less likely to consider the interests of their stakeholders. CSR-related responsibilities were seen as the responsibilities of the government.

In the integration phase, the government increasingly recognized the importance of stakeholders' interests, based on the legal principle that companies are separate legal entities established to make profit, with economic responsibility as the basic corporate responsibility. The perception was that the government should not impose extra responsibility on enterprises of any kind, including SOEs. With pressure from multinational corporations, international organizations and the media, corporations in China started to pay attention to CSR and respond to their stakeholders' needs. In this phase, the main achievement was an integrated understanding of CSR. It was recognized that CSR was a voluntary responsibility that was not related to government policies and enforcement measures.

In the regulatory phase, CSR started to be explicitly mentioned within government legislation and legislative instruments. The most distinct example was article 5 of Chinese Company Law (CCL) 2006, which indicated that 'a company must, when engaging in business activities, abide by the laws and administrative regulations, observe social morals and business ethics, be in integrity and good faith, accept regulation of the government and the public, and undertake social responsibilities'. The CCL confirmed that social morals and ethical issues should be included as part of corporate objectives. Furthermore, even earlier than CCL 2006, there were legislative requirements for directors in terms of their duties

---

[11]   *Ibid.*

towards various stakeholders enshrined in the Code of Corporate Governance for Listed Companies in China 2001. In Chapter 6 of the Code, titled 'Stakeholders', companies are required to 'respect the legal rights of creditors, employees, consumers, suppliers, the community and other stakeholders'.[12] In this phase, the government is trying to establish a unique CSR system with Chinese characteristics through law and regulations, in order to promote corporations in China as more socially responsible, either by giving legitimacy to directors to take account of their stakeholders' interests, or by regulating corporate behaviour through soft law.

In the author's opinion, both approaches mentioned above are accurate, although they are based on different criteria. It is not necessary to judge which approach is more correct in terms of the development of the Chinese corporate governance system and the reform process of SOEs. However, in terms of the development of SOEs, it is worthwhile to discuss the characteristics of the development trends of Chinese CSR. First, CSR is becoming increasingly important, informed by a broader awareness. Secondly, CSR is becoming officially recognized through law and regulations. Thirdly, the attitudes of corporations towards CSR have changed from being passively forced to comply, towards being actively and voluntarily willing to undertake and participate. Fourthly, the government's role has transformed from being a planner to being a regulator. Fifthly, CSR in China is increasingly internationalized, with rapid economic development. Finally, corporate objectives are turning from profit maximization towards combined economic, social and philanthropic objectives, collectively working towards becoming a respected corporate citizen.

3.2   RISE OF CSR IN CHINA

After the systematic structural reform of Chinese enterprise and the opening of China to Western investors in 1978, a period of unprecedented growth took place in China with the economy increasing by an average of 9.5 per cent annually. Since then, China's economy has become the second largest in the world after the United States. The idea of CSR, transported into China in the 1990s mainly through global supply chains, was driven by both social and environmental problems as internal pull issues, and economic interests in the global market as an external push.

---

[12]   Code of Corporate Governance for Listed Companies in China 2001 s. 81.

Global consumer movements and public awareness of CSR in Europe and the United States have led to anti-sweatshop campaigns against socially irresponsible corporate actions in China and other developing countries with emerging corporate governance and CSR strategy in their corporate agendas. Therefore, the Chinese government need to reconsider their policy and economic development goals for the long-term sustainable development of China in order to respond to these external pressures, which are trying to force the implementation of CSR strategy in company strategic management policies and government policies that directly decide the management policies of SOEs.

It is generally believed that Western multinational corporations are still the dominant actors in Asia, including China, in terms of the scope and sophistication of their CSR policies.[13] However, recent initiatives from Chinese companies show that they have become more active in engaging CSR through CSR practices and reports. The emergence of CSR is always associated with two paradigms, namely, good corporate governance and sustainable development, which both enable a socially responsible business outlook. It is increasingly realized that financially sound corporate performance is largely dependent on a 'business case' for responsibility.[14] However, CSR always means different things to different people and corporations in different countries. Discussions and judgement of CSR as a term are still relevant and justifiable in the contemporary economic climate:[15] 'to some it conveys the idea of legal responsibility or liability; to others it means socially responsible behaviour in an ethical sense; to still others, the meaning transmitted is that of "responsible for", in a causal mode; many simply equate it with a charitable contribution'.[16] Despite the ambiguity of the term itself, and especially in China, CSR is broadly recognized to encompass all aspects

[13]   P. Debrox, 'Corporate Social Responsibility and Sustainable Development in Asia: A Growing Awareness' (2009) 8 *Asian Business and Management* 33 at 33–4.

[14]   B. Horrigan, *Corporate Social Responsibility in the 21st Century: Debate, Models and Practice Across Government, Law and Business* (Cheltenham: Edward Elgar, 2010) pp. 269–70.

[15]   Clarkson also held the view that the criticism was valid in the mid-1990s, see M.B. Clarkson, 'A Stakeholder Framework for Analyzing and Evaluating Corporate Social Performance' (1995) 20 *Academy of Management Review* 92 at 96.

[16]   D. Votaw, 'Genius Becomes Rare' in D. Votaw and S.P. Sethi (eds), *The Corporate Dilemma: Traditional Values versus Contemporary Problems* (Englewood Cliffs, NJ: Prentice Hall, 1973) p. 11.

of CSR-related activities. CSR is increasingly accepted both as a term introduced from Western countries and multinational corporations, and as an embryonic term which has been developed in response to customers' demands, government policies, competitive business environments, domestic law and regulations including soft law, and lessons learned from corporate scandals and irresponsible behaviour.

Of course, because China is a socialist country with unique characteristics, the Chinese government needs to play a vital role in pushing CSR as a broadly acceptable and implementable term. It is argued by Holst-Jensen that the Chinese government is trying to submerge the concept under the control of the Party-State.[17] Under a control-based corporate governance model, it remains important to accommodate CSR strategy and CSR-related law in line with the current economic development in China, the development stage of the Chinese legal system, Chinese traditions and the country's history and culture.

3.2.1   CSR as a Result of External Push

In 1984, both Deng Xiaoping and Zhao Ziyang (Premier of China from 1987 to 1989) stated that 'the policy of opening to the outside world is a basic policy of China. Whatever else changes, it can only change towards a more relaxed attitude'. This stressed the new Chinese open door policy. Deng's speech in 1992 began a new era for foreign direct investors by establishing a 'socialist market economy' that gives foreign investors greater confidence to invest in China. This external push to the development of Chinese CSR is a direct result of Chinese markets opening up to Western investors and the increasing number of multinational companies in China, especially since the Chinese entry into the global trading regime of the WTO in 2001.

Globalization of the Chinese economy

China has become more integrated with the global economy. It is obvious that this is a mutual working integration. China's economic power is affecting the global economy, on the one hand, while China also has to adjust itself to the globalized market, on the other.[18] China is now

---

[17]   M. Holst-Jensen, *Serve the People! Corporate Social Responsibility (CSR) in China*, Copenhagen Discussion Paper 2006-6 (2006) p. 15, available at http://openarchive.cbs.dk/bitstream/handle/10398/7405/cdp%202006-006.pdf.
[18]   S.A. Aaronson, 'A Match Made in the Corporate and Public Interest: Marry Voluntary CSR Initiatives and the WOT' (2007) 41 *Journal of World Trade* 629.

characterized as the world 'factory', and plays an important role as a supplier in the global supply chain. Consumers in the United States and Europe are increasingly cognizant that goods and services they purchase are often made in countries where human rights and the environment are inadequately protected. When multinational corporations put an increasing amount of investment into those developing countries who do not have a good CSR record, 'consumers, investors and other stakeholders have begun to pressure executives to monitor their behaviour in these developing countries and make sure they produce goods and services in a socially responsible manner'.[19] The 'go global' policy has been a source of pressure promoting CSR while multinational corporations have mushroomed in the Chinese market. CSR in China is seen as a consequence of globalization. Stakeholders in developed countries want the directors of multinational corporations in China to go beyond simply complying with Chinese law and regulations. Directors have so far responded positively to these demands with a wide range of CSR initiatives.[20] Chinese companies should have better understanding and anticipate the increased importance of CSR in the context of international business.

The globalization of the rapidly expanding Chinese economy has led to lucrative growth markets for businesses, supply chains within companies, and expanding investments and business activities with dramatic social and environmental impacts. In line with these developments, the Chinese government and enterprises are encountering a distinctive set of CSR agenda challenges, especially in areas where extensive and dynamic overseas transactional relationships have been developed with multinational corporations. The companies in these areas are more likely to be socially responsible, demonstrating responsible health and safety practices and more sound labour and environmental credentials in both their immediate operation and supply chains. There will also be a more proactive attitude from the government to encourage public and private

---

[19]   *Ibid.* at 634.

[20]   However, there are many arguments about the inadequacies of these initiatives based on the following reasons: first, the compliance with CSR initiatives by 'second tier' suppliers in order to put CSR initiatives in the appropriate place; secondly, suppliers from whom they procure small amounts unless they partner with other firms sourcing from the same supplier; finally, CSR initiatives designed by the multinational companies' directors often cannot address the root causes of CSR-related violations towards successful remedies. See The Frank Hawkins Kenan Institute of Private Enterprise, *Statement of Findings Promoting CSR in China* (Washington, DC: Kenan-Flager Business School, UNC, 2004).

companies to be active in promoting and engaging CSR.[21] CSR-related researches carried out for Chinese companies have always focused on the social performance of multinational corporations that operate in China. These companies have a transnational character with a recognized international reputation, either positive or negative, which makes it easier to attract public attention. Multinational companies are more likely to engage in the manufacture of a wide range of production lines, and are responsible for a broad spectrum of hazardous and pollution-intensive activities.[22]

Multinational companies which invest in China always regard business development in China as part of their global business strategies. Their business strategic plans always engage in long-term goals which take account of China's potential, rather than immediate short-term economic returns. They are always in a position to introduce more advanced technological innovations to Chinese industry. Multinational companies are always more cautious regarding the social impacts of their corporate actions, in response to concerns such as the pursuit of profit at the expense of a vulnerable workforce and the environment in China.[23] The impacts of their corporate activities and irresponsible corporate decisions are normally much more influential and significant for their corporate image. In order to meet environmental goals and satisfy their stake-holders' expectations, multinational corporations have started to look beyond their own facilities and involve their suppliers in their overall CSR-related initiatives. The good practice of multinational corporations will apply pressure and issue challenges to Chinese corporations, including SOEs, to maintain responsible business practices and partner relationships. The challenges could come from the business organizational level, or from the international organizational level. They could include pressures either from internal voluntary codes of conduct established by

---

[21] L. Zu, *Corporate Social Responsibility, Corporate Restructuring and Firm's Performance* (Berlin: Springer-Verlag, 2009) p. 45.

[22] H. Lu, 'Dirty Industry Migration in China: Lessons for Corporate Social Responsibility' (2005) 2 *US-China Law Review* 37 at 40.

[23] T. Edwards, P. Marginson, P. Edwards, A. Ferner and O. Tregaskis, *Corporate Social Responsibility in Multinational Companies: Management Initiatives or Negotiated Agreement?* (International Labour Organisation, International Institute for Labour Studies, 2007) p. 1.

multinational companies themselves,[24] or from external voluntary standards imposed by non-governmental organizations.[25]

The expansion in coastal provinces like Guangdong, Fujian, Jiangsu and Shandong, where widespread and vibrant international trade has developed with multinational corporations, is a good example to demonstrate the pressure applied by multinational companies on the CSR practice of Chinese companies. Domestic partners, suppliers and components of multinational companies, as well as cooperative companies in these provinces, are always comparatively more exposed to CSR-related issues and are under pressure to demonstrate 'responsible health and safety practices and sound labour and environmental credentials in both their immediate operations and supply chain'.[26] This CSR-focused and stakeholder-friendly practice also makes the local government more exposed to CSR issues, encouraging them to look at corporations in a more progressive manner by encouraging companies to be active in promoting and engaging with CSR. From the point of view of the multinational companies, they will always encourage their suppliers to accommodate CSR policies in their management strategies by applying voluntary codes and workplace standards.

It is argued by Murdoch and Gould that CSR, as an ambiguous concept in the West, should be implemented and developed to construct a Chinese terminology to enhance the indigenization and acceptability of CSR among Chinese citizens, corporate citizens and government institutions.[27] Pressures come from both the micro-level and the macro-level. At the micro-level, Chinese suppliers and companies need to prove that their production standards are consistent with Western CSR standards (mainly in terms of social and environmental issues) in order to maintain the supply-chain and attract more investment to China.[28] Failure to comply with basic standards could expose the business to the risk of being suspended, or losing potential opportunities to maintain or create supply

---

[24]   For example,: Wal-Mart Standards for Vendor Partners; Nike's Code of Conduct.

[25]   For example, SA8000 established by Social Accountability International; Apparel Certification Programme by Worldwide Responsibility Apparel Production; ISO 14001 by the International Organization for Standardization.

[26]   L. Zu, *Corporate Social Responsibility, Corporate Restructuring and Firm's Performance* (Berlin: Springer-Verlag, 2009) p. 45.

[27]   H. Murdoch and D. Gould, *Corporate Social Responsibility in China: Mapping the Environment* (Global Alliance for Workers and Communities, 2004).

[28]   L.W. Lin, 'Corporate Social Responsibility in China: Window Dressing or Structural Change' (2010) 28 *Berkeley Journal of International Law* 64 at 89.

chains. On the other hand, at the macro-level, China needs to respond efficiently to CSR demands within the global market in order to retain economic growth and competitiveness.[29] With the development and transformation from a planned economy to a market economy, CSR is not optional if China is to be seen as an attractive place for investment, and if 'Made in China' is to be a reliable brand for consumers.

International corporate social responsibility standards

International CSR standards have been regarded as a key external push for development of CSR in China. Despite efforts in promoting CSR from central and local government, the understandings on CSR differ dramatically across sectors in China. With China having become the world's top manufacturing nation, accounting for 19.8 per cent of the world's manufacturing output, ending 110 years' leadership from the United States (as confirmed by Mark Killion, IHS's head of world industry services), the international CSR standards seem particularly important to China for its sustainable economic development. The cancellation by multinational organizations of international trade transactions with China due to failure to comply with international CSR standards on the Chinese side could lead to tremendous economics loss for Chinese export trade organizations and Chinese corporations.

With regard to external CSR pushing through international standards, the most popular standard for manufacturers in China is SA8000.[30] This is a set of auditable corporate social accountability standards established in 1997 by the Council of Economic Priorities Accreditation Association, and it is currently supervised by Social Accountability International. SA8000 addresses national law compliance, and incorporates International Labour Organization Conventions, the Universal Declaration of Human Rights, and the UN Convention on the Rights of the Child.[31] SA8000 is now internationally recognized and widely accepted as the most viable and comprehensive workplace management system for ethical issues. The system requires ongoing compliance and continual improvement of the ethical standards of corporations, with involvement from stakeholders, including participation by all key sectors in the SA8000 system, including employees, trade unions, companies, socially responsible investors, non-governmental organizations, the government and the public. As of 30 June 2012, 473 Chinese corporations had been granted a

---

[29]   *Ibid.* at 89.
[30]   See Social Accountability Accreditation Services (SAAS), www.saas accreditation.org.
[31]   See Social Accountability 8000, art. II (2001).

SA8000 certificate, among a total of 3,083 companies altogether.[32] SA8000 is a controversial topic in China, where there are varied opinions about the role of corporate social accountability standards in the global supply chain. SA8000 is either regarded as a technical trade barrier in favour of developed countries, or a passport to the global market.[33] However, it is argued that with modernized awareness and attitudes towards CSR from the Chinese authorities, who now recognize CSR as a way to improve the competitiveness of corporations, the impact of SA8000 on Chinese industry and export-oriented firms has been taken on board.[34]

ISO 26000, the Guidance on Social Responsibility, was introduced by the International Integrated Reporting Council in 2010 as a new approach to corporate reporting, and it has had a significant impact worldwide. It was produced with the intention of developing a practical form of social responsibility in order to support corporations in maintaining a continuously sustainable development agenda. The standard was introduced in a manner that was different from previous international standards in that it did not require third party certification. A Chinese version of ISO 26000 was published in 2011, translated by the Standardization Administration of the People's Republic of China under the authorization of the International Organization for Standardization (ISO).

A few issues were seen as fundamental principles of the social responsibilities outlined in ISO 26000, including accountability, transparency, ethical behaviour, respect for stakeholder interests, respect for the rule of law, respect for international norms of behaviour and respect for human rights. Seven core subjects listed in ISO 26000 were Governmental Organization, Human Rights, Labour Practices, the Environment, Fair Operating Practices, Consumer Issues and Community Involvement and Development. These subjects include various aspects of CSR, and they are closely intertwined with CSR-related scandals in China. The adoption of the standard will have potential effects in terms of the sustainable development of Chinese corporations towards an international level. The establishment of the China ISO 26000 Evaluation and Research Institute, a third party with mission and functions to do with

---

[32]   See SAAS Statistics on Certified Facilities by Country, 30 September 2011, available at www.saasaccreditation.org/facilities_by_country.htm.

[33]   L.W. Lin, 'Corporate Social Accountability Standards in the Global Supplier Chain' (2007) 15 *Cardozo Journal of International and Comparative Law* 311.

[34]   L. Zu, *Corporate Social Responsibility, Corporate Restructuring and Firm's Performance* (Berlin: Springer-Verlag, 2009) p. 45.

research, evaluation and training in the standard, also provides evidence for the market necessity and the impact of international standards on the ethical behaviours of Chinese corporations. According to Professor Youhuan Li, the director of the Institute, the introduction of ISO 26000 can be regarded as an opportunity for China to adopt an internationalized and positive attitude, welcoming CSR through legislation and voluntary standards for the scientific, sustainable and healthy development of the Chinese economy.[35]

Corporate social responsibility reports

Another important external issue that is pushing CSR is the increasingly accepted and implemented corporate responsibility report, especially CSR reports. It is the rationale in Western corporations that CSR reporting ultimately serves the interests of the shareholders, and economic benefits always outweigh ethical duties as the self-identified motivations for the practice of corporate responsibility reporting in the West.[36] A globalized study on corporate responsibility reports carried out by KPMG in 2011[37] surveyed executives at the 250 largest corporations in the world, drawn from the Fortune Global 500 List in 2010 and representing more than a dozen industry sectors, and the 100 largest companies in each of 34 countries, including developed countries such as the United Kingdom, Japan, France, the United States, Italy, Germany and the Netherlands, and some developing countries such as Nigeria, Mexico, India and China. The report indicates that corporate responsibility reporting has become the de facto law for business. It signifies more than just being a good corporate citizen; further, it drives innovation and promotes the growth of businesses as well as their organizational value.[38] It was shown in the survey that 95 per cent of the 250 largest companies in the world now report on their corporate responsibility activities.[39] Of the 100 largest companies in each country, 69 per cent of the publicly traded companies conduct corporate responsibility reporting, compared to

---

[35] Y. Li and Y. Liu, *Bluebook of Corporate Social Responsibility in China 2011* (Beijing: People's Publishing House, 2011) p. 126.

[36] A. J. Sulkowski, S.P. Parashar and L. Wei, 'Corporate Responsibility Reporting in China, India, Japan and the West: One Mantra Does not Fit All' (2008) 42 *New England Law Review* 787 at 790.

[37] KPMG, *KPMG International Survey of Corporate Responsibility Reporting 2011* (2011), available at www.kpmg.com/Global/en/IssuesAndInsights/ArticlesPublications/corporate-responsibility/Documents/2011-survey.pdf.

[38] *Ibid.* at 2.

[39] *Ibid.* at 10–11.

just 36 per cent of family-owned enterprises and close to 45 per cent for both cooperatives and companies owned by professional investors, such as private equity firms.[40]

As for China, almost 60 per cent of China's largest companies already report using corporate metrics.[41] Based on the data, China, as a country with an emerging economy and corporate governance framework, has a limited focus on corporate responsibility reporting and Chinese companies could 'strengthen their credibility and reputation by putting additional focus on the communication side of the work'.[42] The pressures from countries classified as 'leading the pack', with top scores in terms of the professionalism of their internal systems and external accountability, can be regarded as external pushes for Chinese corporations, especially those which have not adopted a sound corporate responsibility reporting system, encouraging them to promote their CSR practice through responsible reporting.

3.2.2   CSR as a Result of Internal Drivers

People's understanding of CSR changed with the transformation of the Chinese economy and the economic reform of China. Since China's opening up and reform policies enacted in 1978, the goal of economic freedom and individual wealth grew rapidly in importance as the former Confucian and Maoist values have decreased. Increasing attention was paid to profit, productivity and returns but CSR and moral standards were ignored. Businessmen were keen to make immediate returns from their investments as their primary overriding objective, while the importance of CSR dimmed and the phenomenon of money-worship grew.[43] With very severe market competition, corporations paid a great deal of attention to profit-making and left loopholes in balancing profits and moral standards.[44] This competitive business atmosphere has enabled China to undergo rapid economic growth since the 1980s. However, it is commonly agreed that growth comes with social and environmental costs that the Chinese people and the Chinese government cannot afford in the long term.

---

[40]   *Ibid.* at 6.
[41]   *Ibid.* at 10.
[42]   *Ibid.* at 10.
[43]   L. Zu, *Corporate Social Responsibility, Corporate Restructuring and Firm's Performance* (Berlin: Springer-Verlag, 2009) p. 47.
[44]   *Ibid.* at 47.

Worrying CSR practices in China

There are industries which have been highly profitable, but which have been highly polluting and have offered low wages and minimal health and safety standards to non-unionized rural migrant workers who are continually willing to come to urban Chinese cities despite the poor working conditions.[45] It is undeniable that China has always been regarded as a source of an inexhaustible supply of cheap labour from rural areas. However, according to a government report, the poor working conditions and extremely low salaries have led to a shortage in labour within the major exporting areas since 2004, especially in areas such as the Pearl River Delta and the Chang Jiang Delta. This shortage might persuade corporations to be more socially responsible towards their employees.[46] Furthermore, competition for foreign investment among local governments in China also highlights the need for CSR culture, in circumstances when the Chinese government grants regulatory exemptions to attract external investment in sacrifice of the protection of the natural environment. The corporations' responsibilities for social issues are starting to be regarded as one of the standards used to assess overall corporate performance. It is recognized that corporate actions might do harm and have negative influences on stakeholders, including employees, the environment and local communities.

Apart from the concerns about the protection of employees, environmental degradation is an issue that needs careful and full attention from governments, corporations and individuals. Rapid industrial development and power in China has created a legacy of environmental damage that may take decades and a great deal of public wealth to undo. It is claimed that such severe environmental degradation has increasingly caused domestic and international repercussions that pose a heavy long-term burden for the Chinese public and a serious political challenge for the Chinese

---

[45]   N. Young, 'Three C's: Civil Society, Corporate Social Responsibility and China' (2002) 29 *China Business Review* 34; see also J.L. Gonzalez, 'Corporation-Community Collaboration for Social Development: An Overview of Trends, Challenges, and Lessons from Asia' in M.E. Contreras, *Corporate Social Responsibility in Promotion of Social Development: Experiences from Asia and Latin America* (Washington, DC: Inter-American Development Band and Free Hand Press, 2004).

[46]   See Ministry of Labour and Social Security (*Laodong Baozhang Bu*), *A Report on Shortage of Labour from Rural Areas of China* (*Guanyu Mingong Duanque De Diaocha Baogao*), available at www.gddx.gov.cn.

government and ruling party.[47] It is reported on the Chinese government's Official Web Portal that environmental pollution cost China losses of 511.8 billion Yuan (about US$64 billion) in 2004, which amounted to 3.05 per cent of the Chinese GDP in 2003.[48] Zhu Guangyao, deputy chief of the State Environmental Protection Agency, used statistics from more recent and general sources to estimate that environmental damage cost the government about 10 per cent of GDP in 2005 (US$2.26 trillion).[49]

Therefore, governments at both central and local levels are putting increasing emphasis on CSR-related issues. In terms of internal influences, the emergence and popularity of CSR in China are a combinative force arising both from the awakening of individual corporations and entrepreneurs, and promotion and awareness from governments. Therefore, governments at different levels have been organizing publicity campaigns to encourage CSR, to widen the responsiveness and understanding of the entire society and encourage more involvement in the process. Meanwhile, the government will play a supervisory role in reinforcing CSR by making regular assessments and enforcing observance of the laws.[50] Based on some collaborative research carried out by the Chinese State Environmental Protection Administration (SEPA) and the World Bank, 'implementation of environmental pollution control policies – particularly command-and-control measures, but also economic and voluntary measures – have contributed substantially to levelling off or even reducing pollutions loads, particularly in certain targeted industrial sectors'.[51]

However, various statistics also indicate the seriousness of environmental problems in China: it is suggested that 500 million people in rural areas of China do not have access to piped water, while 300 million people in rural areas cannot get safe drinking water. About 47 billion

---

[47]   J. Kahn and J. Yardley, 'As China roars, pollution reaches deadly extremes', *New York Times*, 26 August 2007.

[48]   Chinese Government's Official Web Portal, 'Pollution Costs China 511.8b Yuan in 2004', available at http://english.gov.cn/2006-09/07/content_381756.htm.

[49]   'Pollution cost equal 10% of China's GDP', *China Daily*, 6 June 2006, available at www.chinadaily.com.cn/china/2006-06/06/content_609350.htm.

[50]   See Speech of Mr Yi Xiaozhun, Assistant Minister of Ministry of Commerce, People's Republic of China; X. Yi, 'Improving Corporate Responsibility Competitiveness to Promote Harmonious Society', available at www.wtoguide.net/html/2005Sino-European/14_36_14_633.html.

[51]   State Environmental Protection Administration of China and World Bank, *Cost of Pollution in China: Economic Estimates of Physical Damages* (2007), available at http://siteresources.worldbank.org/INTEAPREGTOPENVIRONMENT/Resources/China_Cost_of_Pollution.pdf.

cubic metres of water below quality standards was supplied to households; about 100 billion cubic metres of the water supply in China
(approximately 20 per cent) was contaminated; and only 1 per cent of
560 million urban residences in China are able to breathe air of
satisfactory quality according to the current EU safety standards.[52] These
environmental problems around clean air and drinking water inevitably
lead to health problems and deaths. It was estimated in the same report
that approximately 350,000 to 400,000 premature deaths were caused by
outdoor air pollution, while approximately another 300,000 to 400,000
were caused by indoor air pollution.[53] These problems triggered numerous petitions about environmental problems. The environmental agency
nationwide filed 414,122 cases in 2006.[54] In fact, environmental problems have become a threat to the stability of society and the unwavering
control of the Chinese Communist Party. Environmentally irresponsible
corporate actions are now subject to public scrutiny in China.[55]

Domestic regulations and guidelines
The internal push towards corporations becoming more socially responsible also emanates from stock exchanges in China. The Shenzhen Stock
Exchange released 'Social Responsibility Guidelines for Listed Companies' and adopted CSR into its general principles in official documents
that regulate the public companies that are listed on the stock exchange.
'In accordance with the Company Law, the Securities Law, Law of the
People's Republic of China on State-Owned Asserts of Enterprise and
other laws, administrative regulations and the rules of competent authorities', the Guidelines have been formulated 'for the purpose of implementing a scientific outlook on social development, building social
harmony, accelerating sustainable economic and social development and
promoting commitment to social responsibility'.[56] Social responsibilities

[52]   *Ibid.*
[53]   *Ibid.*
[54]   Z. Tong, 'Thoughts on Protests Arising from Environmental Pollutions in
China (*Dui Woguo Huanjing Wuran Yinfa Quntixing Shijian De Sikao*)' in D.
Yang (ed.), *Crisis and Turning Point in Environmental Problems in China
(Zhongguo Huanjing de Weiji yu Zhuanji)* (Beijing: Social Sciences Academic
Press, 2008) pp. 149–56.
[55]   L.W. Lin, 'Corporate Social Responsibility in China: Window Dressing or
Structural Change?' (2010) 28 *Berkeley Journal of International Law* 64 at 89.
[56]   Shenzhen Stock Exchange, Social Responsibility Guidelines for Listed
Companies (2006) art. 1.

were defined, in a manner which is closely related to corporate responsibility towards various stakeholders, as obligations that should be assumed by listed companies for social development 'for the natural environment and resources and for the interests of parties including their shareholders, creditors, employees, customers, consumers, suppliers and communities'.[57] Furthermore, social policies and the legal rights of stakeholders were also closely related to the Guidelines, while the listed companies are required to proactively protect 'the legitimate rights and interests of their creditors and employees, be honest and trustworthy towards their suppliers, customers and consumers, and commit themselves to social welfare services like environmental protection and community development in order to achieve social harmony'.[58] In conclusion, in line with the requirements in the CCL, especially the corporate objective stipulations within article 5, and according to the Guidelines produced by the Shenzhen Stock Exchange, listed companies must protect the interests of various stakeholders while pursing economic results. Adhering to the policy of establishing a Harmonious Society, corporate responsibilities are a mixture of legal responsibilities, economic responsibilities and ethical responsibilities. Furthermore, it is also stated that more socially responsible companies will improve corporate governance structure and treat shareholders fairly,[59] and enable stakeholders to enjoy their rights and interests provided in laws, regulations and rules[60] through the provision of CSR and CSR reports.[61]

Apart from the Guidelines issued by the Shenzhen Stock Exchange, CSR issues have been increasingly recognized as an important issue for many other domestic government bodies when they either independently published CSR-related rules and guidelines, or adopted CSR into their general guidelines. The State-owned Assets Supervision and Administration Commission of the State Council (SASAC) issued the 'Guidelines to the State-Owned Enterprises Directly under the Central Government on Fulfilling Corporate Social Responsibilities'; the Chinese Academy of International Trade and Economic Cooperation, a subsidiary of the Ministry of Commerce, issued 'Guidelines on Corporate Social Responsibility Compliance by Foreign Invested Enterprises'; the Shanghai Stock Exchange issued a 'Notice on Strengthening Listed Companies' Assumption of Social Responsibility and Guidelines on Shanghai Stock

---

57   *Ibid.* art. 2
58   *Ibid.* art. 3.
59   *Ibid.* ch. II.
60   *Ibid.* chs II–VI.
61   *Ibid.* ch. VII.

Exchange Listed Companies' Environmental Information Disclosure'; furthermore, in 2007, the Ministry of Commerce and the former Closer Economic Partnership Arrangement issued a 'Circular on Enhancing Environmental Surveillance on Exporting Enterprise' to restrict socially irresponsible enterprises from conducting foreign trade.[62]

Taking the 'Guidelines on Corporate Social Responsibility Compliance by Foreign Invested Enterprises' as an example, the document contains indications that the government is willing to favour corporations that it considers to be socially responsible. 'The Guidelines suggest that China intends to take a global lead in making CSR strategies a prerequisite for companies doing business within its borders. Moreover, the Guidelines have a decidedly Sino-centric focus, focusing on issues in China today and CSR programs with "Chinese characteristics"'.[63] The Guidelines cover four areas, including an 'objective for CSR in China, a definition of CSR for foreign invested companies, the essentials of CSR and the implementation of CSR strategy'. The most important element, closely related to the policy of foreign invested companies, appears to be the implementation of CSR strategy. Regarding this aspect, foreign invested companies are advised to comply with operational needs (abiding by laws, regulations and business ethics); stakeholder engagement (assuming a holistic approach to management decisions by taking employee and community impacts into account); and proactive contributions to development (engaging in projects that are in the interests of social, economic and environmental development).[64] It can be seen that CSR-compliant companies, from the criteria generated in the Guidelines, must consider their economic, social and environmental impacts, and they are advised to incorporate CSR elements into their corporate mission, vision and operations as well as striving for improvements against measurable

---

[62]   Guangzhou Yu, Vice Minister of Commerce, 'Strengthen CSR for Harmonious Society', speech at the Sino-Swedish CSR High-level Forum, 14 April 2008, available at http://wss2.mofcom.gov.cn/aarticle/translatorsgarden/famous speech/200806/20080605573007.html.

[63]   C. Pearson, 'Corporate Social Responsibility Compliance for Foreign Invested Enterprises in China' (2009), available at www.dlapiper.com/foreign_enterprises_csr_compliance.

[64]   Ministry of Commerce of the People's Republic of China, Guidelines on Corporate Social Responsibility Compliance by Foreign Invested Enterprises (*waizi touzi qiye lvxing shehui zeren zhidaoxing yijian*), available at www.mofcom.gov.cn/.

criteria.[65] The Guidelines can be regarded as an internal push for foreign investors to be socially responsible in China. It can also indirectly encourage other corporations in China to act in line with competitive ethical levels.

Furthermore, regarding the impact of the Guidelines on domestic corporations, it is proposed that SOEs should fulfil CSR to be consistent with the principle of human-orientation and the Scientific Outlook on Development, and act responsibly towards stakeholders to achieve a balance between the growth of enterprise, social benefits and environment protection.[66] The direct requirement on SOEs from central government to comply with CSR covers the interests of various stakeholders and different levels of corporate responsibility. SOEs are required to do business legally and honestly to make sustainable profits.[67] They are also required to improve product services, quality and safety for customers; strengthen resource conservation and environmental protection; protect the legal rights of employees; and participate in social public welfare programmes.[68] A broad range of stakeholders, including customers, the environment, employees and the public, were covered in the content of CSR undertakings of SOEs. The contents of the Guidelines also fit into the four dominant themes of CSR suggested by Lockett and others[69] (social, environmental, ethical and stakeholders), although such a classification will include some overlaps and lacunae. Regarding measures for the enforcement of CSR, five approaches have been suggested, including establishing awareness of CSR; completing systems and mechanisms for fulfilling CSR; building CSR information release systems; enforcing inter-enterprise communication and international cooperation; and systematizing the organizational role of the Communist Party of China in encouraging CSR within SOEs.[70] Enforcement approaches that have been

---

[65]   C. Pearson, 'Corporate Social Responsibility Compliance for Foreign Invested Enterprises in China' (2009) p. 3, available at www.dlapiper.com/foreign_enterprises_csr_compliance.

[66]   SASAC, Guidelines to the State-Owned Enterprises Directly under the Central Government on Fulfilling Corporate Social Responsibilities, s. 1(1), available at www.sasac.gov.cn/n2963340/n2964712/4891623.html.

[67]   *Ibid.* s. 3(8)–(9).

[68]   *Ibid.* s. 3(10) –(15).

[69]   A. Lockett, J. Moon and W. Visser, 'Corporate Social Responsibility in Management Research: Focus, Nature, Salience and Influence' (2006) 43 *Journal of Management Studies* 115 at 117.

[70]   SASAC, Guidelines to the State-Owned Enterprises Directly under the Central Government on Fulfilling Corporate Social Responsibilities, s. 4(16)–(20), available at www.sasac.gov.cn/n2963340/n2964712/4891623.html.

the subject of academic discussion in an international context include CSR-related information disclosure, public awareness of CSR, and the encouragement of international corporations through soft law; all these measures were explicitly suggested in the Guidelines. The guideline-based analysis of the nature and scope of CSR also suggested that enforcement measures could be regarded as internal pushing forces, not only directly in favour of CSR practice in SOEs under central government control, but also indirectly for companies in other categories as the result of supply chains and competition.

Legal reform

Legal reform in China has always been an internal force influencing the development of CSR as an acceptable policy in China. Stone distinguished two types of legal responsibility: 'responsibility one', which emphasizes following the law; and 'responsibility two', which emphasizes deliberation and preparedness to give reasons for one's actions in terms that admit of generalization.[71] While responsibility one refers to the letter of the law that requires obedience, responsibility two refers to the spirit of the law by approaching the legal framework through socially appropriate considerations which place a premium on autonomous choice.[72] CSR-related legal obligations in employment law, consumer protection law, environmental law and insolvency law are always related to responsibility one, which places emphasis on following and obeying the law in order to be more socially responsible. In China, a number of statutes have been passed to protect the rights of various stakeholders, including Labour Contract Law 2008, Environmental Protection Law 1989, Law on the Protection of Rights and Interests of Consumers 1994, Property Law 2007, Corporate Income Tax Law 2008, Antimonopoly Law 2007 and Enterprise Insolvency Law 2007. The enactment of these laws was the government's response to various types of irresponsible action. These CSR-related legal responsibilities include such matters as restrictive compliance, opportunistic compliance, avoidance of civil litigation, and anticipation of changes in legislation, such as the moral duty to justify the minimum standards of corporate conduct.[73] Most of these

---

[71] C.D. Stone, *Where the Law Ends* (New York: Harper and Row, 1975) pp. 97–102.

[72] A. Geva, 'Three Models of Corporate Social Responsibility: Interrelationships between Theory, Research and Practice' (2008) 113 *Business and Society Review* 1 at 25.

[73] M.S. Schwartz and A.B. Carroll, 'Corporate Social Responsibility: A Three-Domain Approach' (2003) 13 *Business Ethics Quarterly* 503 at 515.

corporate activities are seen not only as legal requirements, but also have an ethical dimension and an economic incentive. Responsibility one towards various stakeholders can be collectively regarded as an internal push for promoting a comprehensive and far-reaching CSR framework in China.

Responsibility two approaches the law through socially appropriate considerations, with the morality of aspiration and an exhortation to realize one's fullest potential.[74] This responsibility makes it necessary to think about the general good in situations where legal controls over company actions are ineffective and may even be counterproductive.[75] Corporations, under this type of responsibility, want to adopt CSR into their corporate strategy and their company with the associated legal obligations. They have this desire not because of the threat of liability and litigation, but because these obligations have been internalized as guiding standards for their decisions and actions.[76] Therefore, the regulations are not only necessary but also desirable.[77] Support from the corporate side for the government's regulations encourages the voluntary nature of CSR. The general corporate objective of Chinese corporations is stipulated in CCL 2006. A commendable legislative initiative of this policy is article 5, which requires companies to 'undertake social responsibility' in the course of conducting business. The voluntary nature of this article illustrates the internal nature of corporate action in this area. The collective view of corporations and competition between companies can also be seen as internal pushes towards the effective adoption of CSR policies.

Domestic CSR management standard
Similar to SA8000 and ISO 26000 but in reference to a specific industry sector, China developed its first CSR management standard, the China Social Compliance 9000 (CSC9000), to apply to the textile and apparel

---

[74]   C.D. Stone, *Where the Law Ends* (New York: Harper and Row, 1975) p. 101.
[75]   A. Geva, 'Three Models of Corporate Social Responsibility: Interrelationships between Theory, Research and Practice' (2008) 113 *Business and Society Review* 1 at 25.
[76]   J. Aharony and A. Geva, 'Moral Implications of Law in Business: A Case of Tax Loopholes' (2003) 12 *Business Ethics: A European Review* 378 at 380–1.
[77]   A. Geva, 'Three Models of Corporate Social Responsibility: Interrelationships between Theory, Research and Practice' (2008) 113 *Business and Society Review* 1 at 26.

sector based on Chinese law and regulations as well as relevant international conventions.[78] This standard has gained worldwide recognition, and aims to ensure the protection of employees' legal rights, assist companies to improve their CSR record, facilitate the sustainable development of enterprise, and ultimately promote the international reputation of Chinese textile manufacturers.[79] It was emphasized that the standard is also designed to 'materialize the idea of building a Harmonious Society in the Chinese textile sector'.[80] This impact of the standard is not limited only to the internal context. The World Bank included CSC9000 in its Key Corporate Responsibility Codes, Principles and Standards as an example of a country-specific set of standards.[81] Despite the fact that this standard only applies to the textile and apparel industry, the drafting, implementation and international impact of the standard has had a positive effect on CSR practice and the awareness of CSR in China, and it can be regarded as an important internal impetus for the development of CSR.

[78]   International Trade Centre, CSC9000T Standard, available at http://cms. standardsmap.org/publish/itc_standards/csc9000/resources/files/1067/Final_CSC 9000T_EN.pdf.

[79]   CSC9000 Responsible Supply Chain Association, 'General Description of CSC9000T', available at www.csc9000.org.cn/en/AboutCSC9000T.asp.

[80]   CSR-China, 'China Social Compliance 9000 for the Textile and Apparel Industry (CSC9000T)', available at www.csr-china.net/templates/node/index. aspx?nodeid=39dc8010-662b-44e2-aeb3-24957bcf92b6&l=en&page=contentpage& contentid=9a20544a-1b9a-4e50-bb70-b9fa93e81dd7.

[81]   World Bank Virtual Resource Centre, 'Key Corporate Responsibility Codes, Principles and Standards', available at http://web.worldbank.org/WBSITE/ EXTERNAL/WBI/WBIPROGRAMS/CGCSRLP/0,,contentMDK:20719568~page PK: 64156158~piPK:64152884~theSitePK:460861,00.html.

4. A unique corporate governance model in China, including a unique corporate social responsibility policy

Before engaging in discussions of the legality of corporate social responsibility (CSR) and related regulations and enforcement problems in China, it is worth paying attention to the existing corporate governance model in China and discussing the agency relationships within the actors of the company, namely, directors, shareholders and various stakeholders. The causality and dynamics between Chinese corporate governance practices and institutional constraints from various sources should be discussed in order to gain a deeper understanding of 'what portfolio of governance mechanisms can be better adapted to China's increasingly challenging institutional settings and generate the largest benign impact'.[1] The involvement of the Chinese government in business raises a unique set of corporate governance issues, and makes the improvement of Chinese corporate governance difficult.

Corporate governance in China has emerged and developed with the shift of the Chinese economy from a planned to a market economy. It has been argued that the development of China's corporate governance has demonstrated a number of internal weaknesses which make the stock market less effective in controlling shareholders, protecting minority shareholders and stakeholders, and fostering long-term performance for businesses. It is problematic that the governance model gives unpoliced power and plenty of leeway to the controlling shareholders, expropriates the minority shareholders, and undermines the confidence of the public in the Chinese stock market.[2] It is important to suggest some corporate governance reform measures that might help to establish a more effective business environment and promote CSR in China. While there is a large number of factors affecting the efficiency and effectiveness of a particular

---

[1] Q. Liu, 'Corporate Governance in China: Current Practices, Economic Effects and Institutional Determinants' (2006) 52 *CESifo Economic Studies* 415 at 419.
[2] *Ibid.* at 418.

corporate governance model, several important pillars should always be included in this list. These factors are: the existence of a wide range of stakeholders within corporations; the board of directors and its responsibilities; disclosure and transparency; and the rights of shareholders, including their equitable treatment. These factors should be taken into account in corporate governance reform with the purpose of promoting increased regional and international recognition of Chinese corporations and increasing overall prosperity.[3]

Chinese officials have engaged in research on corporate governance ever since they launched the Shanghai and Shenzhen stock exchanges in December 1990 and April 1991, respectively. The concept and origin of corporate governance were first researched and discussed in detail by the staff of the Research and Development Centre of the Shanghai Stock Exchange in 1997. This early research was carried out as a result of influences from corporate governance research in the United States, as well as the OECD corporate governance principle.[4] Over a period of 20 years, reforms were introduced to change the Chinese economy from a centralized and fully planned economic system, with the result that the economy of China is now set to become a decentralized market economy. According to an OECD survey in 2010,[5] China has stabilized her position as the third biggest economy after the United States and Japan, based on an average annual GDP growth rate of 9 per cent and a total GDP of over RMB 30 trillion in 2008.

Domestically, around 200 to 300 million people in the People's Republic of China are investing, either directly or indirectly, in the stock market. Internationally, the Chinese stock market, which was officially established in the late 1990s, has grown to be the eighth largest in the world in less than 15 years,[6] and the Shanghai Stock Exchange and Shenzhen Stock Exchange are ranked as the sixth and seventh largest stock exchanges by trade value and market capitalization in 2011. Over

---

[3]   J.V. Feinerman, 'New Hope for Corporate Governance in China?' (2007) 191 *China Quarterly* 590 at 591.

[4]   R. Hu, 'The Concept and Importance of Corporate Governance' in G. Tu and C. Zhu (eds), *Corporate Governance: International Experience and China Practice* (Beijing: People's Press, 2001) pp. 15–18.

[5]   Organisation for Economic Co-operation and Development, *Economic Survey of China – 2010* (OECD, 2010), available at www.oecd.org/document/43/ 0,3746,en_2649_34571_44477419_1_1_1_1,00.html.

[6]   Q. Liu, 'Corporate Governance in China: Current Practices, Economic Effects and Institutional Determinants' (2006) 52 *CESifo Economic Studies* 415 at 416.

the last decade, much attention has been given to Chinese corporate governance, both in practice and in theory, as a worldwide research topic. It has become a concept that has increasingly engaged the minds of corporate regulators and the stock exchange in China. Attention is mostly focused on the debate concerning how China can develop an effective corporate governance system to improve the performance of its listed companies and protect their minority shareholders and stakeholders. The improvement of corporate governance for Chinese corporations is an ongoing battle that calls for the participation of parties such as regulators, market participants and academics.[7]

In light of the granting of permanent normal trade relations with China from other WTO members, and also of China's induction into the WTO in December 2001, many more investment opportunities in China are becoming available and the potential market is massive. China has entered a new stage of economic transformation and integration within the world economy.[8] At the same time, Chinese legislation on corporate law has been subject to increasing pressure for reform. The implementation of new laws in the form of a new Company Law in 2006, a Securities Law also in 2006, and the new Bankruptcy Law in 2005, is evidence of progressive legislative reform. Additionally, numerous regulations have been issued by the China Securities Regulatory Commission (CSRC) and other ministries concerning disclosures, mergers and acquisitions, accounting, related party transactions, independent directors and securities litigation, in order to establish a substantial legal framework for corporate governance.[9] Therefore, research on the framework, style and reconstruction of corporate governance in China is becoming more and more important and has accompanied the steady opening up of the Chinese economy to greater market-based fair competition and enhanced market monitoring.

---

[7] *Ibid.*

[8] S. Voss and Y.W. Xia, 'Corporate Governance of Listed Companies in China', paper presented at Track 8 of IFSAM VIIIth World Congress 2006, hosted by VHB, Berlin, September 2006, p. 11, available at www.ctw-congress.de/ifsam/download/track_8/pap00750.pdf.

[9] L.H. Tan and J.Y. Wang, 'Modeling an Efficient Corporate Governance System for China's Listed State-Owned Enterprises: Issues and Challenges in a Transitional Economy' (2007) 7 *Journal of Corporate Law Studies* 143 at 145.

Corporate governance is the system of laws, rules and factors that control activities in a company.[10] The Chinese corporate governance model includes characteristics from practices and experiences of various jurisdictions. Partly as the result of political interference from the government, 'corporate governance in China was developed by a combination of top-down and bottom-up approaches'.[11] The top-down approach was implemented by the Chinese Communist Party in such a way that every major corporate governance plan had first to be endorsed by the Chinese Communist Party before it could be drafted into law by the National People's Congress or a Standing Committee. For example, the establishment of a modern corporate system within state-owned enterprises (SOEs) was first published as a Resolution of the Chinese Communist Party before it was incorporated into CCL 1994. On the other hand, the bottom-up approach is the natural choice of any market economy, and the establishment of corporate governance is the result of adopting and borrowing from Western models that are enforceable in China until they are explicitly banned by the controlling Communist Party. It has been argued that the top-down approach has been dominant over the bottom-up approach, and the outcome is the result of the absolute leadership of the Chinese Communist Party.[12]

It has further been argued that neither the 'outsider system' nor the 'insider system' of corporate governance will be suitable for application in China because of the country's unique transitional economy.[13] China needs a unique system of its own, shaped by the socialist market economy and with Chinese characteristics. Both the outsider model and the insider model have particular characteristics describing both internal governance and external governance. Internal governance is primarily concerned with ownership and control, the characteristics and composition of the board of directors and executive compensation, while external governance is concerned with the production market, the take-over

---

[10]   S.L. Gillan and L.T. Starks, 'Corporate Governance Proposals and Shareholder Activism: The Role of Institutional Investors' (2000) 16 *Pacific-Basin Finance Journal* 591.

[11]   J. Fu, *Corporate Disclosure and Corporate Governance in China* (London: Kluwer Law International, 2010) p. 6.

[12]   *Ibid.*

[13]   L.H. Tan and J.Y. Wang, 'Modeling an Efficient Corporate Governance System for China's Listed State-Owned Enterprises: Issues and Challenges in a Transitional Economy' (2007) 7 *Journal of Corporate Law Studies* 143 at 182.

market and the state regulatory system.[14] As the largest transitional economy and an emerging market, China has become a focus for corporate governance research in recent years. China has a unique socialist market-oriented economy, and the government has done much to improve the corporate governance of listed companies. However, it is unclear whether the corporate governance model in China is an insider network-oriented model or an outsider market-oriented model. If the typical characteristics of the insider model are termed 'CAI' and the typical characteristics of the outsider model 'CAO', it can be demonstrated that features of both CAI and CAO can be found in the Chinese corporate governance model.

However, in terms of the debate between the shareholder and stakeholder theories, it is legitimate to ask if the current Chinese corporate governance model belongs to any of the archetypical models, or whether it forms a hybrid model.[15] In this section a few traits of Chinese corporate governance will be discussed and classified according to whether they are CAI or CAO. The purpose of this analysis is to enable a discussion of the protection of stakeholders' interests in China in the current hybrid corporate governance model, in which the protection of stakeholders is not being addressed at a satisfactory level. This is an issue which is becoming more and more important because of recent and current corporate ethical problems, human rights problems and social responsibility scandals, including cases of very serious pollution.

4.1 CONCENTRATED SHAREHOLDING

Before discussing the pattern of concentrated share ownership in China, it is important to clarify the different shares in China, which constitute a unique characteristic of the shareholding ownership structure. Shares in listed companies have been comprised of non-tradable and tradable shares because of the expectation of control from the state over most listed companies. Tradable shares include A-shares, B-shares, H-shares and N-shares. A-shares are shares traded in Yuan (Chinese currency) on the Shanghai and Shenzhen Stock Exchanges. B-shares of companies

---

[14] M.R. Huson, R. Parrino and L.T. Starks, 'International Monitoring Mechanisms and CEO Turnover: A Long Term Perspective' (2001) 56 *Journal of Finance* 2265.
[15] For discussions on the hybrid corporate governance model see J. Zhao, 'Modernising Corporate Objective Debate towards a Hybrid Model' (2011) 62 *Northern Ireland Legal Quarterly* 361.

listed on the Shanghai Stock Exchange are quoted and traded in US dollars, and quoted and traded in Hong Kong dollars for companies listed on the Shenzhen Stock Exchange. Although A-shares and B-shares are quoted and traded in different currencies, shareholders have same rights to dividends and voting. H-shares and N-shares are shares of companies in mainland China that are listed on the Hong Kong Stock Exchange and the US Stock Market, respectively. Despite the fact that A-shares were designed for domestic investors while B-shares were designed for investors from outside mainland China, there have been some changes and there is leeway to make purchasing and floating shares easier and to enhance the market economy in China. Since 20 February 2001, domestic investors have been allowed to invest in B-shares, and A-shares have been made available to Qualified Foreign Institutional Investors since 23 May 2003. This was done in order to enhance the strength of institutional investors in the market and to come into alignment with the commitments made in China's agreement with the WTO.[16]

The biggest factor that affects corporate governance in China is state ownership. The Chinese state owns about half of all the shares in listed companies.[17] Based on the database of the China Centre for Economic Research at Peking University, more than half of the listed company shares were owned by the government at the end of 2009.[18] According to a statistical analysis carried out by Li in 2011, 54 per cent of equity in listed companies belongs to the state or to state-owned corporate entities. Among the 1,104 listed companies on the Shanghai and Shenzhen Stock Exchanges, the proportion of shares owned by the largest shareholder reached 45 per cent, while the second largest shareholder owned 8 per cent[19] The government defines SOEs as 'enterprises in which all assets are owned by the state'.[20] Generally speaking, the term 'listed company' in China is identical to the term 'listed SOEs' since the majority of the

---

[16] J. Yang, J. Chi and M. Young, 'A Review of Corporate Governance in China' (2011) 25 *Asian-Pacific Economic Literature* 15 at 16.

[17] Based on the data from CEIC Data, China Premium Database, available at www.ceicdata.com/China.html.

[18] Based on the calculations of Yang, Chi and Young; see J. Yang, J. Chi and M. Young, 'A Review of Corporate Governance in China' (2011) 25 *Asian-Pacific Economic Literature* 15 at 17.

[19] H. Li, 'Capital Structure on Agency Cost in Chinese Listed Firms' (2011) 1 *International Journal of Governance* 295 at 299–300.

[20] National Bureau of Statistics, *General Survey Definitions: Management of Registration of Corporations Guidelines* (2002).

listed companies in China are SOEs.[21] There are normally two types of SOEs: SOEs that are centrally owned, including entities managed by the State-owned Assets Supervision and Administration Commission of the State Council (SASAC), which are state-owned financial institutions supervised by the China Securities Regulatory Commission (CSRC), as well as entities managed by other central government ministries such as the Ministry of Commerce, Ministry of Education, Ministry of Science and Technology and other ministries; or SOEs owned by provincial or local governments. It is argued by Lee that central SOEs have become increasingly important in comparison with local SOEs.[22] In the China Corporate Governance Report,[23] a study of the Shanghai Stock Exchange, the high ownership concentration was described as 'excessive'.[24]

Together with 'legal person' shares, state-owned shares belong to one of the two major classes of non-tradable shares which comprise two-thirds of the shares on the market. In a typical Chinese listed company, 30 per cent of its shares are state-ownership shares and 30 per cent 'legal entity' shares, with the remainder being individual shares.[25] The legal entities in the 'legal entity' shares are companies or economic entities, with the classification of legal person including a number of heterogeneous entities, ranging from solely SOEs to private corporations.[26]

The Report took the Shanghai Stock Exchange as a research object, and demonstrated that in the annual reports for 2002, 'each largest shareholder possessed 44.3 per cent of its company's shares in all 734 companies'. Concentrated shareholding is a typical characteristic of the

---

[21]   J.Y. Wang, 'Dancing with Wolves: Regulation and Deregulations of Foreign Investment in China's Stock Market' (2004) 5 *University of Hawaii Asian-Pacific Law and Policy Journal* 1 at 3.

[22]   J. Lee, 'State Owned Enterprises in China: Reviewing the Evidence' (Organisation for Economic Cooperation and Development Working Group on Privatisation and Corporate Governance of State Owned Assets, 2009) pp. 8–9, available at www.oecd.org/dataoecd/14/30/42095493.pdf.

[23]   See Shanghai Stock Exchange Research Centre, *Zhongguo Gongsi Zhili Baogao* (*China Corporate Governance Report*) (Shanghai: Fudan University Press, 2003).

[24]   *Ibid.* at 45.

[25]   D.K.K. Fan, C.M. Lau and M. Young, 'Is China's Corporate Governance Beginning to Come of Age? The Case of CEO Turnover' (2007) 37 *Pacific-Basin Finance Journal* 105 at 110.

[26]   G. Chen, M. Firth and L. Xu, 'Does the Type of Ownership Control Matter? Evidence from China's Listed Companies' (2009) 33 *Journal of Banking and Finance* 171.

insider corporate governance model. However, the largest shareholder in China, in contrast to the overwhelming institutional shareholders in other countries, normally refers to the state, which dominates the shareholding in listed SOEs. This very high concentration of ownership is directly linked to control from the board of directors, which is regarded as a critical link between ownership and control in the current Chinese corporate governance scheme.[27]

Efforts have been made by the Chinese government to reduce the overly-high concentration of state shareholding. Notwithstanding a general objective to create a more dispersed and competitive shareholding structure, corporatization and ownership diversification have also led to the emergence of new owners such as individual minority shareholders, institutional investors and employee shareholders.[28] China's SOEs have restructured and a few of them are among the largest companies globally. However, state ownership still prevails in most listed enterprises where the state still holds a high percentage of the shares.[29]

Many problems arise if the state acts as the controlling shareholder of corporations. When SOEs are listed, the local office of the Bureau of State Asset Management or its subsidiaries (local state asset management companies) will be the largest shareholders of the listed companies. The chairman of the board of directors is normally a representative from the Bureau of State Asset Management. The chairman of the company will consult with the board and nominate the directors and managers of the SOEs, who will make the corporate decisions.[30] Therefore, the decisions made by the board of directors will focus on the largest shareholders' interests. This fits within the shareholder primacy norm, and is therefore classified as CAO.

---

[27]   L.H. Tan and J.Y. Wang, 'Modelling an Efficient Corporate Governance System for China's Listed State-Owned Enterprises: Issues and Challenges in a Transitional Economy' (2007) 7 *Journal of Corporate Law Studies* 143 at 147.

[28]   S. Tenev, C. Zhang and L. Brefort, *Corporate Governance and Enterprise Reform in China: Building the Institutions of Modern Markets* (Washington DC: World Bank and the International Finance Corporation, 2002) pp. 2–3.

[29]   S. Vob and Y. W. Xia, 'Corporate Governance of Listed Companies in China', paper presented at Track 8 of IFSAM VIIIth World Congress 2006, hosted by VHB, Berlin, September 2006, pp. 110–16, available at www.ctw-congress.de/ifsam/download/track_8/pap00750.pdf.

[30]   J.F. Huchet and X. Richer, *China in Search of an Efficient Corporate Governance System: International Comparison and Lessons*, Centre for Economic Reform and Transformation, Herriot-Watt University Discussion Paper No. 99/01 (1999).

However, the shareholder primacy norm in China is completely different from the classic shareholder primacy model. In China, the directors of SOEs, namely, the Bureau of State Asset Management officers, are aiming to maximize the interests of the state since the state is the biggest shareholder. They are civil servants employed by the government, whose remunerations are not related to the performance of the corporations they manage. Therefore, there is no incentive for them to maximize the interests of shareholders and promote the success of SOEs. Furthermore, the bosses of the SOE directors are the local governments, and directors will 'align their interests with the local government, whose political interests may be to preserve employment rather than increase the efficiency of the listed SOEs'.[31] In comparison, under the Anglo-American model the directors' remunerations are closely tied to the performance of their corporations. It is the directors' duty to maximize the interests of the shareholders. Although managerial shareholdings have been widely recognized as a functional corporate governance mechanism in Western countries, given their low occurrence in China and the close relationship between the directors and the controlling shareholders in SOEs,[32] the importance of managerial shareholdings is not as high as has been reported.[33] It can be concluded from the shareholding structure of Chinese corporations that it is not possible to classify the Chinese corporate governance model into either of the classic frameworks.

4.2 TWO-TIER BOARD STRUCTURE AND INDEPENDENT DIRECTORS

The reform of Chinese corporate governance offers an interesting context for investigating the determinates of board structure, size and

[31] L.H. Tan and J.Y. Wang, 'Modelling an Efficient Corporate Governance System for China's Listed State-Owned Enterprises: Issues and Challenges in a Transitional Economy' (2007) 7 *Journal of Corporate Law Studies* 143 at 149.
[32] J. Yang, J. Chi and M. Young, 'A Review of Corporate Governance in China' (2011) 25 *Asian-Pacific Economic Literature* 15 at 16.
[33] For discussions on the positive effects of managerial shareholding on firm performance, see L. Gao and G. Kling, 'Corporate Governance and Tunnelling: Empirical Evidence from China' (2008) 16 *Pacific-Basin Finance Journal* 591; J. Chen, 'Ownership Structure as Corporate Governance Mechanism: Evidence from Chinese Listed Companies' (2001) 34 *Economics of Planning* 53; D.H. Li, F. Moshirian, P. Nguyen and L.W. Tan, 'Managerial Ownership and Firm Performance: Evidence from China's Privatizations' (2005) 21 *Research in International Business and Finance* 396.

independence. Board size is primarily driven by firm complexity, and board independence and structure are mainly driven by law and regulations.[34] According to Chinese Company Law, 'a limited liability company shall have a supervisory board composed of no less than three members. Where a limited liability company has a small number of shareholders or is comparatively small in scale, it may have one or two supervisors instead of a supervisory board'.[35] The supervisory board shall supervise 'the acts of the directors and senior executives performing their functions'.[36] Besides this, board members should exercise their function and power 'to bring the proposal to dismiss those directors and senior executives violating the law, administrative regulations, the articles of association of the company or the resolutions of the shareholders meetings'[37] and to 'demand directors and senior executives to make corrections if any of their acts are found to have damaged the interests of the company'.[38] Additionally, they can 'bring a lawsuit against the directors or senior executives in accordance with the provisions of Article 152 of Company Law 2006'.[39] Furthermore, based on the Code of Corporate Governance for Listed Companies in China issued by the CSRC in 2002, the duty of the board of supervisors is to supervise the corporate finance of listed companies. They are responsible for the appropriateness and accuracy of the company's financial statements.[40] The supervisory boards shall be 'accountable to all shareholders'. The board 'shall supervise the corporate finance, the legitimacy of directors, managers and other senior management personnel's performance of their duties, and shall protect the company's and the shareholders' legal rights and interests'.[41]

It can be concluded from the requirements above that a quasi-two-tier board structure has been adopted in China, which is very similar to the

---

[34]   C. H. Chen and B. Al-Najjar, 'The Determinants of Board Size and Independence: Evidence from China' (2011) 21 *International Business Review* 831 at 831–2.

[35]   CCL 2006 art. 52.

[36]   *Ibid.* art. 54(2).

[37]   *Ibid.* art. 54(2).

[38]   *Ibid.* art. 54(3).

[39]   *Ibid.* art. 54(6).

[40]   Code of Corporate Governance for Listed Companies in China 2002 s. 68.

[41]   *Ibid.* s. 59.

German corporate governance model.[42] The supervisory board, as an independent board, offers independent opinions on corporate decisions and monitors the directors' executive management, while the board of directors makes the main decisions on the day-to-day operation of the corporation. However, it was shown in a recent survey carried out by the Chinese Centre for Corporate Governance, entitled *Developing Effective Boards of Directors of SOEs*,[43] that members of the supervisory board are encountering difficulties in performing their duties. They are civil servants, and their education levels and qualifications are normally lower than those of the directors on the main board.[44] They normally have limited knowledge about the company itself. Moreover, they are not independent from the board of directors. It is not surprising in Chinese listed companies that internal directors and senior management teams have *guanxi*[45] (a close relationship) with the supervisors, and sometimes individuals even act both as internal directors and supervisors (or part-time supervisors) on the supervisory board.[46] Statistically, among all the reported cases in China since the formation of the first listed company, there has been no case in which the supervisory board has reported illegal actions or misbehaviour of the company to the board meeting before the problems were actually revealed in legal proceedings in court. The supervisory boards in companies do not have the right to vote on executive decisions or the right to vote for directors and financial officers of the companies. This lack of voting rights makes the related provisions a law without teeth. Also, in practice, most of the chairmen of supervisory boards in SOEs are secretaries of the Chinese Communist Party, or else they are civil servants who usually lack the professional expertise to enable them to make efficient business judgements. This

---

[42]   Centre for Financial Market Integrity, *China Corporate Governance Survey* (2007) p. 8.

[43]   Chinese Centre for Corporate Governance and Chinese Academy of Social Science, *Developing Effective Boards of Directors of SOEs* (2005).

[44]   Corporate Governance Research Group of Nan-kai University and Chinese Commission of Economy and Trade, *The Internal Corporate Governance Survey of Chinese Listed Corporations* (2005).

[45]   For discussions on '*guanxi*' and Chinese corporate governance see U. Braendle, T. Casser and J. Noll, 'Corporate Governance in China: Is Economic Growth Potential Hindered by *Guanxi*?' (2005) 16 *Business Strategy Review* 42; T.W. Dunfee and D.E. Warrren, 'Is Guanxi Ethical? A Normative Analysis of Doing Business in China' (2004) 32 *Journal of Business Ethics* 191.

[46]   Y. Li, 'Comparative Studies on Supervisory Board of Limited Corporations' in S. Shen (ed.), *Essays on International Commercial Law II* (Beijing: Law Publishing, 2002) p. 265 (in Chinese).

method of appointing chairmen violates market forces regarding the selection of human capital with professional skills within the field of business.

The roles of independent directors are easy to overlook due to the existence of the supervisory board. The allocation of power and how to reconcile the relationship between the independent directors and the supervisory board are important problems in the development of the Chinese corporate governance model.[47] It has been argued by Firth and others that larger and more active supervisory boards will help to raise the quality of accounting information.[48] Reforms regarding the size and composition of supervisory boards are key to make the system effective in China.

Since reforms and opening up to the world in 1978, China has also begun to reform its own internal economy and has sought to establish a 'modern enterprise system' since the 1990s.[49] One of the results of moving towards a modernized system is that the government has directed policy as regards corporate governance towards employing independent directors for companies. The system of independent directors has been introduced in China in order to improve the level of corporate governance for listed firms and offer better protection to minority investors. The Guidelines for Introducing Independent Directors to the Board of Directors of Listed Companies, issued by the CSRC in 2001,[50] was a landmark document formally establishing the independent director system in China. The Guidelines recommended that all companies listed on China's stock exchange should revise their articles of association, and made it mandatory for all listed corporations that a minimum of one-third of their board members should be independent directors.[51] In spite of a lack of practical and theoretical bases underpinning the Guidelines, regulators, directors and the government all have big ambitions for the independent director scheme and hope it will be a panacea for the corporate

---

[47]   *Ibid.* at 87–8.
[48]   M. Firth, P.M.Y. Fung and O.M. Rui, 'Corporate Performance and CEO Compensation in China' (2006) 12 *Journal of Corporate Finance* 693.
[49]   C. Lau, D.K.K. Fan, M. Young and S. Wu, 'Corporate Governance Effectiveness during Institutional Transition' (2007) 16 *International Business Review* 425.
[50]   See China Securities Regulatory Commission, Guidelines for Introducing Independent Directors to the Board of Directors of Listed Companies, Zhengjianfa No. 102 (2001).
[51]   *Ibid.*

governance problems currently affecting Chinese listed corporations.[52] In January 2002, the CSRC State Economic and Trade Commission re-affirmed the independent director system when it promulgated the Code of Corporate Governance for Chinese Listed Companies.[53] The system was also incorporated in company law, and it is required by CCL 2006 that 'a listed company shall have independent directors, and the concrete measures shall be formulated by the State Council'.[54]

The independent director system is regarded as an important aspect of US corporate governance, and the adoption of the system in China is regarded as evidence of the internalization of the American corporate governance model. In the United States, corporate governance has evolved towards a market-oriented system with shareholder dominance over boards of directors and managerialism.[55] The independent director system in the United States was partly adopted to solve the problems of managerialism.[56] It is a system designed to solve the problems of managerial indiscretion and the agency costs inherent in the separation of ownership and control.[57] The United States is a country typifying the external corporate governance model, with widely dispersed shareholding

---

[52]   M. Gu, 'Will an Independent Director Institution Perform Better than a Supervisor? Comments on the Newly Created Independent System in the People's Republic of China' (2003) *Journal of Chinese and Comparative Law* 59.

[53]   Code of Corporate Governance for Chinese Listed Companies 2002 s. 46.

[54]   CCL 2006 art. 123; the third draft of the CCL initially stated that listed companies *may* have independent directors, but the final version of the CCL enforced in 2006 changed the language to state that companies should do this, and made the independent director system compulsory.

[55]   J. Yuan, 'Formal Convergence or Substantial Divergence? Evidence from Adoption of the Independent Directors System in China' (2007) 9 *Asian-Pacific Law and Policy Journal* 71 at 75–6.

[56]   See B.D. Baysinger and H.N. Butler, 'Revolution Versus Evolution in Corporate Law: The ALI's Project and the Independent Director' (1984) 52 *George Washington Law Review* 563.

[57]   See American Law Institute, *Principles of Corporate Governance and Structure: Restatement and Recommendations* (1982); D. Machesani, 'The Concept of Autonomy and the Independent Directors of Public Corporations' (2005) 2 *Berkeley Business Law Journal* 315; M. Bainbridge, 'Independent Directors and the ALI Corporate Governance Project' (1993) 61 *George Washington Law Review* 1034. See also D.C. Clarke, 'The Independent Director in Chinese Corporate Governance' (2006) 36 *Delaware Journal of Corporate Law* 125.

structures, shareholders' rational apathy[58] and free-riding.[59] However, most listed companies in China are former SOEs, and the largest shareholder has strong control over the shareholders' general meeting and the decisions of the board of directors.

Guanxi and the limited rights of the supervisory board and independent directors made both systems weak and ineffective, and they appear to exert little influence over the decisions of directors. The mission of boards of supervision is to serve as watchdogs in Chinese corporate governance. However, they are selected at general shareholders' meetings, and they are always 'loyal' to the controlling shareholder in order to make sure they are reappointed. Comparatively speaking, supervisory boards in Germany and Japan play a more effective role[60] without interference from *guanxi* and the power of controlling shareholders. For example, in Germany, the German Stock Corporation Act 2009 gave supervisory boards the power to appoint members of the management board.[61] Furthermore, if the members of the board of directors breach their duties, are unable to manage the company or where there has been a vote of no confidence by the shareholders, the supervisory board has the power to revoke their appointment.[62]

---

[58]   R.C. Clark, 'Vote Buying and Corporate Law' (1979) 29 *Case Western Reserve Law Review* 776 at 779–83.

[59]   J.H. Choper, J.C. Coffee and R.J. Gilson, *Cases and Materials on Corporations*, 6th edn (New York: Panel Publisher, 2004).

[60]   See C. Liao, *The Governance Structure of Chinese Firms: Innovation, Competitiveness and Growth in a Dual Economy* (London: Springer, 2009); see also A.R. Pinto, 'Globalization and the Study of Comparative Corporate Governance' (2005) 23 *Wisconsin International Law Journal* 477; H. Schmidt and J. Drukarczyk, *Corporate Governance in Germany* (Baden-Baden: Nomos, 1997); S. Kaplan, 'Corporate Governance and Corporate Performance: A Comparison of Germany, Japan, and the U.S.' (1997) 9 *Journal of Applied Corporate Finance* 86; C.L. Wade, 'Commentary: Corporate Governance in Japan, Germany and Canada: What Can the U.S. Learn from Other Countries?' (2002) 24 *Law and Policy* 441. Of course, there are also discussions of the efficiency of the German-Japanese model in terms of their dual board systems; these discussions are always accompanied by discussions about the convergence of corporate governance models towards the Anglo-American model. See C. Lane, 'Changes in Corporate Governance of German Corporations: Convergence to Anglo-American Model?' (2003) 7 *Competition and Change* 79; M. Goergen, M.C. Manjon and L. Renneboog, 'Is the German System of Corporate Governance Converging towards the Anglo-American Model' (2008) *Journal of Management and Governance* 37.

[61]   German Stock Corporation Act 2009 art. 84(1).

[62]   *Ibid.* art. 84(2).

In addition, the independent director system in the United States is established within a unitary board structure where decision-making, oversight and supervisory roles are carried out by a single board of directors. The system is designed to strengthen the directors' independence so they can perform their supervisory function. The function of independent directors in the United States is very similar to that of the supervisory board in China. This is why, under the unique Chinese controlling corporate governance model, the roles of the supervisory board and the independent directors overlap to a great extent.[63] Therefore, the design and function of the independent director system are different, and it is difficult to classify the system as a classic model. Legal reform in China needs to focus on reconciling an independent director system originally developed for a US single-tier board, adapting it to China's dual board structure. It was argued by West that a substantial statutory convergence to the US model is unlikely, although a limited form of convergence may occur with regard to enabling rules.[64]

4.3 EMPLOYEE PARTICIPATION AND COMPANY TRADE UNIONS

Employee participation is a broad term, including possible co-determination measures like employee representation on the corporate board, employee representation through works councils, collective bargaining arrangements, or employee share ownership. The 'employee participation' theory asks us to reconsider traditional shareholder value corporate law theory. According to the theory, shareholders are not the only owners of the company, since the employees have similar rights of possession over the corporation.[65] Consequently, employees' interests and shareholders' interests should be considered simultaneously by the board of directors. Employees also have rights of control and management over

---

[63] J. Yuan, 'Formal Convergence or Substantial Divergence? Evidence from Adoption of the Independent Director System in China' (2007) 9 *Asian-Pacific Law and Policy Journal* 71 at 85.

[64] M. West, 'The Puzzling Divergence of Corporate Law: Evidence and Explanations from Japan and the United States' (2001) *University of Pennsylvania Law Review* 527 at 594.

[65] See J. Summers and J. Hyman, *Employee Participation and Company Performance: A Review of the Literature* (York: Joseph Rowntree Foundation, 2005) pp. 33–6.

the corporation in the same way as the directors do. Employee participation has been adopted in the CCL since the early 1990s when the first Company Law was drafted. It is argued that the employee participation provided in CCL 1994 was more of a political and economic path-dependent product, in order to be consistent with the theme of the Chinese socialist ideology that celebrates workers.[66] The initial legislative incentive and philosophy also came from the Constitution of the People's Republic of China, which made it clear that 'the country is led by the proletariat and is based on the alliance of workers and peasants'.[67]

CCL 2006 set out a series of new stipulations concerning employee participation. As far as limited liability companies are concerned, based on Article 45, 'the members of the board of directors of a limited liability company invested in and established by two or more State-owned enterprises, or by two or more other State-owned investment entities, shall include representatives of the staff and workers of the company. Other limited liability companies can include representatives of the staff and workers of the company'.[68] Compared to the old Company Law, the new Company Law enlarges the scope of employees as internal directors in all forms of companies. As far as joint stock limited companies are concerned, according to article 109 of CCL 2006, 'the members of the board of directors may include the representatives of the staff and workers of the company. The representatives of the staff and workers on the board of directors shall be democratically elected by the staff and workers of the company through the staff and workers' congress, workers' assembly or other forums'. This legislation ensures that the voice of the employee will be heard and employees' interests will be considered at board meetings when decisions are made.

Moreover, trade unions also play an important role in promoting the interests of employees in the Chinese corporate governance model. Under article 18, a company's employees will organize a trade union to carry out trade union activities and safeguard the lawful rights and interests of the employees. The company will provide necessary conditions for its labour union to carry out activities.[69] 'The labour union shall, on behalf of the employees, sign collective contracts with the company with respect to the remuneration, working hours, welfare, insurance, work safety and

---

[66] L.W. Lin, 'Corporate Social Responsibility in China: Window Dressing or Structural Change' (2010) 28 *Berkeley Journal of International Law* 64 at 68.
[67] Constitution of the People's Republic of China 1982 art. 1.
[68] CCL 2006 art. 45.
[69] *Ibid.* art. 18.

sanitation, and other matters'.[70] To make a decision about restructuring or any major issues concerning the business operation or the formulation of important rules and regulations, a company shall solicit the opinions of its trade union, and solicit the opinions and suggestions of its staff and workers through the staff and workers' congress or other forums.[71]

This provision enhances employee participation in the governance of the company by enabling employees to enforce their democratic controlling rights over the company's decisions. Compared to the old Company Law, this provision legitimates the employees' rights to participate in corporate governance. It also affirms the improvement of Chinese government policy on CSR as far as employees' interests are concerned. However, this article is only a primary principle-based provision, and it only focuses on the major issues in corporate actions. Chinese corporate law still has a long way to go in order to reach a systematic and complete provision for employee participation in corporate governance.

Based on the provisions above, it is apparent that Chinese Company Law is following legislative principles adopted in German corporate law by adopting employee participation in the board of directors, in the trade council and in corporate strategy and board decision-making. It also reflects the stakeholder orientation, the fundamental characteristic of insider models, in the type of corporate governance prevalent in China.[72] However, China has created a unique form of board structure – a management board of directors, with some independent outside directors and a board of supervisors comprised of both employees and other members – thereby combining elements of both the insider two-tier board model and the unitary board structure, as well as making use of independent outside directors, and also recognizing China's traditional concept of employees being the 'masters of enterprise'.[73]

From the discussion in 4.1 to 4.3 above, the main traits of the Chinese corporate governance system seem to belong to neither a purely CAO category nor an exclusively CAI category. They operate within a controlled corporate governance model unique to China, because of its state shareholding and long history of unique Chinese culture and tradition. Influences brought by path dependence to the formulation of a Chinese

---

[70]   *Ibid.* art. 18.

[71]   *Ibid.* art. 18.

[72]   M. Roth, 'Employee Participation, Corporate Governance and the Firm: A Transatlantic View Focused on Occupational Pension and Co-Determination' (2011) 11 *European Business Organization Law Review* 51.

[73]   B. Tricker, *Corporate Governance: Principles, Policies, and Practices* (Oxford: Oxford University Press, 2009) p. 194.

corporate governance model seem much stronger than those in typical Anglo-American countries or in Japan and Germany. In such a unique hybrid corporate governance model, how can the interests of stakeholders in modern China be effectively protected?

4.4 CHINESE CORPORATE GOVERNANCE AND PROBLEMS RAISED BY THE CONTROLLING MODEL

The Chinese corporate governance model is unique. Tam compared its characteristics with both the Anglo-American and German-Japanese models, and it is worthwhile to note a few findings, shown in Table 4.1.

It is suggested by Table 4.1 that China's corporate governance model has more in common with German-Japanese models than with the Anglo-American model.[74] However, China has been trying to follow the lead of the Anglo-American corporate governance system.[75] Yet the fact remains that China's listed companies are facing a set of very different ownership, business and financial conditions when compared with the Anglo-American model, and the institutional conditions for the successful operation of that model are either absent or undeveloped.[76] Furthermore, whilst protection for investors has been enhanced, Chinese legal and accounting standards are still far below the international standards.[77] China still needs a more active external corporate control market, an executive labour market and other external monitoring, as well as effective internal monitoring mechanisms.[78]

---

[74] O.K. Tam, 'Ethical Issues in the Evolution of Corporate Governance in China' (2002) 37 *Journal of Business Ethics* 303 at 311.

[75] However, it is the case that in 1996 the Chinese government initiated a limited experiment with the introduction of a governance system from Japan's main bank in a few selected enterprises; see J. Lu, 'Corporate Governance in China: Drawing Lessons from the USA and Japan' in R. Tomasic (ed.), *Corporate Governance: Challenges for China* (Beijing: Law Press China, 2005) ch. 7, p. 131.

[76] O.K. Tam, 'Ethical Issues in the Evolution of Corporate Governance in China' (2002) *Journal of Business Ethics* 303 at 311.

[77] R. La Porta, F. Lopez-de-Silanes and A. Shleifer, 'Corporate Ownership around the World' (1999) 54 *Journal of Finance* 471.

[78] C.K. Low (ed.), *Corporate Governance: An Asia-Pacific Critique* (Hong Kong: Sweet & Maxwell Asia, 2002) p. 282.

Table 4.1 *Comparing the characteristics of the Chinese corporate governance model with the Anglo-American and German-Japanese models*

CG models	Anglo-American models	German and Japanese models	Chinese model
Shareholding ownership	Dispersed ownership	Concentrated ownership with cross-shareholding	Concentrated ownership with state as majority shareholder
Investment horizon (IH)	IH of shareholders is usually short term	IH of shareholders is usually long term	IH of individual shareholders is usually short term
Interests of shareholders vs stakeholders	Shareholder primacy	Multiple stakeholders' interests represented in corporate objective that incorporate social and employment goals	Ineffective shareholder representation and stakeholder protection; corporate objectives subject to government intervention
Capital financing	Reliance on securities market for financing	Reliance on bank credit for corporate financing	Reliance on bank credit from state-owned banks
Market power	Active market for senior managerial manpower	Less active market for senior managerial manpower	Obstacles to development of active power
Composition of board of directors	Board with majority of outside directors	Insider dominated board	Insider manager-dominated board with appointment influenced by the authorities

Source: O.K. Tam, 'Ethical Issues in the Evolution of Corporate Governance in China' (2002) 37 *Journal of Business Ethics* 303 at 309.

Unlike the outsider and insider models, the corporate governance model adopted by Chinese listed firms can best be described as a control-based model, in which the controlling shareholders 'tightly control the list companies through concentrated ownership and management friendly boards'.[79] Consequently, 'there is a lack of timely disclosure of accounting information or complete transparency of operations'.[80] The privileges of the controlling shareholder, namely, the state, within the control-based corporate governance model can be observed within three aspects. First, the state has privileges based on the percentage of the shares it owns within corporations. Central or local government always ultimately controls more than half the shares. The controlling shareholders, such as government agencies, always dominate shareholder meetings. By using their privilege in shareholder meetings these controlling shareholders always divert the capital of listed companies for other purposes.[81] They 'divert the money of listed companies for their personal interests through affiliate transaction, which not only severely affects the normal operation of the listed company but also endangers the faith and credit of the market'.[82] From a speech given by Vice-Minister Jiang of the State Economic and Trade Commission,[83] data from the CSRC revealed that the problem of the diversion of capital by controlling shareholders for other purposes existed in 676 listed companies, amounting to a total value of RMB 96,669 billion (£10,000 billion).

Secondly, the enforcement of the rights of shareholders, stakeholders and directors' duties are also adversely affected by the state. The CSRC, the main enforcement agency of the State Council, is 'susceptible to political influence, local protectionism and other forms of corruption'.[84] Because of the fear of having a negative impact on the performance of companies, the government is reluctant to enforce law and impose

---

[79] Q. Liu, 'Corporate Governance in China: Current Practices, Economic Effects and Institutional Determinants' (2006) 52 *CESifo Economic Studies* 415 at 429.

[80] *Ibid.*

[81] See OECD, 'Overview of Governance of State-owned Listed Companies in China' in *EFC/ERI-OECD 2005 Policy Dialogue on Corporate Governance in China* (Beijing, 19 May 2005) p. 9.

[82] *Ibid.*

[83] See Q. Jiang, Vice-Minister of the State Economic and Trade Commission, 'Standardizing Behavior and Deepening Reform, to be Creditworthy and Responsible Shareholders of Listed Companies', speech at the Meeting on Summarizing the Experience of Establishing a Modern Enterprise System in Listed Companies, 27 December 2002.

[84] C. Anderson and B. Guo, 'Corporate Governance under the New Company Law (Part 2): Shareholder Lawsuit and Enforcement' (2006) *China Law and Practice* (May) 15.

punishment on controlling shareholders.[85] It has been argued by Trifiro that, if all fraudulent and unlawful behaviours were publicized, it could result in a stock market crash and the potential loss of a large amount of State assets,[86] as well as a general loss of trust in security investment.[87] Therefore, the interests of the controlling shareholders and minority shareholders are in conflict – the former's interest lies in maintaining social stability, while the latter is only concerned about economic returns.[88]

Thirdly, the reality of a dual board structure with independent directors has been suggested to have a 'symbolic rather than practical function'.[89] However, the efficiency and effectiveness of the system is severely affected by *guanxi* between directors and government authorities who have excessive power in listed companies in which the state is the controlling shareholder. The preservation of the Party's monopoly supports the strong role of the Party within the company, and uncontested power at the macro-level can easily trigger a voluntary acceptance or even the request for political involvement at the corporate level.[90]

In 2005, the CSRC and SASAC jointly released the Notice on Standardizing Capital Intercourse between Listed Companies and Associated Parties and the Issues of External Guarantee Provided by Listed Companies. This Notice 'strengthens the force to investigate, prosecute and liquidate'[91] holding shareholders or controlling shareholders who

---

[85]   X. Huang, 'Modernising the Chinese Capital Market: Old Problems and New Legal Responses' (2010) 21 *International Commercial and Company Law Review* 223 at 232.

[86]   N. Trifiro, 'China's Financial Reporting Standards: Will Corporate Governance Induce Compliance in Listed Companies?' (2007) 16 *Tulance Journal of International and Comparative Law* 271 at 288.

[87]   S. Opper and S. Schwaag-Serger, 'Institutional Analysis of Legal Change: The Case of Corporate Governance in China' (2008) 26 *Washington University Journal of Law and Policy* 245 at 259.

[88]   N. Trifiro, 'China's Financial Reporting Standards: Will Corporate Governance Induce Compliance in Listed Companies?' (2007) 16 *Tulance Journal of International and Comparative Law* 271 at 286.

[89]   A. Young, 'Conceptualising a Chinese Corporate Governance Framework: Tensions between Traditions, Ideologies and Modernity' (2009) 19 *International Company and Commercial Law Review* 235 at 239.

[90]   S. Opper and S. Schwaag-Serger, 'Institutional Analysis of Legal Change: The Case of Corporate Governance in China' (2008) 26 *Washington University Journal of Law and Policy* 245 at 261.

[91]   See OECD, 'Overview of Governance of State-owned Listed Companies in China' in *EFC/ERI-OECD 2005 Policy Dialogue on Corporate Governance in China* (Beijing, 19 May 2005).

have or are likely to engage in improper behaviour for the appropriation of funds.[92] However, it is not hard to imagine the difficulties in implementing the Notice, because of the complicated social relationships between controlling shareholders and local government, and the *guanxi* between controlling shareholders and company directors.

The Chinese government should refrain from simply adopting either the outsider or the insider model without modification.[93] The Chinese corporate governance model is rightly described as a combination of both models.[94] It is a mixed model, based primarily on the insider model of institutional control, but supplemented by good practice from both the basic models. In terms of the shareholder and stakeholder debate, since the development of Chinese corporate governance is at a very early stage, it is not reasonable for the Chinese government to choose directly between the shareholder and stakeholder systems. According to the Corporate Governance Assessment Report of the 100 Top Chinese Listed Companies 2006,[95] the Chinese government has to face the facts that shareholders' rights are insufficient, stakeholders are being ignored, and the responsibilities of boards of directors are inadequate.[96]

The Chinese government should learn from historical experience within other countries, who have experienced a similar situation to the current state of the Chinese economy. As well as research on corporate governance, interdisciplinary studies on culture, management and business studies in other jurisdictions, especially the United States, the United Kingdom, Japan, Germany, Australia, Korea and Singapore (where state-owned enterprises also play a significant role), will be beneficial in assisting the Chinese government in finding the right way forward. Taking account of this existing research will help the Chinese government avoid the risk of imposing an inefficient corporate governance regime. In any case, a hybrid model with Chinese characteristics seems to be the best option.

---

[92]   *Ibid.*

[93]   C.K. Low (ed.), *Corporate Governance: An Asia-Pacific Critique* (Hong Kong: Sweet & Maxwell Asia, 2002) p. 282.

[94]   S. Vob and Y.W. Xia, 'Corporate Governance of Listed Companies in China', paper presented at Track 8 of IFSAM VIIIth World Congress 2006, hosted by VHB, Berlin, September 2006, p. 11, available at www.ctw-congress.de/ifsam/download/track_8/pap00750.pdf.

[95]   Chinese Centre for Corporate Governance, *Corporate Governance Assessment Report of the 100 Top Chinese Listed Companies in 2006* (2006), available at www.iwep.org.cn/.

[96]   *Ibid.* at 44.

4.5 LACK OF LEGISLATIVE CLARITY

Under the control-based corporate governance model, a systematic and enforceable legal regime is very important to promote the effectiveness of the role of the supervisory board, independent directors and effective employee participation schemes, in order to protect the interests of minority shareholders and other stakeholders who are in a disadvantaged position due to the overly powerful controlling power of the state as the majority shareholder. The application of statutory instruments in China, in terms of civil law jurisdictions, requires much legislative guidance concerning the application of the law.[97] However, corporate governance and CSR-related law are always lacking in sufficient detail or legal definitions.[98] Legislative ambiguity exists throughout the relevant legal instruments. The ambiguity can be classified into the following groups, which all make the law difficult to implement. First, there is language ambiguity; for example, article 20 of CCL 2006 gave an exception to the legal principle that companies are separate legal entities to protect the interests of creditors. It is provided that the creditor's interests need to be 'seriously' damaged in order to pierce the corporate veil. However, there is no monetary amount or practical guidance to define the meaning or degree of the term 'serious'. The 'major issues' in article 18 of CCL 2006, discussed earlier in this chapter, also suffer from this problem. Secondly, there is ambiguity in the lack of numerical requirements; for example, the percentage or the number of employees who can sit on the board of directors should be stipulated in detail, to make requirements more than just provisions without teeth.

Thirdly, there is ambiguity in the related remedies if directors, shareholders or stakeholders within companies are in breach of their contract or duties. For example, the amended CCL clarifies that directors owe a duty of good faith and a duty of care to their companies.[99] Also, the CCL requires companies or boards of directors, who form the deciding minds of companies, to 'observe social morals and business ethics, be in integrity and good faith, accept regulation of the government and the public, and undertake social responsibilities'.[100] However, the law does not explain the meaning of good faith, care, business ethics or social

---

[97] In China, the Supreme People's Court normally plays the role of legislative interpretation.

[98] M. Tsui, 'Corporate Governance in China' (2010) *Corporate Governance eJournal* 1 at 14.

[99] CCL 2006 art. 148.

[100] *Ibid.* art. 5.

responsibility, and does not shed light on the criteria that should be used to judge the reasonableness of care.[101] Moreover, no guidance has been provided as to what remedies shareholders or stakeholders may seek if there is a breach of the duty required by the CCL. In the next chapter, the legality of CSR will be discussed in order to provide an in-depth examination of article 5 of CCL 2006, with suggestions about its enforcement and the overall effectiveness of the enforcement of CSR-related legal requirements in China.

---

[101] For example, should the degree of care be judged by a subjective or an objective test, or a combined subjective and objective test?

5. Stakeholders' interests and legitimacy analysis of corporate social responsibility in China

With certain exceptions, corporate social responsibility (CSR) has always been approached from disciplines other than that of law. However, it is argued that even though CSR ostensibly involves doing more than the law requires, CSR seems to function as soft or informal law and to be based on a set of fundamental principles of commercial and business law.[1] The substance of CSR can always be embedded in the regulations and laws in the abstract and statutory sense. The corporate objectives are always enshrined in the purpose of establishing corporations within corporate governance codes, international corporate governance principles, corporate laws and securities regulations. Governments make use of law to encourage corporations to take corporate actions towards more socially responsible ones by refereeing international law, regulatory standards, and recommendations for supra-national organizations.

> The normative and regulatory trends in and of CSR seem to indicate a shift in certain normative foundation for corporate action and governance. A shift appears to be characterised by an increased expectation that informal norms will be observed by corporations as if they were formally legally binding, with enforcement served not by a state legal enforcement system, but by an informal system of stakeholder sanctions, and formal government regulation is to some extent being replaced by voluntary corporate self-regulation.[2]

This trend fits not all, but many aspects of CSR enforcement in China, including the corporations' awareness and understanding of the corporate objective stipulated in Chinese Company Law (CCL) 2006, CSR-related reports, directors' duties, directors' discretions and CSR-related information discourse through corporate reporting systems.

---

[1] K. Buhmann, 'Corporate Social Responsibility: What Role for Law? Some Aspects of Law and CSR' (2006) *Corporate Governance* 188 at 199.
[2] *Ibid.*

As for the legal norms relevant to CSR, this would include international law and national law regulating various stakeholders, for example, international law on human rights, labour and environmental protection; national legislation concerning non-discrimination, working conditions and safety issues, social and environmental impact assessments and environmental protection; and Codes of Conduct that create enforceable duties and obligations, for example, between a company and its employees, or between a company and its consumers or suppliers.[3] In bringing CSR towards a more regulatory level, the regulation takes a variety of forms and is generated from regulatory bodies at different levels, including the local level, the regional or national level, and the supra-national level based on delegated state government powers, for example the European Union, or international bodies based on state membership, for example the OECD or United Nations.[4] It ranges from formal government regulations and binding laws to recommendations that are designed to have a guiding effect on corporate decisions and corporate behaviours.

5.1 DEBATE ON VOLUNTARY VERSUS MANDATORY RESPONSIBILITY

The role that the law is playing or should play in CSR area is always debatable. This makes it difficult for corporations and scholars to define the nature and scope of CSR accurately. This debate is commonly referred to as the 'voluntary versus mandatory' debate. On the one hand, the voices of companies and business industry organization argue that CSR should not be regulated because regulation would stifle innovation and damage national competitiveness.[5] Instead of being regulated, the corporations will be keen to develop their strategic management policies and collectively raise the bar for industry in general.[6] CSR is regarded as

---

[3] A. Winkler, 'Corporate Law or the Law of Business? Stakeholders and Corporate Governance at the End of History' (2004) 67 *Law and Contemporary Problems* 109 at 111.

[4] K. Buhmann, 'Corporate Social Responsibility: What Role for Law? Some Aspects of Law and CSR' (2006) *Corporate Governance* 188 at 194.

[5] J.A. Zerk, *Multinational and Corporate Social Responsibility: Limitations and Opportunities in International Law* (Cambridge: Cambridge University Press, 2006) p. 33.

[6] European Commission, *Prompting a European Framework for Corporate Social Responsibility*, Green Paper, COM 366 (Brussels, 2001).

comprising corporate discretionary activities that benefit the community and are external to the core business of the company.[7] These voluntary initiatives in CSR are described as benefiting the long-term harmonious relationship with corporate stakeholders. Moreover, the companies' awareness of the financial benefits arising from being socially responsible should make it unnecessary to regulate CSR in law. The voluntarists believe that CSR goes hand in hand with appropriate financial management because unethical corporations tend to be unsustainable in the long run. CSR will be closely related to profit and productivity in the long term. The idea is that a reputable record on CSR and governance will generate long-term benefits for shareholders and this will also makes investors believe in the possibility of financial returns by pursing social, environmental or community goals and agendas.

However, the arguments for the voluntary character of CSR did not convince a significant proportion of campaigners and critics, who argue that explicit recognition of the interests of stakeholders is necessary.[8] It is argued that protection of stakeholders' interests should be made a legal requirement, or at least specifically approved or explicitly permitted under company law through provisions related to directors' duties, shareholders' rights, stakeholders' rights (rights of creditors and employees are particularly suggested), and information disclosure requirements.

---

[7] J. Moon, 'The Firm as Citizen? Social Responsibility of Business in Australia' (1995) 30 *Australian Journal of Political Science* 1.

[8] For example see D. McBarnet, A. Voiculescu and T. Campbell (eds), *The New Corporate Accountability: Corporate Social Responsibility and the Law* (Cambridge: Cambridge University Press, 2007); K. Buhmann, 'Corporate Social Responsibility: What Role for Law? Some Aspects of Law and CSR' (2006) *Corporate Governance* 188; C. Villiers, 'Corporate Law, Corporate Power and Corporate Social Responsibility' in N. Boeger, R. Murray and C. Villiers, *Perspectives on Corporate Social Responsibility* (Cheltenham: Edward Elgar, 2010) p. 85; J. Zhao, 'Promoting More Socially Responsible Corporations through UK Company Law after the 2008 Financial Crisis: Turning of the Crisis Compass' (2011) 22 *International Company and Commercial Law Review* 275; P. Puri, 'The Future of Stakeholder Interests in Corporate Governance' (2010) 48 *Canadian Business Law Journal* 427; J.E. Kerr, 'Sustainability Meets Profitability: The Convenient Truth of How the Business Judgement Rule Protects a Board's Decision to Engage in Social Entrepreneurship' (2007) 29 *Cardozo Law Review* 623; R.I. Patel, 'Facilitating Stakeholder-Interest Maximization: Accommodating Beneficial Corporations in the Model Business Corporation Act' (2010) 23 *St Thomas Law Review* 135; A. Mickels, 'Beyond Corporate Social Responsibility: Reconciling the Ideals of a For-Benefit Corporate with Director Fiduciary Duties in the U.S. and Europe' (2009) 32 *Hastings International and Comparative Law Review* 271.

Furthermore, many non-governmental organizations (NGOs) remain sceptical that the voluntary 'business case' is sufficient to guarantee responsible corporate actions. A number of NGOs, including Amnesty International UK, Friends of the Earth and Action Aid, have established an alliance specifically to campaign for law reform to improve transparency and accountability of corporations.[9] The Corporate Responsibility Coalition (CORE Coalition) believes that the voluntary approach to corporate responsibility has failed: 'We believe the only way Corporate Responsibility will succeed is through new laws which make companies value people and the planet, as much as they value making a profit'.[10] 'There is no rigid separation between soft and hard law, between totally voluntary codes and strictly binding laws.'[11]

Despite the validity of the issues raised, the author agrees with Zerk that the dispute over the nature of CSR has done little to further the debate about the appropriate regulatory responses to CSR-related problems, but has rather tended to render the definition of CSR less helpful and distract attention away from the substantive issues regarding CSR that need more attention.[12] There is no single solution to the various CSR-related problems, many of which call for co-ordinated action at different levels, including regulation on both the national and international level, either by government or self-regulatory approaches.[13] It is important to establish an 'architecture' of normative arrangements that can combine and integrate the various categories of regulation in the most efficient and fruitful manner.[14] Finding the most appropriate regulatory framework which is efficient, enforceable and fits into the national legal system and stage of economic development seems much more sensible than arguing about the nature of CSR, or whether it is truly

---

[9] For example, see Friends of the Earth, 'Hidden Voices: The CBI, Corporate Lobbying and Sustainability', available at www.foe.co.uk/resource/reports/hidden_voices.pdf.

[10] See CORE Coalition, 'Make Business Work for People and Plant', available at http://corporate-responsibility.org/.

[11] S. Picciotto, 'Rights, Responsibilities and Regulation of International Business' (2003) 42 *Columbia Journal of Transnational Law* 131 at 146.

[12] J.A. Zerk, *Multinational and Corporate Social Responsibility: Limitations and Opportunities in International Law* (Cambridge: Cambridge University Press, 2006) pp. 35–6.

[13] S. Picciotto, 'Rights, Responsibilities and Regulation of International Business' (2003) 42 *Columbia Journal of Transnational Law* 131 at 146.

[14] *Ibid.* at 146–7.

voluntary. It is argued by Buhmann that the current normative understanding of CSR may constitute pre-formal law.[15] Regulation focusing on
CSR in a positive and progressive manner would make corporations
'want to do what they should do'.[16] Such legal recognition of CSR would
create institutional constraints on directors' discretion when making
decisions and help direct corporate goals towards the interests of the
wider community of stakeholders in society, the environment and sustainability in the long term.[17]

A series of corporate scandals and failures during the global financial
crisis in 2008 brought the responsibility and accountability of corporations under greater scrutiny.[18] With such corporate failures,[19] the
demand for better control of corporations and more efficient supervision
though regulations has increased in order to prevent such misbehaviour.
The international political focus on the impact on business of the 'triple
bottom line'[20] has resulted in a platform of international and regional
agreements which have encouraged governments to incorporate regulation into national legislation. In China, the judicial recognition and
acceptance of the significance of CSR developed very rapidly in response
to the internal and external push discussed in Chapter 3.

Corporations' voluntary initiatives towards CSR may have significant
legal implications. Corporations are becoming more aware of the need to
publish codes of conduct, corporate responsibility reports and ethical
codes, and to ensure that in their public statements they take responsibility for what they have done and what they will do. It is argued that
legislation may have an impact on the substance, implementation and
commercial profile of CSR, while the current normative understanding of
CSR may constitute pre-formal law, making corporations sincerely want

---

[15]   K. Buhmann, 'Corporate Social Responsibility What Role for Law? Some
Aspects of Law and CSR' (2004) 4 *Corporate Governance* 188 at 192.
[16]   P. Selznick, *The Communitarian Persuasion* (Washington, DC: Woodrow
Wilson Centre Press, 2002) p. 102.
[17]   C. Nakajima, 'The Importance of Legally Embedding Corporate Social
Responsibility' (2011) 32 *Company Lawyer* 257 at 258.
[18]   *Ibid.* at 257.
[19]   C. Nakajima and P. Palmer, 'Anti-Corruption: Law and Practice' in A.
Stachowicz-Stanusch (ed.), *Organizational Immunity to Corruption: Building
Theoretical and Research Foundations* (Charlotte, NC: Information Age Publish-
ing, 2010) p. 99.
[20]   J. Elkington, *Cannibals with Forks: The Triple Bottom Line of the 21st
Century Business* (Gabriola Island: New Society Publishers, 1998); see also A.
Henriques and J. Richardson, *The Triple Bottom Line, Does it All Add Up?
Assessing the Sustainability of Business and CSR* (London: Earthscan, 2004).

to do what they should do.[21] Informal networks and organizations based on trust can also have an impact on the enforcement of CSR, in addition to the government regulating CSR through purely legal obligations.

Therefore, the question arises how to establish the most appropriate regulatory framework to confront CSR-related problems in China. How can the regulatory framework be made efficient and enforceable? What is the nature and scope of the systemic regulatory agenda? Based on the evidence that the approach to CSR has progressively transformed from voluntary to mandatory,[22] are there any international experiences that the Chinese government could learn from? With the rapid development of the Chinese economy, how can a trading network be developed that supports the globalized goals of increasing human dignity, reducing poverty, promoting environmental safety and protection, human rights, consumer protection, well-being and development, labour protection and supplier relationships? Can CSR act as an active response to balance the process of liberalization and the time necessary to elaborate the necessary changes in the international regulatory framework? Can legislation in developing countries, such as China, work together with reform on corporate governance structure to promote CSR?

In order to answer these questions in a systematic manner, it is important to understand that a CSR approach with 'Chinese characteristics' classifies CSR as supplementary to enforcing labour rights and environmental law; this differs widely from most Western approaches and contrasts starkly with the EU concept, where CSR is considered as an issue going beyond compliance with the law. The legal responses to CSR and protection of the various stakeholders must be discussed with reference to China's unique corporate governance and legal system, with its unique legislative, litigation and enforcement procedures.

---

[21]   K. Buhmann, 'Corporate Social Responsibility: What Role for Law? Some Aspects of Law and CSR' (2004) 6 *Corporate Governance* 188; see also C.J. Parker, C. Scott, N. Lacey and J. Braithwaite, *Regulating Law* (Oxford: Oxford University Press, 2004).

[22]   For example, CSR has progressed to being mandatory in Indonesia, the first country to mandate CSR. It is required under art. 74 of Indonesian Limited Liability Corporation Law No. 40, 2007, which defines CSR as an 'obligation of the company which is budgeted and calculated as the cost of the Company', requiring obligatory funding for corporations to implement CSR; for a discussion on the article see P.R. Waagstein, 'The Mandatory Corporate Social Responsibility: Problems and Implications' (2011) 98 *Journal of Business Ethics* 455.

5.2 STAKEHOLDERS' INTERESTS IN CHINA

Since the beginning of the transformation process, China has impressed
the world with its growing GDP, has gained second place among the
world's economies, and become a leading nation in respect of its trading
power. Nevertheless, this rapid economic development has a dark and
negative side. A rapid restructuring process of state-owned industries is
being undertaken in China, however, CSR still remains very unfamiliar to
most Chinese corporations. The pressures of social and environmental
problems, such as pollution, occupational accidents, damage to the health
and safety of employees, use of child labour, poor quality of products and
associated risks to the health and safety of consumers (including numerous food poisoning incidents), corruption, fake reporting and misleading
advertisements in the media of companies and their products, have
increased significantly; these many problems have a serious negative
impact on the development of a sound corporate governance model.

Since China joined the World Trade Organization (WTO), Chinese
companies are now competing and cooperating with their international
counterparts. A poor CSR record will discourage foreign investment in
China, a factor which is becoming increasingly important for the
development of the Chinese economy. That is why the United Nations
and Future 500, an advocate for global sustainability, have separately
called on Chinese business to adopt measures to encourage social
responsibility.[23] Chinese companies have in the past scored poorly on
CSR criteria, both in terms of rigorous compliance with financial and
legal rules, and the embrace of ethical or other actions going beyond
formal requirements.[24] The transition from a planned economy to a
market-oriented economy makes CSR a key corporate strategy in protecting the stakeholders of the company. It would be wise for Chinese
companies to integrate CSR from the start and ensure that their ethical

---

[23]   See Future 500, *Best Practices in CSR Standards, Reporting, and
Performance*, available at www.future500.org/.

[24]   Z. Li, 'Lack of Corporate Social Responsibility Behind Recent China
Accident' (China Watch, World Institute Vision for a Sustainable World, 12
December 2005), available at www.worldwatch.org/node/3859; H. von W.
Hoivik, 'East Meets West: Tacit Messages about Business Ethics in Stories Told
by Chinese Managers' (2007) 74 *Journal of Business Ethics* 457; G.F. Woodbine,
'Moral Choice and the Declining Influence of Traditional Value Orientation
within the Financial Sector of a Rapidly Developing Region of the People's
Republic of China' (2004) 55 *Journal of Business Ethics* 43; P.K. Ip, 'The
Challenge of Developing a Business Ethics in China' (2008) 88 *Journal of
Business Ethics* 211.

codes comply with international norms, in order to promote their global competitiveness. Therefore, systemic protections for stakeholders, not only legislatively but also in business practice, are important for China to promote the success of the company.

In this section, the current legislative and practical protections for stakeholders will be discussed in terms of the book's overall theme of considering the stakeholder and shareholder debate in light of the unique Chinese hybrid corporate governance model. In practice, the Chinese government has not given priority to 'soft issues' such as business ethics.[25] The concerns expressed regarding stakeholders within corporations, especially SOEs, appear to be more a response to the government's political power and control over corporations, rather than addressing how companies should behave towards their stakeholders.

In the *Corporate Governance Assessment Report of the 100 Top Chinese Listed Companies 2006* ranked by FORTUNE China,[26] a scoring system was used to evaluate various corporate governance aspects of 100 companies' performance over the previous year. The combined average score for corporate governance in all the sample companies in 2006 was 56.08. This score was composed of five sections, including shareholder rights (individual average score 37); fairness to shareholders (68.75); information disclosure and transparency (80.8); and responsibilities of the board of directors (45.87); 'roles of stakeholders' scored the lowest, with an average of 21. Most of the indicators relating to the roles of stakeholders scored poorly (i.e. lower than 25), apart from: 'does the company clearly mention safety and welfare for the employees?'.

One of the questions posed was 'does the company describe clearly the roles of stakeholders, including clients, suppliers, creditors, community and employees?'. This question clearly went beyond basic stakeholder requirements since the focus was not merely internal, but also external. The individual average score for 2006 was only 15, and only 15 per cent of companies in China actually gave comprehensive consideration to the roles of various stakeholders as a necessary foundation for good corporate governance. Another question asked was 'does the company state clearly in its information disclosed to the public about environmental protection, company's social responsibilities and charitable activities', a question that again went beyond the basic legal requirements and

[25]   See X. Lu and G. Enderle, *Developing Business Ethics in China* (Basingstoke: Palgrave Macmillan, 2006).
[26]   Chinese Centre for Corporate Governance, *Corporate Governance Assessment Report of the 100 Top Chinese Listed Companies in 2006* (2006), available at www.iwep.org.cn/.

embraced ethical and even philanthropic considerations. The individual average score for 2006 was 19, and the survey revealed that up to 74 per cent of Chinese companies did not offer clear public descriptions of the company's environmental protection, other social responsibilities and charitable activities. A further question worth mentioning was 'do the companies provide an employee share scheme or other long-term employee incentive compensation plan relating to the creation of share-holder value? The individual average score for this question was only 14, revealing that 86 per cent of Chinese companies did not have an employee share scheme, and also highlighting Chinese companies' deficiency in the creation of incentive compensation plans.[27]

It can be concluded from the 2006 survey that, as far as stakeholders' interests are concerned, the actions that Chinese listed companies had taken were limited to the level of basic legal requirements.[28] Regarding voluntary CSR, corporate charitable activities, and company strategy towards various stakeholders, such as suppliers, creditors, local communities, customers and environment, the achievements of Chinese companies were far from satisfactory.

Five years later, the data showed changes in a more stakeholder-friendly direction, but still did not give grounds for too much optimism. In the *Corporate Governance Assessment Summary Report of the 100 Top Chinese Listed Companies for 2012*[29] (published by the Centre for Corporate Governance, the Chinese Academy of Social Science and Protiviti Consulting), a scoring system was used to evaluate various corporate governance aspects of the performance of 100 companies, based on data gathered from official and/or publicly available sources such as annual reports, Articles of Association, websites of the stock exchanges and companies' websites, as on 31 December 2011.[30] References were made to the OECD Principles of Corporate Governance, and the assessment was conducted under the six classic corporate governance

[27]   *Ibid.* at 31.
[28]   *Ibid.* at 8.
[29]   Centre for Corporate Governance, Chinese Academy of Social Science and Protiviti Consulting, *Corporate Governance Assessment Summary Report of the 100 Top Chinese Listed Companies for 2012* (2012), available at http://www.protiviti.it/China-en/Documents/CN-en-2012-Corporate-Governance-Survey-Report.pdf.
[30]   *Ibid.* at 2.

categories,[31] including the 'roles of stakeholders' in corporate govern-ance. The combined average score for corporate governance for all the sample companies in 2012 was 65.9. Figure 5.1 shows that the 'roles of stakeholders' had the forth lowest score, with an average of 60.6. However, this category showed the biggest improvement since 2006 in comparison with the other six categories.[32] For the first time, the scores for the 'roles of stakeholders' (which scored 34.2 in the 2009 assessment) exceeded the scores for the 'responsibilities of supervisors', 'share-holders' rights' and 'responsibility of board of directors'. From the data, it is clear that companies' performances in terms of both stakeholders' interests and 'responsibility of board of directors' are below average. However, the trend towards improvement fits with the development of internationalized corporate governance. Chinese corporate governance is still at a compliance stage. Reform of the corporate governance frame-work in China, instigated by 'active initiative of shareholders and co-management of stakeholders' is plainly necessary.[33]

From the data analysis, it appears that adopting stakeholder theory in corporate management is becoming a more popular strategy in Chinese corporations, and stakeholders are gaining a heightened profile in com-panies. For those directors who are enthusiastic in balancing shareholder and stakeholder concerns, stakeholder theory offers theoretical support and legitimacy to take stakeholders' interests into account by achieving a balance of risks and rewards.[34] Furthermore, from the perspective of

---

[31] These include 'shareholders' rights', 'fairness to shareholders', 'role of stakeholders in corporate governance', 'information disclosure and transparency', 'responsibilities of board of directors' and 'responsibilities of board of super-visors'; see OECD, *OECD Principles of Corporate Governance* (2004).

[32] From 21.0 in the 2006 assessment, 24.9 in the 2007 assessment, 27.3 in the 2008 assessment, 34.2 in the 2009 assessment, 55.6 in the 2010 assessment and 60.6 in the 2012 assessment. The general improvement rate is 17.47%, with a 56.49% improvement for 'shareholders' rights', 8.14% improvement for 'fairness to shareholders', 188.57% improvement for 'role of stakeholders in corporate governance', 4.46% deterioration for 'information disclosure and transparency', 26.58% improvement for 'responsibilities of board of directors', and 41.21% improvement for 'responsibilities of board of supervisors'.

[33] Centre for Corporate Governance, Chinese Academy of Social Science and Protiviti Consulting, *Corporate Governance Assessment Summary Report of the 100 Top Chinese Listed Companies for 2011* (2011), available at www.protiviti.com/zh-CN/Headlines/Documents/CN-2011-Corporate-Governance-Survey.pdf.

[34] J. Dean, 'Stakeholding and Company Law' (2001) 22 *Company Lawyer* 66 at 69; see also as adopted in arts 1 and 5 of CCL 2006.

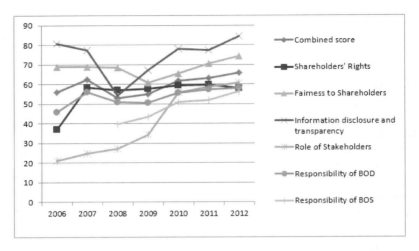

Source: Based on the data provided by the Centre for Corporate Governance, the Chinese Academy of Social Science and Protiviti Consulting, *Corporate Governance Assessment Summary Report of the 100 Top Chinese Listed Companies for 2012* (2012) p. 5.

Figure 5.1 *Distribution of combined sources and individual scores for the seven corporate governance categories for the six years from 2006–2012*

obtaining more enforceable requirements for the consideration of stake-holders' interests, it will be a positive legislative step for China to include various stakeholders' interests in directors' fiduciary duties. It would be sensible to remind directors that as well as the interests of shareholders, they also have to consider the interests of other constituencies who are a part of the company and who have certain claims on the corporation's profits, no matter whether these claims are fixed or residual.

It is argued that against the backdrop of the economic transition, the level of participation of stakeholders in corporate governance is low.[35] Corporations, as a network linking all their stakeholders, have to take their stakeholders' interests into consideration and accord them a proper position within the framework of corporate governance. It is argued that the more funds directors have at their discretion, the less they are

[35] S. Mei, 'The Corporate Governance of Listed Companies in China: Some Problems and Solutions' in R. Tomasic (ed.), *Corporate Governance: Challenges for China* (Beijing: Law Press China, 2005) ch. 19, p. 422 at p. 425.

constrained in their planning and implementation of social strategies in the consideration of relative stakeholders' interests.[36] Resource availability thus determines the 'organisational capacity for creation and implementation of social initiatives'.[37] Currently in China, there are not adequate resources to create a sound mechanism for both internal and external governance in order to establish a corporate governance system which invites the joint participation of all stakeholders.[38] In this case, the transfer from administrative governance to economic governance of SOEs will enhance the possibility for various stakeholders to participate in corporate actions. Furthermore, directors have to believe that CSR might result in better financial performance and therefore place it on the corporate agenda. It is also true that most of the Chinese companies are comparatively new, and the newness of a firm can impact on the stage of its stakeholder engagements. New firms are more likely to lack a well-established formal structure, resources at their discretion and stable relationships with various stakeholder groups.[39]

The consideration of stakeholders' interests enables the creation of long-term favourable conditions for the company to become more competitive. It is useful to regard 'the company as 'the company as a whole', a coherent body in which the various stakeholders are bound together through the business.[40] The long-term focus on creating value for various stakeholders will enable the directors to devote themselves to improving the long-term interests of the corporation, and it does not exclude long-term value-enhancing strategies.[41] Taking social responsibilities into account in the development of corporate strategies is another advantage of adopting the stakeholder theory model. 'The evolution of CSR theory provides a sort of social responsibilities and performance

---

[36] C. Keinert, *Corporate Social Responsibility as an International Strategy* (Heidelberg: Physica-Verlag, 2008) p. 110.

[37] K. Elsayd, 'Re-examining the Expected Effect of Available Resources and Firm Size on Firm Environmental Orientation: An Empirical Study of UK Firms' (2006) 65 *Journal of Business Ethics* 297 at 304.

[38] S. Mei, 'The Corporate Governance of Listed Companies in China: Some Problems and Solutions' in R. Tomasic (ed.), *Corporate Governance: Challenges for China* (Beijing: Law Press China, 2005) ch. 19, p .422 at p. 425.

[39] D.O. Neubaum, M.S. Mitchell and M. Schminke, 'Firm Newness, Entrepreneurial Orientation, and Ethical Climate' (2004) 52 *Journal of Business Ethics* 335 at 339.

[40] J. Parkinson, *Reforming Directors' Duties*, Policy Paper 12 (Political Economy Research Centre, University of Sheffield, 1998).

[41] R. Aggarwal and A. Chandra, 'Stakeholder Management: Opportunities and Challenges' (1990) 40 *Business* 48 at 49.

paradigm that is, in essence, a solid foundation for corporate social management and stakeholder engagement.'[42] Very early discussions of the CSR concept suggested that CSR is about attending to stakeholder rights and taking proactive, voluntary steps to avoid harm or wrongful consequences to stakeholders.[43] CSR theory suggests that corporations should recognize obligations beyond their shareholders, based on stakeholder theory.

A distinct disadvantage of the Chinese derivative claim system stipulated in CCL 2006 is the uncertainty of the scope of the claim, with the possibility of a large number of malicious suits, since shareholders are empowered to bring a claim against directors based on infringements of unclear duties and unclear corporate objectives.[44] Therefore, clearer definitions of the nature and scope of corporate objectives and related responsibilities, with the assistance of stakeholder theory, will have a direct, positive impact on the enforcement of derivative action in China. According to stakeholder theory, many individuals are qualified to be business stakeholders in the modern business environment. There are many individuals or groups who have legitimate interests in or claims on the operations of the firm.[45] It will be beneficial to directors and entire corporations to clarify the question of who are their stakeholders, in order to efficiently and comprehensively manage the entire stakeholder group. This is especially the case in China, a country with a poor record of stakeholder business awareness in practice.

Systematic protections for stakeholders, not only legislatively but also in business practice, will have a direct impact and allow a clearer interpretation of derivative claims in China. It will force directors to have a more thorough understanding of their duties. At the same time, the increasingly important role played by stakeholder engagement will also force shareholders who want to bring a derivative claim to develop a better understanding of the scope of derivative action standing. Therefore,

---

[42]   R.T. Byerly, 'Seeking Global Solutions for the Common Good: A New World Order and Corporate Social Responsibilities' in I. Demirag, *CSR, Accountability and Governance: Global Perspectives* (Sheffield: Greenleaf Publishing, 2005) ch. 7, p. 122.

[43]   See the initial argument for CSR in H.R. Brown, *Social Responsibilities of the Businessman* (New York: Harper & Row, 1953); see also A.B. Carroll, 'The Pyramid of Social Responsibility: Towards the Moral Management of Organizational Stakeholders' (1991) 34 *Business Horizons* 39 at 39–48.

[44]   See CCL 2006 arts 1, 5, 148–50.

[45]   A. Carroll, *Business and Society: Ethics and Stakeholder Management* (Cincinnati, OH: South-Western Publishing, 1993) p. 57.

excessive unmeritorious and frivolous suits could be prevented, especially where the interests of shareholders and stakeholders are in conflict. 'The stakeholder theory is managerial in the broad sense of that term. It does not simply describe existing situations or predict cause-effect relationships; it also recommends attitudes, structures, and practice that, taken together, constitute stakeholder management.'[46] The management style requires simultaneous attention to the legitimate interests of various related stakeholders by the establishment of organizational structures and tailored decision-making processes in individual cases. The inclusion of stakeholder provisions in corporate law will make the law permissive enough to give directors legitimacy and wider discretion to take the interests of stakeholders into account. It is also important to revise and extend the scope of the codified statutory duties in the CCL 2006, and to incorporate article 5 of CCL 2006 into the directors' duties. The adoption of the management philosophy of stakeholders in directors' duties will indirectly benefit the enforcement of a derivative action system in China.[47]

5.3 CSR AND CORPORATE GOVERNANCE CODE 2002

Following the enactment of the Chinese Securities Law 1998, the power of the Chinese Securities Regulatory Committee was strengthened and the Committee played an increasingly active role in monitoring and regulating the corporate governance issues of public companies. In 2002, the Code of Corporate Governance for Listed Companies was released by the China Securities Regulatory Committee State Economic and Trade Commission, based on the principles of the Company Law, the Securities Regulations and other law and regulations issued on 7 January 2001. The Code applies to all listed companies in Mainland China and has become the standard measure in China with which to evaluate the competitiveness of the corporate governance framework. It is argued that the 'magnitude of both discretionary accruals and related-party transactions in Chinese

---

[46] T. Donaldson and L.E. Preston 'The Stakeholder Theory of the Corporation: Concept, Evidence, and Implications' (1995) 20 *Academy of Management Review* 65 at 67.

[47] For discussions on adopting stakeholder theory into directors' duties and enforcement of the duties see J. Zhao, 'Modernising Corporate Objective Debate towards a Hybrid Model' (2011) 62 *Northern Ireland Legal Quarterly* 361; I.L. Fannon, 'The Corporate Social Responsibility Movement and Law's Empire: Is there a Conflict?' (2007) 58 *Northern Ireland Legal Quarterly* 1.

listed firms decreased significantly' after the promulgation of the Code and the Code is 'effective in constraining earnings management in the listed firms'.[48] The Code was drafted according to commonly accepted best corporate governance practices embodied in the OECD Principles of Corporate Governance to promote the establishment and improvement of modern enterprise systems by listed companies, to standardize the operation of listed companies and to bring forward the healthy development of the securities market of China.[49]

The focus on CSR within the Code appears in different aspects. First, CSR-oriented concerns were considered in relation to directors' duties. Article 43 included reference to the interests of stakeholders when directors exercise their duties. The board of directors 'shall earnestly perform its duties as stipulated by laws, regulations and the company's articles of association, shall ensure that the company complies with laws, regulations and its articles of association, shall treat all the shareholders equally and shall be concerned with the interests of stakeholders'.

Further, in line with Part IV (Role of Stakeholders in Corporate Governance) and Part V (Disclosure and Transparency) of the OECD Principles of Corporate Governance, Chapter 6 on Stakeholders and Chapter 7 on Information Disclosure and Transparency were included in the Code in order to achieve the goals of transparency and balancing the interests of shareholders and stakeholders. In Chapter 6, stakeholders' interests are referred to and companies are required to 'respect legal rights of banks and other creditors, employees, consumers, suppliers, the community and other stakeholders'[50] 'provide necessary means to ensure the legal rights of stakeholders'[51] to 'advance company's sustained and healthy development'.[52] The Code places specific emphasis on certain stakeholders, including employees, local communities and the environment. Employees' interests are given special attention, through 'encouraging employees' feedback regarding the company's operating and financial situations and important decisions affecting employees' benefit

---

[48]   J.J. Chen and H. Zhang, *The Impact of the Corporate Governance Code on Earning Management: Evidence from Chinese Listed Companies*, European Financial Management Association Working Paper (2011), available at http://efmaefm.org/0EFMSYMPOSIUM/Renmin-2011/papers/Chen_jean.pdf.

[49]   See Preface to Code of Corporate Governance for Listed Companies, 2001.

[50]   *Ibid.* art. 81.

[51]   *Ibid.* art. 83

[52]   *Ibid.* art. 82.

through direct communications with the board of directors, the supervisory board and the management personnel'.[53] Moreover, the listed company 'shall be concerned with the welfare, environmental protection and public interests of the community in which it resides, and shall pay attention to company's social responsibilities'.[54]

As regards information disclosure requirements to enhance the transparency of corporate governance, a company shall 'voluntarily and timely disclose all other information that may have a material effect on the decisions of shareholders and stakeholders, and shall insure access to information for all shareholders'.[55] Focusing on creditors' information discourse-related rights, companies 'shall provide necessary information to banks and other creditors to enable them to make judgements and decisions about the company's operating and financial situation'. Many requirements on the protection of stakeholders' interests have been turned into legal necessity in CCL 2006.

5.4 CORPORATE SOCIAL RESPONSIBILITY AND CHINESE COMPANY LAW

Debate on CSR in China, compared with the discussion and literature surrounding CSR in general, is rather limited, and the idea of CSR in China is comparatively new to academics, company directors and practitioners. China is infamous for sweatshops, environmental pollution problems and poor working conditions. The recent series of scandals involving substandard Chinese products, including the baby milk scandal, has reminded the world of the shocking fact that many Chinese companies are unscrupulous about making money at the expense of human rights and even human life.[56] China as a product brand has been badly damaged by these irresponsible behaviours, and 'Made in China' products are misleadingly and unconditionally associated with low prices and low quality and socially irresponsible production processes. In a global market, where countries are becoming brands, it is important to promote 'China' as a positive brand through effective corporate governance in

---

[53]   *Ibid.* art. 85.
[54]   *Ibid.* art. 86.
[55]   *Ibid.* art. 88.
[56]   See D. Barboza, 'Why lead in toy paint, it's cheaper', *New York Times*, 7 September 2007; W. Bogdanich, 'Toxic toothpaste made in China is found in U.S.', *New York Times*, 2 June 2007; see also J. Macartney, 'China baby milk scandal spreads as sick toll rises to 13,000', *Sunday Times*, 22 September 2008.

order to attract more institutional shareholders and loyal foreign customers. The negative image of the 'Made in China' brand because of the country's previous irresponsible behaviour could also, ironically, become a major incentive and drive for the development of CSR in China.[57]

From this perspective, many current problems have the potential to cause conflict and damage social harmony, including inequality in regional development, population pressure and environmental pollution, unemployment and income inequality, and low accessibility and quality of health care and social security.[58] It has been stated that solving these problems will be the current primary mission of the Chinese Communist Party. Numerous steps and measure have been adopted to affect a paradigm shift from a qualitative growth model to a more sustainable economic, social and ecological form of development.[59] This shift has led to many new laws, including the revised company law and labour law with additional provisos on protection of the environment and other stakeholders. Legal recognition, and especially the acknowledgment in the CCL 2006 of the direct legal regulation of corporations, will be discussed below.

5.4.1   The Chinese Legal System and Environment for CSR

Just as with its economic achievements, China has also made significant progress in law reform since 1978. Mr Wu Bangguo, Chairman of the National People's Congress of China, declared on 8 March 2009 that the socialist legal system with Chinese characteristics was 'basically formed'. The State Council Information Office released a White Paper at a press conference on 28 October 2011 entitled 'The Socialist System of Law with Chinese Characteristics'.[60] According to the White Paper, as of the end of August 2011, China had enacted 240 laws, 706 administrative regulations, more than 8,600 local regulations, and more than 600 autonomous regional regulations. A variety of legal instruments define a

---

   57   L.W. Lin, 'Corporate Social Responsibility in China: Window Dressing or Structural Change' (2010) 28 *Berkeley Journal of International Law* 64 at 65.

   58   See Sixth General Meeting of the Sixteenth Central Commission of the Chinese Communist Party, Zhonggong Zhongyang guanyu Goujian Shehui Zhuyi Hexie Shehui Ruogan Zhongda Wenti de Jueding (Several Important Resolutions on the Construction of Socialist Harmonious Society by the Central Commission of the Chinese Communist Party).

   59   T. Chahoud, 'Policies on Corporate Social Responsibility' in C. Scherrer (ed.), *China's Labour Questions* (Munich: Rainer Hampp Verlag, 2011) p. 158.

   60   The White Paper is available at http://news.xinhuanet.com/english2010/ china/2011-10/27/c_131215899.htm.

broad range of responsibilities of corporations and their boards of directors to shareholders and stakeholders.[61] Of these laws, regulations and rules enacted in China since 1949, the ones with a direct impact on and relationship with corporate governance and CSR were mainly drafted during the last two decades, as corporate governance and CSR are relatively new terms in China.[62] The emergence of this modernized legislation started from the legal reform of SOEs in the 1990s. The Third Plenary Session of the Fourteenth Chinese Communist Party National Congress was held in Beijing in November 1993, where a Central Committee Resolution on Several Issues Regarding Building a Socialist Market Economy was passed. A modernized enterprise system requires clear ownership, clear rights and responsibility, the separation of government and enterprises, and scientific management, as expressed in Part 4 of the Resolution 'Changing Management Mechanisms of SOEs and Building a Modern Enterprise System'.[63] Based on the provisions in the Resolution, the National People's Congress Standing Committee passed the first Chinese Company Law in 1993, which was regarded as a product of China's economic reform and saw the adoption of Western corporate legislation with the goal of enabling SOEs to build a modern enterprise system.[64] Revisions of Chinese Company Law and Chinese Securities Law have focused new attention on various aspects of corporate governance, including shareholder voting rights, corporate objectives, and fiduciary duties of directors. These laws will bring a new approach to the roles of a corporate board and its directors, the rights of shareholders, the fiduciary duties of directors and officers, and the balance between directors' responsibility and reasonable protection of directors.[65]

Despite the modernized aspects instituted by the reforms in the new CCL 2006, it is argued that amending existing laws and enacting new laws will not be sufficient to meet the needs of reorganizing business

---

[61] See 'Foreword' to State Council Information Office, *The Socialist System of Law with Chinese Characteristics* (Beijing, 2011).

[62] It was not until late 1994 when the corporate governance term was first formally written into the Central Committee of the Communist Party of China's Resolution on Important Issues Regarding Reform and Development of SOEs at the Fourth Plenary Session of the Communist Party of China's Fifteenth National Congress.

[63] Announcement of the Third Plenary Session of the Fourteenth Chinese Communist Party National Congress.

[64] CCL 1994 art. 1.

[65] J.V. Feinerman, 'New Hope for Corporate Governance in China?' (2007) 191 *China Quarterly* 590.

relationships in China to make China a competitive and attractive place for investment on a global scale.[66] The legislation and regulations on business relationships and commercial transactions have always suffered from a lack of clarity and inconsistency with other regulations, which have made the laws imported into China from developed Western jurisdictions difficult to adapt to satisfy the domestic political agenda.[67]

5.4.2   Analysis of CSR-related Provisions in Chinese Company Law

Since the legislative process in China is not transparent, it is not easy to trace the steps towards reform and examine the exact deliberations that drove the legislative process surrounding the new company law. The former CCL, launched in 1994, did not explicitly make reference to CSR. However, the CCL 1994 did adopt certain elements of CSR, particularly regarding the rights of employees' in corporations, where companies were required to consult with trade unions and employees when making decisions about the employees' wages and welfare, and about safe production processes and other issues related to employees' interests. Article 14 also included provisions that were broad enough to cover the elements of CSR, stipulating that 'companies must comply with the law, conform to business ethics, strengthen the construction of the socialist civilization and subject themselves to the Government and public supervisions in the course of their business'.

General principles in CCL 2006 and CSR
Unlike the procedure adopted before the enactment of the CCL 1994, in 2005 a research report was published by a Chinese legal publishing house entitled *A Research Report on the Amendment to Company Law*.[68] The editors of the report included representatives of the Chinese government, including Kangtai Cao (Director of Legislative Affairs Office of State Council), Qiong Zhang (Deputy Director of Legislative Affairs Office of State Council), Keming Hu (Head of Secretary and Administrative Department, Legislative Affairs Office of State Council), Xiaoguang Zhao (Head of Public Relations and Commerce, Legislative Affairs Office of State Council), and a number of distinguished university

---

[66]   A. Young, G. Li and A. Lau, 'Corporate Governance in China: The Role of the State and Ideology in Shaping Reform' (2007) 28 *Company Lawyer* 204.

[67]   *Ibid.*

[68]   K. Cao *et al.* (eds), *A Research Report on the Amendment to Company Law (Xin Gongsi Fa Xiuding Yanjiu Baogao)* (Beijing: China Legal Publishing House, 2005).

professors in the areas of company law and civil law, including Professor Pin Jiang, Professor Jifu Wang, Professor Baoshu Wang and Professor Xudong Zhao.

The editors compiled and collected opinions from corporations, experts and the public that were taken into account in the legislative process. Regarding the opinion of the public, a group of delegates from the National People's Congress in Shanghai suggested the inclusion of CSR in the new company law, proposing that 'in addition to protecting shareholders' interests, companies should also consider other social interests such as the interests of employees, consumers, creditors, local communities, the environment, socially disadvantaged groups, and the general public'.[69] Delegates from the National People's Congress in Guangdong Province proposed that the new company law should include a section defining the relationships between corporations and their stakeholders.[70] The company stakeholders were defined and explained in Volume 2 of the report, alongside some measures proposed to protect their interests in the CCL 2006.[71]

With support from various sources, the legislators finally decided to incorporate CSR into the new company law. Article 5 of CCL 2006 states that 'a company must, when engaging in business activities, abide by the laws and administrative regulations, observe social morals and business ethics, be in integrity and good faith, accept regulation of the government and the public, and undertake social responsibilities'. At the most basic level, companies are required to abide by the law and regulations when they aim to make profits. It is implied in article 5 that apart from the interests of shareholders, employees and other stakeholders, the performance and activities of the company have a deep impact on the economic rules of the marketplace and also on public social interests. Therefore, when company directors and supervisors pursue the interests of their shareholders, they also have to be socially responsible and responsible to internal and external stakeholders.

Moreover, under article 5, corporations are legally required to observe social, moral and business ethics and undertake social responsibilities. Comparatively modern terms such as 'business ethics' and 'social responsibilities' were introduced into the general provisions of Chinese corporate law for the first time in 2006. This corporate responsibility goes beyond economic and legal responsibility, introducing a level of

---

[69] *Ibid.* vol. 1, pp. 13–30.
[70] *Ibid.*
[71] *Ibid.* vol. 2, pp. 68–78.

social and philanthropic responsibility. In addition to article 5, which gives directors legitimacy in considering stakeholders' interests, the rights of employees were also emphasized in the new CCL,[72] which may help to illustrate the philosophy underlying article 5. Moreover, as far as legislative tenets are concerned, it is stipulated in article 1 of CCL 2006 that this legislation was enacted in order to 'standardise the organisation and activities of companies, to protect the legitimate rights and interests of companies, shareholders and creditors, to maintain socio-economic order and to promote the development of the socialist market economy'.[73] The interests of creditors as primary stakeholders were explicitly mentioned in this article, along with the interests of shareholders and the company itself.

Interpretation of CCL 2006 article 5

Academic interpretation of the provisions has always been popular for newly enacted legislation, and the CCL 2006 was no exception, with interpretation of the new CCL being offered in a number of books. It is worth starting from the literature on article 5(1) to establish a coherent understanding on the article. Professor Lou Jianbo argued that the article requires that a company must, first, when engaging in business activities, abide by the laws and administrative regulations. Secondly, a company should observe social morals and business ethics, act in integrity and good faith, and accept regulation of the government and the public, and undertake social responsibilities. Professor Zhao Xudong interpreted the article differently. He argued that the article reaffirmed that corporations are business organizations established for shareholder wealth maximization. However, a company must abide by the law and administrative regulations as the basic requirement when engaging in business activities. Additionally, a company is required to observe social morals and business ethics. This is moral requirement on corporations when they are engaging in business activities. Last of all, corporations should maintain the public interests of society, accept government supervisions and regulation and undertake social responsibility.

However, the corporate responsibilities in respect of the economic, social, moral and legal levels have always overlapped and it is not accurate or logical to place the various responsibilities in an order of importance, for directors to perform a box-ticking exercise one after another. Business activities engaged in by directors are always related to

---

[72]   CCL 2006 arts 17, 18, 52, 117, 118 and 126.
[73]   CCL 2006 art. 1.

multi-stakeholders and the stakeholder groups are different in different corporations. There is always a fine line between moral responsibility and responsibility for public interests. In the author's opinion, it makes more sense to interpret the article by identifying its nature and scope, rather than focusing on its application.

The nature of the article consists in a general requirement for the company and the board of directors to undertake collective responsibility, including legal responsibility and ethical responsibility, while making profits. It is very general in its terms in order to express the overall direction and philosophy of the CCL 2006 on corporate objectives. It adopted the understanding of corporate objectives of the OECD Principles of Corporate Governance which reflect economic, social and legal goals which are commonly regarded as the result of discussions based on best practice experiences. Before clarifying the scope of the article, there are a few terms included in the wording of the article which need further definition, such as 'social morals', 'business ethics' and 'undertaking social responsibilities'. In the literature, 'morality' is defined as 'character or conduct considered as good or evil; ethical; adhering to or directed towards what is right'. Morality consists of 'principles concerning the distinction between right and wrong or good and bad behaviours as a particular system of value and principles of conduct'. In this sense, corporations are required to behave in a socially justified manner towards a 'right' direction.

The terms 'ethics' and 'morality' are generally used interchangeably, but some academic writers have proposed making a distinction between the two. The most commonly offered distinction defines the two terms as follows: 'morality is concerned with norms, values and beliefs embedded in social processes which define right and wrong for an individual or a community, while ethics is concerned with the study of morality and application of reason to elucidate specific rules and principles and determine right and wrong for a given situation. These rules and principles are called ethical theories'. Based on this definition, morality precedes ethics, which in turn precedes ethical theory, and 'ethics represent an attempt to systematize and rationalize morality, typically into generalized normative rules that supposedly offer a solution to situations of moral uncertainty'. Transposed from morality, business ethics, it has been claimed, is an oxymoron bringing together two apparently contradictory terms. This traditional view maintains that there are no ethics in business: that business is in some way inevitably unethical, or at best amoral. Business ethics are defined by Laura Nash as the 'study of how personal moral norms apply to the activities and goals of commercial enterprise. It is not a separate moral standard, but the study of how the business context poses its own unique problems for the moral person who acts as an agent of this system'. It has been argued by Ip that, instead of a single set of business ethics, there will be a whole range of ethical responses which Chinese corporations might adopt, a suite of business ethics approached from various angles to satisfy various stakeholders' interest.

Therefore, the definition of morality and ethics and business ethics within the scope of article 5 of CCL 2006 is very broad. However, it is clear that terms adopted in the article such as 'social morals', 'business ethics' and 'social responsibilities' will overlap. It is not known whether the legislators, in drafting the CCL 2006, simply included these terms to enrich the CSR character of the article, or whether they listed the terms following the logic that ethics rationalizes morality while social responsibility implements and executes business ethics. If that were the case, terms in article 5, including 'social morals', 'business ethics' and 'undertaking social responsibilities' could be interpreted in a coherent order: generation of CSR philosophy, followed by rationalization of CSR philosophy, then execution of CSR philosophy in corporate decisions and corporate actions. In any event, it is clear that the legislators intended corporations to act in a morally justifiable manner which is socially responsible, rather than solely pursuing profits.

Article 5 and the corporate responsibility pyramid

Article 5 does not automatically impose any additional legal responsibility on corporations. The direct effect of the article is limited to increasing the moral justification of the government's call for more socially responsible corporations. According to the corporate responsibility pyramid created by Carroll,[74] the economic components entailed in considering the interests of a company and being committed to maximizing profits are also the bottom level in establishing a successful company that is consistently profitable. At the next level, it is suggested that corporations must perform in a manner consistent with legal requirements, and comply with various regulations as law-abiding corporate citizens.[75] The company is required to offer products and services that meet basic legal

---

[74] A.B. Carroll, 'The Pyramid of CSR: Toward the Moral Management of Organizational Stakeholders' (1991) 34 *Business Horizons* 39 at 40–1; for more discussion on models of CSR, including the pyramid model, see A. Geva, 'Three Models of CSR: Interrelationships between Theory, Research and Practice' (2008) 113 *Business and Society Review* at 1.

[75] A.B. Carroll, 'The Pyramid of CSR: Toward the Moral Management of Organizational Stakeholders' (1991) 34 *Business Horizons* 39 at 40.

requirements. These requirements are consistent with duties towards various stakeholders that are enforced principally by corporate law but also by employment law, consumer protection law, environmental law and insolvency law, in order to validate the positions of stakeholders in corporations. At the higher level of ethical responsibility, companies are required to perform as sound corporate citizens in a manner consistent with the 'expectations of social mores and ethical norms',[76] and to recognize corporate integrity and ethical behaviours beyond their legal requirements. Article 5 of CCL 2006 constitutes an attempt by the Chinese government to move beyond basic levels of corporate responsibility and require companies to observe social morals and business ethics, act in integrity and good faith, accept regulation by the government and the public, and undertake social responsibilities.[77]

At the top of the corporate responsibility pyramid are philanthropic responsibilities, which are generally adopted in order for the corporation to act as a good corporate citizen, by contributing resources to the public and improving the society's quality of life. In this case, company directors will have in mind their stewardship role based on altruism in order to realize their collective responsibility.[78] Philanthropic responsibilities are examples of purely voluntary corporate strategies which act to promote human welfare and goodwill. Moreover, they are factual evidence that companies in countries that are dominated by the shareholder value principle constantly consider stakeholders' interests in their corporate strategy. This responsibility is highly prized and always desirable as a part of CSR.

Based on the corporate responsibility pyramid, article 5 of CCL 2006 could be interpreted as recommending that companies should undertake corporate social responsibilities in the course of doing business. First, companies should comply with laws and administrative regulations (their legal responsibility). Secondly, companies should conform to social morality and business ethics, act in good faith, and subject themselves to government supervision (their ethical responsibility). Their economic responsibility is enshrined in article 1, which emphasizes the interests of

---

[76]   *Ibid.* at 41.

[77]   Likewise, the ESVP in the UK Companies Act 2006 also requires directors to have regard to the interest of various stakeholders beyond the basic requirements in employment law, insolvency law, consumer protection law and environmental law in order make companies more ethical corporations.

[78]   R.V. Aguilera, D. Rupp, C. Williams and J. Ganapathi, 'Putting the S Back in CSR: A Multi-level Theory of Social Change in Organizations' (2007) 32 *Academy of Management Review* 836.

shareholders and the company as a whole. These philanthropic responsibilities, in addition to the broader interpretation of 'social morality' in article 5 of CCL 2006, are also found in other Chinese legislation. Article 186 of Contract Law of the People's Republic of China 1999 clarifies the difference between normal gift contracts and 'gift contracts the nature of which serves public interests or fulfils a moral obligation, such as disaster relief, poverty relief, etc., or any gift contract which has been notarised'.[79] In the latter case, the donor may not revoke the gift prior to the transfer of rights in the gift property. Similarly, the Welfare Donations Law of the People's Republic of China 1999 recites that is was enacted 'for the purpose of encouraging donations and standardising the behaviours of both donation and receipt of donation; protecting the legitimate rights and interests of the donor, the recipient and the beneficiary in order to promote public welfare undertakings'.[80] Furthermore, in article 9 of the Enterprise Income Tax Law of the People's Republic of China 2007, favourable treatment is given to charitable donation expenses: 'of the expenses from charitable donations incurred by Enterprises, the portion within 12 per cent of the total annual profit may be deducted from taxable income'.

5.5   ENFORCEMENT AND EFFECTIVENESS OF CCL 2006 ARTICLE 5

Much has been written on the general issues confronting the implantation of law in China. The enforcement of law in China has always been regarded as the most important but also the most difficult aspect of the legal reform process. This refers to implementation of national legislation together with international law that China is bound by, while international law and treaty obligations are thought to prevail if there is a conflict between domestic law and an obligation of international treaty law binding on China.[81] Although it is already very positive that the government is making initial efforts to realize the importance of CSR and make it legitimate for directors to consider their responsibility

---

[79]   CCL1999 art. 186.
[80]   Welfare Donations Law of the People's Republic of China 1999 art. 1.
[81]   K. Buhmann, 'Corporate Social Responsibility in China: Current Issues and Their Relevance for Implementation of Law' (2005) 22 *Copenhagen Journal of Asian Studies* 62 at 78; J. Chen, Y. Li and J.M. Otto, *Implementation of Law in the People's Republic of China* (The Hague: Kluwer, 2002).

beyond shareholder value maximization, it is still important to identify the approaches by which the Chinese government may enforce these rules.

5.5.1 SA 8000 and Chinese Corporations

Voluntary social responsibilities undertaken by companies themselves, including SOEs, Chinese companies and joint stock enterprises, have played an important role in transforming corporations in China into more responsible bodies. Some international organizations and related standards have also played a positive role in this. The most effective one has been the establishment and application of the Social Accountability 8000 International Standard (SA 8000) in China. The SA 8000 is an international standard for social responsibility initiated by the Council on Economic Priorities Accreditation Agency. The objective of the SA 8000 is to ensure the ethical sourcing of goods and services. The standard may replace or change a company's special social accountability or ethical code. 'This standard is the benchmark against which companies and factories measure their performance. Those seeking to comply with SA 8000 have adopted policies and procedures that protect the basic human rights of workers.'[82] As of September 2010, 339 out of a total of 2,330 Chinese companies had been granted an SA 8000 certificate. Nevertheless, in the author's opinion, despite the positive aspects from an international perspective of Chinese companies obtaining an SA 8000 certificate, the Chinese government and related organizations should also establish domestic standards for social and environmental responsibility, as well as technical regulations based on an evaluation of SA 8000 and the current Chinese economic situation.

5.5.2 Administrative Organization Enforcement

Administrative organization enforcement has always been regarded as an effective way to implement corporate social responsibility. Thus, in the United States, Carroll pointed out: 'Though social activist groups and others throughout the 1960s advocated a broader notion of corporate responsibility, it was not until the significant social legislation of the early 1970s that this message became indelibly clear as a result of the creation of the Environmental Protection Agency (EPA), the Equal Employment Opportunity Commission (EEOC), the Occupational Safety

---

[82] The SA 8000 Standard, available at www.sa-intl.org/index.cfm?fuse action=Page.viewPage&pageId=937&parentID=479&nodeID=1.

and Health Administration (OSHA), and the Consumer Product Safety Commission (CPSC)'.[83] Such enforcement also forms an initial recognition of various corporate stakeholders apart from shareholders.

Chapter V of the new Company Law of the Republic of Indonesia, concerning 'Environmental and Social Responsibility', is a good example of implementing corporate social responsibility by the means of administrative power. It is stipulated in Chapter V article 74 as follows:

(1) Companies doing business in the field of and/or in relation to natural resources must put into practice Environmental and Social Responsibility.

(2) The Environmental and Social Responsibility contemplated in paragraph (1) constitutes an obligation of the Company which shall be budgeted for and calculated as a cost of the Company performance of which shall be with due attention to decency and fairness.

(3) Companies who do not put their obligation into practice as contemplated in paragraph (1) shall be liable to sanctions in accordance with the provisions of legislative regulations.

(4) Further provisions regarding Environmental and Social Responsibility shall be stipulated by Government Regulation.

In comparison with article 5 of CCL 2006, the scope of article 74 above is narrowly focused on 'companies doing business in the field of and/or in relation to natural resources'. However, article 74(2) transforms social and environmental responsibility from a negative and compensatory responsibility to an active one. Under paragraph (2), companies should budget for and calculate the cost of their environmental and social responsibility as a cost of company performance embodied in the annual balance sheet. This legislative attitude has the potential to transform directors' opinions on CSR in 'companies doing business in the field of and/or in relation to natural resources'. Meanwhile, directors have been given explicit legitimacy to take CSR directly into their corporate strategy, which makes administrative power-based enforcement possible.

In the opinion of the author, two positive aspects of article 74 of the new Company Law of the Republic of Indonesia are worth considering in relation to Chinese company law: first, it might be helpful to require companies to include the cost of practising CSR in their corporate budgets in future company law or other related legislation, in order to strengthen the idea of CSR in the minds of corporate directors; secondly, it is important for certain categories of industries to undertake additional social and environmental responsibilities.

---

[83]   A.B. Carroll, 'The Pyramid of CSR: Toward the Moral Management of Organizational Stakeholders' (1991) 34 *Business Horizons* 39 at 40.

5.5.3   CCL 2006 Article 5 and Related Directors' Duties

Experience from the UK Companies Act 2006

The enlightened shareholder value principle (ESVP) is the objective principle currently adopted in UK company law, originally advocated by the Company Law Review Steering Group[84] for the purpose of achieving wealth generation and competitiveness for corporations. It is adopted in the Companies Act 2006 as the 'duty to promote the success of the company' embodied in section 172. This section makes it clear that the purpose of promoting the success of the company is for the benefit of its members as a whole, who are in most cases the shareholders.[85] According to the section, the directors are required to create value for shareholders when considering the long-term interests of the corporation, and also to foster the relationships with suppliers, employees and communities. The result of this definition is that ESVP maintains the shareholder-centred paradigm favoured by those advocating the shareholder value principle.

However, under appropriate circumstances it also requires that consideration be given to a wider range of interests.[86] The adoption of the principle makes it legitimate for directors to look after the interests of stakeholders in order to maximize shareholders' interests and maintain companies in the long term.[87] It legitimizes far-sighted management policies in considering the interests of non-shareholder stakeholders with the goal of fostering the profitability of corporations. Also, it may alleviate the concerns of directors who 'feel that they must operate in a way that is acceptable to society in a common sense way and take into account the interests of primary stakeholders'.[88] The directors will be protected from censure by shareholders when they act in order to promote the long-term competitiveness of the company.

---

[84]   For the evolution of ESVP and enforcement of s. 172(1) of the Companies Act 2006 see A. Keay, *The Enlightened Shareholder Value Principle and Corporate Governance* (Abingdon, UK: Routledge, 2013).
[85]   The wording of s. 172 is intended to cater for the situation of all companies, including guarantee companies that do not have shareholders.
[86]   J. Loughrey, A. Keay and L. Cerioni, 'Legal Practitioners, Enlightened Shareholder Value and the Shaping of Corporate Governance' (2008) 8 *Journal of Corporate Law Studies* 79 at 86.
[87]   A. Keay, 'Tackling the Issues of the Corporate Objective: An Analysis of the United Kingdom's "Enlightened Shareholder Value Approach"' (2007) 29 *Sydney Law Review* 599.
[88]   See J. Dean, *Directing Public Companies: Company Law and the Stakeholder Society* (London: Cavendish Publishing Ltd, 2001) p. 251.

ESVP was seen as a radical reform in UK company law, since it was intended to 'reflect the fundamental assumptions and often long-established principles in company law and practice in Europe, which have yet survived the onslaught of shareholder value ideology'.[89] The UK government has described section 172 as a radical departure in articulating the connection between what is good for a company and what is good for society at large. However, it was argued that the list of matters set out in section 172(1) to which directors were to have regard would lead to all directors' decisions being made only after a formal box-ticking exercise, which in turn would lead to an increased administrative burden but no substantive change in directors' behaviour.[90]

The author agrees with the government's response in Ministerial Statements that the words 'have regards to' are 'absolutely not about ticking boxes', but instead they denote having to 'give proper consideration to'.[91] For the first time in legislation, the UK government adopted the ESVP and protected directors from shareholder pressure to maximize the short-term interests of the corporation at the expense of long-term progress. The Companies Act 2006 gives the first indication that companies whose directors have regard to relevant social and environmental objectives and consider the environment, employees, customers, suppliers, local communities and the public media in their decisions are likely, as far as the long-term interests of the companies are concerned, to perform more successfully than those whose directors do not take account of such matters. Furthermore, it entitles and legitimates the directors in taking corporate social responsibilities into account when making corporate decisions in order to fulfil their ethical and philanthropic responsibilities.

However, in the opinion of the author, although the directors are enabled to take a different approach to managing the company under ESVP, there is still no fundamental movement away from shareholder value in reality.[92] Indeed, there are enlightened factors resulting from the

---

[89]   T. Clarke (ed.), *Theories of Corporate Governance: The Philosophical Foundations of Corporate Governance* (London: Routledge, 2004) pp. 13–14.

[90]   D. Chivers, *The Companies Act 2006: Directors' Duties Guidance* (Corporate Responsibility Coalition, 2007) pp. 6–7.

[91]   DTI, *Companies Act 2006 Duties of Company Directors: Ministerial Statements* (2007), available at www.BERR.gov.uk/files/file40139.pdf.

[92]   Also see J. Loughrey, A. Keay and L. Cerioni, 'Legal Practitioners, Enlightened Shareholder Value and the Shaping of Corporate Governance' (2008) 8 *Journal of Corporate Law Studies* 79 for concerns expressed by legal practitioners about Companies Act 2006 s. 172 .

principle regarding the promotion of stakeholders' interests and encouragement for directors to make more ethical and socially responsible decisions. The adoption of ESVP can be regarded as the result of a convergence of the corporate governance model in the United Kingdom towards a new hybrid model.

Learning from 'duties to promote the success of the company'

The duty of loyalty in good faith is clearly summarized in Chinese company law, and was amended in 2005 so that 'the directors, supervisors and senior managers shall bear the obligations of fidelity and diligence to the company'.[93] The amended CCL 2006 clarified the requirement that directors owe their duties to their company. The former CCL 1994 did not expressly impose the duty of good faith and duty of care upon directors, but it is stipulated in the CCL 2006 that directors have the following duties: a duty of good faith, a duty to disclose, a duty to maintain secrecy, a duty to compensate the company for breach of duty, a duty not to carry on a competing business, and a duty not to deal with the assets of the company fraudulently.[94] After the amendments, the CCL 2006 unequivocally states that directors owe a duty of good faith and a duty of care to their companies.[95] In civil law systems, the duty of good faith normally requires directors to fulfil their duties faithfully, uphold the interests of the company, and exercise a reasonable degree of care.[96] At the same time the duty of good faith also requires directors to actively pursue the best interests of the company, and forbids directors to use their positions to seek personal gains.[97] It appears that the duty of good faith includes duties that are equivalent to the fiduciary duty, based on the intention of the law-makers to interpret the duty of good faith based on the civil law doctrine.[98]

In order to integrate this legislative attitude into the provisions regarding directors' duties to enforce CSR more efficiently, the duty in good faith, namely, the fiduciary duty in CCL 2006, would appear to be the relevant provision to extend. Because ESVP is itself still a subject of

---

[93]   CCL 2006 art. 148.

[94]   *Ibid.* arts 148–50.

[95]   *Ibid.* art. 148.

[96]   Y. Wei, 'Directors Duties under Chinese Law: A Comparative Review' (2006) 3 *University of New England Law Journal* 31 at 49.

[97]   H. Zhou, 'Directors' Duty of Good Faith' in P. Jiang and Z. Yang (eds), *Civil Law and Commercial Law Forum* (Beijing: China University of Political Science and Law Press, 2004) 434 at 437.

[98]   *Ibid.* at 447.

controversy in the United Kingdom, it might not be logical or reasonable to give a definite answer about the validity and effectiveness of the adoption of such an approach in Chinese law surrounding directors' duties. However, in the author's opinion, it would be a positive legislative step for China to include various stakeholders' interests in the directors' fiduciary duties. It would be sensible to remind directors that as well as the interests of shareholders, they also have to consider the interests of other stakeholders who are parts of the company and have certain claims, either fixed or residual, on the corporation's profits.

However, the enforcement of such a provision would not be easy. In civil law systems, laws regarding directors' duties are, to some extent, different from the common law system. Directors' duties are fully codified in China, where there is a civil law system without common law to interpret the codified statutes. Furthermore, another key factor is that China endorses a two-tier board system, an employee participation system and an independent directors system, which under certain circumstances may result in some managerial powers being shared by the supervisory board, the employees, independent directors and the board of directors. Furthermore, regarding creditors' interests, Chinese insolvency law still has a long way to go to match the well-developed insolvency law in the United Kingdom or bankruptcy law in the United States, not only in terms of statutes but also the common law. Therefore, with the development of Chinese insolvency law, the extent of directors' duties towards creditors should become more specifically defined based on the financial circumstances of the corporations.

5.6 CSR AND CHINESE LABOUR LAW

China has always been regarded as an attractive place to do business due to its low labour costs which enable companies to manufacture various products very cheaply. However, the serious problems in labour rights and human rights have hindered the sustainable development of corporations in China. The innovative strategies and programmes to address labour law violations are best understood in the context of the Chinese Labour Law (CLL) 1995.[99] The first Labour Law came into force in 1995 in response to the reform of the socialist market economy and the

---

[99] R.J. Rosoff, 'Beyond Codes of Conduct' (2004) 31 *China Business Review* 6.

growing labour market created thereafter.[100] The enactment of CLL 1995 was also regarded as a response to the privatization of SOEs and the removal of the secured permanent 'iron rice bowl' in SOEs through the employment contract system, made necessary by the huge deficits they had accumulated. However, the CLL 1995 proved unsuitable for the rapid development of the Chinese economy and it was criticized for serious shortcomings with regard to the increasing complexity in employment formats.[101] First, there were no provisions in the CLL 1995 regulating informal employment and the proliferating forms of non-standard employment such as labour hire and casual work, which had become increasingly important and numerous since early 1990. Secondly, the Law's focus was on the termination of the labour contract, without paying enough attention to when or how a contract came into formation.[102] Thirdly, it was argued that the CLL 1995 did nothing to inhibit a range of emerging contracting practices which could lead to abuse by employers.[103]

These shortcomings of the CLL 1995 led to the most significant reform of the law regulating industrial and employment relationships, namely, the enactment of the new Chinese Labour Contract Law (CLCL) in 2008. Chinese labour law follows the guidance produced by the International Labour Organization (ILO) despite the fact that legislation on labour standards and practices goes beyond the minimum requirements suggested by the ILO.[104] Furthermore, the CLCL 2008 substantially changed the conditions under which employees can enter into employment contracts and has had a significant impact on the ability of employees to shape their working conditions.[105] It regulates the establishment, performance, variation and termination of the labour contract and is regarded as a distinct improvement on the legal framework regulating

---

[100]   S. Cooney, S. Biddulph, K. Li and Y. Zhu, 'China's New Labour Contract Law: Responding to the Growing Complexity of Labour Relations in the PRC' (2007) 30 *UNSW Law Journal* 786 at 787–8.

[101]   *Ibid.* at 787.

[102]   See CLL 1995 arts 16–17 and 23–32.

[103]   A. Chan, 'Globalization, China's Free (Read Bonded) Labour Market and the Chinese Trade Unions' (2000) 6 *Asia Pacific Business Review* 260 at 261–2.

[104]   For example, beyond the requirements imposed by the ILO's guidance, employees in China are entitled to more days of leave and longer maternity leave.

[105]   T. Lan and J. Pickles, *China's New Labour Contract Law: State Regulation and Worker Rights in Global Production Networks*, Economic and Social Upgrading in Global Production Network Working Paper 5 (2011), available at www.capturingthegains.org/pdf/ctg-wp-2011-05.pdf.

employment relations.[106] The new CLCL is also designed to respond to the rapid urbanization and pro-industrialization policies and the increasing demand of labour. With in excess of 230 million migrant workers moving from rural areas to cities, the relationship between employees and corporations became one of the most difficult and controversial problems for China, and the CLCL, if efficiently enforced, should function as a legislative base for employees to rely on to protect their interests. The Law prescribes when employees can be dismissed[107] and introduced requirements regarding work hours, rest and leave, wages and social insurance.[108]

In a further development, in line with common globalized legislative practice, the Chinese Employment Protection Law was enacted and came into force in January 2008. This Law prohibited employment-related discrimination based on the ethnicity, race, gender, religious belief, age, physical disability or health of employees.[109] Simultaneously, this legislation also responded to the worrying situation of migrant workers by prohibiting discrimination against migrant workers by providing that those who seek employment in cities must be given the same rights as those of urban workers.[110] The enforcement of the Law was also supported by the reorganization of the institutional framework through the establishment in 2008 of a new central government department, the Department of Migrant Workers' Affairs, to 'safeguard the rights of migrant workers, help them get training and ensure safe working conditions'.[111] Wang Zhihong, director of this new department, stated that the mission of the unit is to 'carry on the government's unremitting efforts to protect the legal rights of migrant workers'. The unit is regarded as a landmark in the government's efforts to bridge the widening urban-rural divide.

The new CLCL 2008 and Employment Protection Law 2008 addressed the issues of protection of legitimate rights of employees, by putting

---

[106] See CLCL 2008 art. 2, in which the scope of the CLCL 2008 is defined as covering private sector and non-profit-making firms as well as governmental agencies where they have established a labour relationship.

[107] CLCL 2008 arts 21, 44, 48 and 87.

[108] CLCL 2008 arts 4, 17 and 51.

[109] Employment Protection Law of China 2008 arts 3, 25, 26, 27, 28, 29 and 30.

[110] Employment Protection Law of China 2008 art. 31.

[111] 'Special unit to fight for migrant workers', *China Daily*, 22 July 2008, available at www.china.org.cn/government/news/2008-07/22/content_16045546. htm.

emphasis on offering satisfactory, fair and non-discriminatory working conditions and opportunities to all employees in China. The legislative reforms can be regarded as demonstrating the government's intentions to give protection to employees, as the internal and primary stakeholders. These protections are regarded as the reconstruction of the regulatory framework in China to promote the basic interests of employees without discrimination. The enactment of the two Laws is designed to assist and complement the growing CSR movement in China by promoting the use of collective employment contracts in Chinese companies and multinational corporations. The goal of more socially responsible corporations is consistent with three principal objectives pursued in the protection of the contractual rights of employees, namely, mobilizing workers to participate in collective bargaining so that they can play an active role in protecting their own rights; efficiently implementing the CLCL, trade union legislation and relevant standards from the ILO; and providing a new and effective means by which multinational companies can realize their commitment to the principles of social accountability.[112] Thus, protection of employees' contractual rights is transposed from the code of conduct as a moral responsibility into a legal standard as enforceable obligations. Employees will play a more active and participatory role through this transformation.

5.7 CORPORATE SOCIAL RESPONSIBILITY IN CHINA AFTER THE 2008 FINANCIAL CRISIS: NEW TRENDS AND NEW CHALLENGES

Even from a historical perspective, the 2008 financial crisis was unique. Unlike the Asian and Latin American crises in the 1980s, this financial crisis was truly global, and countries such as Iceland and Pakistan have been threatened with bankruptcy. In Japan, the country has been hit by huge volatility in the markets. Since 2008, nations have been grappling to make use of every possible economic policy instrument to curb the crisis and improve national welfare. The global financial crisis, which had been brewing for a while, began to show its effects from the middle of 2007 and continued through 2008, 2009 and 2010, and even into 2011. Subsequently, China has been suffering as a result.

---

[112] 'Chinese Labour Bulletin's Corporate Social Responsibility Initiatives', *Chinese Labour Bulletin*, 2 January 2008, available at www.clb.org.hk/en/node/100187.

5.7.1   The 2008 Financial Crisis and China

The 2008 global financial crisis put the entire financial market system in turmoil and resulted in severe losses and a possible slowdown of the whole world economy since 2007. This financial crisis was initiated in the United States, where there had been a sustained period characterized by growing loan incentives, declining lending standards, and rising housing prices. According to the statistics, the total value of US subprime mortgages amounted to US$1.3 trillion as of March 2007.[113] Around 7.5 million first-lien subprime mortgages were outstanding at that time, accounting for about 14 per cent of all first-lien mortgages.[114] An acceleration of defaults and foreclosures in the subprime market triggered a liquidity crisis and subsequently the global financial crisis. Heralded by the bankruptcy of Lehman Brothers, a 158-year-old investment bank, on 14 September 2008, the financial crisis deepened towards the end of 2008 and the entire banking system came close to collapse. The bankruptcy of Lehman Brothers, a major Wall Street investment bank, sent the prices of financial assets in a massive downward spiral and banks' shares were especially badly affected because of 'the freezing of the inter-bank loan market, inadequate disclosure and massive doubt about the state of the banks' balance sheets'.[115] The United States, the United Kingdom and most of the other EU nations were forced to piece together massive bank rescue packages and a considerable number of banks in these jurisdictions were nationalized.

China has not been immune from the economic turndown, and like most of the rest of the world it fell victim to the global financial crisis to a certain extent. Although it may have seemed that China remained relatively unscathed initially, 'it was hit hard by second-order effects, as exports suddenly collapsed'. World trade volume dropped by 12 per cent in 2009. Exports from China, a country which is increasingly integrated with the globalized economy, were badly hit during the recession, with the total export value dropping by 16 per cent in 2009 relative to 2008. Before 2008, the average annual rate of GDP growth was 9.8 per cent with a peak growth rate of 13 per cent in 2007. However, the GDP

---

[113]   B.S. Bernanke, 'The Subprime Mortgage Market', paper delivered at the Federal Reserve Bank of Chicago's 43rd Annual Conference on Bank Structure and Competition, Chicago, Illinois, 17 May 2007.

[114]   *Ibid.*

[115]   E. Avgouleas, 'The Global Financial Crisis, Behavioural Finance and Financial Regulation: In Search of a New Orthodoxy' (2009) 9 *Journal of Corporate Law Studies* 23.

growth rate fell, gradually at first in 2008, and then in a dramatic fashion after the collapse of Lehman Brothers. The development trend of GDP growth rate in the first half, third quarter and fourth quarter of 2008 and the first quarter of 2009 dropped from 10.4 per cent to 9 per cent, to 6.8 per cent, and finally to 6.1 per cent, respectively, proving the impact of the crisis on China's economy. Moreover, the share prices of individual Chinese companies plummeted by more than 50 per cent in just eight months.

China was drawn into the financial chaos due to a massive decrease in demand from abroad. The most important impact of the global financial crisis on the Chinese economy came from the fall in global demand, which reflects China's extremely high export dependency. This has meant the closure of factories and severe job losses in China. In the Pearl River Delta, tens of thousands of workers were forced to return to their homes in the countryside in 2008. The Chinese government considered various ways to ease the impact of the financial crisis, including legal responses to boost market confidence. The government fully realized the danger of not tackling structural problems for China's long-term growth, and it began to take measures to execute structural adjustments. These attempts included subsidies, the introduction of a RMB 4 trillion stimulus fund for 2009 and 2010, the adoption of an expansionist monetary policy to support the expansionist fiscal policy, and a regulatory framework reconstruction for companies and banks.

The Chinese government also enhanced its capability to promote CSR, reflected in government policy transformation and supervision of the fulfilment of CSR through law. After the enactment of the CCL 2006 and the financial crisis of 2008, it is interesting to note corporate responses to these legal requirements regarding CSR, as well as the impact of the global business climate on CSR in China. In the current hard times faced by the world, caused by the worst financial crisis in recent years, do people sincerely care about CSR? It might seem logical that attention should turn to profit-making and profit maximization, in order to reduce the negative effects on the economy brought about by the financial crisis. However, can China afford to profit at the expense of CSR? Environmentalists and other pluralists in the areas of corporate law and corporate governance are worried that sustainability and increased corporate responsibility towards social and philanthropic concerns are being removed from the boardroom agenda as companies tighten their belts in the face of turbulent stock markets, the 'credit crunch' and a looming economic slowdown. Irresponsible corporate actions will eventually burst the risk balloon; the lesson to be learnt from the financial crisis of 2008 is to regulate risk management and act responsibly in line with public interests. The issuing of Guidelines on Performing Social Responsibility of Central Enterprises by the State Asset Supervision and Administration Commission and Draft Guidelines on Performing Social Responsibility of Foreign Invested Enterprises by the Chinese Academy of International Trade and Economic Cooperation, both in 2008, can be regarded as long-term plans to encourage corporations in China to integrate CSR into their business best practice in the post-crisis environment.

5.7.2 Corporate Governance and Financial Crisis: Lessons for Chinese Corporations and Legislators

'We know a lot about what has happened, but less about how or why.'[116] A great body of academic literature and official reports has attempted to identify the origins and implications of the worldwide financial crisis in order to minimize its negative impacts.[117] As yet, there is no consensus about the implications of the crisis, but neither is there any contradiction among academics or analysts about the fact that an unprecedented number of financial institutions have collapsed or been bailed out by governments worldwide since the onset of the global financial crisis in 2008.[118] Although there is a lack of uncontroversial evidence as to the

---

[116] P. Moxey and A. Berendt, *Corporate Governance and the Credit Crunch*, ACCA Discussion Paper (2008) p. 3.

[117] Related research is from all disciplines, although mainly from the legal, business and management fields. See J.C. Coffee, 'What Went Wrong? An Initial Inquiry into the Causes of the 2008 Financial Crisis' (2009) 9 *Journal of Corporate Law Studies* 1; A. Arora, 'The Corporate Governance Failings in Financial Institutions and Directors' Legal Liability' (2011) 32 *Company Lawyer* 3; P. Rose, *Regulating Risk by 'Strengthening Corporate Governance'*, Public Law and Legal Theory Working Paper Series No. 130, (Ohio State University Moritz College of Law, 2010); M.K. Brunnermeier, 'Deciphering the 2007–2008 Liquidity and Credit Crunch' (2009) 23 *Journal of Economic Perspective* 77; M.J.B. Hall, *The Sub-prime Crisis, the Credit Crunch and Bank 'Failure': An Assessment of the UK Authorities' Response*, Discussion Paper Series (Department of Economics, 2008); G.F. Udell, 'Wall Street, Main Street and a Credit Crunch: Thoughts on the Current Financial Crisis' (2009) 52 *Business Horizons* 117; V. Finch, 'Corporate Rescue in a World of Debt' (2008) *Journal of Business Law* 756; R. Tomasic, 'Corporate Rescue, Governance and Risk-taking in Northern Rock' (Parts I and II) (2008) 29 *Company Lawyer* 297.

[118] The list of these casualties includes Bear Stearns, Citigroup, Lehman Brothers, Merrill Lynch (in the United States); HBOS and RBS (in the United Kingdom); and Dexia, Fortis, Hypo Real Estate and UBS (in continental Europe).

true reason for this, many observers[119] attribute these events to failures in corporate governance, such as lax board oversight, under-qualified directors, inefficient non-executive directors and flawed executive compensation practices that encouraged aggressive risk-taking. As a result, regulators provide regulatory support towards vigorous markets benefiting from more efficient corporate control, imposing new regulations or reconstructing corporate governance mechanisms that limit managerial discretion and/or enhance directors' accountability.

There is no doubt that the current regulations, policies and practice within the two archetypal corporate governance models will also be challenged and developed in the aftermath of the recent economic crisis. Of all the destabilizing factors leading to this social-economic crisis, many seem to be inextricably linked to failures in existing corporate governance practice; for instance, the lack of common understanding of the purpose and scope of corporate governance among board members, shareholders and stakeholders; the unaccountability of boards towards shareholders and stakeholders; poor directors' performance; and poor corporate monitoring and corporate control.[120] It has been argued that corporate governance failed during the 2008 financial crisis – some observers believe that ultimately the crisis is not a risk management problem but a larger crisis in corporate governance.[121] Rebuilding confidence for the future means preventing regulatory overkill that would damage the entrepreneurialism needed to secure economic growth. Therefore, the global authorities should work with market participants to develop enhanced governance practice that will underpin other actions being taken to address the current problems.[122]

From the international perspective, the current turmoil suggests a need for the OECD, through the Steering Group on Corporate Governance, to re-examine the adequacy of its corporate governance principles in these key areas.[123] Advice and examples contained in the OECD's methodology for assessing the implementation of the OECD Principles of Corporate

---

[119]   For example, the OECD.

[120]   P. Moxey and A. Berendt, *Corporate Governance and the Credit Crunch*, ACCA Discussion Paper (2008) p. 2.

[121]   B. Cheffins, 'Did Corporate Governance "Fail" During the 2008 Stock Market Meltdown? The Case of the S&P 500' (2009) 65 *Business Lawyer* 1.

[122]   International Corporate Governance Network, *Statement on Global Financial Crisis* (2008) p. 4.

[123]   G. Kirkpatrick, 'The Corporate Governance Lessons from the Financial Crisis' (2009) 96 *Financial Market Trends* 2.

Governance might also need to be revised.[124] Without exception, it is accepted that a fundamental factor leading to this crisis was that the directors of banks and financial institutions failed to perform basic good corporate governance.[125] A lack of accountability both within financial institutions and among management, shareholders and stakeholders (such as banking customers) was also one of the root causes of the global financial crisis.[126] For corporations and institutions, accountability and risk management are among the most fundamental concerns of directors, forming the basic elements of internal control systems.[127] In addition, an excessive concentration on short-term considerations, the result of a problematic remuneration and bonuses structure that encouraged excessive short-termism by ignoring stakeholders' interests, is another reason for rapid financial growth in the last decade and the ongoing worldwide crisis. This short-term motivation has led to the pursuit of reckless short-term business strategies and insufficient risk management. The financial failures proved the pathology of the shareholder model, under which company directors focus on short-term considerations. The fact that management vacancies tend to be filled via an external open labour market,[128] as well as the fact that managers' performance over a relatively short-term period has a critical effect on their career prospects, have also become significant factors in further stimulating managers to increase their firm's short-term financial performance, mostly by increasing the share price of the company.

Currently, most corporate governance recommendations made in response to the crisis concern the future role and responsibilities of the directors of banks and financial institutions.[129] Nevertheless, it is anticipated that this improvement in corporate governance in the banking and financial sectors will also provide new guidance for the performance of public company directors. It has been frequently argued that the main

---

[124]   *Ibid.*
[125]   P. Moxey and A. Berendt, *Corporate Governance and the Credit Crunch*, ACCA Discussion Paper (2008); Association of Chartered Certified Accountants (ACCA), *Climbing Out of the Credit Crunch*, ACCA Policy Paper (2008).
[126]   ACCA, *Climbing Out of the Credit Crunch*, ACCA Policy Paper (2008) p. 3.
[127]   T. Clarke, *International Corporate Governance: A Comparative Approach* (Abingdon: Routledge, 2007) p. 60.
[128]   R.V. Aguilera and G. Jackson, 'The Cross-national Diversity of Corporate Governance: Dimensions and Determinants' (2003) 28 *Academy of Management Review* 447 at 458.
[129]   A. Yip, 'Risk Governance as Part of Corporate Governance' (2008) 23 *Journal of International Banking Law and Regulation* 493.

reason underlying the 2008 financial crisis and related problems was the mispricing of risk, or mistakes and wrong decisions made by irresponsible corporations leading practice all the way down the chain.[130] While some academicians have focused on the failure of risk management as the reason for the 2008 crisis,[131] others have identified broader reasons, in particular short-termist pressure placed on directors as a result of demands by shareholders for unsustainable earnings growth, possible only by way of the shortcuts such as over-leverage, reduced investment and danger-ously excessive risk.[132] Although it cannot be concluded that failures of risk management are ultimately corporate governance failures, there is a consensus that lessons should be learned from current and potential problems in the existing corporate governance system in the aftermath of the 2008 financial crisis, and that companies need to be regulated more efficiently to overcome these weaknesses and support a sounder implementation of related law and principles. The OECD Steering Group on Corporate Governance has argued that weak governance across the spectrum of companies was a major cause of the financial crisis.[133] CSR is one of the most important elements requiring reconsideration and regu-lation post-crisis.

There are two progressive suggestions that could be referenced as good lessons for China through investigation of the interrelations between the financial crisis, related economic downturn, and the possible develop-ment trend of corporate governance models after the crisis: (1) long-termism, and (2) more responsible corporations, including more responsible banking, executives and capitalism. It suggests that the extensive responsibility of various stakeholders, including shareholders, in promoting the success of a company in the long term will be significant and even intensified after the crisis.

---

[130] C. Jordan and A. Jain, *Diversity and Resilience: Lessons from the Financial Crisis*, Research Paper (Centre for Corporate Law and Securities Regulation, University of Melbourne, 8 September 2009) p. 5.

[131] W. Sahlman, *Management and the Financial Crisis (We have Met the Enemy and He is Us…)*, Harvard Business School Working Paper No. 10-033 (2009) p. 4, available at www.hbs.edu/research/pdf/10-033.pdf.

[132] A. Keay, 'The Duty to Promote the Success of the Company: Is it Fit for Purpose?' in J. Loughrey, *Directors' Duties and Shareholder Litigation in the Wake of the Financial Crisis* (Cheltenham: Edward Elgar, 2013 p. 50).

[133] G. Kirkpatrick, 'The Corporate Governance Lessons from the Financial Crisis' (2009) 96 *Financial Market Trends* 1.

5.7.3   CSR in China After the 2008 Financial Crisis

The turbulent state of the global economy has brought many uncertainties to financial stability, economic well-being and the social contract between business, government and their stakeholders, including local communities and society at large.[134] In the environment of 'emerging social structures at risk of succumbing to a wave of financial hardship and changes', 'corporate commitment to socially responsible practice assumes heightened importance'.[135] Wayne Visser, the CEO of CSR International, has argued that the financial crisis will have a substantial impact on CSR. However, the impact will vary for the different types of CSR being practised. Philanthropic CSR is likely to be the worst hit, with strategic CSR probably less affected, while embedded CSR may be largely unaffected.[136] On this view, philanthropy such as charities, donations, sponsorships, will suffer substantial cuts. However, compared to this immature version of CSR, strategic CSR may well pay dividends for its users in the aftermath of the financial crisis, since the 'more closely tied a social issue is to a company's business, the greater the opportunity to leverage the firm's resources – and benefit society'.[137] Those corporations which have adopted strategic management policies consistent with CSR practices will be more likely to achieve their business initiatives. As regards embedded CSR, Visser has argued that CSR can only survive the 'vagaries of fickle markets, fluctuating profits, financial crisis and leadership whims if it is totally embedded in the corporate culture, strategy and governance system'.[138]

---

[134]   K.H. Darigan and J.E. Post, 'Corporate Citizenship in China: CSR Challenges in the 'Harmonious Society'' (2009) 35 *Journal of Corporate Citizenship* 39.

[135]   *Ibid.*

[136]   W. Visser, 'CSR and the Financial Crisis: Taking Stock', Official Blog of CSR International, 4 November 2008, available at http://csrinternational. blogspot.co.uk/2008/11/csr-and-financial-crisis-taking-stock.html.

[137]   M. Porter and M.R. Kramer, 'Strategy and Society: The Link between Competitive Advantage and Corporate Social Responsibility' (2006) 84 *Harvard Business Review* (12 December).

[138]   W. Visser, 'CSR and the Financial Crisis: Taking Stock', Official Blog of CSR International, 4 November 2008, available at http://csrinternational. blogspot.co.uk/2008/11/csr-and-financial-crisis-taking-stock.html.

Visser has taken a different view on Carroll's classic pyramid.[139] He has changed the emphasis assigned to various responsibilities and reconstructed the order of the corporate responsibility pyramid for developing countries by placing philanthropy as the second highest priority after economic responsibilities, followed by legal and then ethical responsibilities.[140] He has argued that the philanthropic responsibility jumped the queue as the result of strong indigenous traditions of philanthropy in developing countries and companies' reliance on philanthropy as the direct way to improve the prospects of the communities in which their businesses operate.[141] Therefore, in developing countries like China, the impact of the financial crisis on philanthropic responsibility will likely not be as severe as in developed countries. The attitudes and ingrained culture towards philanthropic responsibility is strong, and companies sometimes even equate CSR with philanthropy.[142] However, Visser has suggested that corporations in China should pay more attention to strategic CSR and embedded CSR after the financial crisis. This reflects the lessons learned from corporate governance deficiencies in the aftermath of the financial crisis, so that corporations need to focus on long-term behaviour in terms of CSR through strategic management policies, rather than short-term success and immediate returns; and it will be necessary to understand thoroughly the unique stakeholder groups in each company before it will be possible to take their interests into consideration in such policies. In order to achieve the goal of responsible corporations, attention to CSR must 'bring about a change in business culture so that sustainability objectives become an integral part of corporate strategic planning and routine operational performance'.[143]

---

[139]   A.B. Carroll, 'The Pyramid of Corporate Social Responsibility: Toward the Moral Management of Organizational Stakeholders' (1991) 34 *Business Horizons* 39.

[140]   W. Visser, 'Corporate Social Responsibility in Developing Countries' in A. Crane, A. McWilliams, D. Matten, J. Moon and D. Siegel (eds), *The Oxford Handbook of Corporate Social Responsibility* (Oxford: Oxford University Press, 2008) 473 at 480, 488–92.

[141]   *Ibid.* at 490.

[142]   W. Visser, *The Age of Responsibility: CSR 2.0 and the New DNA of Business* (Chichester: John Wiley & Sons, 2011); see also M. Huniche and E.R. Padersen, *Corporate Citizenship in Developing Countries: New Partnership Perspectives* (Abingdon: Copenhagen Business School Press, 2006).

[143]   F. Martin, 'Corporate Social Responsibility and Public Policy' in R. Mullerate (ed.), *Corporate Social Responsibility: The Corporate Governance of the 21st Century* (London: Kluwer Law International, 2005) ch. 5, p. 77 at p. 78.

Working within Confucian philosophy, the more progressive and enlightened corporate culture will enhance the embedded CSR in China, integrating CSR as another part of the board's responsibility.

Gefei Yin, Director and Vice-President of the China WTO Tribunal and the Development Centre for Chinese CSR, stated in an interview with CSR Europe at the Fourth International CSR Forum, Beijing 5 June 2009, that 'despite the impact of the economic crisis, more and more Chinese enterprises are taking steps to integrate corporate social responsibility into their business practices'.[144] China's economic development is heavily dependent on investment flows and the global trading system's markets. The 2008 financial crisis led to a decrease in demand from abroad and seriously affected China's exports, making the export market more competitive. The negative news and bad press about CSR in China in recent year had a devastating and disproportionate effect on the potential global market.[145] Adoption of CSR, responding to public expectations of CSR and provision of CSR-related information to various stakeholders will not only promote 'Made in China' products globally, but also help attract more investors, especially socially responsible investors, to invest in China. The implementation of CSR will mitigate the conflicts between Chinese companies and their non-domestic and international stakeholders. It will also integrate CSR and corporate citizenship into business strategy and practice in China, to help create important social capital to assist communities to adjust to the harsh realities of global change and enable business to interact with government and non-profit organizations towards a more Harmonious Society.[146]

---

[144]   CSR Europe, 'CSR in China: Building Responsible Competitiveness in Global Supply Chains' (28 May 2009), available at www.csreurope.org/news.php?type&action=show_news&news_id=2368.

[145]   X. Shen and G. Fleming, *'Made in China' and the Drive to Include CSR*, GFC Working Paper 200803 (Centre for Global Finance, Nottingham University, Ningbo), available at www.nottingham.edu.cn/en/gfc/documents/research/gfc research/2008/gfcworkingpaper200803shenximadeinchinaenglish.pdf.

[146]   K.H. Darigan and J.E. Post, 'Corporate Citizenship in China: CSR Challenges in the "Harmonious Society"' (2009) 35 *Journal of Corporate Citizenship* 39 at 40.

6. Promoting more socially responsible corporations through corporate governance and a regulatory framework in China

Mirroring the rapid growth in the Chinese economy, there is an emerging consensus among many leading companies that stakeholders' interests should be protected at least to a certain extent in order to avoid bad publicity and gain a competitive position against their Western counterparts.[1] Following the discussions in the previous chapters on corporate governance and related regulatory responses to corporate social governance (CSR) in corporate law, corporate governance codes, employment law and other regulatory instruments in China, it is clear that the defects and inefficiencies in the Chinese legal system and corporate governance model hinder the effective enforcement of relevant laws. Despite the fact that Chinese companies, especially state-owned enterprises (SOEs) and export-oriented companies, are aware of the growing concerns with respect to CSR, and that the Chinese government has been incorporating CSR standards into the legal system, problems still exist. Occupational accidents, industrial pollution and food poisoning incidents remain common.[2] It is becoming increasingly important to answer the question as to how CSR and stakeholder protection should be dealt with in business practice for the proper management and further development of companies in China through corporate governance model reconstruction and corporate law reform, with developments in other legislative instruments.

Looking back to the definition of CSR itself, one of the first attempts to define CSR suggested that CSR involved a 'relative shift from government to companies as the source of social improvement and the

---

[1] X. Jia and R. Tomasic, *Corporate Governance and Resource Security in China: The Transformation of China's Global Resources Companies* (Abingdon, UK: Routledge, 2010).

[2] D.C. Nicholas, 'China's Labour Enforcement Crisis: International Intervention and Corporate Social Responsibility' (2009) 11 *Scholar* 155 at 170.

means to promote specific items of social welfare'.[3] On the other hand, it is also important to build an environment that will ensure that the CSR strategy is embedded within the company culture while the companies discharge their corporate responsibility in the various levels of the corporate responsibility pyramid. CSR has gradually moved away from purely being regarded as ethical or a commitment to society or local commitments. It has been seen as a means to retain competitiveness and properly manage risk, and even to enhance corporate financial performance.[4] This chapter aims to offer a detailed discussion on promoting more socially responsible companies in China based on the current corporate governance structure, regulatory framework, culture, traditions and stage of economic development. Reform seems necessary in order to make substantial changes to enable corporations and government to implement CSR standards in China more efficiently and effectively.

6.1 DEVELOPING A JOINT AND EFFECTIVE CORPORATE GOVERNANCE SYSTEM

6.1.1 The Hybrid Corporate Governance Model in China

Reforms in legislation such as corporate law, employment law, consumer protection law, media law, insolvency law and environmental law are important in order to provide an institutional guarantee for the realization of the special scheme that makes stakeholder participation possible and achievable. On the one hand, company directors have to consider the interests of various stakeholders when making corporate decisions in order to make profits while observing social morals and business ethics. On the other hand, it is necessary for various stakeholders to understand their positions in the corporation and heighten their awareness in order to protect their lawful rights and interests, and be encouraged to participate actively in corporate decisions where their opinions should be taken into account to promote the success of the company. In addition, directors

---

    [3] M.E. Beesley and T. Evans, *Corporate Social Responsibility: A Reassessment* (London: Taylor & Francis, 1978) p. 13.
    [4] See D.E. Hawkins, *Corporate Social Responsibility: Balancing Tomorrow's Sustainability and Today's Profitability* (Basingstoke: Palgrave Macmillan, 2006); see also J. Hancock, *Investing in Corporate Social Responsibility: A Guide to Best Practice, Business Planning and the UK's Leading Companies* (London: Kogan, 2005).

need to establish an incentive mechanism to promote the attachment of stakeholders to their long-term interests.

The overall objective is not to place limits on the protection of the legitimate interests of stakeholders. This extends to promoting the company in a much more socially responsible and ethical manner, in order to enhance its overall long-term success. The maintenance of long-term success within an individual company is a precondition of a sound corporate governance model. Therefore, in a joint corporate governance model, the interests of shareholders can be legitimately protected by receiving dividends while the stakeholders' lawful interests can also be protected by the creation of a more ethical corporate governance model.

Corporate governance convergence, and pressures from this convergence trend, should enable companies to reconfigure their governance structure towards a more efficient model. Convergence is the result of many factors, including the increasingly large percentage of institutional investors in the shareholder structure; the growing integration of financial and capital markets; increasing numbers of cross-border mergers and acquisitions; and the adoption of statutes for a European company, the so-called *Societas Europaea*. Supporters of the hybrid model have claimed that the reason for convergence is global competition between the corporate governance models.[5] It is believed that the two main models possess equal competitive fitness, so that they will merge into a hybrid model.[6] Such a convergence of archetypal corporate governance models will lead towards a hybrid model that borrows from both the traditional stakeholder and shareholder models, with the right mix of market discipline, corporate regulation and power for corporate stakeholders. This seems to be the direction in which developments in corporate governance convergence are leading, with the purpose of promoting the success of corporations according to the most efficient and responsible measures.

The purpose of establishing this convergent model is essentially to establish a more sound and efficient corporate governance model, which will direct governments and legislators in formulating a unique corporate governance model based on best practice principles. Under this model, the interests of both shareholders and stakeholders, although not always given the same amount of attention, will be considered by company

---

[5] J. Zhao, 'Modernising Corporate Objective Debate towards a Hybrid Model' (2011) 62 *Northern Ireland Legal Quarterly* 361.

[6] R. La Porta, A. Shleifer and R.W. Vishny, 'Legal Determinants of External Finance' (1997) 52 *Journal of Finance* 1131.

directors in order to promote the long-term success of the company as the ultimate purpose of establishing the corporation. Directors should maximize shareholders' gains while corporate decisions should be made in a socially responsible manner and the interests of shareholders should be primarily (but not exclusively) considered. Directors of the company, as the deciding mind of the company, should realize the legal rights of various stakeholders stipulated in employment law, consumer protection law and environmental law. Legislative permission should be given to directors to consider the interests of stakeholders in maximising the long-term interests of the company. The theory of path dependence suggests that governments should employ these principles to establish an ideal corporate governance model which suits their traditions, culture and stage of economic development.

In the case of China, in the broader picture, it is important to establish a mode of joint corporate governance suitable for the reality of modern China, which involves the active and comprehensive participation of various stakeholders, in order to promote the success of the company in the long term.[7] Although there is no doubt that Chinese capitalism has been reshaped and transformed by globalization, the shift in its forms of corporate governance should not necessarily converge towards the dominant model of Anglo-American capitalism. Instead, such a shift opens up new possibilities for a strategic combination of both the old and the new norms and practices, a process leading to the emergence of a hybrid model.[8]

6.1.2   More Effective Corporate Governance Model in China to Accommodate CSR

Just like other countries with transition economies and emerging corporate governance systems, China faces major challenges to establish an effective corporate governance model for its SOEs to ensure that they are competitive and can adapt to the changing demands of the markets.[9] This effective corporate governance system is a modernized one developed by

---

    [7]   S. Mei, 'The Corporate Governance of Listed Companies in China: Some Problems and Solutions' in R. Tomasic (ed.), *Corporate Governance: Challenges for China* (Beijing: Law Press China, 2005) ch. 19, p. 422 at p. 428.
    [8]   H.W.C. Yeung, *Chinese Capitalism in a Global Era: Towards a Hybrid Model* (London: Routledge, 2004) p. 188.
    [9]   L. Zu, *Corporate Social Responsibility, Corporate Restructuring and Firm's Performance* (Berlin: Springer-Verlag, 2009) p. 174.

the authorities to accommodate the profit-oriented and stakeholder-engaged corporate activities, in line with the interests of corporations and social wealth. Reconstruction of the corporate governance model to accommodate CSR has become a key goal for reform, aiming to ensure that SOEs function effectively under a hybrid corporate governance model. Especially following China's entry into the World Trade Organization (WTO) and the integrative forces of economic globalization, corporate governance reform is a key element to enable China to take on a prominent role in the global community. A report by the World Bank and International Finance Corporation, entitled *Corporate Governance and Enterprise Reform in China*,[10] pointed out that corporate governance will continue to be weak in many Chinese SOEs if the role of state ownership remains ambiguous and internal control practices and regulatory supervision are still weak.[11] China's enterprises need to upgrade their decision-making mechanisms in line with international practices and standards, to deal with the increased competition from other member states within the WTO and to attract more capital and investors from the global stock markets.[12]

The governance and structural reform of the SOEs, which suffer from the imposition of non-commercial objectives by the state, will be the main problem in this reform agenda. A key question is how to give directors of SOEs more incentives for them to manage the SOEs more efficiently and overcome the potential problem of managerialism. This difficulty is primarily caused by the ambiguity of property rights related to state ownership without a clearly accountable representative of the state to monitor the performance of the directors in SOEs.[13] The separation of state ownership interests in SOEs from the government's regulatory function, and the setting up of internal governance mechanisms to provide incentives and accountability for directors to act in the interests of the shareholders to promote the success of the corporation,

[10] S. Tenev, C. Zhang and L. Brefort, *Corporate Governance and Enterprise Reform in China: Building the Institutions of Modern Market* (Washington, DC: World Bank and International Finance Corporation, 2002).
[11] *Ibid.* at 59.
[12] See also L. Wong, 'Corporate Governance in China: A Lack of Critical Reflexivity?' in C.R. Lehman, T. Tinker, B. Merino and M. Neimark (eds), *Corporate Governance: Does Any Size Fit?* (Oxford: Elsevier, 2005) p. 117 at p. 118.
[13] S. Estrin, 'State Ownership, Corporate Governance and Privatization' in OECD (ed.), *State-owned Enterprises and Privatization* (Paris: OECD, 1998); D. Pannier, *Corporate Governance of Public Enterprises in Transitional Economies* (Washington, DC: World Bank, 1996).

are regarded as two major objectives in this revolutionary reform.[14] However, achieving these goals is not an easy task in China. In the emerging corporate governance system, reforms to SOEs are particularly challenging due to lack of support for internal governance practices from external disciplinary mechanisms, such as efficient financial markets and competitive product and factor markets, and a lack of efficient gate-keepers, which in developed legal systems include enforcement mechanisms and accounting and auditing frameworks.[15]

The transformation of SOEs under the pressure of intense market competition has been regarded as an important pathway to solve the inherent inefficiencies and agency problems in the emerging corporate governance markets.[16] The creation of various new business organizations with different combinations of state and non-state shareholders, including cooperative enterprises, companies limited by shares and limited liability companies, are important signs of this transformation. In line with this transformation, separation of the state's ownership function from its regulatory function is one of the most direct objectives in the SOE reforms. This could be carried out by creating separate non-conflict-of-interests agencies to manage state assets according to commercial principles, with the government delegating its ownership responsibility in order to maintain efficient management and the internal government mechanism function.[17] A systematic reform has been carried out in China to oversee and manage state assets by creating a three-tier institutional network at the national, provincial, and municipal government levels. First, at the highest national level, the State Council serves as the owner of assets of SOEs while the National Administrative Bureau of the State-Owned Property acts as the administrative arm for the Council. Secondly, at the provincial and municipal levels, State Asset Management Committees, organized as a government department composed of heads of major departments of the municipality and chaired by the mayor, act

[14] L. Zu, *Corporate Social Responsibility, Corporate Restructuring and Firm's Performance* (Berlin: Springer-Verlag, 2009) p. 174.

[15] C. Lin, *Corporatisation and Corporate Governance in China's Economic Transition*, Department of Economic Discussion Paper Series (Oxford: Oxford University Press, 2000).

[16] S. Li, J. Xia, C.X. Long and J. Tan, 'Control Modes and Outcomes of Transformed State-owned Enterprises in China: An Empirical Test' (2011) 8 *Management and Organization Review* 1; see also W.L. Megginson and J.M. Netter, 'From State to Market: A Survey of Empirical Studies on Privatization' (2001) 36 *Journal of Economic Literature* 321.

[17] L. Zu, *Corporate Social Responsibility, Corporate Restructuring and Firm's Performance* (Berlin: Springer-Verlag, 2009) p. 177.

as similar upper-level bodies that are responsible for preserving and increasing the value of state assets which oversee many state-holding companies. The state-holding companies (which accounted for 57 per cent of the 2,154 large industrial companies in 2004), have been constituted by transforming the traditional government bureaus and manage the assets of SOEs entrusted to their responsibility.[18]

6.2   REFORM OF THE SOCIAL SECURITY SYSTEM IN CHINA

With the reform of corporate governance and shareholding structures, various employment-related CSR problems have become the main concern of the government and enterprises. These problems include a large number of redundancies and lay-offs arising as the result of the restructuring process and the transformation of the economy, and the question of reform of health and pension programmes, which is essential to reduce the burdens on enterprises and in the light of China's ageing society.

6.2.1   Reforms Concerning Lay-offs and Redundant Workers

Following the reconstruction of the corporate forms and corporate privatization, three key social dimensions need to be addressed by the Chinese government, including enhanced social service provision through transfer of social assets from state industrial enterprises to non-state operators or municipalities; dealing with unemployment problems; and the funding of social security liabilities. Redundancies and lay-offs arising out of corporate restructuring and privatization have eroded the state workers' secured permanent contract, the 'iron rice bowl'. In order to improve the efficiency and productivity of SOEs, one of the major approaches was the reconstruction of the lifelong employment policy. In order to control overstaffing while avoiding social unrest from widespread redundancies, many SOEs adopted extremely gradual transitional measures, while a common practice has been to lay off surplus worker but treat them as 'internal retirees' who receive only a very basic level of salary plus associated welfare benefits. The numbers of workers laid off in the years 1996 to 2000 were 7.2, 7.87, 6.1, 6.5 and 6.57 million,

---

[18]   'State-holding companies represent 57 per cent of China's large enterprises', *Xinhua News Agency*, 21 October 2005, available at http://english. peopledaily.com.cn/200510/21/eng20051021_215899.html.

respectively.[19] It was reported that 4.1 million workers had been laid off by SOEs, along with 2 million or so from non-state enterprises, by the end of 2002.[20] According to statistics published by Xie, career opportunities for the laid-off workers were not very favourable. The re-employment rate for those laid off by SOEs declined from 42 per cent in 1999, to 36 per cent in 2000, to 30 per cent in 2001, and the number of registered jobless in cities reached 7.1 million (4 per cent of the overall labour force) by the end of 2002.[21] These statistics demonstrate the need for social security reform to reduce the financial burden on corporations, and to provide a secure social security system to deal with the side-effects of economic reform and industrial restructuring in China and ensure basic necessary living expenses for a transitional period for redundant workers.

The initial strategy in China for providing for the basic needs of laid-off workers relied heavily on 're-employment centres'. Working through re-employment agencies jointly managed by local government labour and finance bureaus and trade unions, these centres had three principal functions: providing basic living expenses; training or retraining the workers to enhance their employability; and assisting them to find new jobs. However, in practice their priorities were not clearly set out, and they were used mostly for distributing living allowances rather than providing re-employment services.[22] The main aim of their establishment was to facilitate a better allocation of support between companies and the government. Based on figures published by the Ministry of Labour and Social Security, more than 6 million workers were registered with re-employment centres by the end of 1998, and that number had increased to 11.9 million by the end of 1999.[23]

The re-employment centres were replaced in 2002 by new unemployment insurance arrangements, although the system was first established in 1985 to ensure that urban unemployed workers had a basic living

---

[19]   H.Y. Lee, '*Xiagang*, the Chinese Style of Laying off Workers' (2000) 40 *Asian Survey* 914.

[20]   F. Xie, 'Employing the unemployed', *China Daily*, 8 August 2003.

[21]   *Ibid.*

[22]   G.O.M. Lee and M. Warner, 'The Shanghai Re-employment Model: From Local Experiment to Nation-wide Labour Market Policy' (2004) 177 *China Quarterly* 174.

[23]   See Ministry of Human Resources and Social Security of People's Republic of China, 'Policy and Statistics (*Guihua Yu Tongji*)', available at www.mohrss.gov.cn/page.do?pa=8a81f3f1314779a101314ab910170566.

allowance.[24] With the expansion and reform of the system, the ultimate goals of the unemployment insurance system is to provide interim support for unemployed workers, relax constraints on corporations' ability to adjust labour forces, and improve labour market integration and labour mobility.[25] Regulations on Unemployment Insurance of People's Republic of China were adopted at the Eleventh Executive Meeting of the State Council on 26 December 1999, to 'guarantee basic living of the unemployed during the unemployment period and promote their re-employment'.[26] The participants in the unemployment insurance scheme are urban and rural enterprises and institutions, as well as their workers. Under these Regulations, coverage has been extended to all urban and rural workers, including those in SOEs, collectively owned enterprises, enterprises with foreign investment and private companies.[27] It is stipulated that enterprises must pay unemployment insurance at a rate of 2 per cent on the basis of their total amount of salaries, while the workers must pay 1 per cent of their salary though a payroll deduction.[28] Despite the adoption of the Regulations and internalization of the Chinese unemployment insurance system, it still faces many important policy dilemmas and changes.[29] Like the establishment of CSR in Chinese corporations, the unemployment insurance system developed with the transformation of the Chinese economic structure and the privatization of SOEs. Resources and Social Security of China have identified three main phases of the unemployment insurance system: phase 1 on establishment of the basic framework (1986 to 1993); phase 2 on further adjustment of the unemployment insurance system (1993 to early 1999); and phase 3 on the gradual improvement of the unemployment insurance system (early 1999 to present).

In order to continue the Chinese economic transformation while at the same time enhancing social development, the Chinese government should consider reform and improvement of China's existing unemployment

---

[24]   M. Vodopivec and M. H. Tong, *China: Improving Unemployment Insurance*, Social Protection and Labour World Bank Discussion Paper No. 0820 (2008) pp. 1–2.

[25]   L. Zu, *Corporate Social Responsibility, Corporate Restructuring and Firm's Performance* (Berlin: Springer-Verlag, 2009) p. 187.

[26]   Regulations on Unemployment Insurance of People's Republic of China 1999 art. 1.

[27]   *Ibid.* art. 2.

[28]   *Ibid.* art. 6.

[29]   M. Vodopivec and M.H. Tong, *China: Improving Unemployment Insurance*, Social Protection and Labour World Bank Discussion Paper No. 0820 (2008) p. 1.

insurance system by learning from international experiences.[30] Deficiencies of the system which fail to meet the current requirements include the narrow coverage of the unemployment insurance; the low level of benefits and incomplete items for unemployment insurance fund expenditure; the weak role of the system in promoting re-employment; the fact that the unemployment insurance system plays no role in stabilising employment and preventing unemployment; and difficulties in dealing with regional differences.[31] Considering these problems as a whole, it is important to make changes to the scheme in the areas of scope of insurance coverage; level of security;[32] efficient use of unemployment insurance funds in employment promotion; increasing the capacity of the system to promote employment stabilization; and enhancing the flexibility of the existing system in local conditions.[33] The reforms should be carried out with the objectives of reducing unemployment, and efficiently pooling the social funds to guarantee the basic livelihood of those workers who are temporarily unemployed through a moderate level of benefits, administered by efficient unemployment insurance management agencies.[34]

6.2.2   Reforms of the Health and Pension Systems

Health and pension programmes in China are now largely confined to urban workers and residents. Before the privatization, SOEs were fully responsible for the medical costs of their employees under a full

---

[30]   Z. Wang, 'Major Issues to be Addressed in the Establishment and Development of China's Unemployment Insurance System' in *EU-China Social Security Reform Co-operation Project, Unemployment Insurance Reform Seminar* (2008) p. 13 at p. 17.

[31]   J. You, 'The Basic Situation of China's Unemployment Insurance System' in *EU-China Social Security Reform Co-operation Project, Unemployment Insurance Reform Seminar* (2008) p. 30 at p. 32.

[32]   Based on the current employment, the unemployment insurance benefit is normally only 60–80 per cent of minimum pay.

[33]   Z. Wang, 'Major Issues to be Addressed in the Establishment and Development of China's Unemployment Insurance System' in *EU-China Social Security Reform Co-operation Project, Unemployment Insurance Reform Seminar* (2008) p. 13 at p. 17.

[34]   See Z. Qu, *The Historical Review and Current Reflections on Unemployment Insurance (Zhongguo Shiye Baoxian Lishi Huigu Jiqi Sikao)* (Shanghai: Shanghai Social Science Academy Press, 2009); S. Guo, *Unemployment Insurance System and Reemployment in China (Zhongguo Shiye Baozhang Zhidu Yu Zaijiuye)* (Shanghai: Shanghai University of Finance and Economics Press, 2008).

reimbursement system (*baoxiao zhidu*) and SOEs were compensated for these expenses by government appropriations until the mid-1980s. After that, the SOEs became responsible for their own expenses and profitability and the government in principle withdraw the reimbursement for medical care. A new health reform plan was drafted in 1993 in order to reduce the financial burdens on SOEs and increase the employees' responsibility for the cost of their own health care. The plan involves a two-tier system of benefits, comprising an individual medical account through contribution of 2 per cent of employees' salaries, and a community pool through further contributions from corporations worth 6 per cent of employees' salaries (30 per cent of this contribution goes into the individual account and the remainder into the community pool). Payment of medical expenses is made from the individual account and employees are responsible for additional expenses. As regards the Chinese government's policy on health care, it has been argued that China is going too far with privatization and is 'beginning to discover that market forces alone cannot produce good health care'.[35] Therefore, a combined model somewhere between a purely government delivery model and a model driven purely by profit incentives has been suggested for China's health system, to suit China's hybrid economy.[36] On the government side, the government with the Central Committee of the Communist Party announced a major comprehensive health reform taking effect in April 2010 and committed RMB 850 billion over three years to the hybrid health system.[37] The multiple stakeholders of society, government and private health sectors make this a leading initiative for CSR-related issues.[38] Many discussions have been focused on the relationship between CSR and epidemic diseases, and other serious diseases that need

---

[35] 'Where are the Patients?', special report, *The Economist*, 21 August 2004, p. 20 at p. 24.

[36] C. Ho, 'China's Health Care Reform: Background and Policies' in C.W. Freeman and X.L. Boynton, *Implementing Health Care Reform Policies in China: Challenges and Opportunities, A Report of the CSIC Freeman Chair in China Studies* (Centre for Strategic International Studies, 2011).

[37] China Information Centre, *Opinions of the Central Committee of the Chinese Communist Party and the State Council on Deepening the Health Care System Reform* (Communist Party of China Central Committee, State Council, National Development and Reform Commission, 2009).

[38] S. Lee, *Implementing Corporate Social Responsibility in Health Sector*, EU-China Business Management Training Project Research Project No. 003 (2005).

special attention from the public and private sectors.[39] Many CSR policies and programmes fit together with the government's priorities in various spheres, including health care. Despite the fact that the general public may not be aware of the existence of enterprises' CSR initiatives, health care-related policies have become part of corporate responsibilities that are driven by the relationship with government.[40] In the opinion of the author, a model which blends the twin poles of 'market' and 'government' is most likely to work in the long term to enable the Chinese government to achieve its goals with sufficient balance at the different levels.

Nearly half of all Chinese now live in cities, and the proportion of the population above the age of 60 had risen to 13.3 per cent by 2010, up nearly 3 per cent since 2000.[41] The demographics of China present formidable problems for the pension programme and related reforms. Until the late 1980s, China had always maintained an urban- and enterprise-based 'pay as you go' pension system that covered mainly SOEs and some large collective enterprises.[42] In 1991, Document No. 33 of the State Council called for the establishment of a three-tier system, with a supplementary pension scheme funded by mandatory contributions from enterprises and individuals. Since 1993, major reforms in pension schemes have been instituted by the authorities in order to achieve goals including providing a more sustainable funding mechanism to meet current needs, reducing the burdens on SOEs as the result of the pension schemes, and extending the coverage of the pension programme to non-state sectors.[43] By 1999, the new pensions network had been expanded to cover millions of retirees, including in the non-state sectors. However, the reforms had not helped to reduce the financial burdens on SOEs from pension schemes.

---

[39]   K.M. Leisinger, 'The Corporate Social Responsibility of the Pharmaceutical Industry: Idealism without Illusion and Realism without Resignation' (2005) 15 *Business Ethics Quarterly* 577; A.K. Nussbaum, 'Ethical Corporate Social Responsibility and the Pharmaceutical Industry: A Happy Couple?' (2009) 9 *Journal of Medical Marketing* 67.

[40]   J. Mullich, 'Corporate Social Responsibility Emerges in China' (2010) *Wall Street Journal*, available at http://online.wsj.com/ad/article/chinaenergy-responsibility.

[41]   'China census shows population aging and urban', *BBC News*, 28 April 2011, available at www.bbc.co.uk/news/world-asia-pacific-13218733.

[42]   J. Ma and F. Zhai, 'Financing China's Pension Reform', paper prepared for Conference on Financial Sector Reform in China (2001) p. 1.

[43]   L. Zu, *Corporate Social Responsibility, Corporate Restructuring and Firm's Performance* (Berlin: Springer-Verlag, 2009) p. 189.

By the end of 2008, around 40 per cent of the 775 million workers in China were covered by the Basic Old Age Insurance system, the rural pension system or the pension plans of the state organization and public institutions, while the remaining individuals were covered by the Minimum Life Security system.[44] The success of further pension reform still requires the combined support from enterprises, individuals and local governments. Although not seemingly directly related to the issue of CSR, progress in the reforms of the pension schemes and health system will require help from enterprises and corporations to make the benefits more enforceable and effective and to satisfy the basic needs of their employees.

6.3   CAPITALIZATION ON HUMAN CAPITAL

Investment in human capital contributes significantly to productivity growth, especially for high technology science companies. It is one of the huge successes of the modern corporation to be able to attract the talent of workers, who might otherwise have been independent entrepreneurs, without offering them ownership or control, or even an obligation on directors to consider employees' interests.[45] The employees, as providers of human capital, play a key role in fostering innovation and alteration within the company.

In the new economy, the information obtained by consumers will create demand for customized products, which will inevitably result in a more demanding role for employee initiative and creativity. The value of intellectual property is becoming increasingly crucial in the knowledge-driven economy. The knowledge, talent and technology of employees, like electricity, are in a form that exists only when it is being used.[46] Employees make valuable investments in the wealth-creating activities of the company through the accumulation of non-transferable knowledge.[47]

---

[44]   Ministry of Human Resources and Social Security of China (MOHRSS) database, available at www.mohrss.gov.cn/SYrlzyhshbzb/zwgk/szrs; see also World Bank, *Urban Di Bao in China: Building on Success* (World Bank Report, 2007).
[45]   C.L. Fisk, 'Knowledge Work: New Metaphors for the New Economy' (2005) 80 *Chicago-Kent Law Review* 839 at 843.
[46]   P. Drucker, 'Leadership: More Doing than Dash' in P. Drucker, *Managing for the Future* (London: Butterworth-Heinemann, 1992) ch. 15, pp. 119–25.
[47]   A.M. Robinson and H. Zhang, 'Employee Share Ownership: Safeguarding Investment in Human Capital' (2005) 43 *British Journal of Industrial Relations* 469 at 471.

Without proper incentives, employees would be discouraged from committing themselves to investment in non-transferable skills, preferring instead to make investments in more generic skills that they can take elsewhere.[48] Corporations, in the new economy, should encourage and protect their valued human capital and make them prosper.[49] Company directors should identify and encourage the development of their 'human assets' in terms of individuals, in order to contribute to the company's success, taking into account their employees' highly subjective tastes and idiosyncratic ways of thinking.[50] Therefore, directors should pay special attention to employees as key stakeholders, in order to secure their legal rights. It is important to connect the interests of shareholders, employees and managers through human capitalization to ensure that the owners of the human capital promote the interests of the entire business organization as well as shareholders.

In countries like China, where development of corporate governance is in its early stages, employees should be offered more information about the company. Also, training sessions should be offered to directors to enable them to understand both domestic and international legal requirements, and should give their local managers sufficient training in relevant legal requirements and local regulations.

6.4   REFORM OF EMPLOYMENT PARTICIPATION

Under articles 45 and 109 of Chinese Company Law (CCL) 2006, for the first time, non-SOEs are allowed to include representatives of their employees on the board of directors. These articles correct the misunderstanding that employees are 'hosts of the country' who are only allowed to participate in corporate governance decisions if employed in SOEs. The CCL reconfirms the important position of employees as a primary stakeholder group in all forms of company in China. However, despite making provision allowing the company to include representatives of its employees on the board of directors, the CCL 2006 contains no stipulations regarding the percentage or exact number of employee directors on the board, which could render the employee director provision a purely

---

[48]   *Ibid.* at 471.
[49]   *Ibid.* at 469–70.
[50]   J. Aoi, 'To Whom Does the Company Belong? A New Management Mission for the Information Age' in D.H. Cew (ed.), *Studies in International Corporate Finance and Governance System: A Comparison of the U.S., Japan, and Europe* (Oxford: Oxford University Press, 1997) p. 244 at p. 247.

token gesture. The percentage or the number of employees who can sit on the board of directors should therefore be stipulated in detail, to ensure that these requirements are more than just hollow provisions which are difficult to implement.

Since the enactment of the first CCL in 1994, there has been a shift in the form of employee participation, from corporate management participation to capital management participation. There have been a series of local legislative instruments concerning employees' stock ownership.[51] With respect to employees' stock ownership plans, the system in China focuses more on raising capital for the corporation rather than for the employees themselves. This misunderstanding about the purpose of employee participation makes the development of stock ownership difficult and slow in China.

There is a new stipulation in CCL 2006 on employee incentives through an employee share ownership scheme, which has always been regarded as one of most important forms of employee participation in the United States and Japan. The employee shareholder ownership plans (known as ESOPs) have attracted the interest of policy-makers, managers and employees for a variety of reasons. ESOPs are believed to be effective in enhancing social cohesion and equality by distributing the fruits of economic success more directly.[52] According to CCL 2006 article 143:

'a company shall not purchase its own shares except under any of the following conditions: ... (3) where the company is to offer its shares to its staff and workers as a reward ... The shares of the company purchased by the company in accordance with the provisions of Item (3) of Paragraph 1 shall not exceed 5% of the total amount of the shares issued by the company; ... the shares purchased shall be transferred to the staff and workers within one year upon the purchase.

Apart from the relevant stipulation in the CCL, the Measures for the Administration of the Equity Incentives of Listed Companies were

---

[51]   These local legislative instruments included: Temporary Stipulations on Employees' Stock Ownership, 6 March 1996; Temporary Stipulations on Committee of Employees' Stock Ownership in Tianjin City, 23 May 1996; and Temporary Stipulations on Internal Employees' Stock Ownership in SOEs in Shenzhen City, 20 September 1997.

[52]   See D. Kruse, 'Economic Democracy or Just another Risk for Workers? Reviewing the Evidence on Employee Ownership and Profit Share', paper presented at Columbia University Conference on Democracy, Participation and Development (1999).

introduced in 2006. According to these Measures, listed companies may use their own shares as the subject matter of long-term incentives provided to their directors, senior management and core technological professionals, and other employees may benefit from the related incentives.

Unlike in developed countries, managerial and employee shareholdings are extremely small in China.[53] For the first time in the CCL 2006, the ownership of shares by employees was legalized and an employee stock ownership scheme was created. The provision directly connects the employees' interests with the economic profits of the company in order to promote alterations and innovation within the company (provided primarily by employees). This provision can be regarded as another big step forward by the Chinese government in corporate decision-making in order to promote stakeholders' interests and enhance CSR in China. However, this provision is only a soft stipulation, which is limited to permitting employee stock ownership schemes, without powers of enforcement. The scheme stipulated in CCL 2006 is still far from being a systemic scheme compared to a well-developed employee share ownership system. The stipulations in CCL 2006 concerning employee participation should be as detailed as possible to minimize the opportunism of directors in avoiding these provisions. More detailed legislation dealing with employee participation will be required not only in company law but also in employment law, state regulation and legislative explanation from courts to strengthen employment participation schemes in China.

6.5 ENHANCING THE PUBLIC REGULATION OF CORPORATE SOCIAL RESPONSIBILITY

6.5.1 Justifications and Rules for Public Regulation

Public regulation of CSR in the current situation in China means that government authorities, social organizations and citizens[54] regulate, supervise and encourage behaviours and decisions of companies which

---

[53] J. Yang, J. Chi and M. Young, 'A Review of Corporate Governance in China' (2011) 25 *Asian-Pacific Economic Literature* 15 at 17.

[54] The government is actively encouraging individual citizens to supervise corporate activities. For example, it is stipulated in art. 4 of the Law against Unfair Competition in China that 'all the regulations on unfair competitions by individuals should be encouraged, supported and protected by government'; also it is stipulated in art. 6 of the Consumer Protection Law of China that 'all the

observe CSR and pursue ethical purposes, according to the law, company policy and ethical codes. This supervision and regulation plays an active role in improving companies' social behaviour and enhancing their social responsibilities to ensure companies are responsive to public social interests. With economic power coming from the public, a corporation, in promoting the company's interests, thereby also promotes the public interest of the entire society, and corporations should therefore willingly and actively accept public regulation. This will not only act to remind and affirm ethical corporations in fulfilling their social responsibilities, but will also enable the setting of minimum standards for those corporations with poor ethical behaviours and prevent them from acting unethically.

There are a few rules which should be followed in the process of public regulation. First, the individuals or organizations who are entitled to regulate companies' social behaviour should be specifically authorized government authorities, administrative authorities or legal authorities. Alongside those authorities, other non-profit-making organizations, such as committees for product quality control, committees for customers and the media, can also play a regulatory role, although the form of regulation is different due to their differing legal relationships with the company. Secondly, the authorized individuals or organizations, apart from supervising various corporate production and management activities such as manufacturing, procurement of raw materials, selling the product, promotional advertisement, competitions and external corporate investment, should also consider the strategies the company adopts in promoting or overriding CSR. Finally, public regulation should be carried out strictly according to the law.

6.5.2 Forms of Public Regulation

Technical regulation
Both metrology regulation and quality regulation are included in technical regulation. Metrology regulation includes 'establishing national primary standards of measurement, conducting metrological verification, and the manufacture, repair, sale or use of measuring instruments'[55] in order to 'strengthen the metrological regulation and administration, to ensure the uniformity of the national system of units of measurement and

---

regulations on legal rights of consumers by individuals should be encouraged, supported and protected by government'.
[55] Metrology Law of the People's Republic of China 1986 art. 2.

the accuracy and reliability of the values of quantities, so as to contribute to the development of production, trade and science and technology, to meet the needs of socialist modernisation and to safeguard the interests of the state and the people.[56] Although the Metrology Law 1986 has a series of stipulations concerning standards of measurement, metrological verification, administrative control of measuring instruments and metrological regulation, with the development of highly accurate scientific technology and the introduction of new measuring instruments, the current Metrology Law needs updating.

In the case of quality regulation, the body of Law on Product Quality has been 'enacted to strengthen the regulation and control over product quality, to define the liability for product quality, to protect the legitimate rights and interests of users and consumers and to safeguard the socio-economic order'.[57] However, specific legislation on quality regulation is badly needed. It is apparent that self-regulation and government quality regulation using public authorities are of limited utility. Therefore, public awareness of product quality regulations is significant for quality regulation.

Financial regulation
Accounting regulation and certified public accountant (CPA) regulation are included in financial regulation. Accounting regulation means that the accounting department and the accountant of each company supervises and inspects the business and corporate actions according to the rights and programmes stipulated by accounting law. Accounting regulation is the internal regulation of the company's accounting procedures, while CPA regulation forms an external regulation of the company. They work together for the purposes of 'standardising accounting behaviour, ensuring the authenticity and completeness of accounting documents, strengthening economic management and financial management, improving economic effects and safeguarding the order of socialist market economy'.[58]

In practice, and in the light of the specific economic transactions and operational matters, accounting regulation includes inspection of original accounting vouchers, a financial records audit, and identifying any illegal income and expenses.[59] CPAs are professionals who have 'obtained the certificate of certified public accountant according to law and are

---

[56] *Ibid.* art. 1.
[57] Law on Product Quality of People's Republic of China 2000 art. 1.
[58] Accounting Law of the People's Republic of China 1999 art. 1.
[59] *Ibid.* arts 27–35.

commissioned to offer auditing, accounting consultancy and other accounting services'.[60] It is important to enhance regulation by the CPA in order to promote public social interests and the interests of investors. Apart from accounting consultancy and accounting services,[61] registered public accountants also undertake audit services, including (1) examining the accounting statements of enterprises and producing audit reports; (2) verifying the capital of enterprises and producing capital verification reports; (3) dealing with audit services in matters of merger, division or liquidation of enterprises and production of the relevant reports; and (4) other audit services stipulated by relevant laws and administrative rules and regulations.[62]

Government auditing regulation
Government auditing regulation is a typical regulation procedure in China, in which the government plays a key role in the public regulation of CSR. In government auditing regulation, auditing institutions conduct regulation through audit in accordance with their functions and powers, as well as the procedures prescribed by law.[63] Specifically, these institutions should supervise the authenticity, legality and beneficial results of budgetary revenues and expenditures or financial revenues and expenditures.[64] Government auditing regulation, working with CPA regulation as a complete social auditing system in China, aims to maintain the financial and economic order of the country and to build an uncorrupted government.

Furthermore, modern legislators focus on both the stipulations themselves and the justice of the legislative procedure. According to article 5 of the Audit Law and articles 91 and 109 of the Constitution of the People's Republic of China, audit institutions should exercise their powers of regulation through auditing in accordance with the law independently, without interference by any administrative organ, public organization or individual. Government auditing institutions should avoid abuse of their auditing rights or neglecting to execute their rights in order to achieve an efficient auditing result.

---

[60] Law of the People's Republic of China on Certified Public Accountants 1993 art. 2.
[61] *Ibid.* art. 15.
[62] *Ibid.* art. 14.
[63] Audit Law of the People's Republic of China 2006 art. 3.
[64] *Ibid.* art. 4.

6.6   RECENT CHINESE CORPORATE SCANDALS AND THE FUTURE OF CSR IN CHINA

The challenge of developing a structure for business ethics in China in response to today's increasing demands for CSR can be examined within the context of recent business scandals, food scares,[65] labour issues[66] and environmental degradations.[67] From 14 to 16 September 2008, He Bei Province, where San Lu Milk Powder Company is situated, destroyed 5,936 tons of milk as waste.[68] And 700 tons of San Lu baby milk powder had been contaminated with melamine, to meet company requirements for protein content in the short-term interests of the shareholders. As a result of consuming the contaminated milk, infants allegedly suffered diseases such as kidney stones. According to incomplete statistics, nearly 7,000 infants were involved in this scandal, some of whom were in hospital for a prolonged period, 150 had serious kidney failure after consuming the milk powder, and three infants died. On 25 September 2008, more than 700 dairy enterprises in China made a quality commitment to consumers following the San Lu scandal through the General Administration of Quality Supervision, Inspection and Quarantine.

---

[65]   M. Liu, 'Unsafe at any speed: the downside of China's manufacturing boom: deadly goods wreaking havoc at home and abroad', *Newsweek*, 16 July 2007, pp. 14–17; Z. Li, 'Lack of corporate social responsibility behind recent China accident', *China Watch, World Institute Vision for a Sustainable World*, 12 December 2005, available at www.worldwatch.org/node/3859.

[66]   'Several hundred bereaved families of 166 miners killed in Shanxi coal mine explosion protest false death toll and news blockade', *China Labour Bulletin*, 30 May 2007; J. Kahn, 'Making trinkets in China and a deadly dust', *New York Times*, 18 June 2003.

[67]   See 'A Great Wall of Waste, Special Report: China's Environment', *The Economist*, 21 August 2004; E.C. Economy, *The River Runs Black: The Environmental Challenge to China's Future* (Ithaca, NY: Cornell University Press, 2001); M. Forney, 'Pouring Cash' (2004) *Time* (October) 18 at 36–9; H.W. French, 'Chinese success story chokes on its own growth', *New York Times*, 19 December 2006; B. Walsh, 'Choking on Growth', *The New York Times*, 13 December 2004 at 16–23.

[68]   Of course, this is a recent case, but food and drug safety has always been a worrying issue in China. In August 2007, Mattel twice recalled millions of toxic toys manufactured in China; in May 2007, China probed reports that contaminated toothpaste had been exported to the United States; in March 2007, melamine was found in wheat gluten made in China for use in pet food in at least 100 pet food brands; in August 2006, after eating partially cooked snails in a chain of restaurants, around 40 people in Beijing contracted meningitis; in 2004, 13 babies died of malnutrition as a result of consuming bad-quality milk powder.

Former Premier Wen Jiabao reassured the world that China will continue to offer safe products at home and abroad in the aftermath of the tainted milk scandal, in his speech at the World Economic Forum in Tianjin on 27 September 2008. As the representative of the government, he helpfully acknowledged that 'the incident is not over yet and it is not just food or milk[69] made in China that should be made safe for consumers. Wen also admitted the weaknesses in production supervision in China[70] and regarded the scandal as a reminder to the government that they should pay more attention to business ethics and social morality.[71]

This scandal may have had its basis in failures in health and safety requirements for products which fall outside the scope of CSR. However, the pursuit of short-term corporate profits regardless of customers' rights is the result of ignoring stakeholders' interests and CSR. The blame for this ignorance should not only rest with the milk powder provider; the entire supply chain should all be held at least partly responsible. Government authorities, organizations and citizens should regulate, supervise and encourage behaviours and actions of companies which observe CSR and which pursue corporate ethical purposes according to the law, company policies and ethical codes. The scandal also suggests that, although seemingly a hybrid corporate governance model has been adopted in China and directors are required under the CCL 2006 to consider the interests of stakeholders, and observe business ethics and social morality, the enforcement of these requirements and the practical social responsibility level in China is far from satisfactory.

Such irresponsible behaviour by corporations has not only brought bad consequences for customers, it has also left shareholders with no return on their investments. Furthermore, the serious social consequences of such scandals can result in broad negative effects, not only for the company's stakeholders but also for the international reputation of other companies operating a similar business. When countries become brands, changing the image of a nation is neither easy nor quick.[72] It is

---

[69] Quoted from the speech of former Premier Wen Jiabao to the World Economic Forum, Annual Meeting of the New Champions of 2008, Tianjin, 27–28 September 2008.

[70] As to supervision and regulation of corporations to protect the interests of stakeholders and promote business ethics and sustainability of corporations, see 6.4.4 above.

[71] This is consistent with new legislative principles set out in the CCL 2006; for more detailed arguments see 6.2.1 above.

[72] S. Anholt, *Brand New Justice: The Upside of Global Branding* (Oxford: Butterworth-Heinemann, 2003) ch. 5.

influenced by many factors including 'wars, religion, diplomacy or the lack of, international sporting triumphs or disasters, famous and infamous sons and daughters'.[73] It is important to promote 'China' as a positive brand through effective corporate governance, in order to attract more institutional shareholders and loyal foreign customers. Moreover, it will be easier for China to attract high-quality employees if 'China becomes recognized as a good brand in which to invest human capital. Globalization and the new economy have raised serious questions about the continuing viability of traditional governance practices in Chinese capitalism.[74] The Chinese corporate governance model, instead of converging with any of the archetypal models, is opening up new possibilities for an evolutionary process that could lead to a unique hybrid model. This currently immature model will need to be based on hybrid model principles in order to help Chinese corporations to deal with social and ethical problems[75] and gain credibility and legitimacy in the international business and finance community through their enrolment in globalizing actor-networks.[76] The integration of ethical rules in the practices of Chinese corporations will promote 'China' as a brand.

While its emerging economic system resembles those economies which reject a planned framework,[77] China is arguably more multifaceted, and far less willing to accept Western notions regarding workers' individual rights, democracy in the workplace and many of the social demands developed in the West.[78] However, China is still searching for

---

[73]   *Ibid.* at 116.
[74]   H.W.C. Yeung, *Chinese Capitalism in a Global Era: Towards a Hybrid Model* (London: Routledge, 2004) p. 188.
[75]   Such as corruption, concerns over intellectual property rights, environmental abuses, labour unrest, and other social equality issues.
[76]   H.W.C. Yeung, *Chinese Capitalism in a Global Era: Towards a Hybrid Model* (London: Routledge, 2004) p. 188; see also H.W. Yeung, 'International/ Transnational Entrepreneurship and Chinese Business Research' in L.P. Dana (ed.), *The Handbook of Research on International Entrepreneurship* (Cheltenham: Edward Elgar, 2004) p. 73.
[77]   See P.C. Wright, W.F. Szeto and S.K. Lee, 'Ethical Perceptions in China: The Reality of Business Ethics in an International Context' (2004) 41 *Management Decision* 180; G.F. Woodbine, 'Moral Choice and the Declining Influence of Traditional Value Orientation within the Financial Sector of a Rapidly Developing Region of the People's Republic of China' (2004) 55 *Journal of Business Ethics* 43.
[78]   H. von W. Hoivik, 'East Meets West: Tacit Messages about Business Ethics in Stories Told by Chinese Managers' (2007) 74 *Journal of Business Ethics* 457 at 459.

new ways to improve the present ethical situation[79] in order to promote the long-term success of its companies. With her unique hybrid corporate governance model, China still has a long way to go in order to match internationally competitive levels of ethical and social responsibility. Advanced ethical codes and other management systems and tools (especially strategic management systems) do not necessarily function equally well in China unless they are reassessed and adapted.[80] It is left to the Chinese government and individual company directors to identify the differences between the Chinese economy and the West, and to look for common perspectives in order to identify the usefulness of such tools and 'find the most pragmatic approach to align the differences without compromising either'.[81] Realistically speaking, the present stage of development should focus on extensive learning, sustained by long-term adaptation in a dialogue-based process. Efforts have to be made both from government and individual business organizations to establish integrity in business, social trust in corporations both domestically and internationally, and the harmonization of the entire society.

---

[79] This can be demonstrated by a survey about Chinese managers' understanding of CSR, see Z. Lu, H.von W. Hoivik and L. Wang, 'Chinese Managers' Perception of Corporate Social Responsibility: What is the Status Quo in China?', paper presented at the World Business Ethics Forum, Hong Kong, 1–3 November 2006.

[80] H. von W. Hoivik, 'East Meets West: Tacit Messages about Business Ethics in Stories Told by Chinese Managers' (2007) 74 *Journal of Business Ethics* 457 at 467.

[81] *Ibid.*

7. Promoting socially responsible listed companies in China through mandatory information disclosure requirements

Corporate social responsibility (CSR)-related disclosure by means of reports is far from being a recent phenomenon; indeed, it can be traced back to the beginning of the twentieth century.[1] However, the issue first gained real prominence in the 1970s as a result of the debate then raging concerning the role of the company in society at a time of rising social expectations and emerging environmental awareness.[2] A growing awareness of CSR is always reflected by an increase in the number of CSR or sustainability reports, as well as in the provision of CSR-related information.[3] CSR is a multidimensional process concerned with the communication of the social and environmental effects of corporations' economic actions to particular interests within society as well as society at large;[4] this process is achieved largely through information disclosure.[5]

---

[1] J. Guthrie and L.D. Parker, 'Corporate Social Reporting: A Rebuttal of Legitimacy Theory' (1989) 1 *Accounting and Business Research* 343. A good example would be Hogner's examination of the annual reports of US Steel for the years 1901 to 1980, documenting comments, statistical records, yearly comparisons and the nature of the company's activity related to CSR; see R.H. Hogner, 'Corporate Social Reporting: Eight Decades of Development at US Steel' (1982) 4 *Research in Corporate Performance and Policy* 243.

[2] D.L. Owen and B. O'Dwyer, 'Corporate Social Responsibility: The Reporting and Assurance Dimension' in A. Crane, A. McWilliams, D. Matten, J. Moon and D. Siegel (eds), *The Oxford Handbook of CSR* (Oxford: Oxford University Press, 2008) p. 384 at p. 386.

[3] A. Kolk, 'Environment Reporting by Multinationals from the Triad: Convergence or Divergence' (2005) 45 *Management International Review* 145.

[4] R.H. Gray, D.L. Owen and K.T. Maunders, *Corporate Social Reporting: Accounting and Accountability* (Hemel Hempstead: Prentice Hall, 1987).

[5] L. Cecil, 'Corporate Social Responsibility Reporting in the United States' (2008) 1 *McNair Scholars Research Journal* 43 at 44.

CSR-related or corporate social disclosure includes details about environmental, energy, human resources, products and community matters, and can be defined as the provision of non-financial information relating to a corporation's interactions with social and environmental factors as stated in its annual reports or its separate social reports.[6] This information is regarded as a route by which directors are able to discharge their CSR beyond their direct decisions regarding various stakeholders.

The growing importance of socially responsible investment and media are converging, and an increasing awareness of companies' social, ethical and environmental performance calls for greater transparency in reporting.[7] Transparency has been regarded as a critical component of corporate governance regimes, and openness can be achieved through clear disclosure and reporting and through engagement and dialogue among directors, shareholders and stakeholders. There are a number of reasons for corporations to publicize their corporate decisions and actions to stakeholders and the public. One of the most convincing is derived from political cost theory, which suggests that managers are concerned with political considerations, including the avoidance of explicit or implicit taxes or regulatory actions.[8] By disclosing information on the social and environmental performance of corporations, directors are able to minimize the cost of the interactions between the companies and their natural and societal environments; these have been referred as the political costs.[9] The disclosure of this information will reduce the likelihood of negative political or societal behaviours, minimizing the resulting cost

---

[6]   J.E. Guthrie and M.R. Matthews, 'Corporate Social Accounting in Australia' (1985) 7 *Research in Corporate Social Performance and Policy* 251.

[7]   N. Dando and T. Swift, 'Transparency and Assurance: Minding the Credibility Gap' (2003) 44 *Journal of Business Ethics* 195 at 195–6.

[8]   See P.M. Healy and K.G. Palepu, 'Information Asymmetry, Corporate Disclosure, and the Capital Markets: A Review of the Empirical Disclosure Literature' (2001) 31 *Journal of Accounting and Economics* 405; see also R.L. Watt and J.L. Zimmermann, 'Towards a Positive Theory of the Determination of Accounting Standards' (1978) 53 *Accounting Review* 112; E. Yip, C. Van Saden and S. Cahan, 'Corporate Social Responsibility Reporting and Earnings Management: The Role of Political Costs' (2011) 5 *Australasian Accounting Business and Finance Journal* 17; M.J. Milne, 'Positive Accounting Theory, Political Costs and Social Disclosure Analysis: A Critical Look' (2002) 13 *Accountancy and Business Law* 369.

[9]   T.D. Fields, T.Z. Lys and L. Vincent, 'Empirical Research on Accounting Choice' (2001) 31 *Journal of Accounting and Economics* 301.

and allowing corporations to generate moral capital.[10] This moral capital will bring positive profits for corporations who adhere to more stringent social constraints and engage in more public exposure than other companies.[11] CSR-related information disclosure makes it possible for profitable companies to show that their business operations and decisions have been performed within the norms of society, and demonstrate that they are fully aware of the costs of breaching society's expectations.[12] Communication between the company and society through disclosure will convince the public that the corporation is meeting its social expectations, and the level of the disclosure can be regarded as a standard for building legitimacy and a criterion by which companies improve their environmental and social conduct and reputation.[13]

Corporate disclosure is one of the most common means of ensuring adherence to corporate governance principles such as fairness and transparency. Justice Louise Brandeis first emphasized the importance of corporate disclosure by using the analogy that 'sunshine is said to be the best of disinfectants; electronic light the most efficient policeman'.[14] Disclosure makes the securities market transparent, and it is effective in maintaining the confidence of investors who trade on the basis of securities information. Securities markets have always regarded information disclosure as a fundamental issue.[15] Furthermore, corporate disclosure also has the effect of raising corporate governance standards with the purpose of building business aims and principles, since it

---

[10]   P.C. Godfrey, 'The Relationship between Corporate Philanthropy and Shareholder Wealth: A Risk Management' (2005) 30 *Academic of Management Review* 777.

[11]   R.W. Hulthausen and R.W. Leftwich, 'The Economic Consequences of Accounting Choice' (1983) 5 *Journal of Accounting and Economics* 77 at 79–80.

[12]   K. Bewley and Y. Li, 'Disclosure of Environmental Information by Canadian Manufacturing Companies: A Voluntary Disclosure Perspective' (2000) 1 *Advances in Environmental Accounting and Management* 201 at 203.

[13]   D. Neu, H. Warsame and K. Pedwell, 'Managing Public Impressions: Environmental Disclosure in Annual Reports' (1998) 23 *Accounting, Organizations and Society* 265 at 267–8; G. O'Donovan, *Legitimacy Theory as an Explanation for Corporate Environmental Disclosure* (Ph.D thesis, Victoria University of Technology, 2000), available at http://vuir.vu.edu.au/15372/.

[14]   L.D. Brandeis, *Other People's Money and How the Bankers Use It* (Chevy Chase: National Home Library Foundation, 1933) p. 62.

[15]   J. Fu, *Corporate Disclosure and Corporate Governance in China* (Alphen: Kluwer Law International, 2010) pp. 23–4.

enhances accountability.[16] The Code of Corporate Governance for Listed Companies in China 2002, in line with the OECD Principles of Corporate Governance, included 'information disclosure and transparency' as a single chapter and urged listed companies to 'truthfully, accurately, completely and timely disclose information as required by laws, regulations and the company's articles of association'.[17]

Information disclosure requirements are particularly important for China, where *Guanxi* and government control are regarded as key elements for business transactions. This also makes systematic and strict mandatory information disclosure requirements important and necessary for state-owned enterprises (SOEs). Therefore, the question arises of how to establish an effective and efficient CSR information disclosure system in China, incorporating both mandatory and voluntary elements to fit with the progressive corporate objective requirement under article 5 of Chinese Company Law (CCL) 2006.

This chapter sets out to explore the emerging practice of CSR reporting in China, using the lens of stakeholder theory to examine whether current practice is motivated by the purpose of discharging accountability to relevant stakeholders, and also whether it is helpful to transplant the legislative experience of 'business review' in the UK Companies Act 2006[18] to China. It is important to discuss why the CSR reporting scheme is important to China in order to promote CSR and a harmonious society, and how to enforce the scheme by mandatory regulations and voluntary guidelines. If a CSR-reporting system is established, there is likely to be resistance to major regulatory changes. It would be desirable to maintain a balance between efficient disclosure and increased burdens for companies, in order to achieve the ultimate purpose of boosting the competitive advantages of companies through increased transparency via corporate disclosure.

7.1   THE EMERGING CSR INFORMATION DISCLOSURE SYSTEM

CSR-related reporting, while not mandatory in most countries, has been accommodated and adopted in many corporations around the world.

---

[16]   A. Cadbury and I.M. Millstein, *The New Agenda for ICGN*, Discussion Paper No. 1 for the ICGN Tenth Anniversary Conference (London: July 2005) p. 13, available at www.icgn.org/403.
[17]   Code of Corporate Governance for Listed Companies in China s. 87.
[18]   UK Companies Act 2006 s. 417.

There are a variety of competing global standards for non-financial reporting, such as the Global Reporting Initiative (GRI)[19] and the UN Global Compact.[20] Although it can be initially traced back to the 1970s,[21] CSR reporting re-emerged from the mid-1990s in research and practice in the fields of corporate governance, accounting and auditing. The terms 'CSR reporting' or 'CSR-related information disclosure reporting' have also been referred to as sustainability reporting, social responsibility accounting,[22] social accounting[23] and corporate social disclosure,[24] and they have been popularized using the acronym SEAAR (social and ethical accounting, auditing and reporting).[25]

Before proceeding to a discussion of CSR reporting in China, it might be helpful to define the term. The author agrees with the definition of CSR reporting provided by Gray, Owen and Adams: 'the process of communicating the social and environmental effects of organisations' economic actions to particular interest groups within society and to society at large'.[26] It is logical to understand the system as the external reporting of ethical, social and environmental aspects of a corporation, while corporations try to achieve information disclosure aspects beyond the traditional role by providing a financial account to the shareholders under the assumption that companies have and will carry out responsibilities beyond making profits. In response to increasing public concerns about corporate social performance and social responsiveness, companies are becoming increasingly open about the social and environmental impacts of their business activities, especially with the growing number

---

[19]   For more information see www.globalreporting.org/Pages/default.aspx.

[20]   For more information see www.unglobalcompact.org/.

[21]   A.R. Belal, *Corporate Social Responsibility Reporting in Developing Countries: The Case of Bangladesh* (Aldershot: Ashgate, 2008) p. 6.

[22]   M.R. Mathews, 'A Suggested Classification for Social Accounting Research' (1984) 3 *Journal of Accounting and Public Policy* 199.

[23]   R. Gray, 'Current Developments and Trends in Social and Environmental Auditing, Reporting and Attestation: A Review and Comment' (2000) 4 *International Journal of Auditing* 247.

[24]   A.R. Belal, 'A Study of Corporate Social Disclosures in Bangladesh' (2001) 16 *Managerial Auditing Journal* 274.

[25]   C. Gonella, A. Piling and S. Zadek, *Making Values Count: Contemporary Experience in Social and Ethical Accounting* (London: ACCA, 1998).

[26]   R. Gray, D. Owen and C. Adams, *Accounting and Accountability: Changes and Challenges in Corporate Social and Environmental Reporting* (Hemel Hempstead: Prentice Hall, 1996) p. 9.

of multinational corporations and their acceptance and awareness of global CSR reporting standards.[27]

The emergence and popularity of CSR reporting are regarded as a trend for economic development in a globalized environment. First, CSR reporting is increasingly regarded as a result of the debate over corporate governance in emerging markets, and in the United Kingdom and the United States in particular, taking into account corporate scandals such as WorldCom, Enron and the recent 2008 financial crisis, with the purpose of promoting transparency, accountability and an ethical stance on the part of corporations. It is concluded that increased transparency in corporate disclosure, especially in the aftermath of the financial crisis, will boost the competitive advantages of companies which aim for it.[28]

Secondly, the Association of Chartered Certified Accountants (ACCA) established the CSR Reporting Award Scheme,[29] which can be seen as another motivating element to influence the increasing number of companies who are making social and environmental disclosures. The award scheme has now been renamed as the Sustainability Reporting Awards, originating from the launch of the Environmental Reporting Awards in the United Kingdom in 1991, and it has now been rolled out globally in European countries, the United States, Canada, Australia, New Zealand, Pakistan, Hong Kong, Singapore, Sri Lanka and Malaysia.[30] The scheme would promote CSR reporting in China if it were to be extended to the country, recognizing excellence in transparent environmental, social and sustainability reporting.

Finally, CSR reporting is closely related to standards and codes that help companies in their development of CSR strategy. The most widely accepted ones are SA8000, AA1000 or the Global Reporting Initiatives that have been developing through consultation and which have a very

---

[27] S. Chen and P. Bouvain, 'Is Corporate Responsibility Converging? A Comparison of Corporate Responsibility Reporting in the USA, UK, Australia and Germany' (2009) 87 *Journal of Business Ethics* 299 at 300.

[28] O. Aiyegbayo and C. Villers, 'The Enhanced Business Review: Has It Made Corporate Governance More Effective?' (2011) *Journal of Business Law* 699 at 720.

[29] See M. Hopkins and R. Crowe, *Corporate Social Responsibility: Is There a Business Case?* (2003), available at www2.accaglobal.com/pdfs/members_pdfs/publications/csr03.pdf.

[30] ACCA, *ACCA Sustainability Reporting Award*, available at www2.accaglobal.com/vpalgore/acca_approach/asra.

wide impact on companies and their stakeholders.[31] SA8000 was initiated by the US-based Social Accountability International in 1997, and is based on the International Labour Organization and human right conventions. The focus of the Global Reporting Initiative Guidelines or AA1000 rests on employees and communications, and the 'triple bottom line' of CSR through a multi-stakeholder engagement process.[32]

Corporate responsibility reporting has established its position as the de facto law for business, delivering a compelling insight into the expectations that companies face.[33] Based on the KPMG International Survey of Corporate Responsibility Reporting of the G250 companies, drawn from the Fortune Global 500 List and representing more than a dozen industry sectors, there has been an upward trend in CSR reporting. It was found that the most prominent type of reporting has changed from environment, health and safety reporting[34] to sustainability reporting.[35] Of the G250 companies, 95 per cent reported on their corporate responsibility activities in 2011, compared with 64 per cent in 2005, 45 per cent in 2002 and 35 per cent in 1999.[36] As far as the reporting guidelines are concerned, in 2011 80 per cent of the G250 companies claimed to have followed the Global Reporting Initiative Guidelines. Furthermore, 46 per cent of them had utilized formal assurance, compared with 30 per cent in 2005, reflecting a long-term improvement in data quality and value.[37]

China was a new entry to this survey in 2001, and appears to have undertaken a full-out sprint to catch up with the traditional leaders in the field, with almost 60 per cent of the China's largest companies reporting on corporate responsibility metrics in 2011. It is predicted that China will

---

[31]   A.R. Belal, 'Stakeholder Accountability or Stakeholder Management: A Review of UK Firms' Social and Ethical Accounting, Auditing and Reporting (SEAAR)' (2002) 9 *Corporate Social Responsibility and Environmental Management* 8.

[32]   A.R. Belal, *Corporate Social Responsibility Reporting in Developing Countries: The Case of Bangladesh* (Aldershot: Ashgate, 2008) p. 4; see also J. Elkington, *Cannibals with Forks, the Triple Bottom Line of 21st Century Business* (Oxford: Capstone, 1998).

[33]   KPMG, *KPMG International Survey of Corporate Responsibility Reporting 2011* (2011) p. 2.

[34]   KPMG, *KPMG International Survey of Corporate Responsibility Reporting 2002* (2002).

[35]   KPMG, *KPMG International Survey of Corporate Responsibility Reporting 2011* (2011) p. 20.

[36]   *Ibid.* at 7.

[37]   *Ibid.* at 27.

institute a widespread reporting system in the future.[38] Furthermore, a proprietary model has been created to assess a number of elements, including information systems and processes, assurance, restatements, multiple channel communication, the use of GRI standards and integrated reporting.[39] China is categorized into the 'Getting it Right' group, which indicates that companies in China are taking a 'conservative path to becoming members of the leaders' quadrant', focusing on 'building their information systems and processes first before over-communicating on achievements they may not be able to continuously demonstrate'.[40] It has been shown that companies in China do take corporate social responsibility seriously, with effective stakeholder communications an important achievement to better control future performance by broadening external assurance.[41]

7.2   EMERGING LEGISLATIVE ATTEMPTS AT CSR-RELATED INFORMATION DISCLOSURE

The transplantation of foreign law, including laws on information disclosure requirements, always needs to ensure that the new system fits into the cultural, legal, historical and political environment of China. However, corporate practices have demonstrated that the disclosure laws borrowed heavily from Western securities markets often do not fit the Chinese system, losing their function and effectiveness and suffering from widespread breaches of the law and rules. The securities market in China is accurately described as an emerging and transitional market, with unique characteristics that are substantially different from those of the mature and complex securities markets of the United States and Europe.[42]

Corporate social and environmental disclosure has become an important component of efficient CSR implementation. Despite the fact that non-financial CSR reporting is usually prepared and published on a voluntary basis, some countries have issued regulatory requirements to make these disclosures on CSR issues mandatory. If there are not enough

---

[38]   *Ibid.* at 10.
[39]   *Ibid.* at 4.
[40]   *Ibid.* at 5.
[41]   *Ibid.* at 5.
[42]   W.L. Hong, *Securities Regulations: Theory and Practice (Zhengquan Jianguan: Lilun yu Shijian)* (Shanghai: Shanghai University of Finance and Economics Press, 2000) pp. 104–5.

incentives for companies to report on their CSR impact in a voluntary manner based on market forces, the local government can make it a legal requirement for companies to produce these reports through corporate law, stock listing regulations, tax law, pension fund regulations or even separate compulsory disclosure laws, setting precise standards for corporate reporting, including requirements for lists of metrics, formats for reports and the frequency of reporting.[43] In order to make this legal system complete and enforceable, the information disclosed should be calculated, evaluated and studied by government agencies or independent third parties, for example KPMG, for verification and assurance. Additionally, there should be stipulated mandatory sanctions for the failure to report any of these compulsory data.[44]

In 2010, KPMG, the Unit for Corporate Governance in Africa, the Global Reporting Initiative and the United Nations Environment Programme published a joint publication entitled *Carrots and Sticks – Promoting Transparency and Sustainability: An Update on Trends in Voluntary and Mandatory Approaches to Sustainability Reporting*. This was an update of the 2006 version of a similarly-named publication produced by the United Nations Environment Programme and KPMG, which gave an overview of sustainability reporting in a selection of countries worldwide.[45] It was reported that the global regulatory landscape has evolved substantially, introducing more codes and regulatory measures, while 'a review of mandatory and voluntary sustainability reporting standards and legislation in thirty countries has revealed that both international and national standards for codes and guidelines, as well as legislations for sustainability reporting, have been strongly evolving'.[46]

---

[43] C. Noronha, S. Tou, M.I. Cynthia and J.J. Guan, 'Corporate Social Responsibility Reporting in China: An Overview and Comparison with Major Trends' (2012) 20 *Corporate Social Responsibility and Environmental Management* 29 at 30.

[44] *Ibid.*

[45] KPMG, Unit for Corporate Governance in Africa, Global Reporting Initiative and United Nations Environment Programme, *Carrots and Sticks – Promoting Transparency and Sustainability: An Update on Trends in Voluntary and Mandatory Approaches to Sustainability Reporting* (2010).

[46] *Ibid.* at 4.

In the United States, the Securities and Exchange Commission (SEC) made the disclosure of certain environmental and climate change information mandatory in the SEC filing.[47] The information disclosure requirements start off with a comprehensive array of statutes and international treaties, including numerous federal statutes regulating corporate behaviours such as the Civil Rights Act of 1964,[48] the Occupational Safety and Health Act,[49] the Safe Drinking Water Act,[50] the Consumer Product Safety Act,[51] and the Foreign Corrupt Practices Act.[52] The disclosure of certain CSR-related information is required within the framework of the financial and non-financial disclosure regimes, especially in relation to the issues of environment and climate change.[53] CSR-related issues are incorporated in Regulation S-K of the Securities Act 1933. In particular, it is worth mentioning item 101, which requires the disclosure of the company's business in general and expressly requires the disclosure of the material cost of complying with environmental law.[54] In addition, item 103 requires the disclosure of any material legal proceedings in progress against the company,[55] and item 303 prescribes the disclosure of the management's discussion and analysis of financial conditions and result of operations, which itself requires the disclosure of any trends, events, demands, commitments and uncertainties that are reasonably likely to have a material effect on the company's financial condition and performance.[56] Finally, item 503 requires the disclosure of the risk factors relevant to the company, including risks related to the environment and climate change, which make any investment in the company speculative or risky.[57]

---

[47]   Securities and Exchange Commission, Commission Guidance regarding Disclosure related to Climate Change (2010) (17 CFR Pts 211, 231 and 241).

[48]   See Civil Right Act 1964, 42 U.S.C. s. 1981 (1994).

[49]   See Occupational Safety and Health Act 1970, 29 U.S.C. s. 651 (1994).

[50]   See Safe Drinking Water Act 1970, 42 U.S.C. ss. 7401–7671 (1994).

[51]   See Consumer Product Safety Act, 15 U.S.C. s. 2065 (1994).

[52]   See Foreign Corrupt Practices Act 1977, 15 U.S.C. s. 78dd-r (1994); see also M. Freedman and B. Jaggi, 'The SEC's Pollution Disclosure Requirements: Are They Meaningful' (1981) *California Management Review* 60.

[53]   It was established by the Securities Act 1993 and Exchange Act 1934; see Securities and Exchange Commission, Commission Guidance regarding Disclosure related to Climate Change (2010).

[54]   *Ibid.* at 12–13.

[55]   *Ibid.* at 13–14.

[56]   *Ibid.* at 16–17.

[57]   *Ibid.* at 15.

Similarly to the United States, in Europe there are CSR-related information disclosure requirements under the existing framework which are applicable to both listed and other types of company. The Transparency Directive regulates the ongoing periodic disclosures of listed companies, making it mandatory for companies to draw up their annual reports (or management reports for listed companies) in accordance with the provisions of the accounting company law Directives concerning annual reports.[58] The Accounts Modernization Directive modifies the company law Directive on annual accounts, making the disclosure of certain non-financial key performance indicators mandatory under EU law, including the annual report on environmental and employee issues.[59] EU legislation also makes the disclosure of certain non-financial key performance indicators mandatory, including information related to the environment and employees.[60]

In the United States, the passing of the National Environment Policy Act 1969 required the SEC to consider environmental effects in its disclosure requirements for publicly held companies.[61] However, in the European Union, the Modernization Directive narrows the scope of the information that needs to be disclosed by including an additional condition on the information only 'to the extent necessary for an understanding of the company's development, performance or position'[62] and to give a fair review of the development and performance of the company.[63] In UK legislation, under section 417 of the Companies Act 2006, directors are obliged to include in the business review 'a fair review of the company's business and a description of the principal risks and uncertainties facing the company'.[64] The purpose of the business review is 'to inform members of the company and help them assess how the directors have performed their duty under Section 172 (duties to promote the success of corporations)'.[65]

---

[58] Directive 2004/109/EC of the European Parliament and of the Council of 15 December 2004 on the harmonization of transparency requirements in relation to information disclosure, art. 4(5) ('Transparency Directive').

[59] Directive 2003/51/EC of the European Parliament and of the Council of 18 June 2003, amending Directives 78/660/EEC, 83/349/EEC, 86/635/EEC and 91/674/EEC ('Accounts Modernization Directive').

[60] *Ibid.*

[61] Securities and Exchange Commission, Securities Act Release Nos 33-6130 and 34-16224 (27 September 1979).

[62] Accounts Modernization Directive, arts 1(14)(a) and 2(10)(a).

[63] *Ibid.*

[64] UK Companies Act 2006 s. 417(3).

[65] *Ibid.* s. 417(2).

7.3 ADVANTAGES OF MANDATORY APPROACHES TO REPORTING AND TWO-WAY COMMUNICATION WITHIN THE REPORTING SYSTEM

There is a range of methods to evaluate possible legislative protection for stakeholder groups, with relevant factors such as the introduction of provisions that mandate (or at least permit) the relevant behaviour with appropriate enforcement measures. Information disclosure at a mandatory level is one part of a combination that makes CSR possible and enforceable. Despite the fact that companies are increasingly disclosing CSR information, it is questionable whether the current annual, stand-alone CSR reports on social and environmental factors can satisfy the increasing demand for corporate accountability.[66] In the above-mentioned *Carrots and Sticks – Promoting Transparency and Sustainability: An Update on Trends in Voluntary and Mandatory Approaches to Sustainability Reporting*, a number of reasons were listed for mandatory approaches to CSR-related reporting, including 'changing the corporate culture, incompleteness of voluntary reports, comparability, non-disclosure of negative performance, legal certainty, market failures, cost savings, standardisation and equal treatment of investors'.[67] Beattie and McInnes argued that mandatory rules will help to produce narrative disclosures of a higher quality, which will lead to an increase in the amount of disclosure and reduce variability by an absolute amount attributable to the size of the company.[68]

Companies need more mandatory standards and rules as well as voluntary guidelines to achieve uniformity in CSR reporting.[69] CSR

---

[66]   See C.A. Adams, 'The Ethical, Social and Environmental Reporting-Performance Portrayal Gap' (2004) 17 *Accounting, Auditing and Accountability Journal* 731; M.J. Milne and R. Gray, 'Future Prospectus for Corporate Sustainability Report' in J. Unerman, J. Bebbington and B. O'Dwyer (eds), *Sustainability Accounting and Accountability* (Abingdon: Routledge, 2007) p. 184.

[67]   KPMG, Unit for Corporate Governance in Africa, Global Reporting Initiative and United Nations Environment Programme, *Carrots and Sticks – Promoting Transparency and Sustainability: An Update on Trends in Voluntary and Mandatory Approaches to Sustainability Reporting* (2010) p. 8.

[68]   V. Beattie and B. McInnes, *Narrative Reporting in the UK and the US: Which System Works Best?* Institute of Chartered Accountants in England and Wales Briefing (London: Centre for Business Performance for ICAEW, 2006) p. 15.

[69]   D.L. Owen, T.A. Swift, C. Humphrey and M. Bowerman, 'The New Social Audit: Accountability, Managerial Capture or the Agenda of Social Champion?' (2000) 9 *European Accounting Review* 81.

disclosure is regarded as being reactive to environmental and social factors, since disclosures legitimize action.[70] This legitimate action could be regarded as evidence of an assessment of the company's corporate citizenship, and as responses to social contracts where corporations agree to perform various socially desirable actions in return for approval of their corporate objectives as a reward for their ultimate survival.[71] The legitimacy of their actions via disclosure will make the corporations justify their continued existence.[72]

While the reporting system is still underdeveloped, it is necessary to further enhance sustainability reporting and CSR reports in a more enforceable manner, adopting a more systematic and standardized format in comparison with traditional economic reporting.[73] Looking at the current practices in most jurisdictions, producing mandatory or voluntary reports on social and environmental issues are not normally exclusive options; in fact they are highly complementary. Disclosure practice by companies may be driven by the need to legitimize their corporate activities. It is for the government to decide the most appropriate approach for reporting, with different levels of minimum mandatory requirements based on different criteria, including business nature, and the size or type of the corporation.[74] Mervyn King, the chairperson of the Global Reporting Initiative, encouraged the regulatory role played by government when it comes to minimum levels of disclosure when he addressed the environmental, social and corporate governance (ESG)

---

[70]　See R.H. Hogner, 'Corporate Social Reporting: Eight Decades of Development at US Steel' (1982) 4 *Research in Corporate Performance and Policy* 243; C.K. Lindblom, *The Concept of Organizational Legitimacy and its Implications for Corporate Social Responsibility Disclosure*, American Accounting Association Public Interests Section Working Paper (1983).

[71]　J. Guthrie and L.D. Parker, 'Corporate Social Disclosure: A Rebuttal of Legitimacy Theory' (1989) 19 *Accounting and Business Research* 343 at 344; see also R. Gray, R. Kouhy and S. Lavers, 'Constructing a Research Database of Social and Environmental Reporting by UK Companies' (1995) 8 *Accounting, Auditing and Accountability Journal* 78.

[72]　C. Lehman, *Stalemate in Corporate Social Responsibility Research*, American Accounting Association Public Interest Section Working Paper (1983).

[73]　A.R. Belal and V. Lubinin, 'Corporate Social Disclosure (CSD) in Russia' in S.O. Idowu and W.L. Filho (eds), *Global Practice of Corporate Social Responsibility* (Berlin: Springer Verlag, 2008) p. 165.

[74]　KPMG, Unit for Corporate Governance in Africa, Global Reporting Initiative and United Nations Environment Programme, *Carrots and Sticks – Promoting Transparency and Sustainability: An Update on Trends in Voluntary and Mandatory Approaches to Sustainability Reporting* (2010) p. 8.

disclosure workshop hosted by the European Commission in 2010. He stated that 'after decades of voluntary *laissez-faire* reporting, the time is ripe for stronger regulatory action and to follow the good example of several EU governments who have introduced binding measures or legislation on ESG disclosure for some portion of their corporate sectors'.[75]

It is argued that CSR-related communications between corporations and their stakeholders were carried out in the form of the annual CSR reports, or via the presence of some CSR information in financial reports.[76] These reports transfer CSR-related information from the company to stakeholders, and are only issued and disclosed after the achievement of the CSR-related activities.[77] The process of transferring the information is based on a one-way communication route, and is predictable, insufficient and generally not transparent enough regarding comments and timeliness to give stakeholders a good understanding of the corporation's CSR decisions and actions. It is suggested that two-way communication, via a system under which information can be transferred between the company and its stakeholders in a bidirectional manner, should be established to make the CSR information disclosure system more efficient.[78] Under such a scheme, the 'informing' direction transmits CSR-related messages to stakeholders via reports and other media in order to involve them in the sustainable development of the company. This involvement will enable them to provide voluntary sustainable support for socially responsible corporate behaviours. The 'listening' direction will help the company to adapt to the needs of stakeholders by listening to their voices through questionnaires, surveys, consulting sessions and collective opinion pools. The company can then make changes to upgrade the sustainable support for its CSR activities, and these adjustments can be disseminated through reports on more efficient CSR-related developments and strategies. The importance of informing

---

[75]   See Global Reporting Initiative, *Beyond Voluntary Laissez-Faire Reporting: Towards a European ESG Disclosure Framework: Submission to the European Commission by the Global Reporting Initiative* (2010), available at   http://ec.europa.eu/enterprise/policies/sustainable-business/corporate-social-responsibility/reporting-disclosure/swedish-presidency/files/written-submissions/global_reporting_initiative_en.pdf.
[76]   M. Liu, 'Corporate Social Responsible Actions and Consumer Respondents' (2006) 25 *China Industry Economy* 64.
[77]   H. Chen and H. Zhang, 'Two-way Communication Strategy on CSR Information in China' (2009) 5 *Social Responsibility Journal* 440 at 441.
[78]   *Ibid.* at 442.

stakeholders about CSR-related information should be given equal weight to communication with and support from stakeholders, in order to make the information more attractive, useful and dynamic. A two-way communication system will promote good relations between various stakeholders and corporations through 'identification', which makes stakeholders feel they are being integrated, acknowledging their individualized value and ultimately promoting the company.[79]

This positive reaction of internal and external environments to CSR communication strategy will ensure a positive strategic management policy, boosting CSR within corporations and enforcing the enlightened corporate objectives by mapping stakeholder relationships and stakeholder coalitions, assessing the nature of each stakeholder's interests and power, constructing a matrix of stakeholders' priorities, creating a matrix of corporate responsibility towards stakeholders, and making the corporate objectives in the CCL 2006 more enforceable.[80] In this sense, a two-way disclosure system will propose a solid set of coherent principles and enforcement measures and processes, enhancing the integration of CSR initiatives as a key element of corporate culture and corporate value. Such a two-way strategy will help corporations to decide what to disclose, and will encourage them to keep updating the information to make their CSR strategy fit their stakeholders' needs. To accommodate CSR projects that need a relatively long period of time for their implementation, a systematic two-way disclosure regime is key for the company in obtaining and disseminating updated social and environmental information.

7.4   CURRENT REQUIREMENTS ON INFORMATION DISCLOSURE AND CSR IN CHINA

The phenomenon of CSR is attracting increasing attention internationally from academics, practitioners, CEOs, non-governmental organizations (NGOs) and legislators. Expanded social disclosure generally starts with the information on the products a company produces, extending to the company's legal compliance structure, its domestic and global labour practices, its supplier/vendor standards and global environmental

---

[79]   S. Brammer and S. Parvelin, 'Building a Good Reputation' (2004) 19 *European Management Journal* 704.

[80]   J. Zhao, 'Modernising Corporate Objective Debate towards a Hybrid Model' (2011) 62 *Northern Ireland Legal Quarterly* 361 at 386.

effects.[81] As for legislators, their attentions focus on making CSR-related information disclosure mandatory through different kinds of documents, including periodic disclosure documents such as financial statements, accompanying notes, annual reports and corporate governance reports, or even as a part of other publicized documents available to stakeholders and the public.[82]

With the development and integration of the world economy, Chinese companies, especially public companies, are under an increasing amount of pressure to disclose their CSR-related information from the last few decades.[83] As well as attention from government, media, business and society, academics are also becoming increasingly concerned with corporate social reporting.[84] The rapid economic expansion in China has been accompanied by serious social and environmental problems. CSR-related information disclosure, encouraging or requiring corporations to publish their social responsibility reports, possibly alongside their annual reports, may allow some discretion regarding the extent of the information released. A question arises about whether it is possible for directors and policy-makers to exploit annual reports, using them as a tool to legitimize CSR conduct as a complementary practice in support of a CSR marketing strategy. Disclosure requirements are helpful to measure the congruence between the social values suggested by CSR activities

---

[81]   C.A. Williams, 'The Securities and Exchange Commission and Corporate Social Transparency' (1999) 112 *Harvard Law Review* 1197 at 1201–2.

[82]   D.G. Szabo, *Disclosure of Material CSR Information in the Periodic Report: Comparison of the Mandatory CSR Disclosure System for Listed Companies in the EU and the US*, Nordic and European Company Law, LSN Research Paper Series No. 10-20 (2010) pp. 1–2.

[83]   R. Hooghiemstra, 'Corporate Communication and Impression Management: New Perspective on Why Companies Engage in Corporate Social Reporting' (2000) 27 *Journal of Business Ethics* 55 at 56.

[84]   See A.A. Ullmann, 'Data in Search of a Theory: A Critical Examination of the Relationship among Social Performance, Social Disclosure, and Economic Performance of U.S. Firms' (1985) 10 *Academy of Management Review* 540; R. Gray, R. Kouhy and S. Lavers, 'Corporate Social and Environmental Reporting: A Review of the Literature and a Longitudinal Study of UK Disclosure' (1995) 8 *Accounting, Auditing and Accountability Journal* 47; D.M. Patten, 'Media Exposure, Public Policy Pressure, and Environmental Disclosure: An Examination of the Impact of Tri Data Availability' (2002) 26 *Accounting Forum* 152; W.G. Blacconiere and W.D. Northcut, 'Environmental Information and Market Reactions to Environmental Legislation' (1997) 12 *Journal of Accounting, Auditing and Finance* 149.

and the social norms, judging the legitimacy of the actions.[85] Compared with accommodating CSR elements into directors' duties, legal requirements on information disclosure are more enforceable and allow less discretion for company decision-makers.

The existing mandatory requirements on information disclosure in relation to social and environmental issues at the government legislation level are disappointing in China. Listed companies are required to disclose regular reports, including annual reports, half-year reports and quarterly reports, on a timely basis under the CCL 2006[86] and the Securities Law 2006.[87] However, the content of these mandatory reports has always focused on the financial issues of the company. For example, a company is required by the CCL 2006 to formulate a financial report and have it checked by an accounting firm according to law, administrative regulations and provisions of the Treasury Department of the State Council.[88] The listed companies are required to submit interim reports under the Securities Law 2006, which contain information including financial accounting reports; business reports; details of any major lawsuits; and changes in shares and corporate bonds. They are also required to submit annual reports which contain information including the company profile; financial accounting reports; business reports; profiles of directors, supervisors and senior management personnel and their shareholdings; existing shares and corporate bonds; and details of anyone in actual control of the company.[89] These mandatory information disclosure requirements are specifically focused on the financial aspects of the companies and on corporate shares and bonds. In the Chinese provisions, information about non-financial issues such as environmental matters, employees and social and community issues have been ignored, while such issues have been included in the legislation in other jurisdiction.[90]

Despite the lack of mandatory requirements in the CCL or Securities Law, several CSR disclosure initiatives have been launched by the

---

[85]   J. Dowling and J. Pfeffer, 'Organizational Legitimacy: Social Values and Organizational Behavior' (1975) 18 *Pacific Sociological Review* 122.

[86]   CCL 2006 arts 34, 98, 146, 165 and 166.

[87]   Chinese Securities Law 2006 arts 14, 52, 65, 66 and 68. There are also related requirements in Administrative Measures on Information Disclosure by Listed Companies and the Measures for the Administration of Material Asset Reorganisation by Listed Companies at non-government legislation level.

[88]   CCL 2006 art. 165.

[89]   *Ibid.* art. 166.

[90]   For example, UK Companies Act 2006.

Chinese government to facilitate a more efficient enforcement of social responsibility in China. As a sign of the full implementation of article 5 of the CCL 2006 regarding the requirements of socially responsible corporations, a series of regulations and guidelines for CSR-related information disclosure were introduced in China after 2006. The State-owned Assets Supervision and Administration Commission (SASAC) published a directive entitled Guidelines to the State-Owned Enterprises Directly under the Central Government on Fulfilling Corporate Social Responsibilities in January 2008, strongly encouraging SOEs to adopt sound CSR practices and issue efficient CSR reports. This directive is regarded as a powerful regulatory instrument due to the position and impact of the Commission. SOEs are strongly encouraged, according to the Guidelines, to publish CSR or sustainability reports, with information on the status of their CSR practices, planning and measures to improve CSR, and to enhance their communication and dialogue mechanisms to facilitate responses to opinions and suggestions of stakeholders in the wider society.[91] The requirement for non-financial information disclosure is not only limited to SOEs in China; the Draft Guidelines on Performing Social Responsibility of Foreign Invested Enterprises, published by the Investment Ministry of Commerce, also introduced a plan to encourage foreign companies to integrate best practice standards, including those on CSR information disclosure, to advance China's social fabric, having regard to their social and environmental impact on Chinese society.[92]

The Ministry of Environmental Protection, in partnership with the China Securities Regulatory Commission, launched the 'Green Security' policy in 2008, making it harder for polluters to raise capital by requiring companies listed on the stock exchange to disclose more information about their environmental record.[93] The State Environmental Protection Administration (SEPA)[94] has issued a series of regulations and requirements upon corporations in terms of their corporate environmental reporting. The SEPA promulgated the Regulations on Environmental Information Disclosure (in a trial edition) in 2007, and the Regulations

---

[91]   See SASAC, Guidelines to the State-Owned Enterprises Directly under the Central Government on Fulfilling Corporate Social Responsibilities s. 18.

[92]   WTO Guide, *Research Report on Corporate Social Responsibility of Foreign Invested Enterprises in China (Zai Hua Waishang Touzi Qiye Shehuizeren Baogao Yanjiu)* (28 March 2012), available at www.wtoguide.net/html/2012-03/1079.html.

[93]   'China imposing Green Policy on companies', *New York Times*, 5 December 2008.

[94]   It is now known as the Ministry of Environmental Protection of China.

took effect on 1 May 2008. Under this new legislation, environmental agencies and heavily-polluting companies are required to disclose certain environmental information to the public.

When a company is on the SEPA's list of companies whose pollutant emissions exceed national or local standards, the company will be mandated to disclose the following information to the public: (1) the names, discharge methods, discharge densities, aggregate amounts and excess amounts of major pollutants; (2) the construction and operation of environmental protection facilities; and (3) emergency plans for environmental disasters. Under the regulations, companies are required to disclose this information to the public via the local media within 30 days from when the SEPA releases the list, and the agency itself is required to disclose lists of heavily-polluting companies. These compulsory disclosure requirements, in conjunction with environmental law, should ensure that potentially environmentally harmful companies listed by the SEPA are reasonably supervised by law, the public, government and media.

Under article 19 of the Regulations, companies are encouraged to disclose the following information on a voluntary basis concerning their environmental policies: (1) environmental guidelines, annual environmental goals and results; (2) annual resources consumption; (3) the condition of their environmental investment and environmental technology development; (4) the types, discharge amounts and densities of pollutants; (5) the construction and operation of their environmental protection facilities; (6) waste processing and recycling; (7) any voluntary agreements with environmental agencies concerning environmental protection; (8) their performance of corporate social responsibility; and (9) any other environmental information. These environmental concerns may be considered when companies draft their corporate social responsibility reports, disclosing their past behaviours and the ethical codes that regulate their future corporate behaviour.

Mr Yue Pan, Vice Minister of the SEPA, emphasized three important consequences of the introduction of the first ever Regulations for information disclosure.[95] First, the introduction of the Regulations was intended as a significant measure towards the creation of a Harmonised

---

[95]   See 'The Introduction of the First Regulation on Environmental Disclosure and Enforcement of Information Disclosure for Environmental Agencies and Heavy-Pollution Companies. Mr Yue Pan is appealing for in-depth public participation to minimize pollution and emissions' (*Shoubu Huanjing Xinxi Gongkai Banfa Chutai Qiangzhi Huanbao Bumen he Wuran Qiye Gongkai Huanjing Xinxi: PanYue Huyu yi Gongzhong Shendu Canyu Tuidong Wuran Panjian*), 25 April 2008.

Society (as described by former President Hu Jintao), especially since environmentally-related complaints were increasing by 30 per cent every year. It was hoped that the disclosure requirements would build a communication bridge between the public and the government, by which the public could exercise their environmental rights to monitor development projects and polluting companies. Secondly, the introduction of the Regulations was seen as necessary for building a socialist democracy and the rule of law, to enable public participation in environmental policy-making. Thirdly, environmental discourse was necessary to strengthen administrative reform and build a service-oriented government. Therefore, the government should establish institutional mechanisms for public participation, enabling environmental discourse as an important institutional underpinning.[96]

Both the Shenzhen Stock Exchange and the Shanghai Stock Exchange have also taken the initiative in promoting social and environmental disclosure, releasing the 'Shenzhen Stock Exchange Social Responsibility Instruction to Listed Companies', the 'Guide to Environmental Information Disclosure for Companies Listed on the Shanghai Stock Exchange', and the 'Notice on Strengthening the Social Responsibility of Listed Companies'. These guides were based on the CCL 2006 and the Securities Law 2006, with the purposes of 'achieving scientific development, building a harmonised society, advancing towards economic and social sustainable development and promoting corporate social responsibility.[97]

7.5 SCOPE AND MEASUREMENT OF DISCLOSED CSR INFORMATION

It is important to identify the scope and dimensions of CSR before deciding on the parameters for CSR information disclosure. There are many different ways to consider what should be included in CSR and what it embraces. Dahlsrud identified a number of elements as the most frequent factors in CSR, including: the stakeholder dimension, social factors, economic dimensions, the voluntary factor and environmental issues.[98] CSR activities under all these dimensions may promote

---

[96] *Ibid.*

[97] Shenzhen Stock Exchange, Social Responsibility Instruction to Listed Companies 2006 art. 1.

[98] A. Dahlsrud, 'How Corporate Social Responsibility is Defined: An Analysis of 37 Definitions' (2008) 15 *Corporate Social Responsibility and Environmental Management* 1 at 4.

companies' reputations and their relationships with creditors, investors and government officials, and these improved relationships may well be translated into economic benefits.[99] When considering the scope of CSR information disclosure, Guthrie and Parker analysed corporate and social disclosure practices in the United States, the United Kingdom and Australia in 1983, discussing disclosures related to the environment, energy, human resources, products and community involvement.[100]

The scope of CSR information disclosure has been broadly discussed from different angles, but the discussions have arrived at similar conclusions. Some think that CSR information disclosure is concerned with providing information about, *inter alia*, pollution control, employee relations and community involvement, not only for investors, but also for employees, consumers and the public at large.[101] Gray and others identified several CSR categories employed in the disclosure project, including the environment, customers, energy, community, charitable and political donations, employees, charities and shareholders.[102] Trotman and Bradley examined the scope of CSR-related information disclosure in Australia through empirical studies and identified six aspects, including:

- the environment, including pollution control, protecting and improving the environment, environmentally friendly design, environmental impact studies, land reclamation and reforestation, recycling and conserving resources;
- energy, including using energy more efficiently, utilizing waste materials for energy, disclosures about companies' efforts towards reducing energy consumption and increasing energy efficiency with research directed at reducing energy consumption;
- human resources, including promoting employees' health and safety, working conditions and training;

---

[99]   J. McGuire, A. Sundgreen and T. Schneeweis, 'Corporate Social Responsibility and Firm Financial Performance' (1988) 31 *Academy of Management Journal* 854.

[100]   J.E. Guthrie and L.D. Parker, 'Corporate Social Disclosure Practice: A Comparative International Analysis' (1989) 3 *Advances in Public Interest Accounting* 159; N. Elias and M. Epstein, 'Dimensions of Corporate Social Reporting' (1975) 57 *Management Accounting* 36.

[101]   T. Yamagami and K. Kokubu, 'A Note on Corporate Social Disclosure in Japan' (1991) 4 *Auditing and Accountability Journal* 32.

[102]   R.H. Gray, R. Kouhy and S. Lavers, 'Methodological Themes Constructing a Research Database of Social and Environmental Reporting by UK Companies' (1995) 8 *Auditing and Accountability Journal* 78 at 95–100.

- products, including safer manufacturing processes and the improved recyclability of products in order to reduce polluting effects;
- community involvement, including donations, charities, universities, hospitals, public health project sponsorship and opening companies' facilities to the public; and
- other institutions, including the acknowledgment of CSR and providing for aboriginal welfare.[103]

The contents of CSR or sustainability reports have also been prescribed by international accounting firms and non-profit organizations. Ernst and Young published a report that focused on the status of the sustainability reporting of the top 20 European financial services organizations based on a review of their sustainability reports issued in 2010.[104] The report was published in the context of the 2008 financial crisis, which altered the basis of trust between stakeholders and corporations and made long-term business strategy more important than ever.[105] It was reported that the content of CSR information disclosures should include topics such as socially responsible investment, customers, stakeholder dialogues, the environment, corporate donations, employees and risk management-related issues.[106]

Furthermore, the Global Reporting Initiative framework and G3 Sustainability Reporting Guidelines were followed by many companies when deciding the content of their CSR and sustainability reports. These content principles include materiality, stakeholder inclusiveness, sustainability context and completeness.[107] Materiality refers to the information in the report, which should reflect significant impacts from corporations towards society and the environment; stakeholder inclusiveness means that reports should respond to stakeholders' reasonable expectations and

---

[103]   K.T. Trotman and G.W. Bradley, 'Association between Social Responsibility Disclosure and Characteristics of Companies' (1981) 6 *Accounting, Organizations and Society* 355 at 359; see also J.E. Guthrie and M.R. Mathews, 'Corporate Social Accounting in Australasia' (1985) 7 *Corporate Social Performance and Policy* 251.

[104]   Ernst & Young, *The Financial Sector from a Non-Financial Perspective: The Path Forward* (2011), available at www.ey.com/Publication/vwLUAssets/The_path_forward/$FILE/The%20Path%20Forward.pdf.

[105]   *Ibid.* at 5.

[106]   *Ibid.* at 17.

[107]   Global Reporting Initiative, see Defining Report Content of G3 Online, s. 1.1, available at www.globalreporting.org/reporting/guidelines-online/G3Online/DefiningReportContentQualityAndBoundary/Pages/DefiningReportContent.aspx.

interests; suitability context clarifies that the purpose of the report is to show how the company is helping to improve environmental, social and other conditions over the long term; and completeness requires that reports reflect significant impacts of the business and enable stakeholders to assess its performance in the reporting period.[108]

From the discussions above regarding the content and dimensions of CSR-related reporting systems in different countries and international organizations, it is clear that the definition of the scope of CSR information disclosure varies. However, it most often comprises a combination of the following six categories: environment, energy, employees, local community, the public, and products, services and customers. Shareholders' interests were not normally mentioned in these reports because CSR requires corporations to have regard to issues beyond profit maximization. The only CSR issues that are related to shareholders will be information disclosure requirements regarding socially responsible investments (sometimes called ethical investments) which involve directors' concerns for the ethical, social and environmental performance of companies selected for investment as well as their financial performance.

CSR-related information disclosure in China is a unique area, just like the corporate governance model in China, because of the unique Chinese history, stage of economic development, shareholding structure, culture and traditions. It is logical to start the discussions by examining government instruments. The scope of Chinese stakeholders is described in section 81 of the Code of Corporate Governance for Listed Companies in China to include 'banks and other creditors, employees, consumers, suppliers, the community and others'. Information disclosure requirements are clearly indicated in section 86, where companies are required to 'be concerned with the welfare, environmental protection and public interests of the community in which it resides, and ... pay attention to the company's social responsibility'. This concerns information disclosure to primary stakeholders including creditors, employees, consumers, suppliers, and the community, who partly fit into the six categories described above. Furthermore, the scope of CSR information disclosure is also described in the Social Responsibility Guidelines for Listed Companies released by the Shenzhen Stock Exchange, including the interests of 'shareholders, creditors, employees, customers, consumers, suppliers and communities'.[109] Ge and Lin argued that apart from corporate reporting

---

[108]   *Ibid.*
[109]   Shenzhen Stock Exchange Social Responsibility Instruction to Listed Companies 2006 art. 2.

on financial aspects, accountants should disclose CSR-related information to stakeholders, governments and the public, e.g. information on environmental protection, employee career development and training, non-discriminatory treatment of employees, health and labour insurance, and relationships with local communities.[110]

Based on the discussions in Ge and Lin, Li[111] and the CSR Blue Book 2011, which reports research on the CSR information disclosure of the top 100 companies in China in different categories (including the top 100 SOEs, the top 100 private companies and the top 100 foreign invested companies),[112] it can be concluded that CSR information disclosure normally includes the following six categories in China: environmental concerns, including pollution control, environmental restoration, energy conservation, waste materials recycling and environmentally friendly products; employee concerns, including health and safety issues, employee training, pensions, insurance and re-employment; community concerns; consumers' concerns such as the improvement of product quality and the health and safety of the products; creditors' concerns; and concerns about general social problems such as medical treatment, education, public safety and charity. These elements will generally fall into one category, or a combination of categories, classified in the Blue Book. However, just as in other emerging markets, problems such as health and safety of products, charity and the environment will be comparatively more important than the other issues in China.

7.6 BUSINESS REVIEW IN THE UNITED KINGDOM AND THE FEASIBILITY OF TRANSPLANTING THE SAME REQUIREMENT INTO CHINESE LAW

Corporate disclosure has long been regarded as an important way of enhancing corporate accountability and improving the transparency of corporate activities. In light of the growing awareness of long-term

---

[110] J. Ge and S. Lin, *Western Financial Accounting Theory (Xifang Caiwu Kuaiji Lilun)* (Xiamen: Xiamen University Press, 2001).

[111] Z. Li, *Research on Corporate Social Responsibility Information Disclosure (Qiye Shehui Zeren Xinxi Pilu Yanjiu)* (Beijing: Economic Science Press, 2008) pp. 67–8.

[112] J. Chen, Q. Huang, H. Peng and H. Zhong (eds), *Research Report on Corporate Social Responsibility of China 2011* (Beijing: Social Science Academic Press, 2011).

development and stakeholder considerations, there has been an increasing demand for corporations to produce reports detailing their commitment to social and environmental issues. A significant modification in the UK Companies Act 2006 was the abolition of the operating financial review (OFR)[113] for quoted companies[114] for financial years beginning on or after 1 April 2005. The statutory requirement to produce an OFR, which had been the subject of much consultation and discussion, was abolished and replaced by the business review.[115] This was in line with the minimum requirements of the EU Accounts Modernization Directive which called for the company's annual report to include 'both financial and, where appropriate, non-financial key performance indicators relevant to the particular business, including information relating to environmental and employee matters (when necessary)'.[116] The Directive was regarded as the response to introduction of the programme of sustainable business development by the European Commission, with a Recommendation on environmental disclosures that led to the inclusion of a fair review of the business in the accounts.[117] After the enactment of section 417 of the Companies Act 2006, the directors' report and business review became the central narrative reporting document in the corporate disclosure regime.[118] The government's intention was to use an enhanced directors' report, specifically the business review, in order to satisfy EU and investor requirements. The general idea was that the business review's requirements for directors 'will be less onerous on companies but still useful for investors and other stakeholders'.[119] The amendment placed an obligation on the directors of public companies to include in their annual business review anything that might be a liability to the company's profits through danger to its reputation, such as

---

[113]   The OFR requirement was amended on 21 March 2005 by Sch. 7ZA to the Companies Act 1985.

[114]   Companies with economic power are referred to as major companies.

[115]   Regulations to repeal the requirement for OFR were published on 21 December 2005 and came into force on 12 January 2006. It was replaced by the business review requirement.

[116]   Accounts Modernization Directive arts 14, 46.

[117]   See European Commission, *Towards Sustainability*, COM(92)235 (1992).

[118]   O. Aiyegbayo and C. Villers, 'The Enhanced Business Review: Has It Made Corporate Governance More Effective?' (2011) *Journal of Business Law* 699.

[119]   A. Reese, *Operating and Financial Review and the Business Review* (London: WSP Environmental, December 2005).

contracts with stakeholders that could potentially expose the company to risk through social or environmental harm.[120]

Based on a government Table comparing the requirements of the business review and the OFR,[121] differences between the OFR and the business review mainly rest on the following aspects: first, while the OFR was applicable to all UK quoted companies, the business review applies to all UK and EU companies except 'small' companies; secondly, while both reports require a balanced and comprehensive review, the business review covers only performance and development through the year, rather than requiring an analysis of the wider trends affecting the business which was a part of the OFR; thirdly, the only essential element of the business review is a summary of principal risks and uncertainties, without the commentary on business objectives, capital structure and resources that the OFR required; fourthly, in terms of measures, the business review does ask companies to include financial and non-financial key performance indicators (including where appropriate environmental and employee matters) 'to the extent necessary', but it does not require the inclusion of social and community issues, receipts and returns to share-holders and persons with whom the company has key relationships. The business review, prepared by the directors from their perspective and understanding of the business, is designed to provide descriptions and analyses of the company as a separate business entity as well as reporting on how the company's activities and operations impact on society, the environment and its local community, and the future prospects of these engagements.[122]

Legally, under section 417 of the Companies Act 2006 which focuses on the content of the business review of corporate annual reports, directors are obliged to include in the business review 'a fair review of the company's business and a description of the principal risks and uncertainties facing the company'.[123] The purpose of the business review is 'to inform members of the company and help them assess how the

---

[120]   D. Arsalidou, 'The Withdrawal of the Operating and Financial Review in the Company Bill 2006: Progression or Regression?' (2007) 28 *Company Lawyer* 131 at 134.

[121]   The Table is available at http://webarchive.nationalarchives.gov.uk/+/http://www.dti.gov.uk/bbf/corp-gov-research/page21369.html.

[122]   O. Aiyegbayo and C. Villers, 'The Enhanced Business Review: Has It Made Corporate Governance More Effective?' (2011) *Journal of Business Law* 699 at 705.

[123]   UK Companies Act 2006 s. 417(3).

directors have performed their duty under section 172'.[124] The obligations imposed on quoted companies are more onerous in comparison. Their business review must 'to the extent necessary for an understanding of the development, performance or position of the company's business', include 'the main trends and factors likely to affect the future development, performance and position of the company's business and information about environmental matters, the company's employees, [and] social and community issues'.[125] In other words, information concerning environmental, employment and community issues does not have to be included in the review if it does not contribute to an understanding of the development, performance or position of the company, and there is no indication or explanation as to what weight directors are to give to any material relating to these matters. Therefore, it is debatable whether the review will constitute a genuine account of the stewardship of all relationships in which the company is involved.[126]

This provision does not offer any hint about the degree of understanding which will be necessary, or how directors should decide to what extent these matters are needed for a full understanding of the business.[127] Similar to the efficiencies of the enlightened shareholder value principle embedded in section 172, the UK courts may be reluctant to find directors liable for not disclosing certain information simply because the legal requirements are unclear and indeterminate. If discretion is involved, directors will need to put 'good faith' as the criteria for making business decisions to promote the success of the company, using their power to decide whether or not to disclose information.

In China, the harmonious development between corporations and society has been regarded as a key theme for the government since the establishment of the goal of a Harmonious Society in 2005. Because the government still owns more than half of the shares of listed companies,

---

[124]   *Ibid.* s. 417(2).

[125]   *Ibid.* s. 417(5).

[126]   A. Keay, 'Tackling the Issue of the Corporate Objective: An Analysis of the United Kingdom's "Enlightened Shareholder Value Approach"' (2007) 29 *Sydney Law Review* 577 at 604.

[127]   O. Aiyegbayo and C. Villers, 'The Enhanced Business Review: Has It Made Corporate Governance More Effective?' (2011) *Journal of Business Law* 699 at 707.

the government also plays a critical role in CSR information disclosure.[128] A number of regulatory instruments have been introduced in China to create incentives for promoting CSR practices and standards for corporate information among listed companies, with a series of standards and guidelines to encourage sustainability reporting by corporations in a voluntary or mandatory manner.[129] Both the Shanghai and Shenzhen Stock Exchanges have instituted regulatory policies for CSR information disclosure, however, companies operating under these two exchanges are subject to different requirements regarding disclosure.[130] Chinese government agencies, regulators, trade associations and NGOs have all established various systems of rules and norms with regard to CSR information disclosure, all with the consistent purpose of promoting the practice of CSR in China. However, the different policies sometimes mean that enterprises are required to perform repetitive exercises in writing CSR reports, with companies having to include the same CSR issues in more than one report, involving unnecessary burdens and costs. It will in future be necessary to integrate CSR information disclosure systems across the different agencies to establish a more systematic, scientific and efficient national legal standard.[131] Given the different requirements of regulatory instruments from various sources, legislation at the national level is vital to make CSR information requirements for listed companies enforceable.

---

[128]   P. Wang, F. Wang, J. Zhang and B. Yang, 'The Effect of Ultimate Owner and Regulation Policy on Corporate Social Responsibility Information Disclosure: Evidence from China' (2012) 6 *African Journal of Business Management* 6183.

[129]   For example, the Corporate Governance Code in China, CCL 2006, the Environmental Information Disclosure Act 2007, Guidelines on Environmental Information Disclosure by Companies Listed on the Shanghai Stock Exchange 2008, the Chinese Corporate Social Responsibility Reporting Guidelines (CASS CSR 1.0), the Chinese Sustainability Reporting Guidelines for Apparel and Textile Enterprises (CSR-GATEs) 2008, and CSC9000T Management 2005.

[130]   P. Wang, F. Wang, J. Zhang and B. Yang, 'The Effect of Ultimate Owner and Regulation Policy on Corporate Social Responsibility Information Disclosure: Evidence from China' (2012) 6 *African Journal of Business Management* 6183; see also Shenzhen Stock Exchange, Social Responsibility Instructions to Listed Companies, Shanghai Stock Exchange, Notification to Listed Companies Concerning Reinforcement of Social Responsibility Work of Listed Companies, and Shanghai Stock Exchange, Environmental Information Disclosure Instruction to Listed Companies.

[131]   J. Wang, S. Qin and Y. Cui, 'Problems and Prospects of CSR System Development in China' (2010) 5 *International Journal of Business Management* 128 at 132.

Despite the fact that the corporate objectives of Chinese companies are guided and directed by article 5 of the CCL 2006, requiring them to practise social responsibility and observe business ethics, there are no supporting provisions in the directors' duties and information disclosure requirements, as is the case in UK company law or often forms a separate part of legislation in other jurisdictions.[132] According to a study published online, as of 30 June 2011, only 24.14 per cent of the listed companies (531 listed companies, compared with 483 in 2010 and 371 in 2009) in both the Shenzhen and Shanghai Stock Exchanges had disclosed and produced CSR reports.[133] Although there has been an increasing trend for disclosure, the legislative requirements in the CCL 2006 will be important to encourage more transparent corporate information disclosure on social and environmental issues in order to mitigate negative impacts such as corporate scandals, and to promote and establish the centrally-planned Harmonious Society. The legal requirements will also be of value to society more generally, either to better gauge the development of policy or to supplement the enforcement of policy by regulatory organizations.[134]

In the author's opinion, the legislative experiences of the 'business review' introduced in the UK Companies Act 2006 could partially be adopted in Chinese company law, with the addition of supplementary enforcement measures, such as quantitative information requirements and

---

[132]   See UK Companies Act 2006 ss. 172 and 417; also in Sweden, Spain and Finland, state-owned companies are required to report on different aspects of their non-financial performance, e.g. Government Resolution of State Ownership Policy 2011 (Finland), Spanish Sustainable Economy Law 2011 art. 39 and Guidelines for External Reporting by State-owned Companies 2007; the German Reform Act on Accounting Regulations 2004 requires that companies examine and report on key financial and non-financial indicators that materially affect the development or performance of the company in their annual report; the French Grenelle II Act art. 225 imposed a CSR reporting and social and environmental information obligation for listed companies and other companies based on the number of employees and balance sheet total; further, with the aim of motivating and inspiring Danish business to take an active position on CSR, the Danish Parliament (Folkertinget) passed a Act in 2008 as an amendment to the Danish Financial Statement Act. As a result, approximately 1,100 large businesses in Denmark are now legally required to include reports in their annual report on three dimensions, including CSR policies, how these policies are translated into actions and what the business has achieved as a result of working with CSR, and expectations for the future.

[133]   See www.csr-china.net/report.aspx.

[134]   M.J. Rhodes, 'Information Asymmetry and Socially Responsible Investment' (2010) 95 *Journal of Business Ethics* 145 at 148.

corporate accounting standards reporting for annual reports. First, as regards the regulated entities, under the Companies Act 2006 'a quoted company' must include information about environmental matters, employees, and social and community issues in its business review.[135] In the proposed article on CSR-related information disclosure in the CCL 2006, the same requirements should be imposed on companies listed on stock exchanges in China. This approach would make information disclosure more practical and attainable, as CSR practised by these listed companies would have a greater impact on stakeholders. The activities of listed companies are likely to have a significant impact on society and the community since they have multi-stakeholder groups, which in turn will have a further effect on CSR information disclosure. Listed companies generally play an active role in society, and their activities are closely followed by the public and regulated by the government, with associated high political costs and attention.[136] They are thus more likely to disclose information in detail in order to reduce political concerns and relieve political and supervisory pressure.[137] Therefore, companies listed on the stock exchanges should be the regulatory target for mandatory CSR disclosure, as the size of such corporations should prompt them to decrease social pressure by disclosing to the public, with positive effects.

As well as identifying common regulated entities, the CSR-related activities that are required to be disclosed in China should be consistent with the requirements in UK law, namely, environmental, social and community issues. Addressing basic concerns surrounding environmental, social and community issues will help corporations to establish a reputable corporate image, gain understanding and support from local communities and other stakeholders, and enhance the credibility of their reports. This legal requirement would partly solve the problem of the lack of a unified mandatory social responsibility information disclosure format, replacing the current inadequate qualitative and quantitative information that results in questionable reliability and poor comparability of CSR information between companies.[138]

---

[135]   UK Companies Act 2006 s. 417(5).

[136]   R. Watt and J. Zimmerman, 'Towards a Positive Theory of the Determination of Accounting Standards' (1978) 53 *Accounting Review* 112 at 115–16.

[137]   S.S. Cowen, L.B. Ferreri and L.D. Parker, 'The Impact of Corporate Characteristics on Social Responsibility Disclosure: A Typology and Frequency-based Analysis' (1987) 12 *Accounting, Organizations and Society* 111 at 113–14.

[138]   Y. Tang and D. Chen, 'Analysis of Present Situation, Foundation and Content about Corporate Social Responsibility Information Disclosure in China' (2012) *M & D Forum* 96 at 98.

Further, the concept of 'key performance indicators', defined as factors by reference to which the development, performance or position of the company's business can be measured effectively,[139] should be also introduced into the CCL 2006, in order to require disclosure of information relating to environmental and employee matters as non-financial information disclosure targets. This requirement fits within the 'triple bottom line' framework, which includes environmental issues (energy, water, waste and legal compliance); social issues (recruitment, employees' rights, health and safety, training and education, non-discrimination, child labour, bribery and community investment); and economic issues.[140] A focus on the last of these three factors remains vital, so that corporations are able to achieve their operational targets and economic goals; this can be regarded in practice as the precondition for effective CSR, because corporations with poor economic performance are unlikely to undertake CSR or engage in CSR information disclosure.[141] In order to promote CSR in China in a systematic manner, an evolving CSR reporting system should be established with different levels of performance indicators.[142] In line with China's policy on the Harmonious Society and sustainable development, the adoption of key performance indicators would help to create desirable and responsible corporate citizenship.

The transplanting of the legislative experience from the UK Companies Act 2006 will enable China to improve the breadth of disclosure to satisfy both stakeholders' needs and corporate values. Working with the mandatory requirements proposed in company law, the unique mix of a Chinese CSR information disclosure system should be consistent with the 'Notice on Strengthening Listed Companies Assumption of Social Responsibility' and the 'Guidelines on Listed Companies' Environmental Information Disclosure', both issued by the Shanghai Stock Exchange in May 2008. The system should include the following characteristics:

---

[139]   See UK Companies Act 2006 s. 417(6).

[140]   International Finance Corporation and Shanghai Stock Exchange, *Sustainability Reporting Guidelines: Mapping & Gap Analyses for Shanghai Stock Exchange* (2011) pp. 3–4, available at www1.ifc.org/wps/wcm/connect/19231 a804886585bb596f76a6515bb18/SSE_IFCReport%2BEnglish.pdf?MOD=AJPE RES&CACHEID=19231a804886585bb596f76a6515bb18.

[141]   J.L. Campbell, 'Why Would Corporations Behave in a Socially Responsible Way? An Institutional Theory of Corporate Social Responsibility' (2007) 32 *Academy of Management Review* 946.

[142]   J. Wang, S. Qin and Y. Cui, 'Problems and Prospects of CSR System Development in China' (2010) 5 *International Journal of Business Management* 128 at 133.

- Listed companies should be strongly encouraged to disclose non-financial information in CSR or sustainability reports.
- The content of the report should include information about the environment, employees, consumers, creditors and the public.
- The report should be endorsed by the board of directors and the audit committee.
- The system should make explicit the circumstances and conditions in which listed companies are mandatorily required to disclose CSR or sustainability reports.

7.7 UNIQUE REQUIREMENTS OF THE CSR INFORMATION DISCLOSURE SYSTEM IN CHINA

As discussed above, legislative experience from the UK Companies Act 2006 seems to be useful for making rules at a national level to promote CSR and CSR information disclosure in China. However, as suggested by path dependence theory, which attributes national differences in corporate law and corporate governance models to divergent historical and social underpinnings in different jurisdictions, 'the lesson of history … is that while markets have always been there, they have always operated in the context of geography, religion, language, folk ways, families, armies, and government, never in a vacuum'.[143] The enforcement of legal and regulatory systems for corporate information disclosure will be very different in China than they are elsewhere, due to the complicated social relationships between controlling shareholders and local government, and the *guanxi* between controlling shareholders and company directors.[144] China is the first Communist nation in the world to have a stock exchange, and since 1990 it has been the only socialist country to initiate the creation of a market-style modern enterprise system, achieved through a corporatization and shareholding framework, but without fully privatizing its state-owned enterprises.[145] China needs a unique CSR system of its own, shaped by the 'socialist market economy with Chinese

---

[143] K. Moore and D. Lewis, *Foundations of Corporate Empire: Is History Repeating Itself?* (New York: Prentice Hall, 2000) p. 219.
[144] J. Zhao and S. Wen, 'Gift Giving, *Guanxi* and Confucianism in a Harmonious Society: What Chinese Law Could Learn from English Law on Aspects of Directors' Duties', (2013) 34 *Company Lawyer* 381.
[145] See C. Yao, *Stock Market and Futures in the People's Republic of China* (New York: Oxford University Press, 1998).

characteristics'. By extension, this is also the case for a putative Chinese CSR information disclosure system.

7.7.1 Combined Legislation and Regulations from Various Sources

In the current international economic climate, in which a considerable number of multinational companies are preparing and producing CSR reports, there is a growing emphasis on gathering CSR information and making it an important factor when considering corporate credit and strength from the point of view of investors and the public. This is also the case for emerging markets, such as the market in China. Strengthening their CSR systems is a key part of corporate strategy for Chinese companies, partly by reputable CSR information disclosure in order to win trust and credibility from government and the public. However, it is necessary to integrate an efficient and comprehensive CSR information system both at a corporate level and at a national framework level. Therefore, a hybrid CSR information system, incorporating both legislative elements from company law, suggested above and informed by the legislative experience from the UK Companies Act 2006, as well as other regulatory instruments from the stock exchanges, central and local government authorities and agencies in other forms, is likely to work best for China, in combination with its unique corporate governance model.

A good example is the Guidelines for Corporate Environmental Reports, introduced in Shandong province in 2008. After the Guidelines were issued, corporations in Shandong province were required to disclose environmental information, beginning with selected companies as test units, and based on 50 basic factors and 45 selected factors.[146] The Guidelines required the selected corporations to write environmental reports reflecting the company's position from 24 aspects. Following the issuing of the Guidelines, a series of training sessions were also offered to the companies to ensure that the Guidelines had been understood and could be enforced in practice. The Guidelines proved to be an effective way, in a local area, of achieving disclosure of environmental information to the community and the public, through establishing a corporate environmental reporting system and providing technical guidance. Although the enforcement scope of the Guidelines was restricted to Shandong province, the scheme can be regarded as a start, and as the

---

[146] Guidelines for Corporate Environmental Reports in Shandong Province 2008 (*Shandongsheng Qiye Huanjing Baogaoshu Bianzhi Zhinan*) DB37/T 1086-2008, available at www.jnepb.gov.cn/moudle%5Cdown.aspx?id=631.

foundation of a system for corporate disclosure of environmental information in China. Such a system urgently needs to be established in order to achieve short-term targets, such as the national economy's Eleventh Five-Year Plan for energy saving, as well as long-term targets to promote CSR practices and sustainability in Chinese corporations.

7.7.2 Forms of Disclosure

In order to enforce the mandatory requirement for business reviews, it is important to clarify the forms of CSR information disclosure that may be further required in other regulatory instruments from government agencies or authorities. Regarding forms of CSR-related information disclosure in China, the argument against adopting a one-size-fits-all corporate governance model and a related regulatory approach suggests that it will also hamper the development of CSR-related reporting practices for both directors and shareholders. In terms of the forms of information disclosure, various types of document have been utilized, including annual reports, individualized reports, and non-report vehicles such as advertisements and company brochures.[147] Of these public domain sources, it is argued that annual reports were the most important,[148] being treated both as a stewardship tool[149] and as an investment tool.[150]

Generally speaking, there are four types of information disclosure in China: generalized information disclosure through annual reports; individualized information disclosure through annual reports; individualized information disclosure separated from annual reports; and information disclosure through the public media and press releases. All these forms of information disclosure can be produced at a descriptive, junior or senior

---

[147]   D. Campbell and A.C. Beck, 'Answering Allegations: The Use of the Corporate Website for Restorative Ethical and Social Disclosure' (2004) 13 *Business Ethics: A European Review* 100; see also D. Zeghal and S.A. Ahmed, 'Comparison of Social Responsibility Information Disclosure Media Used by Canadian Firms' (1990) 3 *Accounting, Auditing and Accountability Journal* 38.

[148]   T.A. Lee and D.P. Tweedie, 'Accounting Information: An Investigation of Private Shareholder Usage' (1975) 5 *Accounting and Business Research* 280.

[149]   *Caparo Industries Plc v Dickman* [1990] 2 AC 605, HL, per Lord Oliver of Aylmerton at 630–1.

[150]   PricewaterhouseCooper, *Corporate Reporting – A Time for Reflection: A Survey of the Fortune Global 500 Companies' Narrative Reporting* (London, 2007) p. 6; see also O. Aiyegbayo and C. Villers, 'The Enhanced Business Review: Has It Made Corporate Governance More Effective?' (2011) *Journal of Business Law* 699 at 700.

level. For generalized information disclosure, the information sources may be various documents such as corporate governance reports, ethical reports, financial statements or their appendices, or directors' meeting reports where there is not a separate information disclosure report. This is currently the most popular form of information disclosure in China, although there is a trend towards separate CSR reports.[151]

Taking CSR reporting among Chinese petrochemical corporations (generally referred to as the 'Sinopec Group') as an example, in comparison with CSR reports in 2003 which were produced in a scattered manner in five separate sections, the same report in 2011 was produced in a separate document and addressed issues including 'continuous energy supply, premium customer services, safe and stable operation, green and low-carbon growth, care for employees and rewarding society'.[152] The Sinopec CSR report identified the main stakeholders and mapped the relationships and coalitions among its stakeholders, as well as assessing the nature of each stakeholder's interest. The report successfully constructed a matrix of stakeholder priorities. It did not stop at a descriptive level; rather, it also assessed and disclosed CSR in a quantitative way and evaluated CSR-related actions from a monetary point of view, which is regarded as the junior statement type. However, the report also goes beyond this level by examining CSR development in the future and internationally, which places it at the senior level of CSR information disclosure.

A generalized CSR information disclosure system always makes it troublesome and time-consuming for investors and other stakeholders to find the useful and necessary information. In contrast, individualized CSR reports make the information clear, understandable, systematic and approachable. It is reasonable for corporations to keep their reports at a 'think small' level, showing their consideration towards minority investors and stakeholders by keeping their CSR reports informative but straightforward and easy to understand and avoiding overly complicated social income statements, value-added sheets or balance sheets. In terms of the future, it will be beneficial to corporations to offer training to corporate accountants about the international experience of CSR information disclosure. While CSR is an important topic on highly regarded corporate agendas, with companies recognizing it as a major business

---

[151]   Z. Li, *A Research on Corporate Social Responsibility Information Disclosure (Qiye Shehui Zeren Xinxi Pilu Yanjiu)* (Beijing: Economic Science Press, 2008) p. 143.

[152]   See www.sinopecgroup.com/english/Pages/ResponsibilityReport2012032 5_en.pdf.

driver, the Institute of Chartered Accountants in England and Wales (ICAEW) believes that that 'the accountancy profession has a central role to play in corporate responsibility and cannot afford to ignore it'.[153] With the joint efforts of both corporate insiders and gatekeepers, a framework such as that described in the 'Comprehensive Report' by Bouten and others seems workable in China. Under this system, a CSR information disclosure report should include the enterprise's corporate vision and goals, management approaches and performance indicators.[154] This is a framework that allows two important aspects of accountability, namely, completeness and comprehensiveness, to be easily, directly and simultaneously assessed.[155]

7.7.3 Government Interference and Information Disclosure

Overall, states whose governments have 'good corporate governance, regular certainty and an appropriate mix of policy tools including clear and enforceable regulatory standards, economic instruments and voluntary initiatives'[156] will be hugely attractive when companies are selecting the location of new investments in order to promote and strengthen their prospective business case for sustainable development. On the other hand, the government also has an interest in the company. For example, the government will outline various aspects of fiscal policies, such as capital allowances, incentives for investing in different industries or different parts of the company, and taxation raised from companies. Besides these considerations, governments always endeavour to ensure that companies act in a socially responsible way by taking account of social, ethical and moral considerations.[157] Of course, it is also the responsibility of the company to analyse corporate trends for various

---

[153] ICAEW Centre for Business Performance, *Corporate Social Responsibility and the Professional Accounting Firm: Insights from Firm's Disclosure* (Angus Duff and Xin Guo, 2010).

[154] L. Bouten, P. Everaet, L.V. Liedekerke, L.D. Moor and J. Christiaens, 'Corporate Social Responsibility Reporting: A Comprehensive Picture' (2011) 35 *Accounting Forum* 187.

[155] *Ibid.* at 202.

[156] R. Cowe, *Developing Value: The Business Case for Sustainability in Emerging Markets* (London: Sustainability, International Finance Corporation and Ethos Institute, 2002) p. 5.

[157] S. Sheikh, *Corporate Social Responsibilities: Law and Practice* (Abingdon and New York: Routledge, 1996) pp. 168–9.

purposes, including employment levels, monetary policies and market supply and demand for goods and services.[158]

The development of CSR in China has to be achieved by informing the public and raising awareness of CSR-related issues.[159] Furthermore, the importance of environmental discourse should also be addressed, with the government's institutional mechanism for disclosure as an important institutional underpinning for socialist democracy.[160] Following the publication of the Guidelines to the State-Owned Enterprises Directly under the Central Government on Fulfilling Corporate Social Responsibilities introduced by SASAC, the situation regarding CSR information disclosure in SOEs has improved dramatically. In his speech on 3 August 2010, entitled 'The Efforts made by the SOEs Directly under Control of Central Government to Fulfil their CSR', in response to the SASAC Annual Review 2010, Mr Huang Shuhe, the Deputy Director of SASAC, urged all SOEs directly under the control of central government to release CSR reports or sustainability reports to the community and public within three years, in order to strengthen communication with various stakeholders and consider opinions and suggestions from society, with timely responses to the concerns of stakeholders.[161]

Pressure from central government has improved the quality and quantity of CSR reports from SOEs directly under the control of central government (65 companies, 54.2 per cent of SOEs), while more than half of the SOEs followed the CASS-CSR 1.0,[162] which closely referenced

---

[158]   C.A. Mallin, *Corporate Governance*, 3rd edn (Oxford: Oxford University Press, 2010) pp. 66–7.
[159]   'Corporate Social Responsibility in China: One Great Leap Forward, Many More Still Ahead', Knowledge@Wharton (2009).
[160]   In a positive move, the Shenzhen and Shanghai Stock Exchanges have taken environmental disclosure on board and released the Guide to Listed Companies' Social Responsibility (Shenzhen Stock Exchange), and Guide to Environmental Information Disclosure for Companies Listed on the Shanghai Stock Exchange.
[161]   The whole speech is available in Chinese at the official SASAC website, www.sasac.gov.cn/n1180/n13307665/n13307681/n13307705/13352083.html.
[162]   Chinese Academy of Social Science, Corporate Social Responsibility 1.0; for the full version of the Guidelines see H. Zhong, X. Sun, C. Zhang and T. Zhang, *Corporate Social Responsibility (CSR) Report Preparation Guide 1.0 (Zhongguo Qiye Shehuizeren Baogao Bianxie Zhinan 1.0)* (Beijing: Economy and Management Publishing House, 2009). An updated version of the Guidelines has been published; see H. Peng, H. Zhong, C. Zhang and X. Sun, *Corporate Social Responsibility (CSR) Report Preparation Guide 2.0 (Zhongguo Qiye*

the GRI Guidelines.[163] The government's influence over SOEs will have a knock-on effect on their competitors, suppliers and customers. Their CSR reports are normally very widely disclosed in various ways, especially via official websites. This enhanced periodic disclosure will win public confidence and increase awareness of the CSR practices of the company, as well as promote the company's long-term interests of sustained development and improved reputation.

Despite the fact that sustainability reporting is essentially an exercise in favour of promoting stakeholder accountability, a notion to which many reporting organizations apparently subscribe, it would appear that economic considerations still provide its main driving force.[164] Following this logic, disclosure will attract more institutional investors who will compare investment opportunities and the environment before making investments based on factors including future forecasts, reputation and the long-term development potential of the company. They will also monitor companies' performance on issues involving CSR, primarily through CSR reports, in order to convey a picture of corporate responsiveness to key societal concerns.[165]

7.8 BLUEPRINT FOR SUGGESTED REFORM

In order to promote stakeholders' interests, companies should incorporate stakeholder-friendly business strategies by providing quantitative assessments of reporting practices, indexes and ratings that link governance with social responsibility.[166] Corporate social reporting, a crucial part of

---

Shehui Zeren Baogao Bianxie Zhinan 2.0) (Beijing: Economy and Management Publishing House, 2011).

[163]   J. Chen, Q. Huang, H. Peng and H. Zhong (eds), *Research Report on Corporate Social Responsibility of China 2011* (Beijing: Social Science Academic Press, 2011) pp. 169–70.

[164]   D.L. Owen and B. O'Dwyer, 'Corporate Social Responsibility: The Reporting and Assurance Dimension' in A. Crane, A. McWilliams, D. Matten, J. Moon and D. Siegel (eds), *The Oxford Handbook of CSR* (Oxford: Oxford University Press, 2008) p. 384 at p. 396.

[165]   J. Armour, S. Deakin and S.J. Konzelmann, 'Shareholder Primacy and the Trajectory of UK Corporate Governance' (2003) 41 *British Journal of Industrial Relations* 531 at 545.

[166]   A. Kolk, 'Sustainability, Accountability and Corporate Governance: Exploring Multinationals' Reporting Practice' (2008) 18 *Business Strategy and Environment* 1; see also C. Deegan, 'The Legitimizing Effect of Social and

CSR, discloses non-financial information on the various activities undertaken by companies in order to discharge their social responsibilities.[167] In order to protect the interests of various stakeholders from unlawful depletion of corporate funds, the disclosure of this specific information has been partly enshrined in legislation. In fact, many of the world's largest companies have started to produce social, environmental or sustainability reports in addition to their financial reports.[168]

The purpose of legal enforcement of CSR information disclosure with the support from local regulatory frameworks is to maintain a good corporate image, avoid unnecessary legal proceedings and consumer resistance, improve the efficiency of production, and optimize the management of supply chains in a socially responsible manner. These aspects are key, from the point of view of the corporations, in supporting the enforcement of corporate objectives stipulated in the CCL 2006 in terms of CSR and business ethics, in order to achieve the ultimate goal of establishing a genuinely Harmonious Society.

The combination of the incorporation of a 'business review' requirement in the CCL 2006, together with additional regulatory instruments and guidelines from government and agencies, seems to offer an efficient way to maintain a good balance and persuade companies to disclose their non-financial information. Despite the positive trend towards increasing levels and better quality of CSR reporting from Chinese companies, with associated progress towards a more comprehensive and competitive reporting system, the author recommends the adoption of the 'Comprehensive Report' framework to facilitate the completeness and comprehensiveness of reports and improve corporate accountability towards readers of the reports as well as shareholders who are potentially willing to invest. Government plays a particularly important role in CSR reporting, not only as regards SOEs which are directly controlled by central government, but also in respect of their suppliers and customers.

This book focuses on the unique characteristics, content and purpose of the CSR information disclosure system in China. Figure 7.1 is intended to assist in making the arguments clearer, and to provide a more vivid representation of the suggestions made throughout this book.

Environmental Disclosure: A Theoretical Foundation' (2002) 15 *Accounting, Auditing and Accountability Journal* 282.

[167]   S. Sheikh, *A Practical Approach to Corporate Governance* (London: LexisNexis, 2003) p. 176.

[168]   C.A. Williams and J.M. Conley, 'An Emerging Third Way? The Erosion of the Anglo-American Shareholder Value Construct' (2005) 38 *Cornell International Law Journal* 493 at 497.

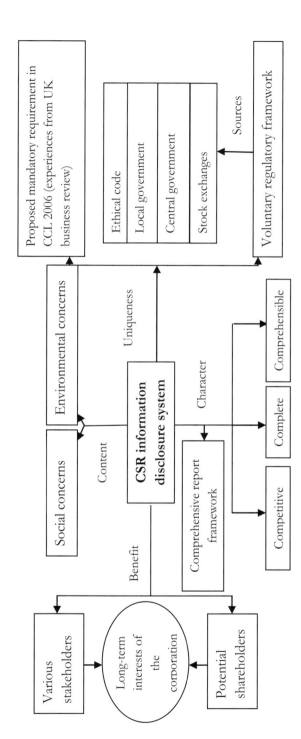

Figure 7.1 China's unique CSR information disclosure system

8. Enforcement of corporate social responsibility in a Harmonious Society

In 2005, former Chinese President Hu Jintao instituted the 'Harmonious Society' policy by establishing a new approach towards development in China. Hu instructed the country's leading officials and Party cadres to place 'building a Harmonious Society' at the top of their agendas, in order to build a society which puts people first. The programme is based on the goals of building a well-off society and creating a new socialist situation.[1] The purpose of building the Harmonious Society is to overcome the drawbacks of the immature and incomplete market within the Chinese socialist market economy, and to solve current and potential problems facing 'rural areas, farmers and agriculture, the drainage of farmland, heavy pressure in the workplace and an incomplete social security system'.[2] It is a policy to tackle a formidable challenge: managing 1.3 billion people with enormous diversity and across a massive territory.[3]

Over 2000 companies are listed on stock exchanges in China; most of these have been converted from state-owned enterprises (SOEs). With its recent rapid economic progress, China has now replaced Japan as the world's second largest economy.[4] Business evolution and development and corporate behaviours in China will certainly continue to capture the attention of many during the next decade. There is plenty of evidence which shows that the Chinese government is seeking to foster cooperation between business and society with an expectation of positive responses from companies. Highly visible community partnership opportunities were created by the 2008 Olympic Games held in Beijing, and

[1] 'Harmonious Society', *People's Daily*, 29 September 2007.
[2] *Ibid.*
[3] H.C. de Bettignies, 'CSR "Fatigue" and China's Performance' (2011) *GRLI Partner Magazine* (January) 31.
[4] At the end of 2010 China's economy was worth close to US$5.8 trillion, while Japan's economy was worth US$5.474 trillion.

there was significant business participation in the massive relief efforts after the devastating Wenchuan earthquake in Sichuan province, such as when Wang Lao Ji, one of China's most well-known and highly esteemed herbal tea and soft drinks companies, donated RMB 100 million on 18 May 2008. A series of major product safety scandals, such as where infant milk products were found to be contaminated with melamine, spotlighted industry failure and the urgent need for regulatory reform. Furthermore, in response to protests in August 2011, the municipal committee of the Chinese Communist Party and the Government of Dalian city ordered an immediate shutdown of the Fujia chemical plant which produced the potentially toxic chemical paraxylene. Former Premier Wen Jiabao reaffirmed this decision by stating that 'we must not any longer sacrifice the environment for the sake of rapid growth and reckless rollouts'.

Corporate social responsibility (CSR) has become an integral part of business management strategy and practice in China. Current thinking about the scope of CSR in China is often divided into two camps: the first interprets CSR in a broad sense, encompassing all corporate responsibilities including economic responsibilities; while the second delivers CSR more narrowly and relates it to corporate responsibilities excluding economic responsibilities, but including social, environmental, philanthropic and public services responsibilities, for example in relation to local communities.[5] It was suggested by Du that CSR can be divided into compulsory CSR and voluntary CSR, although it is widely accepted that CSR is normally defined as voluntary responsibilities beyond those required by legislation.[6] Du further suggested that compulsory CSR included measures against child labour, well-managed legal working hours and working environments, and fair treatment for employees without discrimination.[7] It is recognized that corporations will benefit from having a reputation as a company that 'does good' through contributing to society in multiple ways; such a reputation might facilitate permission to open and operate business activities, foster a better business reputation, improve employee recruitment, morale and retention,

---

[5]   L. Zhao, 'The Transformation and Trend in Corporate Social Responsibility in China' (2005) 2 *Management Research* 7 at 7–8.

[6]   Z. Du, 'Corporate Social Responsibility and Measures for Enforcement (*Qiye de Shehui Zeren Jiqi Shixian Fangshi*)' (2005) 4 *Journal of Renmin University of China (Zhongguo Renmin Daxue Xuebao)* 39 at 42–4.

[7]   *Ibid.* at 43.

influence consumer preference for products in terms of sales and switching, and bring cost savings from both suppliers and manufacturing.[8]

Questions naturally arise as to what, if any, linkage there might be between the Harmonious Society and CSR, and what possible contributions could the emphasis on a Harmonious Society offer to corporations in terms of their ethical improvement. In other words, this chapter will explore whether the Harmonious Society will be relevant and influential in the upgraded and increased CSR engagement that has broadly been adopted in Chinese corporations. If actions drawn up and taken by the government in response to a more Harmonious Society increase the level of CSR in China and make the Harmonious Society a more relevant factor in economic development, might there be ways to accomplish this more efficiently through corporate law? The author recognizes CSR as generally referring to voluntary corporate actions. However, many corporate actions are a precursor to legal regulations, and many types of socially responsible corporate behaviours are also legally required. It is agreed that CSR is not a substitute for regulation or relevant national and international legislation.[9] However, the enforcement of CSR will enhance

---

[8]   K.H. Darigan and J.E. Post, 'Corporate Citizenship in China: CSR Challenges in the "Harmonious Society"' (2009) 35 *Journal of Corporate Citizenship* 39 at 42; for more discussions on the potential benefits for corporations which are socially responsible, see L.W. Lin, 'Corporate Social Accountability Standards in the Global Supply Chain: Resistance, Reconsideration, and Resolution in China' (2007) 15 *Cardozo Journal of International Comparative Law* 321; A.F. Alkhafaji, *A Stakeholder Approach to Corporate Governance: Managing in a Dynamic Environment* (New York: Quorum Books, 1989); J.W. Anderson, *Corporate Social Responsibilities* (New York: Quorum Books, 1984); J.J. Brummer, *Corporate Responsibility and Legitimacy: An Interdisciplinary Analysis* (New York: Greenwood Press, 1991); S.N. Brenner and E.A. Molander, 'Is the Ethics of Business Changing' (1977) 58 *Harvard Business Review* 54; A. Carroll, *Business and Society: Ethics and Stakeholder Management* (Cincinnati, OH: South-Western Publishing, 1993); L.S. Munllia and M.P. Miles, 'The Corporate Social Responsibility Continuum as a Component of Stakeholder Theory' (2005) 110 *Business and Society Review* 371; A.L. Friedman and S. Miles, *Stakeholders: Theory and Practice* (Oxford: Oxford University Press, 2006).

[9]   There are also arguments that CSR represents a step toward standards which will eventually be regulated, or which view CSR as an antidote to over-regulation; see I.L. Fannon, 'The Corporate Social Responsibility Movement and Law's Empire: Is there a Conflict?' (2007) 58 *Northern Ireland Legal Quarterly* 1 at 4–9; see also S. Learmount, *Corporate Governance: What Can be Learned from Japan?* (Oxford: Oxford University Press, 2002); I. Hill, 'How

the implementation of relevant statutory obligations, and moreover it will encourage positive corporate decisions as regards social welfare benefits, beyond mere compliance with regulatory norms. It is argued that most corporate governance scholars have recognized the connection between 'good behaviour towards stakeholders to whom no legal duty is owed and fulfilment of the shareholder primacy obligation required in corporate law and the role the courts have played in guiding the way'.[10]

This chapter aims to demonstratesthat CSR has become institutionalized in China, and it also seems that the dominance of the Harmonious Society policy reaffirms and enhances the significance of ethical issues in Chinese companies. Additionally, links and overlapping aims will be found between the target of establishing a Harmonious Society by 2020 and corporate objectives in a socially responsible corporation. The expectations of stakeholders will be discussed in terms of their potential links with the proposed characteristics of corporations in a Harmonious Society. The final section analyses stakeholders' interests and changes in the Chinese legal system after recent shifts in government policy towards a more Harmonious Society. Special attention will be given to Chinese

---

Finance Can Help Move CSR up the Agenda' (2006) 16 *Cost and Management* 5; see also arguments from a common law perspective: *Evans v Brunner Mond Company Ltd* (1921) 1 Ch. 359; *A.P. Smith Manufacturing Co. v Barlow* (1953) 13 NJ 145; *Shlensky v Wrigley*, 237 N.E.2d 776 (III. App. Ct. 1968); *Green v Hamilton International*, 437 F.Supp. 723, 729 (New York, 1977); *R (on the application of People and Planet) v HM Treasury* [2009] EWHC 3020 (Admin); *Re West Coast Capital (LIOS) Ltd* [2008] CSOH 72, 16 May 2008 (Outer House, Court of Sessions, Scotland, Lord Glennie) at para. 21; *Stone & Rolls Ltd (In Liquidation) v Moore Stephens (A Firm)* [2009] UKHL 39; for the interests of creditors (as important external stakeholders) see *Diplock in Lonrho Ltd v Shell Petroleum Co. Ltd* [1980] 1WLR 627; *Lonrho Ltd v Shell Petroleum Co. Ltd* [1980] 1 WLR 627; *Re Horsley & Weight Ltd* [1982] 3 All ER 1045; *Brady v Brady* [1988] 3 BCC 535; *Liquidator of West Mercia Safetywear Ltd v Dodd* (1988) 4 BCC 30; *Percival v Wright* [1902] 2 Ch. 421; *Multinational Gas and Petrochemical Co. v Multinational Gas and Petrochemical Services Ltd* [1983] Ch. 258; *Peskin v Anderson* [2000] BCC 1110; *Yukong Lines Ltd of Korea v Rendsburg Investments Corp.* [1998] BCC 870; *Spies v The Queen* [2000] 201 CLR 603; [2000] 173 ALR 529; *Kinsela v Russell Kinsela Pty Ltd* [1986] 4 NSWLR 722; *Re New World Alliance Pty Ltd; Sycotex Pty Ltd v Baseler* [1994] 51 FCR 425; *Grove v Flavel* [1986] 43 SASR 410; *Jeffree v National Companies and Securities Commission* [1989] 7 ACLC 556; *Re Trizec Corp.* [1994] 10 WWR 127; *Re Saul D. Harrison & Sons plc* [1995] 1 BCLC 14; *Re Welfab Engineers Ltd* [1990] BCLC 883.

[10]   I.L. Fannon, 'The Corporate Social Responsibility Movement and Law's Empire: Is there a Conflict?' (2007) 58 *Northern Ireland Legal Quarterly* 1 at 16.

company law and to attempts to discover harmonious elements adopted in the new Chinese Company Law (CCL) 2006.

Enforcement of the Law will be also discussed in the context of an analysis of data concerning corporations' performance regarding stakeholders' interests from 2006 to 2011. Further suggestions for the future of legal enforcement of CSR-related laws will be offered during an examination of three case studies, focusing on the three main stakeholders in building a Harmonious Society within a corporation, namely, the company's employees, customers and environment.

8.1   THE HARMONIOUS SOCIETY AND THE GOVERNMENT'S POLICY SHIFT

The idea of building a Harmonious Society is not new for China. There is evidence of a variety of attempts to build a Harmonious Society in different dynasties in Chinese history. The concept is perfectly compatible with Chinese history and tradition.[11] It is described as a 'scientific development concept'[12] which shifts China's primary focus from a model based purely on economic growth to a more balanced, Confucian-style approach aimed at maintaining growth while addressing daunting social concerns.[13] The modernized society policy was suggested by the Chinese government in the Chinese Communist Party's Sixteenth National Party Congress in November 2002. It was emphasized that building a harmonious socialist society is one of the six goals to create a well-off society.

The SARS crisis occurred in 2003 and the global financial crisis began in 2008, while concerns about social inequalities became a hot topic on the political agenda, thus foreshadowing the political project to develop a

---

[11]   M. Anthony, 'The New China: Big Brother, Brave New World or Harmonious Society' (2007) 11 *Journal of Future Studies* 15 at 31.

[12]   Former President Hu Jintao, 'Scientific Outlook Development', lecture for Yale University, 24 April 2006; in the lecture, Hu clarified that 'China will pursue a scientific outlook on development that makes economic and social development people-oriented, comprehensive, balanced and sustainable. We will work to strike a proper balance between urban and rural development, development among regions, economic and social development, development of man and nature, and domestic development and opening wider to the outside world; it is also rooted in the culture heritage of the Chinese nation'.

[13]   J.P. Geis and B. Holt, 'Harmonious Society: Rise of the New China' (2009) *Strategic Studies Quarterly* 75.

Harmonious Society.[14] Concerns about social inequalities and a perceived 'justice gap' in reforming policies were influenced by the intensifying and evolving nature of protests since the late 1990s,[15] and by the need, recognized by the Chinese leadership, to reach out to the common people.[16] The leadership of China responded to the unacceptable social costs and political risks of reforms implemented since the late 1970s by placing social justice at the centre of political attention. The Harmonious Society was seen as a departure from the model that emphasized socialist market reform and economic growth, towards one in which economic aims are balanced against the urgent need to tackle pressing societal and environmental[17] problems in China. It responded to the negative connotations of the pronouncement that 'to get rich is glorious',[18] attributed to former President Deng Xiaoping, who was the driving force behind the move to capitalism after Mao's death, and the focus on GDP and the economy in modern China.

In the Party School, former President Hu confirmed that the Chinese Communist Party and the central government had made building a Harmonious Society into a priority because 'China is facing thorny domestic issues, as well as a complicated and volatile international situation'.[19] Consequently, building a socialist Harmonious Society was officially noted as one of the five major capabilities of the Communist Party of China during the Fourth Plenum of the Sixteenth National Party Congress in September 2004. Recommendations made in the Eleventh Five-Year Plan were adopted by the National Party Congress during the Fifth Plenary Session of the Sixteenth National Party Congress in October 2005. In the Recommendations, more specific plans for the grand blueprint for a Harmonious Society were designed in order to promote social harmony and expand employment, with the purpose of

---

[14]   A. de Haan, 'The Financial Crisis and China's "Harmonious Society"' (2010) 2 *Journal of Current Chinese Affairs* 69 at 82–3.

[15]   D. Kelly, 'Guest Editor's Introduction' (2006) 38 *Contemporary Chinese Thought* 3; see also C. Wong, 'Rebuilding Government for the 21st Century: Can China Incrementally Reform the Public Sector?' (2009) 200 *China Quarterly* 929.

[16]   J. Yu, 'Social Conflict in Rural China' (2007) 3 *China Security* 2.

[17]   G. See, 'Harmonious Society and Chinese CSR: Is there Really a Link?' (2008) 89 *Journal of Business Ethics* 1 at 1–2.

[18]   For discussions on Deng's declaration and the Harmonious Society see also G.K. Sims, 'The River Runs Black: The Environmental Challenge to China's Future' (2006) 65 *Journal of Asian Studies* 403.

[19]   'Building Harmonious Society crucial for China's progress: Hu', *People's Daily*, 27 June 2006.

improving the social security system, regulating income distribution more rationally, and ultimately enriching the spiritual and cultural life of the Chinese people.

The CPC Central Committee approved the Resolution on a number of major issues for the CPC Central Committee regarding the building of a harmonious socialist society in the Sixth Plenum of the Sixteenth National Party Congress in October 2006.[20] The Resolution clarified the steps towards enforcing Harmonious Society decisions regarding ideology, objectives, tasks, principles and major deployments to build a socialist harmonious society by 2020. The Resolution highlighted the 'importance, guidelines, goals and principles of building a socialist harmonious society: coordinated development; social equity and justice; cultural harmony and the ideological and ethical foundations of social harmony; and the need to improve public administration to build a vigorous and orderly society'.[21] It was affirmed in the Resolution that the concept of a Harmonious Society would be regarded as an official policy of the Chinese Communist Party.

8.2 CSR IN CHINA AND THE POSSIBLE LINK WITH THE HARMONIOUS SOCIETY

As a result of concerted efforts by the government, various Chinese corporations, including SOEs and privately owned companies, are producing sustainability and CSR reports. However, the concept of CSR in China is not new. In the centrally planned economic era after the inception of New China in 1949, corporations always performed good works to benefit society at large, and SOEs used to provide wider employee benefits such as primary and secondary education for the children of their staff. In the field of human endeavour, three subdivisions can be distinguished: 'economic, political and social activity – that is, business, government and society – in every civilization throughout

---

[20] 'China publishes its Resolution on Building a Harmonious Society. State Council Information Office of the People's Republic of China February 15, 2006', *Xinhua News Agency*, available at State Council Information Office of the People's Republic of China, www.scio.gov.cn/zgxwybd/en/2006/22/200612/t103742.htm.

[21] 'China publishes "Harmonious Society" Resolution', *Xinhua News Agency*, available at www.china.org.cn/english/2006/Oct/184810.htm.

time'.[22] The interplay between businesses, society and government regulation creates an environment in which businesses can cooperate smoothly. On the other hand, socially responsible corporations, where businesses act responsibly in relation to both the economic and the non-economic environment, will also have a tremendous impact on the creation of a Harmonious Society in China.

At first glance, a few possible links between CSR and the Harmonious Society can immediately be observed. First, the directors of corporations need to make legitimate and fair decisions, and comply with rules regarding fair competition, social norms, business ethics and regulations against bribery. Secondly, corporations need to respect people's rights, especially in their strategic management policies. Thirdly, the philanthropic contributions of corporations to society at large also fit into the theme of a Harmonious Society, as does the protection of the environment, plants and animals.

Looking at the Harmonious Society from a theoretical standpoint, the term was defined by former President Hu as a society 'which gives full play to modern ideas like democracy, the rule of law, fairness, justice, vitality, stability, orderliness and harmonious co-existence between humankind and nature',[23] in a speech given during the event marking the sixtieth anniversary of the United Nations on 15 September 2005. It is viewed as a revolutionary change in mode for the development of China, and it has attracted growing interest from government and academics. Li regarded this policy change as a renewed focus on addressing social and environmental challenges, with a reduced priority given to economic growth where it conflicts with these non-economic objectives.[24] The concept combines aspects of traditional Chinese culture and metaphysics, including Confucian and Taoist thought, with the reality of a modernized and increasingly globalized China. Given the negative fact that greed and self-interest are overriding the traditional Chinese concepts of harmony, family and working together as a group, the emphasis on the Harmonious

---

[22] J.F. Steiner and G.A. Steiner, *Business, Government, and Society: A Managerial Perspective, Text and Cases*, 13th edn (New York: McGraw-Hill, 2012) p. 4.

[23] See 'Harmonious Society concept draws world attention', *People's Daily*, available at http://english.peopledaily.com.cn/200512/14/eng20051214_227940. html.

[24] P. Li, 'Scholar explores Harmonious Society concept', available at www. china.org.cn/english/2005/Mar/121746.htm.

Society is collectively a positive move.[25] It is a strong response to problems in China such as 'income disparity, the urban and rural development imbalance, unemployment, an aging population and environmental pollution'.[26] The idea of the Harmonious Society reaffirmed its corporate aspects by placing emphasis on corporate responsibility and accountability towards a wider group of constituencies than shareholders, namely, corporate stakeholders.

As for the future of the policy for the development of a Harmonious Society, a deadline was set in the Sixth Plenum of the Sixteenth Central Committee of the Communist Party to achieve the policy by 2020, overcoming a number of listed disharmonious elements including:[27]

- widening of the gap between urban and rural development and development between different regions;
- people's rights and interests to be granted concrete respect and guarantees;
- unequal income distribution patterns;
- employment rate is relatively high, but absence of a social security system covering both urban and rural households;
- basic public service system should be further improved;
- efficiency in utilization of resources needs to be enhanced;
- need for improvement in environmental management;
- need to foster a sound moral atmosphere and harmonious interpersonal relationships.

Looking at the targets listed above, primary stakeholders,[28] including consumers, employees, local communities and the environment, will be

---

[25]   M. Anthony, 'The New China: Big Brother, Brave New World or Harmonious Society?' (2007) 11 *Journal of Future Studies* 15 at 31.

[26]   P. Li, 'Scholar explores Harmonious Society concept', available at www.china.org.cn/english/2005/Mar/121746.htm.

[27]   See Communiqué of the Sixth Plenum of the Sixteenth CPC Central Committee, *People's Daily*, available at http://english.peopledaily.com.cn/200610/12/eng20061012_310923.html.

[28]   For more discussions on stakeholders see R.E. Freeman, *Strategic Management: A Stakeholder Approach* (Boston and London: Pitman, 1984); B. Mescher, 'The Law, Stakeholders and Ethics: Their Role in Corporate Governance' (2011) 8 *Macquarie Journal of Business Law* 37; K. Mitchell, B.R. Agle and D.J. Wood, 'Toward a Theory of Stakeholder Identification and Salience: Defining the Principle of Who and What Really Counts' (1997) 22 *Academy of Management Review* 853; M. Evan and R.E. Freeman, 'A Stakeholder Theory of the Modern Corporation' in M. Snoeyenbos, R. Almeder and J. Humber (eds), *Business Ethics*, 3rd edn (New York: Prometheus Books, 2001).

regarded as parties whose interests should be taken into account in order to overcome disharmonious elements by 2020. It is also reemphasized that the policy for a Harmonious Society is a person-centred governmental idea, placing people first and (from a corporation's point of view) focusing on stakeholders' interests in order to promote a more harmonized and supportive working environment and create opportunities for sustainable development.

The policy was introduced in recognition of the social and environmental problems that arose as a result of rapid economic development in China.[29] Undeniably, many of these problems are closely related to the protection of stakeholders' interests by companies, which is a direct result of directors' duties stipulated and required under the CCL 2006. Consistent with corporate objectives enshrined in article 1 and article 5, the scope of fiduciary duties of fidelity and diligence to the company embedded in article 148 have become broader, giving directors legitimacy in taking into account social morality and business ethics. The target also fits with the requirements of ISO 26000,[30] which is widely recognized by the government and corporations in China. It is reaffirmed by results from the questionnaires from the roundtable 'Challenges and Opportunities for CSR Service Providers in China: Warming up for ISO 26000'.[31] Chinese export-oriented companies and companies in coastal areas are most likely to apply ISO 26000. The guidance identified and set a few core subjects as priorities that a business organization should address when integrating corporate social responsibilities in their corporate strategies; these include 'organizational governance, human rights, labour practices, the environment, fair operating practices, consumer issues and community involvement and development'.[32] Therefore, the target and aims of a Harmonious Society would be consistent with the objectives of corporations as far as their social responsibilities are concerned. These are core subjects described in the Guidelines that are

---

[29] W.T. Woo, *Reframing China Policy: The Carnegie Debates; Debate 2: China's Economy – Arguing for the Motion* (Carnegie Endowment for International Peace, Central University of Finance and Economics, Beijing, Brookings Institution, Washington, DC and University of California, Davis, CA, 2006).

[30] For more regarding the International Organization for Standardization, see www.iso.org/iso.

[31] For more information on the roundtable, see the Sino-German Corporate Social Responsibility Project website at www.chinacsrproject.org/News_Show_EN.asp?ID=90.

[32] ISO 26000: Guidance on Social Responsibility (ISO 2010) ch. 6.

closely related to corporate actions and stakeholders' expectations. However, it is also suggested in the Guidelines that social responsibilities are dynamic issues that reflect the evolution of current and future social, environmental and economic concerns.[33]

'The turbulent state of the global economy threatens the financial stability, economic well-being and social contract between business, government and society.'[34] In China, the emerging social structure seems to be at risk of succumbing to waves of financial hardship and change, although economic growth has been regarded as the theme of the past three decades. CSR and corporate citizenship created significant social capital which assists communities in adjusting to the harsh realities of global change, and enables businesses to interact with government and non-profit organizations to help people and build a more harmonious community relationship.[35] The corporations are clearly expected to deliver good products and excellent services; but they should also aim to 'pursue values, not just value; and to help make the world a better place'.[36] The 'organic model' argues that a company should function as a social institution with an independent existence, rather than as the private property of its shareholders.[37] According to this model, 'ownership', 'control' and 'public interests' should be separate from each other in the exercise of corporate power.[38] This gives the directors the right to exercise some latitude to pursue other goals in their daily performance, particularly those which are more socially responsible than the pure pursuit of shareholder wealth maximization.

Applying the organic model in the case of China, the relationship between the targets of establishing a Harmonious Society by 2020 and the social and environmental aspects of corporate objectives can be explicitly

---

[33]   *Ibid.*

[34]   K.H. Darigan and J.E. Post, 'Corporate Citizenship in China: CSR Challenges in the "Harmonious Society"' (2009) 35 *Journal of Corporate Citizenship* 39.

[35]   *Ibid.* at 40.

[36]   J. Bakan, *The Corporation: The Pathological Pursuit of Profit and Power* (London: Constable & Robinson, 2004) p. 31.

[37]   J. Dean, 'Stakeholding and Company Law' (2001) 22 *Company Lawyer* 66 at 66–7; see also M. Stokes, 'Company Law and Legal Theory' in W. Twining (ed.), *Legal Theory and Common Law* (Oxford: Blackwell, 1986) p. 155; D. Millon, 'Theories of the Corporation' (1990) 39 *Duke Law Journal* 201; M. Horwitz, 'Santa Clara Revisited: The Development of Corporate Theory' (1985) 88 *West Virginia Law Review* 173.

[38]   J.E. Parkinson, *Corporate Power and Responsibility: Issues in the Theory of Company Law* (Oxford: Clarendon Press, 1993) p. 23.

demonstrated, as shown in Figure 8.1. It is obvious that the Harmonious Society policy and CSR are interrelated, with the core norm or value of corporate social responsibility lying in constructing a human-oriented Harmonious Society.[39] While the targets of establishing a Harmonious Society have a direct impact on a company's management strategy with regard to social responsibilities, raising the level of CSR, it is also the case that CSR can be used as a tool for creating a Harmonious Society in China,[40] by putting emphasis on the goal of common prosperity under the banner of serving the people to improve their quality of life.

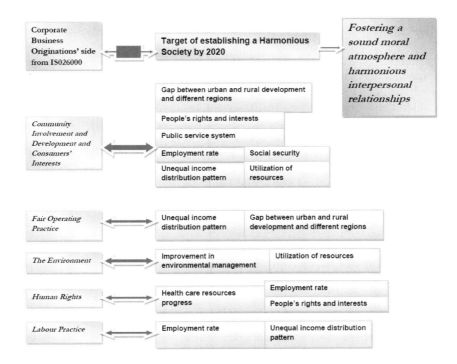

Figure 8.1   CSR and the target of building a Harmonious Society

---

[39]   D. Huang, Y. Kong and Z. Hua, 'Symposium on China's Peaceful Development and International Law' (2006) 5 *Chinese Journal of International Law* 261 at 268.

[40]   See D. Karlsson, *Corporate Social Responsibility: A Tool for Creating a Harmonious Society in China* (Brussels: European Institute for Asian Studies, 2011).

Responsible business is good business in the long term, having positive effects on customer relations, employee attitudes, and ultimately the share price and the cost of capital.[41] The adoption and application of the stakeholder theory can result in increased wealth for the whole of society, and when businesses correctly implement the strategy it has been likened to a win-win situation.[42] The instrumental power of stakeholder theory suggests that stakeholder management can be employed to achieve shareholder value, and a balance between the interests of the different stakeholder groups is essential in ensuring that an organization continues to be viable and achieves other performance goals.[43] If the proposition is correct, namely, that a link exists between CSR and the Harmonious Society, it is important to satisfy stakeholders' expectations in order to build a Harmonious Society at large. For a general commercial company, stakeholders' expectations in relation to the company and the company's potential accountability to stakeholders are analysed in Table 8.1.

Possible reform actions were also suggested in the Sixth Plenum to tackle these disharmonies, including the following measures:

- Social equity and justice as a basic condition of social harmony.
- Accelerated construction of a system to ensure social equity and justice, to guarantee people's rights and interests in political, economic, cultural and social fields and to guide citizens to exercise their rights and fulfil their obligations according to the law.
- Institutional construction should be enhanced and social equality and justice should be safeguarded.
- Development of cultural causes and cultural industries should be accelerated.
- Environmental protection and pollution control should be strengthened.

In addition, three logical approaches were suggested for the attainment of a Harmonious Society in China today:[44] first, the government should take

[41] B. Tricker, *Corporate Governance: Principles, Policies, and Practices* (Oxford: Oxford University Press, 2009) p. 352.

[42] S. Cooper, *Corporate Social Performance: A Stakeholder Approach* (Aldershot: Ashgate, 2004) p. 13.

[43] N.A. Shankman, 'Reframing the Debate between Agency and Stakeholder Theories of the Firm' (1999) 19 *Journal of Business Ethics* 319.

[44] See ideas and approaches suggested by Chen and Hu in K. Chen, 'The Importance of Building a Civilised Society in Building a Harmonious Society' (2006) 33 *Minjian (Civil Society Circular)*; and A. Hu, 'China in 2020:

Table 8.1   Stakeholders' expectations in relation to the company

Stakeholder	Expectations of company	Nature of accountability by the company	Form of legitimacy relationship
Human resources (employees)	Remuneration and other conditions of employment; working conditions, opportunities for advancement and training	Company reports, employment news, bargaining information	Employment and contract law
Suppliers of funds (creditors)	Liquidity and solvency of company; value of security; cash generation; reliable repayment	Cover ratios, collateral, cash forecasts	Insolvency law, security regulations and (bank) lending regulations
Suppliers	Contractual payment of indebtedness and enduring relationship	Payment according to terms	Contract law, company law
Customers	Quality; service; safety; delivery; value for money; product development	Sales literature, advertising, servicing	Sale of Goods Act, contract law
General public and local community	Safety of operations; contribution to the community	Safety reports, press reports	Environmental law, company law and tax law

Sources: D.G. Woodward, F. Edwards and F. Birkin, 'Organizational Legitimacy and Stakeholder Information Provision' (1996) 7 *British Journal of Management* 340; S. Turnbull, 'Corporate Governance: Its Scope, Concerns and Theories' (1997) 5 *Corporate Governance* 180.

steps to reduce inequalities by implementing a more balanced develop-ment strategy to ensure a more progressive redistribution of income through social welfare and services; secondly, the government should develop a fair and legitimate system to promote democracy and resolve social conflicts; and thirdly, it is also important to promote the idea of tolerance when addressing diversity in modern society, since people

Comprehensive Well-off and the Goal of a Socialist Harmonious Society' in J. Zhou, A. Hu and S. Wang (eds), *Building a Harmonious Society: The Experiences of Europe and the Exploration of China* (Beijing: Tsinghau University Press, 2007) p. 165.

should learn to respect differences not just in religious beliefs and lifestyles, but also in the political dimension.[45]

The Chinese government responded positively in terms of encouraging more socially responsible corporations. The leaders of China and Chinese SOEs are becoming more conscious of the importance of improving awareness of CSR in the context of an increasingly complex relationship between the government, enterprises and civil society. Chinese leaders are fully aware that there are problems behind the shining statistical figures describing China's economic growth and expansion. China's impressive economic achievements in the past three decades have cost Chinese society many precious historical characteristics. In New York at a luncheon held in his honour by the National Committee and the US-China Business Council on 23 September 2008, former Premier Wen Jiabao stated that 'China will learn from the baby milk scandal and seize the opportunity to overhaul food safety control and promote better business ethics'. Premier Wen emphasized the importance of the enhancement of social morals, and suggested that 'businessmen should run their business with the blood of morality'.[46] He stated that China will adopt strong measures to ensure more responsible products. On a more generalized level, he also pointed out that 'degradation of morality and lack of integrity has become a serious problem which would eventually hamper the rise of China'.[47] In an online chat on 27 February 2010, Premier Wen reconfirmed that Chinese entrepreneurs must have 'moral blood', and criticized those that cross the line for their own short-term interests because they hurt the interests of the whole of society.[48]

---

[45]   K.M. Chan, 'Harmonious Society' in H.K. Anheier and S. Toepler (eds), *International Encyclopedia of Civil Society* (New York: Springer, 2009) p. 821 at pp. 822–3.

[46]   See 'Wen Jiabao attends welcoming luncheon of American Friendly Organizations and delivers speech on China-U.S. Relations', Ministry of Foreign Affairs of People's Republic of China at www.fmprc.gov.cn/eng/wjdt/zyjh/ t514790.htm.

[47]   See 'Wen Jiabao criticised milk Clenbuterol: a serious moral decline', available at www.cnkeyword.info/wen-jiabao-criticized-milk-clenbuterol-a-serious-moral-decline.

[48]   'News analysis: China looks to central SOEs to back low-income housing project', *Xinhua News Agency*, available at http://news.xinhuanet.com/ english2010/china/2011-05/05/c_13860819.htm; in particular, the Premier issued a moral sermon towards real estate developers, stating that 'as members of society, real estate developers should have social responsibilities and moral blood'. He reaffirmed that 'within the body of every businessman should flow the blood of morality'.

8.3 AN EFFECTIVE LEGAL ENVIRONMENT TO PROMOTE A HARMONIOUS SOCIETY

It is important to build a stakeholder-friendly legal environment so that managers are able to adopt socially responsible practices, assisting non-shareholder groups in their battles against corporate decisions that ignore stakeholders' interests. 'Law's discourse has already signposted the way to consider and resolve corporate governance problems in the broader social responsibility context.'[49] CSR is increasingly being appreciated as a crucial component of companies' 'intangible assets', which are taking on greater significance in determining how investors view the present and future health of companies.[50] CSR practices are not designed to transfer the aim of profit maximization to social purposes. Conversely, CSR supports a rationale that justifies profit maximization. If company directors take social responsibilities into account, it is more sensible to define the ultimate purpose of directors' duties as the 'maximization of the total creation of wealth'.[51] Company directors are required to consider the long-term view of social development in order to establish a healthy ecosystem for their stakeholders and themselves, as well as a favourable natural and business environment for the survival of the company. It is argued that, from the start, voluntary CSR has been socially and economically driven.[52] Under the banner of CSR, it has to be realized that success and shareholder value cannot be achieved 'solely through maximizing short-term profit but instead through responsible

---

[49] I.L. Fannon, 'The Corporate Social Responsibility Movement and Law's Empire: Is there a Conflict?' (2007) 58 *Northern Ireland Legal Quarterly* 1 at 3; see also O. Hart, 'Norms and the Theory of the Firm' (2001) 149 *University of Pennsylvania Law Review* 1701.

[50] K. Howell, 'Introduction' in *Business and Society: Developing CSR in the UK* (London: DTI, March 2001) p. 1. Around 50 per cent of FTSE-100 companies published formal environmental reports in 2000, and this figure has increased steadily in recent years.

[51] For more discussion on the corporate objectives of social welfare and total wealth creation, see G. Kelly and J. Parkinson, 'The Conceptual Foundation of the Company: A Pluralist Approach' in J. Parkinson, A. Gamble and G. Kelly (eds), *The Political Economy of the Company* (Oxford: Hart Publishing, 2000) p. 113 at p. 131.

[52] D. McBarnet, 'Corporate Social Responsibility beyond Law, through Law, for Law: The New Corporate Accountability' in D. McBarnet, A. Voiculescu and T. Campbell (eds), *The New Corporate Accountability: Corporate Social Responsibility and the Law* (Cambridge: Cambridge University Press, 2007) p. 9 at p. 12.

behaviour', and attention to CSR must 'bring about a change in business culture so that sustainable objectives become an integral part of corporate strategic planning and routine operational performance'.[53]

8.3.1 Stakeholders' Interests: The Key to Building a Harmonious Society from the Corporate Perspective

Like the idea of CSR itself, the role played by the law in CSR's form, implementation and communication has been a topic that has been discussed broadly.[54] It is recognized that CSR seems to work as an informal set of rules, but it also seems to be based on a set of fundamental principles in law. Specific instruments of international law, national law and standards all accommodate the main tenets of CSR.[55] Statutory laws are used by governments as instruments to make corporations undertake specific types of responsibilities, specifically by requiring corporations to report on CSR-related topics. Companies in the United States and the United Kingdom are recruiting the services of CSR consultancies to produce CSR codes, write or verify CSR reports, train staff in CSR and market their CSR credentials.[56] Legal requirements will play an increasingly important role in enforcing voluntary corporate policies. New legal developments are directly or indirectly fostering voluntary stakeholder policies and market pressure, to make what business previously perceived to be voluntary, or beyond the law, in fact legally enforceable.[57] Legal doctrines and processes are employed by

---

[53] F. Martin, 'Corporate Social Responsibility and Public Policy' in R. Mullerate (ed.), *Corporate Social Responsibility: The Corporate Governance of the 21st Century* (London: Kluwer Law International, 2005) p. 77 at p. 78.

[54] See J.E. Kerr, 'The Creative Capitalism Spectrum: Evaluating Corporate Social Responsibility through a Legal Liens' (2008) *Temple Law Review* 831; J.E. Kerr, 'A New Era of Responsibility: A Modern American Mandate for Corporate Social Responsibility' (2009) 78 *University of Missouri–Kansas City Law Review* 327; B. Choudhury, 'Serving Two Masters: Incorporating Social Responsibility into the Corporate Paradigm' (2008) 11 *University of Pennsylvania Journal of Business Law* 631.

[55] K. Buhmann, 'Corporate Social Responsibility' (2006) 6 *Corporate Governance* 188 at 199.

[56] D. McBarnet, 'Corporate Social Responsibility beyond Law, through Law, for Law: The New Corporate Accountability' in D. McBarnet, A. Voiculescu and T. Campbell (eds), *The New Corporate Accountability: Corporate Social Responsibility and the Law* (Cambridge: Cambridge University Press, 2007) p. 9 at p. 11.

[57] *Ibid.* at 31.

corporations as part of their strategy, and market forces are stimulated and facilitated by legal measures.[58]

The legal environment consists of legislation, regulation and litigation. The general trend in the legal environment, with all three aspects on the increase, is towards the constraint of business behaviour.[59] With the growth of large and public corporations since the nineteenth century and an increase in the number and complexity of related laws and regulations, companies find themselves with continuously expanding duties to protect the rights of stakeholders, including employees, consumers, the public and even their competitors. Despite the fact that the requirements for ethical behaviour and CSR go beyond legal duties, 'they are plucked from the voluntary realm and encoded into law'.[60] Furthermore, corporations have always needed to anticipate expanding liabilities with necessary training for directors because of rapid technological change and the emergence of new laws and regulations.

When corporate directors are held responsible for their misbehaviour due to their lack of respect for human rights, labour rights and environmental protection, NGOs, investors, current or future employees, consumers, the local community, media and other stakeholders, it is necessary for the government to reassess the law, including its underlying principles.[61] While some progressive scholars and reformers have attempted to protect stakeholders by changing corporate law, others have looked to other legal regimes to regulate corporate behaviour. Directors will be required by laws outside of corporate law to consider the legal rights of various stakeholders. Corporate governance practices are typically influenced by an array of legal domains, such as securities regulation, accounting and auditing standards, tax law, contract law, employment law, environment law, consumer protection law and insolvency law.[62] All these decisions are made under the mandatory legal rules embodied by these legislative instruments. Those duties towards various stakeholders are the fiduciary duties of company directors, and are inseparable from corporate law and corporate governance. As a result,

---

[58]   *Ibid.*

[59]   J.F. Steiner and G.A. Steiner, *Business, Government, and Society: A Managerial Perspective, Text and Cases*, 13th edn (New York: McGraw-Hill, 2012) p. 42.

[60]   *Ibid.* at 41.

[61]   K. Buhmann, 'Corporate Social Responsibility' (2006) 6 *Corporate Governance* 188 at 199.

[62]   OECD, *OECD Principles of Corporate Governance* (2004) p. 2, available at OECD website www.oecd.org.

directors will, when they manage a corporation, find 'their decision tree considerably trimmed and their discretion decidedly diminished by mandatory legal rules enacted in the name of protecting stakeholders'.[63]

An article in the *China Daily* provided the following examples of the development of CSR in China: Liu Rui from Shanghai was relieved when he realized that it was illegal for his boss to refuse to sign a labour contract with him, and his rights were protected by the Labour Contract Law 2008;[64] and Suan Xian from Beijing was pleased that his interests were acknowledged in the government's proposals for drafting employment promotion regulations, which would prohibit discrimination against physically challenged and disabled people in the workplace, giving him confidence that he would be able to find a job after years of struggle. Such examples were described as demonstrating that reforms in the law and regulations have changed the daily life of Chinese people for the better, illustrating the country's critical shift from regulating economic matters to resolving social problems.[65]

The changes in the legal system aimed at building a Harmonious Society come from various sources, but all the changes focus on people's rights, and put people at the centre of society. The statutory changes that took place before and after the government's Harmonious Society policy were implemented were regarded as legislative evidence of building a people-centred society. It was explicitly stated in a constitutional amendment[66] that 'the State respects and protects human rights'.[67] The requirements of the Chinese Criminal Law regarding the final verdict in all death sentences in the Supreme People's Court were also regarded as evidence of the Chinese government's commitment towards a Harmonious Society. The relevant provision stipulates that 'the death penalty shall only be applied to criminals who have committed extremely serious crimes. All death sentences except for those according to law should be decided by Supreme People's Court, [and] shall be submitted to the Supreme People's Court for verification and approval'.[68] Similarly, other

---

[63]   A. Winkler, 'Corporate Law or the Law of Business? Stakeholders and Corporate Governance at the End of History' (2004) 67 *Law and Contemporary Problems* 109 at 111.

[64]   See Chinese Labour Contract Law 2008 art. 14.

[65]   Z. Zhe, 'Toward Harmonious Society through Rule of Law', *China Daily*, 10 March 2008.

[66]   Approved by the Second Session of the Tenth National People's Congress.

[67]   See Constitution of the People's Republic of China art. 33.

[68]   Chinese Criminal Law 1997 art. 48.

evidence can be found in the CCL 2006, Labour Contract Law 2008, Environmental Protection Law 2008, Trade Union Law of China (amended in 2001), Law on Consumer Interest Protection 1994, Law on Air Pollution (amended in 2000), Food Safety Law 2009, Circular Economy Promotion Law 2009, Renewable Energy Law 2006, Law on Prevention and Control of Water Pollution (amended in 2008), and other secondary regulations including Regulations on Supervisors over Labour Rights and Security, Rules on Minimum Wages, CSR Guidelines for State-owned Enterprises published by the State-owned Assets Supervision and Administration Commission (SASAC) in 2008, and Regulations on Administrative Penalties for Damage to the Environment.

It is especially noticeable in the response to the financial crisis of 2008 that 'to ensure the fulfilment of social responsibility by commercial banks'[69] was listed as a main purpose of government bodies in banking regulatory works. This was stated in the New Guidelines on Corporate Governance of Commercial Banks in China (Consultative Document), put forward in July 2011 and formulated in accordance with the CCL 2006. In addition, in the same Guidelines the sound corporate governance of commercial banks was refined to include 'a scientific development strategy, values and codes of conduct as well as social responsibilities'.[70] Furthermore, in Chapter 4 of the Guidelines, 'Development Strategies, Value Criteria and Social Responsibilities', the importance of CSR in commercial banks is once again reaffirmed through emphasis on consideration of the interests of depositors and other stakeholders within the bank.[71] It is significant to note that this legislative instrument has gone one step further compared to previous documents, by putting a 'focus on the mid- to long-term development plans, strategic goals, business philosophies, market positioning, capital management and risk management and so on'. Mid- to long-term development of strategic management goals in conjunction with valuable business philosophies are being carried out in parallel for the first time in Chinese legislative instruments aimed at prompting more socially responsible commercial banks in China.

CSR and economic goals are related closely in both directions, since good CSR policies can also bring 'the enhancement of competitive advantage, better reaching market segments like ethical consumers and socially responsible investors, and enhanced opportunities for strategic

---

[69] Guidelines on Corporate Governance of Commercial Banks in China (Consultative Document, August 2011) art. 5.

[70] *Ibid.* art. 7.

[71] *Ibid.* art. 70.

alliance or other partnership as major business opportunities for corporations with external constituencies, and, from an internal point of view, enhancement of labour relations and employee commitment, and the achievement of overall better financial and strategic results.'[72] The approach adopted in legislation rests on the level of business organization governance, since directors are required to interconnect various stakeholders' interests in the formation of their strategic management policy. The emphasis on CSR extends the reach of strategic planning towards people, particularly bank employees, by adopting Harmonious Society policies into the guidelines and putting people at the centre of society. Commercial banks are required to 'set up sound value criteria, corporate culture and business philosophies that highlight social responsibility so as to motivate employees to better fulfil their responsibility'.[73] Apart from the internal stakeholders' interests, the interests of external stakeholders were also considered in the guidelines in relation to the public at large. Commercial banks are required to 'fulfil their social responsibility in the economy, environment and social welfare', together with a disclosure requirement regarding their 'social responsibility to report to the public on a regular basis'.[74]

The legislative progress mentioned above demonstrates that the Chinese government also realizes the importance of the long-term sustainable development of business. It is argued that recent developments in CSR theory have provided a socially responsible performance paradigm, establishing a solid foundation for stakeholder-oriented strategic management policies.[75] Recent developments in relation to CSR, such as corporate strategic policies, environmental stewardship and sustainability, may all be viewed as implementations of stakeholder theory.[76] Ignoring CSR in the post-crisis context would demonstrate a

---

[72]   C. Keinert, *Corporate Social Responsibility as an International Strategy* (Heidelberg: Physica-Verlag, 2008) p. 90.
[73]   Guidelines on Corporate Governance of Commercial Banks in China (Consultative Document, August 2011) art. 77.
[74]   *Ibid.* art. 80.
[75]   J. Zhao, 'Promoting More Socially Responsible Corporations through UK Company Law after the 2008 Financial Crisis: Turning of the Crisis Compass' (2011) 9 *International Commercial and Company Law Review* 275 at 283–4.
[76]   S. Zambon and A. Del Bello, 'Towards a Stakeholder Responsible Approach: The Constructive Role of Reporting' (2005) 5 *Corporate Governance: International Journal of Business in Society* 130.

serious lack of understanding of the nature of business, since this ethical crisis is not unprecedented but its severity is.[77]

8.3.2 Enforcement of Corporate Law to Promote More Socially Responsible Corporations within a Harmonious Society

As discussed above, the theme and policy of 'building a Harmonious Society' was implemented by the Chinese Communist Party in 2006 following former President Hu's 2005 vision of introducing a Harmonious Society. Despite the fact that the vision and the policy do not explicitly refer to CSR, it is clear that CSR was initially, and is still, considered to be instrumental in achieving the socio-economic goals of this new policy.[78] A distinct body of comparative corporate law and regulations relating to CSR has become a key emergent trend in research on corporate governance and law in a number of jurisdictions.[79] International political moves that draw attention to the impact of corporations on a triple bottom line (environmental, social and economic)[80] have produced a plethora of international regional agreements, encouraging governments to implement them through national legislations.[81] This is also the case in China. Chinese corporate law and regulation have reached new levels during the national engagement with CSR.[82] The move towards the adoption of CSR in the regulations is not an intentional

---

[77] C. Pedamon, 'Corporate Social Responsibility: A New Approach to Promoting Integrity and Responsibility' (2010) 29 *Company Lawyer* 172.

[78] C.C. Pinney, 'Why China will Define the Future Corporate Citizenship' (Centre for Corporate Citizenship, Boston College, Carroll School of Management, 2008), available at www.bcccc.net/index.cfm?fuseaction=Page.ViewPage &PageID=1905.

[79] B. Horrigan, '21st Century Corporate Social Responsibility Trends: An Emerging Comparative Body of Law and Regulation on Corporate Responsibility, Governance, and Sustainability' (2007) 4 *Macquarie Journal of Business Law* 85.

[80] See J. Elkington, *Cannibals with Forks: The Triple Bottom Line of the 21st Century Business* (Gabriola Island: New Society Publishers, 1998).

[81] C. Nakajima, 'The Importance of Legally Embedding Corporate Social Responsibility' (2011) 32 *Company Lawyer* 257.

[82] X. Huang, *Corporate Social Responsibility: Theory and Practice in China (Qiye Shehui Zeren: Lilun Yu Zhongguo Shijian)* (Beijing: Social Sciences Academic Press, 2010) pp. 190–1; see also J.H. Liu, 'Some Thinking about Strengthening CSR' in J. Lou and P. Gan, *Studies on Corporate Social Responsibility* (Beijing: Peking University Press, 2009) p. 199; J. Shi and W. Yang, 'Legal Reanalysis of CSR' in J. Lou and P. Gan, *Studies on Corporate Social Responsibility* (Beijing: Peking University Press, 2009) 243.

result of rational individual or group decisions, but has occurred spontaneously since 2005 with rapid economic growth and the change to a market economy within the emerging framework of the Harmonious Society.[83] It is recognized by mainstream economic and legal scholars that the business world involves more than just corporate profit maximization, free competition and enabling laws.[84] CSR concerns challenges to justice in the social, economic and environmental arenas, involving those who are affected by the behaviour of businesses. Local CSR initiatives in China are part of the global governance scheme, which not only creates a huge business space for corporations but also helps national legislators to regulate more unusual areas.[85] The Chinese government has given increasing attention to CSR, while the Chinese regulatory and legislative authorities are suggesting that a commitment to CSR policy should be adopted as a condition of approval for business licences. 'Civil awareness' campaigns on CSR are also aimed at building business compliance.[86]

After the enactment of the CCL 2006 and the financial crisis of 2008, it is interesting to note corporate responses to these legal requirements regarding CSR, as well as the impact of the global business climate on CSR in China. In the current hard times faced by the world, caused by the worst financial crisis in recent years, do people sincerely care about CSR? It might seem logical that attention should turn to profit-making and profit maximization, in order to reduce the negative effects on the economy brought about by the financial crisis. However, can China afford to profit at the expense of CSR? Environmentalists and other pluralists in the areas of corporate law and corporate governance are worried that sustainability and increased corporate responsibility towards social and philanthropic concerns are being removed from the boardroom

---

[83]   M. Feng, Z. Chen and Z. Wang, *Corporate Social Responsibility of SOEs in China in a Harmonious Society* (*Zhongguo Guoyou Qiye Shehui Zerenlun: Jiyu Hexie Shehui de Sikao*) (Beijing: Economic Science Press, 2009) pp. 46–8.

[84]   J. Liu, *Corporate Social Responsibility* (Beijing: Law Press, 1999) pp. 85–6.

[85]   L.W. Lin, 'Corporate Social Responsibility in China: Window Dressing or Structural Change' (2010) 28 *Berkeley Journal of International Law* 64 at 67.

[86]   P.B. Potter, 'Co-ordinating Corporate Governance and Corporate Social Responsibility' (2009) 39 *Hong Kong Law Journal* 675 at 686.

agenda as companies tighten their belts in the face of turbulent stock-markets, the 'credit crunch' and a looming economic slowdown.[87] Irresponsible corporate actions will eventually burst the risk balloon; the lesson to be learnt from the financial crisis of 2008 is to regulate risk management and act responsibly in line with public interests.[88] However, a question arises as to how effective the CCL 2006 has been in giving stakeholders in China 'stakeholder legitimacy' through the business sector's impact on environmental and social issues.

Common regulation elements between establishing a Harmonious Society and socially responsible concerns in corporate law

Creating a Harmonious Society has been recognized as a driving force behind the growth of CSR. It is important to provide specific principles, laws, regulations and rules in order to place the development of a Harmonious Society in a prominent position. It is obvious that CCL 2006 adopts elements of the Harmonious Society policy into corporate legislation in order to promote stakeholders' interests in a more socially responsible manner. Apart from the link illuminated in Figure 8.1 (see above), there are also overlaps in the following areas: regulating purposes, regulating philosophy, regulating the environment and controlling the regulatory body. It is obvious that the related purposes of both CSR and the Harmonious Society rest on social and environmental concerns, shifting away from the primacy of wealth maximization and economic growth. Both aspects of government policy are a response from the Chinese government to the fact that its social and environmental burdens have outweighed its rapid economic growth in the last 25 years. The common ultimate purpose of both is to ensure the long-term interests of social welfare in a sustainable manner.

Part of the appeal of CSR is that it can lead to tremendous benefits for corporate identity and integrity when done in a sustainable manner. It is a win-win strategy for the mutual benefit of corporations and society.[89] As far as the regulating philosophy is concerned, Chinese traditions and

---

[87]   See T. Macalister, 'A change in the climate: credit crunch makes the bottom line the top issue', *The Guardian*, 6 March 2008; B.F. Souto, 'Crisis and Corporate Social Responsibility: Threat or Opportunity?' (2009) 2 *International Journal of Economic and Applied Research* 36.

[88]   'Social responsibility helps business fight crisis', *Xinhua News Agency*, 9 April 2009, available at www.china.org.cn/china/opinion/2009-04/09/content_17578054.htm.

[89]   Z. Xu and N. Liu, 'Research on Win-Win Management Control Mode of CSR Based on Society Harmony and Corporate Sustainable Development',

Chinese history, including Confucian thought, Taoism and *guanxi* between people, the government and business institutions, all have a deep impact on CSR and the Harmonious Society, and make the social function of corporate law in China unique in the global field of corporate governance, especially when compared to classic market-oriented or network-oriented corporate governance models.

As for regulating the environment, both CSR and the Harmonious Society have become increasingly important since 2005, when the government realized the negative effects of over-emphasizing GDP figures and economic growth, shifting focus instead to recognize the importance of establishing a more people-centred, unprejudiced and sustainable environment to make China a safe, reliable and attractive place to do business. The economic environment in modern China will not allow the Fortune 500 companies that existed 25 years ago to function today, because they failed to adopt a strategy of sustainability.[90] The Chinese Communist Party is the controlling regulatory body for both CSR and the Harmonious Society. It is a central theme that will be implemented in law, regulation, social policy, management style and people's realization and understanding across the whole of society.[91]

Enforcement of CSR-related law in China: Challenges and opportunities for building a Harmonious Society

It is commonly accepted in China, as a reflection of Confucian philosophy,[92] that if an ideal man likes wealth, let him obtain and use it responsibly; this is claimed to be the origin of CSR in China.[93] In a

---

proceedings of International Conference on Management Science and Engineering (2008), available at www.bmtfi.com/upload/product/200910/2008glhy02a 19.pdf.

[90]   See the speech of William Valentino, General Manager, Corporate Communication, Greater China, Bayer (China) Ltd, at the 27th China Daily CEO Roundtable Luncheon on 'Corporate Social Responsibility and Innovation'.

[91]   Of course, there will be advantages and disadvantages to this approach, and the related arguments are worthy of future research; for a good discussion of the state-centric relational approach and society-centric governance, see S. Bell and A. Hindmoor, *Rethinking Governance: The Centrality of the State in Modern Society* (Cambridge: Cambridge University Press, 2009) pp. 1–20.

[92]   See Kongzi, *Confucian Analects*; it is argued that '*Fu yu gui, shi ren zhi suo yu ye, bu yi qi dao de zhi, bu chu ye* [Wealth and being rich is desired by everyone. However, ideal man should get it responsibly]'.

[93]   G. Whelan, 'Corporate Social Responsibility in Asia: A Confucian Context' in S. May, G. Cheney and J. Roper (eds), *The Debate over Corporate Social Responsibility* (Oxford: Oxford University Press, 2007) p. 105.

Harmonious Society, the idea is that a responsible business person will carry out his or her business in a morally responsible manner. The Westernized concept of CSR was introduced to China back in the mid-1990s. CSR-related elements were accommodated in legislation in China as the result of an external push from multinational corporations, as well as internal driving factors from the modernized role of SOEs and the strong civil society with more demanding consumers, suppliers and local communities. With broader media coverage, more transparent information disclosure and better awareness of CSR, the leaders of government, legislators, civil society and consumers have begun to regard CSR as an important tool with which to engage and challenge business. There has been development in the regulatory environment and an evolution in civil society to act as both watchdog and partner to corporations in China.[94]

Despite the positive reflection from the performance data regarding companies' attitudes towards stakeholders, the rapid development of the Chinese economy also raises many social problems which remain a concern. Over the past few years, media reports have highlighted various incidents that demonstrate poor CSR practice in China. Although the general public seems to be gradually accepting the increasing number of high net worth individuals who have emerged, as well as their continually growing wealth, many people still cannot 'rub off the deeply ingrained prejudice against wealth' because of their traditional beliefs that there is something inherently wrong with being rich.[95] This prejudice can also lead to crises of a lack of confidence and trust from the public towards corporations, which normally act to generate wealth and which are controlled and owned by the rich. These crises of trust damage the stakeholders' moral reliance on corporations' socially responsible actions, and the public starts to be suspicious about whether CSR is a means for more profit and wealth, or an end in itself.

Employee suicides, faulty products for consumers, toxic emissions into the environment, and overworked, underpaid or under-age employees, have all been major topics in the popular press. Attention to CSR is gradually being enhanced in the context of the current economic crisis, and corporations' socially responsible behaviours aimed at protecting their stakeholders from widespread 'waves of layoffs' are winning

---

[94] L. Zu, *Corporate Social Responsibility, Corporate Restructuring and Firm's Performance* (Berlin: Springer-Verlag, 2009) p. 45.

[95] H. Li, 'Don't hate the rich, be one of them', *People's Daily*, 2 April 2009.

universal support.[96] With a poor image of CSR in the globalized market, the willingness from individual companies to perform socially responsible actions will collectively improve the situation by building public trust and enhancing their competiveness in the long term. CSR is seen as a rewarding investment for the future, pointing companies towards a sustainable direction for development. The government and individual companies have adopted numerous environmental and social regulatory policy strategies, on both a mandatory and a voluntary basis.[97] However, 'with these regulations on the book, enforcement has been relatively lax'.[98] It is argued that 'incorporating CSR into law mires CSR in the problems of the Chinese legal system' due to ambiguity and unpredictability in Chinese legislation and deficiencies in implementation.[99] In the author's opinion, although it is too early to judge, incorporation can fundamentally change the poor CSR records and practices in China; the data discussed above has already suggested an improvement since 2006.

However, there has been no shortage of controversy in China involving CSR-related issues when corporate actions seriously harm the rights of stakeholders, and the law seems very weak and inefficient in dealing with these cases. In the following paragraphs, the position and treatment of the main stakeholders in the process of building a people-centred Harmonious Society, including employees, the environment and consumers, will be discussed with the use of case studies to investigate the Chinese government's commitment to CSR.

As regards the interests of employees, as important stakeholders recognized in CSR strategies with the aim of moving towards a Harmonious Society,[100] the enactment of the Chinese Labour Contract Law (CLCL) in 2008 has had a significant impact on the treatment of

---

[96]   'Social responsibility helps business fight crisis', *Xinhua News Agency*, 9 April 2009, available at www.china.org.cn/china/opinion/2009-04/09/content_17578054.htm.

[97]   See L.W. Lin, 'Corporate Social Responsibility in China: Window Dressing or Structural Change' (2010) 28 *Berkeley Journal of International Law* 64 at 67–81.

[98]   J. Sarkis, N. Li and Q. Zhu, 'Winds of Change: Corporate Social Responsibility in China' (2011) *Ivey Business Journal* (January/February) 1.

[99]   L.W. Lin, 'Corporate Social Responsibility in China: Window Dressing or Structural Change' (2010) 28 *Berkeley Journal of International Law* 64 at 67–96.

[100]   According to Chinese Labour Contract Law art. 1: 'This Law has been formulated to improve and perfect the labour contract system, to make explicit the rights and obligations of both parties of the labour contract, to protect the lawful rights and interests of labourers and to build and develop harmonious and stable labour relationships'.

employees, and also on how employees view their rights, offering employees greater and more enforceable rights. However, the requirements embedded in the law also dramatically increased employers' costs, caused some companies to go out of business or leave China for other jurisdictions, and caused many others to show reduced profits. It has been argued that the CLCL 2008 has caused a major shakedown in the Pearl River and Pearl River Delta areas, where more than 8,000 companies went into insolvency or relocated their businesses. Conflict arises between the aim of the CCL 2006 to make China an attractive place for investments, and the CLCL 2008, which made China less attractive because of the duties imposed on employers. The CLCL 2008 poses a considerable challenge for corporations in terms of their competitiveness and business ethics. It is not disputed that the promulgation and effect of this new Labour Law should have a long-term impact on the improvement of labour standards in China. However, the short-term impact of the Law has not been so positive; many of its provisions, such as those on open-ended contracts,[101] set overly high standards that cannot be reconciled with reality, and the Law has had to rely heavily on government intervention for enforcement.[102]

As regards the environment, the recent oil leak case at Bohai Bay in 2011 has stimulated discussions about CSR in China in the context of public interest litigation. The State Ocean Administration estimated that the oil spill had polluted 5,500 square kilometres of Bohai Bay, making it the most serious marine ecological incident in China to date.[103] The spill and subsequent cover-up raised questions about corporate environmental transparency regarding public safety. Misleading statements about the spill were issued by ConocoPhillips, describing the damages caused. Furthermore, there was a gap of one month between the report from ConocoPhillips to the State Ocean Administration and the release of the information to the public. Based on the Chinese Marine Environment Protection Law 1983, the state administrative department of marine affairs should have filed litigation on behalf of the nation against the polluters[104] for the discharging fee, the costs of eliminating the pollution,

---

[101]   Chinese Labour Contract Law 2008 arts 12, 14, 15.
[102]   B. Wu and Y. Zheng, *A Long March to Improve Labour Standards in China: Chinese Debates on the New Labour Contract Law*, University of Nottingham China Policy Institute Briefing Series Issue 39 (2008) p. 8.
[103]   'CNOOC: oil leak in Bohai Bay sealed', *Xinhua News Agency*, 25 October 2011.
[104]   Chinese Marine Environment Protection Law 1983 art. 5.

and compensation for the loss sustained by the state.[105] The SOA declared that it would sue ConocoPhillips China for ecological compensation. However, at the time of writing, some considerable time after the incident, no litigation has been filed. Members of the public could only stand by and watch this happen, since under article 108(1) of Chinese Civil Procedure Law, 'the plaintiff must be a citizen, legal person, or an organisation having a direct interest in the case' in order to meet the conditions for filing a lawsuit. This requirement sets up a legal barrier which prevents NGOs from filing lawsuits in the interests of the public. The Bohai incident has led to discussion of a draft legal amendment, enabling relevant authorities and social groups to file public interest litigation in environmental pollution and food safety cases by including 'related authorities' in the civil procedure law passed by the Standing Committee of the National People's Congress, the legislature in China, on 28 October 2011. In this case, pressure from the public may well play a determining role in law reform and CSR development.

It is obvious that the further development of CSR in China has to be achieved by informing the public, raising awareness of CSR-related issues.[106] Furthermore, the importance of environmental discourse should also be addressed, with the government's institutional mechanism for disclosure as an important institutional underpinning for socialist democracy.[107] According to an official statement by Mr Pan Yue, Vice Minister of the State Environmental Protection Administration, environmental disclosure is a significant measure to establish a Harmonious Society, acting as a bridge for communication between the public and the government through which the public is able to exercise environmental rights to monitor development projects and polluting companies.[108]

As regards faulty products and the health and safety of consumers, the Chinese baby milk scandal discussed in Chapter 6 gave China a timely

---

[105]   *Ibid.* art. 41.

[106]   Knowledge@Wharton, *Corporate Social Responsibility in China: One Great Leap Forward, Many More Still Ahead* (2009).

[107]   In a positive move, the Shenzhen and Shanghai Stock Exchanges have taken environmental disclosure on board and released a Guide to Listed Companies' Social Responsibility on the Shenzhen Stock Exchange, and Guide to Environmental Information Disclosure for Companies Listed on the Shanghai Stock Exchange.

[108]   See Ministry of Environmental Protection of People's Republic of China, 'The Introduction of the First Regulation on Environmental Disclosure and Enforcement of Information Disclosure for Environmental Agencies and Heavy-Pollution Companies: Mr Yue Pan is appealing for in-depth public participation to minimize pollution and emissions' (*Shoubu Huanjing Xinxi Gongkai Banfa*

reminder of the problem of the failure of good CSR practices. Nevertheless, Zhao Lianhai, a Chinese activist who campaigned for better compensation for victims of the scandal and himself the father of a baby victim, was jailed for two-and-a-half years.[109] Zhao started a website called 'home for kidney stone babies', enabling information exchange between the victims of the scandal. The website was later blocked and Zhao was sentenced to imprisonment on a charge of 'causing a serious disturbance'.[110] As for the wrongdoers, the boss of the melamine workshop and his associate were given the death penalty, while the Sanlu dairy chief was sentenced to life imprisonment.[111] However, the sentences for government officials detained after the scandal were never announced.[112]

This example suggests that it is necessary to reconsider the reaction of the public and the government's responses to CSR. It is clear that inefficiency in the enforcement of CSR-related laws is not only a consequence of deficiencies in Chinese law enforcement. The problem is a collective one, with causes ranging from a poor information disclosure system, a disrespect of human rights, and unregulated political power, to a high degree of political inference in the law, corporate governance and CSR.[113] This is worrying if the idea of a Harmonious Society is to help China in fostering a corporate business environment. This was noted by Liu Mengxiong, a member of the national committee of the Chinese People's Political Consultative Conference, who called for Zhao's release: 'the government's decision to jail a man viewed favourably by

---

Chutai Qiangzhi Huanbao Bumen he Wuran Qiye Gongkai Huanjing Xinxi: PanYue Huyu yi Gongzhong Shendu Canyu Tuidong Wuran Jianpai), 25 April 2008.
[109] 'China jails tainted milk activist Zhao Lianhai', *BBC News Asia-Pacific*, 10 November 2010.
[110] Chinese Criminal Law 1997 art. 293.
[111] 'China to execute two over poisoned baby milk scandal', *Guardian World News*, 22 January 2009.
[112] 'China court jails father of "tainted milk child"', *Guardian World News*, 22 January 2009.
[113] For more discussions on political interference and CSR, see P.A. Gourevitch and J. Shinn, *Political Power and Corporate Control: The New Global Politics of Corporate Governance* (Princeton, NJ: Princeton University Press, 2007) chs 4 and 6; W. Li and R. Zhang, 'Corporate Social Responsibility, Ownership Structure, and Political Interference: Evidence from China' (2010) 96 *Journal of Business Ethics* 631.

the public would only cast aspersions on the government and weaken public opinion on the justice system'.[114]

From these three cases studies of corporate behaviours and their impacts, it is clear that Chinese CSR practices are unique, just like the Chinese control-based corporate governance model.[115] The enforcement of the law related to CSR in promoting stakeholders' interests depends heavily on political interference, public awareness, business disclosure of social and environmental issues, and the improvement and support of a sound legal system in China. The purpose of legal enforcement is to maintain a good corporate image, avoid unnecessary legal proceedings and consumer resistance, improve the efficiency of production and optimize the management of supply chains in a socially responsible manner. These aspects are key, from the point of view of the corporation, in supporting the enforcement of corporate objectives stipulated in the CCL 2006 in terms of CSR and business ethics, in order to achieve the ultimate goal of establishing a genuine Harmonious Society.

The current enforcement of CSR-related law is still far from satisfactory. Enforcement is not clear, predictable or effective.[116] Enforcement is largely dependent on political power and government interference.[117] With the unique corporate governance system in China, the government could play an effective role in promoting CSR by adopting a relational approach suggested by Albareda and others; such a framework would apply to public CSR policies, permitting corporations and their stakeholders to analyse the vision and strategy of the government in promoting CSR by taking into account the new relationships that the government is

---

[114] 'Still toxic: father protesting China tainted milk scandal jailed', *China Decoded: Culture, News, and Stories from China*, 18 November 2010, available at www.chinadecoded.com/2010/11/18/still-toxic-father-protesting-china-tainted-milk-scandal-jailed/; see also H. Xie and K. Du, 'Proposal for the Case of Zhao Lianhai from National People's Congress and Chinese People's Political Consultative Conference' (2011), available at www.chinaelections.org/newsinfo.asp?newsid=207026.

[115] For the unique corporate governance model in China, see M. Yan, 'Obstacles in China's Corporate Governance' (2011) 32 *Company Lawyer* 311.

[116] X. Wang, 'Government Function on Cultivating CSR: A Thinking on Loss of Truck Fence' (2010) 5 *International Journal of Business and Management* 162 at 164.

[117] For more discussion on CSR, corporate governance and political interference, see C. Shi, *The Political Determinants of Corporate Governance in China* (Abingdon: Routledge, 2012).

establishing with various social agents, including business and social organizations.[118]

Analysis of the three CSR-related incidents and the government's application of law and regulations in each case shows how broad the scope of CSR-related law is. A common understanding and perception of the concept of CSR within the unique Chinese political framework and implementation strategies is vital for building a harmonious relationship between corporations, their stakeholders and the public at large. The application of CSR within the government's agenda in China is a domestic government-centred approach, with reference to international principles, norms and standards. A clearer blueprint for a CSR framework with Chinese characteristics is dependent on a clearer, broader and more globalized understanding of 'increasing interdependent political, regulatory and commercial exchanges between sectors, and the perceptions and challenges of different stakeholders'.[119] This common understanding will speed up the construction of a system of mutual trust by providing a positive environment for companies to develop and implement CSR. At the same time, the government is obliged to implement regulations and opportunities to foster the development of CSR practices, and to extend the remit of CSR to ease the current crisis of trust in China.

From an international perspective, along with the increasing influence of the 'Made in China' brand and China's formal approval to join the World Trade Organization, many trade protections have already been implemented, such as anti-dumping, quality and technical barriers, and green barriers. From a domestic perspective, in the context of very rapid economic development, the conflict between social and economic benefits in Chinese corporations is becoming more significant. The government should play a leading role in responding to the urgent need for CSR. This role should be composed of a combination of: regulator, establishing and implementing relevant regulations and policies to improve CSR; promoter, raising awareness of social responsibility to promote the country's international and social image; and supervisor,

---

[118] L. Albareda, J.M. Lozano, A. Tencati, A. Midttun and F. Perrini, 'The Changing Role of Government in Corporate Social Responsibility: Drivers and Responses' (2008) 17 *Business Ethics: A European Review* 347 at 359.

[119] *Ibid.* at 360; see also D.A. Detomasi, 'The Multinational Corporation and Global Governance: Modelling Global Public Policy Network' (2007) 71 *Journal of Business Ethics* 321; J. Moon, 'Business Social Responsibility and New Governance' (2002) 37 *Government and Opposition* 385.

strengthening the supervisions and punishing behaviours that are harmful to society and the environment at large.[120]

---

[120]   X. Wang, 'Government Function on Cultivating CSR: A Thinking on Loss of Truck Fence' (2010) 5 *International Journal of Business and Management* 162 at 164.

9. Conclusion and the future of corporate social responsibility in China

This chapter provides some concluding remarks, and aims to bring together all the issues examined in the previous chapters of the book. Just as regards the debate surrounding corporate social responsibility (CSR) in general, the issue of CSR in China has gained significant recognition in the last two decades. While the damage caused by scandals such as Enron and WorldCom West-Watergate in the United States, and Rupert Murdoch and News International in the United Kingdom, have been well publicized, with a great deal of negative discussion and criticism and in some cases the introduction of corresponding legislation, codes of conduct and reports, it is likely that CSR abuses in China may be more widespread and tolerated to a greater degree, being less obvious and more part of the 'normal' business scene.[1] Public companies and multinational companies in China will face increasing challenges with regard to their CSR performance, and will be expected to demonstrate their competitiveness to address national priorities in China, including green development, livelihood improvement, outward development into the West and the integration of Chinese companies into the global market.[2]

It has been argued in the book, mainly in Chapter 2, that CSR in contemporary China has its historical and cultural roots in a country that has been profoundly influenced by Confucian philosophy. There is evidence of CSR practice and CSR-related legislation dating back to the *Qing* dynasty. Since that time, CSR has been adopted using different approaches at different historical periods in China. However, one of the main focuses has always been on the people. People have been included

---

[1] S. Jones, *BRICS and Beyond: Executive Lessons on Emerging Markets* (Chichester: Wiley, 2012) p. 57.

[2] S. Zadek, M. Forstater and K. Yu, *Corporate Responsibility and Sustainable Economic Development in China: Implications for Business* (US Chamber of Commerce, National Chamber Foundation and Asia Department, 2012) pp. 5–6, available at www.uschamber.com/.

as an important element in discussions about CSR since Elkington added a third bottom line, in addition to environment and economics, which focused on serving people. This triple bottom line business model maintains fair and equitable practices among corporations with the goal of a reputable relationship with the corporate stakeholders which whom a company conducts its business.[3] This adoption of the vital role of people within corporate strategy as a measure of corporate success has also been included in Chinese political policies in building a Harmonious Society, with the aim of creating a more balanced, people-centred and sustainable society to address social and environmental concerns. The performance of state-owned enterprises (SOEs) in China has 'deteriorated markedly over the past years'; the majority of them are at best making marginal profits, and many collective enterprises are in serious financial difficulties.[4] Since the early 1990s, the Chinese government has designed and carried out a number of economic reconstruction initiatives and reforms to change the economic situation of China, attempting to speed up corporate reforms in order to promote the competitiveness of Chinese companies. Initial attempts, such as the redundancy of workers in SOEs, the privatization of SOEs, removing the secured permanent 'iron rice bowl' (*tie fanwan*) in SOEs and transforming the corporate structure of the 'working unit' (*danwei*) and their relationships with employees have triggered a number of debates about the corporate objectives of SOEs.

The radical reconstruction of corporate forms and shareholding ownership and the irresponsible behaviour of companies have brought severe problems of social instability and a wide range of stakeholder reactions, including campaigns and protests. The discussion and debate has migrated away from the simple question of whether corporations in China have other responsibilities apart from shareholder wealth maximization. The current debate on this topic focuses on how companies can comply with broader responsibilities through both voluntary initiatives and mandatory requirements, and on the roots of CSR from different perspectives which are unique to China, such as the country's history, culture, traditions, values, corporate governance model and legal system. The promotion of CSR in Chinese companies relies on inputs from companies, government and individual citizens. It can be concluded from Chapter 3 that the growing awareness of CSR in contemporary China has

---

    [3]   J. Elkington, 'Towards the Sustainable Corporation: Win-Win-Win Business Strategies for Sustainable Development' (1994) 36 *California Management Review* 90.

    [4]   L. Zu, *Corporate Social Responsibility, Corporate Restructuring and Firm's Performance* (Berlin: Springer-Verlag, 2009) p. 301.

come about as the result of both external push factors and internal drivers. Pressure has come from the globalization of the Chinese economy and growing cooperation with multinational companies, international codes of conduct, international corporate governance principles, international CSR standards, international and domestic competition, political policies, domestic CSR management standards, and of course related legislation and regulations aimed at encouraging more socially responsible companies in China to achieve long-term sustainable development. China's economic growth and development in the last 30 years has led the country to become the world's workshop, unfortunately involving 'under-cutting and de-prioritising of issues such as the environment and business ethics'.[5]

Another controversial issue in this context is how to regulate CSR and to what extent the law is necessary or effective. Should regulation be carried out according to legislative norms, ethical norms or by using national and international standards? As far as regulating CSR is concerned, the method of establishing a framework, led by corporate law and with the involvement of policy-makers, business leaders, consumers and capital markets including the Shanghai and Shenzhen Stock Exchanges, will be key to incorporate CSR as one of the mainstream concerns in China. An awareness of the need for corporations to be socially responsible is commensurate with increasing corporate power.[6] CSR is key in building sustainable and respectful business relationships and supply chains for Chinese companies, and a good CSR record will not only benefit the corporate image of individual companies but will also promote China as a brand. The goal is for CSR to be increasingly regarded as an embedded aspect of China's own global brand and method of global business practice.

From the discussions in Chapters 4, 5, 7 and 8, it is clear that the Chinese government has begun to realize the importance of CSR and has made a move towards the goal of establishing a regulatory framework for CSR, facilitating legislative measures to aid in the implementation of CSR in a mandatory manner. Indeed, government policy and legislation have been regarded as one of the most important reasons for companies to take CSR seriously. A survey was carried out of the opinions of citizens in 16 major Chinese cities, covering areas including the northeast (Dalian City, Shenyang City), the north (Shijiazhuang City, Tianjin

---

[5]   P. French, 'China Briefing Part 1: Overview – Economic Revolution Brings Responsibility Rethink', *Ethical Corporation*, 2 February 2012.

[6]   A. Adeyeye, 'Universal Standards in CSR: Are We Prepared?' (2011) 11 *Corporate Governance* 107.

City), the north-west (Xi'an City, Lanzhou City), the south (Guangzhou City, Shenzhen City), the mid-east (Wuhan City), the east (Shanghai City, Hangzhou City) and the south-west of China (Chongqing City, Chendu City). The survey results showed that 66 per cent of citizens regarded the government as the major driving force behind CSR in China, and 75.6 per cent of citizens agreed that one of the main reasons for poor fulfilment of CSR obligations was the lack of government regulation.[7]

Remedial efforts have been made at different levels, including the adoption of CSR and business ethics elements in article 5 of the Chinese Company Law (CCL) 2006; issuing Guidelines to the State-Owned Enterprises Directly under the Central Government on Fulfilling Corporate Social Responsibilities; Guidelines on Corporate Social Responsibility Compliance by Foreign Invested Enterprises; Notice on Strengthening Listed Companies' Assumption of Social Responsibility and Guidelines on Shanghai Stock Exchange Listed Companies' Environmental Information Disclosure. In detail, from the corporate law perspective, two main suggestions were made by reference to experience under the UK Companies Act 2006: the introduction of directors' duties towards stakeholders, and an information disclosure requirement on environmental and social issues in the future modified CCL to build more solid and enforceable CSR measure underpinned by law.

From the 1980s to the 1990s, a state-based model of implementing regulatory law has been adopted in China, and state interference has also had a significant impact on commercial law which traditionally used contract and liability norms without the capacity for state implementation.[8] While government enforcement authorities and regulatory agencies have difficulties in enforcing the law, a few additional methods have been suggested to make the enforcement of these regulations more efficient in China, including broadening public awareness and encouraging the adoption of international standards related to CSR.

The Harmonious Society, a political policy deeply rooted in Confucian tradition, has buttressed popular belief in the merits of respecting and caring for the community as part of an extended family. This policy was specifically discussed in Chapter 8 in order to identify the relationship between government policy and CSR, with reflections from legal

---

[7]   S. Li, 'The Crisis Chain on Corporate Social Responsibility (*Qiye Shehuizeren Weiji Lian*)' (2011) 34 *Outlook Week (Liaowang)* 22. (This magazine has a wide impact in China and is under direct supervision of the *Xinhua News Agency*.)

[8]   A.C. Mertha, *The Politics of Piracy: Intellectual Property in Contemporary China* (Ithaca, NY: Cornell University Press, 2007) p. 133.

responses. The application of the function of the family goes beyond the traditional limit of one's relatives, expanding to include the community, the country and society at large. According to the belief system based on these values, 'duty to one's national family is morally espoused and an integral component to achieving the greatest possible good – a harmonious society'.[9] The concept of the Harmonious Society is affirmed as an official policy of the Chinese Communist Party, which has a plan with clear targets to achieve the policy by 2020. This vision shifts China's primary focus towards a more balanced, people-centred and sustainable model, aimed at maintaining growth but also addressing social and environmental concerns. Together with the Harmonious Society and the implementation of a scientific outlook on development which puts people's interests first within an all-round, balanced and sustainable development framework, CSR has achieved an increasingly important position with the support of the political agenda and government policy.

It can be concluded from the arguments in this book that history, politics and culture constitute the foundation for a comprehensive understanding of CSR in China. CSR is increasingly being appreciated as a crucial component of companies' 'intangible assets', which are taking on greater significance in determining how investors view the present and future health of companies.[10] It can be concluded that a link does exist between CSR and the central tenets of a Harmonious Society. The Harmonious Society, under which people's rights are given the highest priority, will be reflected in corporations by an emphasis on stakeholders' interests in order to promote a more harmonized and cooperative working environment with sustainable development strategies for various stakeholders. The CSR movement has been a major factor in shifting corporate governance theory in a stakeholder-friendly direction, by demanding that companies go beyond the creation of short-term shareholder wealth in pursuit of broader objectives, such as sustainable growth, equitable employment practices and long-term social and environmental well-being.[11] This is also the purpose of

---

[9] K.H. Darigan and J.E. Post, 'Corporate Citizenship in China: CSR Challenges in the "Harmonious Society"' (2009) 35 *Journal of Corporate Citizenship* 39 at 45.

[10] K. Howell, 'Introduction' in *Business and Society: Developing CSR in the UK* (London: DTI, March 2001) p. 1. Around 50% of FTSE-100 companies published formal environmental reports in 2000 and this figure has increased steadily in recent years.

[11] C.A. Williams and J.M. Conley, 'An Emerging Third Way? The Erosion of the Anglo-American Shareholder Value Construct' (2005) 38 *Cornell International Law Journal* 493.

building a Harmonious Society from a corporate perspective, with an emphasis on 'fostering a sound moral atmosphere and harmonious interpersonal relationships'. This link also suggests that, on the other side of the coin, the political and social environment has a marked effect on corporations by applying pressure on directors in the development of their strategic management policies.[12]

It has been found that the progressive and enlightened changes involved in adopting social elements in company law, as well as the emphasis on employees' rights, are beneficial in promoting CSR in Chinese companies, not only in SOEs but also in private companies, in order to achieve the target of establishing a Harmonious Society. Legitimacy has been given to the boards of companies to act in a socially responsible manner by recognizing the different tiers of responsibility defined in CCL 2006 article 5, going beyond mere compliance with regulatory norms, for the benefit of the people in the corporation. The government plays a triple role in the enforcement of the law, overseeing CSR as a regulator, a supervisor and a promoter. The constructive relationship between the Harmonious Society, CSR and progressive elements in the CCL 2006 are illustrated in Figure 9.1.

The regulation of morally-oriented responsibility will remind and encourage corporate directors to promote their responsibility towards various stakeholders, and should ensure that people are always placed at the centre of corporate decisions. After the enactment of CCL 2006, despite positive progress between 2006 and 2011 reflected in the data regarding the performance of directors' duties towards stakeholders, the rapid development of the Chinese economy has also resulted in many social problems which are still a cause for concern. The enforcement of CSR-related legal requirements still depends on political interference, public awareness, business disclosure of social and environmental issues, and the improvement and support of a sound legal system in China. After numerous CSR scandals in China, it is time to reconsider how to benefit society through commitment and trust between stakeholders and corporations, not only in China but also globally. The Harmonious Society is still only a start. It is a reminder for every Chinese person of the dangers of irresponsible behaviour, and it also helps Chinese people form a positive opinion about the future of their country.

Corporations, like capitalism more generally, always exist within specific social, legal, cultural and moral environment conditions that need

---

[12]   J. Cramer (ed.), *Corporate Social Responsibility and Globalisation: An Action Plan for Business* (Sheffield: Greenleaf Publishing, 2006) pp. 68–71.

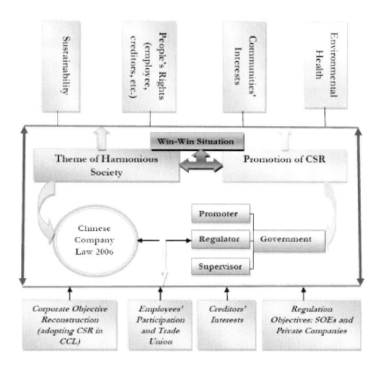

Figure 9.1   Connecting CSR, the Harmonious Society and company law

to be maintained for their existence.[13] Confucian philosophy has an important role to play in increasing the benefits that humanity derives from corporations, acting for the long-term sustainable development of Chinese companies towards a role as custodians of global civilization. The collective effects of these elements in China will help to make CSR a key factor, an important tool of public policy to encourage business to play an active role in contributing to government policies including scientific development and the Harmonious Society. Since the emergence of guidelines and standards produced and sponsored by the state and the enforcement of legislation in China with the aim of promoting CSR

---

[13]   G. Whelan, 'Corporate Social Responsibility in Asia: A Confucian Context' in S. May, G. Cheney and J. Roper, *The Debate over Corporate Social Responsibility* (Oxford: Oxford University Press, 2008) p. 105 at p. 107.

practices, CSR has transformed its image and function from a protectionist threat to Chinese competitiveness into a tool to ensure social suitability with the aim of addressing social and environmental challenges brought about by the rapid growth of the Chinese economy. Attention to CSR has gone beyond the measurement of the competitiveness of Chinese companies, and is moving towards being a measure of the competitiveness of China as a country within the global economy.

As for the potential development of the topic, generally speaking, the agenda and future of CSR will be deeply affected by a number of external factors, including political issues, social factors, environmental factors, technological factors, and the growing significance of Brazil, Russia, India and China (the so-called BRIC countries).[14] Nevertheless, a few trends can be observed which might inform the future of CSR in China. First, it is argued that many of today's CSR practices will become mandatory requirements.[15] This is a trend in the combined character of CSR in China, making it into a mechanism that is both voluntary and mandatory, with a systematic regulatory framework as discussed in the book. Within this regulatory framework, the directors' duties towards stakeholders to promote the long-term interests of the companies and publicly disclose social, environmental and governance data and reports on a mandatory basis can be regarded as two main legislative tools within company law to achieve the goals of fairness, transparency and accountability.

Secondly, in spite of economic liberalization in recent years, the primacy of the state as a regulator and a social provider still remains a distinguishing feature of the Chinese political economy.[16] With government involvement in promoting CSR in China as an important element to endorse the scientific development of a Harmonious Society, CSR will be adopted as a key factor in measuring the competitiveness and advantages of Chinese companies in the global economy. Apart from government intervention, an innovative approach could be adopted in Chinese listed companies, building partnerships with local government and developing the capacity of NGOs in order to gain a better understanding and address CSR-related issues in ways that are tailored for the local community and

---

[14]   H. Ward and N.C. Smith, *Corporate Social Responsibility at a Crossroads: Future of CSR in the UK to 2015* (London: IIED, 2006) pp. 13–14.

[15]   W. Visser, 'Future Trends in CSR: The Next 10 Years' (2012) 11 *CSR International Inspiration Series* 1 at 2.

[16]   J. Moon and X. Shen, 'CSR in China Research: Salience, Focus and Nature' (2010) 94 *Journal of Business Ethics* 613.

specific stakeholders groups within the company. Apart from the government and regulatory framework discussed in detail in this book, the enhancement of CSR in China will rely on support from strengthened corporate approaches that are integrated with business strategies and are responsive to stakeholders' concerns and public awareness, in order to promote CSR in international, domestic and local arenas.

Thirdly, generally speaking it is estimated that reliance on CSR codes, standards and guidelines such as SA 8000 will be seen as a necessary but insufficient way to implement CSR.[17] Although this should be carried out gradually in China, the further development of national standards that are already in place should be increasingly harmonized with international norms through a process of learning from and referencing international standards.[18] With legitimacy from both accountability and expertise, international guidelines and standards set by various stakeholder bodies and NGOs will draw together involvement from public, private and civil society.[19] It is important to ensure that a lack of familiarity and poor compliance with international CSR standards should not be a cause of international or unintended trade barriers. Therefore, a combination of Chinese and international CSR standards is critical to developing national CSR standards and certification systems, with guidance from and reference to international standards such as ISO 26000 with adaptation to the Chinese context.[20] Another area that is worth discussing and developing is one that has been particularly sensitive in China: the domain of human rights. These issues have always had a high profile, and have been one of the most often discussed and criticized aspects in the arguments surrounding CSR. The topic has become even more contentious after China's endorsement of the 'UN Guidelines on Business and Human

---

[17]   W. Visser, 'Future Trends in CSR: The Next 10 Years' (2012) 11 *CSR International Inspiration Series* 1.
[18]   S. Zadek, M. Forstater and K. Yu, *Corporate Responsibility and Sustainable Economic Development in China: Implications for Business* (US Chamber of Commerce, National Chamber Foundation and Asia Department, 2012) p. 5, available at www.uschamber.com/.
[19]   G. Long, S. Zadek and J. Wickerham, *Advancing Sustainable Competitiveness of China's Transnational Corporations* (London: AccountAbility, 2009) p. 8.
[20]   This process has actually started with the Certification and Accreditation Administration of the People's Republic of China. This body is carrying out a project on behalf of the government to investigate the implications and implementation of ISO 26000 and international standards; furthermore, the Regulations of the People's Republic of China on Certification and Accreditation were also introduced in 2003.

Rights', where business and human rights finally came together.[21] In the 'General Principles' section, the Ruggie Guiding Principles are grounded in a recognition of the state's existing obligations to respect, protect and fulfil human rights and fundamental freedoms,[22] which have been regarded as the three pillars of the framework. The endorsement of the Ruggie framework by the United Nations Human Rights Council on 16 June 2011, after years of struggle to develop corporate standards, made the corporate world's responsibility for human rights clear as the foundation for this policy framework.

Fourthly, the global financial crisis which has thrown the entire financial market into turmoil since 2008 has provided a vivid warning about the dangers of short-termism. Although China was able to recover from the crisis at a remarkably brisk pace, it is clear that long-termism is key for sustainable growth, equitable employment practices and social and environmental well-being. When discussing CSR in China, it is vital to highlight the importance of CSR for the long-term success and sustainable development of corporations. This is particularly true for state-owned commercial banks and other financial service institutions, which were involved in the onset of the financial crisis, and which are the reason for China's fast recovery. The performance of banks should not be measured purely by a narrow measure of profitability or allocative efficiency.[23] In the United Kingdom, an independent review by Sir George Cox was commissioned by the Labour Party, entitled *Overcoming Short-termism within British Business: The Key to Sustained Economic Growth*. It was published on 26 February 2013 in the Labour Policy Review as one of the Agenda 2014 policy reports. It concluded that pressure to focus on short-term results is closely linked to the possible detriment of the long-term health of a company, or even a whole industry.[24] What is needed in the twenty-first century, in the context of

---

[21] J. Ruggie, 'Business and Human Rights: Together at Last: A Conversation with John Ruggie' (2011) 35 *Fletcher Forum of World Affairs* 117; for more discussions on China and the international human rights system see S. Sceats and S. Breslin, *China and the International Human Rights System* (Royal Institute of International Affairs, 2012).

[22] Guiding Principles on Business and Human Rights: Implementation of the United Nations 'Protect, Respect and Remedy' Framework.

[23] Y. Liang, 'China's Short-Term and Long-Term Development after the 2007 Global Financial Crisis: Some Critical Reflection' (2012) 45 *China Economy* 3 at 4.

[24] G. Cox, *Overcoming Short-termism within British Business: The Key to Sustained Economic Growth: An Independent Review by Sir George Cox commissioned by the Labour Party* (2013) p. 4, available at Your Britain, the

changes to economic structures and the emergence of new industries, is a strategic approach for the pursuit of long-term growth.[25] This report may also provide some insights for the Chinese economy on the future of CSR and the relationship between long-termism and sustainable business development.

Fifthly, despite the fact that the shareholder primacy ideology and the shareholder wealth maximization principle, which still dominate business and academic circles in some countries today, have been criticized as conflicting with objectives for the successful implementation of stakeholder theory and CSR, a better understanding of the reality of the shareholders' identity and what they really value in China will be critical for a complete understanding of Chinese corporate objectives and CSR. It is argued by Professor Stout that shareholders are 'real human beings with the capacity to think for the future and to make binding commitments, with a wide range of investments and interests beyond the shares they happen to hold in any single firm, and with consciences that make most of them concerned, at least a bit, about the fates of others, future generations and the planet'.[26] With its unique shareholder structure and the dominant position of the state as the majority shareholder in listed companies, discussion of the characteristics and development of shareholders and their rights in China is also critical to the development of CSR. Awareness of CSR in China should go beyond boards of directors and stakeholders, aiming to reach the minds of shareholders, because traditional shareholder primacy harms most shareholders at the same time as it harms stakeholders and the public.[27]

Lastly, the author agrees with Professor Freeman's opinion on the future of CSR and the worthy goal of making the idea of CSR disappear, with a consideration that the roles of responsibility, sustainability and ethics are at least as important as the completion of projects.[28] Former

---

Labour Party Policy Review website, www.yourbritain.org.uk/uploads/.../ Overcoming_Short-termism.pdf.

[25] *Ibid.* at 7.

[26] L. Stout, *The Shareholder Value Myth: How Putting Shareholders First Harms Investors, Corporations, and the Public* (San Francisco, CA: Berrett-Koehler, 2012) p. 6.

[27] *Ibid.* at 6–7.

[28] Speech of Prof. Edward Freeman at Fifth International Conference on Corporate Social Responsibility: The Future of CSR, October 2012, based on the note of the author; see also E. Freeman and A. Moutchnik, 'Stakeholder Management and CSR: Questions and Answers' (2013), uwf Umwelt Wirtschafts Forum, available at http://link.springer.com/article/10.1007%2Fs00550-013-0266-3#.

Premier Wen Jiabao, when designing China's Twelfth Five-year Plan, characterized the current economic model in China as 'unbalanced, unstable, uncoordinated and unsustainable' in an annual meeting in Da Lian on 10 September 2009.[29] With increasing domestic recognition and international pressure in favour of the necessity of transforming the economy in a more sustainable and inclusive direction, CSR should be embedded in order to overcome significant obstacles to the achievement of China's goals in terms of green and inclusive growth. Awareness and understanding of CSR in Chinese companies should be strong enough for corporations to treat it as part of corporate strategic management, thereby enriching a healthy and sustainable corporate culture. This also fits into the stages of CSR development suggested by Zadek and others, moving from defensive, to compliance, managerial, strategic, and ultimately reaching the civil stage by promoting broad industry participation in corporate responsibility, enhancing long-term economic value by over-coming obstacles to sustainable development.[30] With the rapid economic growth in China, Chinese stakeholders such as consumers will be more informed and will demand more active involvement with companies' decisions and strategies. The demands of domestic stakeholders will be more sophisticated and organized, and CSR will be regarded as a part of corporate culture's impact, with recognition and understanding from domestic stakeholders. Gradually, a respect for the legal rights and interests of stakeholders, protection of the environment and the delivery of social responsibility will naturally become part of the accepted code of conduct for business in China.[31]

---

[29]   'Premier: China confident in maintaining economic growth', *Xinhua News Agency*, 16 March 2007, available at http://news.xinhuanet.com/english/2007-03/16/content_5856569.htm.

[30]   S. Zadek, M. Forstater and K. Yu, *Corporate Responsibility and Sustainable Economic Development in China: Implications for Business* (US Chamber of Commerce, National Chamber Foundation and Asia Department, 2012) p. 11, available at www.uschamber.com/.

[31]   OECD, *Corporate Governance of Listed Companies in China: Self-Assessment by the China Securities Regulatory Commission*, OECD-China Policy Dialogue on Corporate Governance (Paris: OECD Publishing, 2011).

Bibliography

Books

Alkhafaji, A.F., *A Stakeholder Approach to Corporate Governance: Managing in a Dynamic Environment* (New York: Quorum Books, 1989)

Anderson, J. W., *Corporate Social Responsibilities* (New York: Quorum Books, 1984)

Anholt, S., *Brand New Justice: The Upside of Global Branding* (Oxford: Butterworth-Heinemann, 2003)

Armour, J. and McCahery, J.A. (eds), *After Enron, Improving Corporate Law and Modernising Securities Regulation in Europe and the US* (Oxford: Hart Publishing, 2006)

Backman, M., *The Asian Insider: Unconditional Wisdom for Asian Business* (Basingstoke: Palgrave Macmillan, 2004)

Bakan, J., *The Corporation: The Pathological Pursuit of Profit and Power* (London: Constable and Robinson Ltd, 2004)

Beesley, M.E. and Evans, T., *Corporate Social Responsibility: A Reassessment* (London: Taylor & Francis, 1978)

Belal, A.R., *Corporate Social Responsibility Reporting in Developing Countries: The Case of Bangladesh* (Aldershot: Ashgate, 2008)

Bell, S. and Hindmoor, A., *Rethinking Governance: The Centrality of the State in Modern Society* (Cambridge: Cambridge University Press, 2009)

Berle, A. and Means, G., *The Modern Corporation and Private Property* (London and New York: Macmillan Co., 1933)

Blowfirled, M. and Murrary, A., *Corporate Responsibility*, 2nd edn (Oxford: Oxford University Press, 2011)

Bosselmann, K., *The Principle of Sustainability: Transforming Law and Governance* (Aldershot: Ashgate, 2008)

Brandeis, L.D., *Other People's Money and How the Bankers Use It* (Chevy Chase: National Home Library Foundation, 1933)

Brown, H.R., *Social Responsibilities of the Businessman* (New York: Haper & Row, 1953)

Brummer, J.J., *Corporate Responsibility and Legitimacy: An Interdisciplinary Analysis* (New York: Greenwood Press, 1991)

Burns, J.M., Goethals, G.R. and Sorenson, G. (eds), *Encyclopedia of Leadership* (Minneapolis: Sage, 2004)

Cane, P., *Responsibility in Law and Morality* (Oxford: Hart Publishing, 2003)

Cannon, T., *Corporate Responsibility* (Harlow: Pearsons Education, 1994)

Cao, K. *et al.* (eds), *A Research Report on the Amendment to Company Law (Xin Gongsi Fa Xiuding Yanjiu Baogao)* (Beijing: China Legal Publishing House, 2005)

Carroll, A.B., *Business and Society: Ethics and Stakeholder Management* (Cincinnati, OH: South-Western Publishing Co., 1993)

Carroll, A.B. and Buchholtz, A.K., *Business and Society: Ethics and Stakeholder Management.* 5th edn (Australia: Thomson South-Western, 2003)

Chen, J., Huang, Q., Pengn H. and Zhong, H. (eds), *Research Report on Corporate Social Responsibility of China 2011* (Beijing: Social Science Academic Press, 2011)

Chen, J., Li, Y. and Otto, J.M., *Implementation of Law in the People's Republic of China* (The Hague: Kluwer, 2002)

Chen, Z. and Yao, L., *Information on Chinese Modern Industrial History (Zhongguo Jindai Gongye Shi Ziliao)* (Beijing: SDX Joint Publishing Company, 1957)

Chien, T., *The Government and Politics of China, 1912–1949* (Cambridge, MA: Harvard University Press, 1950)

Choper, J.H., Coffee, J.C. and Gilson R.J., *Cases and Materials on Corporations*, 6th edn (New York: Panel Publisher, 2004)

Clarke, T., *International Corporate Governance: A Comparative Approach* (Oxford: Routledge, 2007)

Clarke, T. (ed.), *Theories of Corporate Governance: The Philosophical Foundations of Corporate Governance* (London: Routledge 2004)

Cramer, J. (ed.), *Corporate Social Responsibility and Globalisation: An Action Plan for Business* (Sheffield: Greenleaf Publishing, 2006)

Crane, A., Matten, D. and Moon, J., *Corporations and Citizenship* (Cambridge: Cambridge University Press, 2008)

Dean, J., *Directing Public Companies: Company Law and the Stakeholder Society* (London: Cavendish Publishing Ltd, 2001)

Demirag, I. (ed.), *Corporate Social Responsibility, Accountability and Governance: Global Perspective* (Sheffield: Greenleaf Publishing, 2005)

Dou, J., *Researches on Chinese Enterprise System and Thoughts (Zhongguo Gongsi Zhi Sixiang Yanjiu) (1942–1996)* (Shanghai: Shanghai University of Finance and Economic Press, 1999)

Drucker, P., *Managing for the Future* (London: Butterworth-Heinemann, 1992)

Economy, E.C., *The River Runs Black: The Environmental Challenge to China's Future* (Ithaca, NY: Cornell University Press, 2001)

Elkington, J., *Cannibals with Forks, the Triple Bottom Line of 21st Century Business* (Oxford: Capstone, 1998)

Fan, R., *Reconstructionist Confucianism: Rethinking Morality after the West* (London: Springer, 2010)

Feng, M., Chen, Z. and Wang, Z., *Corporate Social Responsibility of SOEs in China in a Harmonious Society (Zhongguo Guoyou Qiye Shehui Zerenlun: Jiyu Hexie Shehui de Sikao)* (Beijing: Economic Science Press, 2009)

Fisher, C. and Lovell, A., *Business Ethics and Value: Individual, Corporate and International Perspective* (Harlow: FT Prentice Hall, 2006)

Freeman, R.E., *Strategic Management: A Stakeholder Approach* (Boston, MA: Pitman, 1984)

Friedman, A.L. and Miles, S., *Stakeholder: Theory and Practice* (Oxford: Oxford University Press, 2006)

Fu, J., *Corporate Disclosure and Corporate Governance in China* (Alphen: Kluwer Law International, 2010)

Ge, J. and Lin, S., *Western Financial Accounting Theory (Xifang Caiwu Kuaiji Lilun)* (Xiamen: Xiamen University Press, 2001)

Gourevitch P.A. and Shinn, J., *Political Power and Corporate Control: The New Global Politics of Corporate Governance* (Princeton, NJ: Princeton University Press, 2007)

Gray, R., Owen, D. and Adams, C., *Accounting and Accountability: Changes and Challenges in Corporate Social and Environmental Reporting* (Hemel Hempstead: Prentice Hall, 1996)

Gray, R.H., Owen, D.L. and Maunders, K.T., *Corporate Social Reporting: Accounting and Accountability* (Hemel Hempstead: Prentice Hall, 1987)

Gu, M., *Understanding Chinese Company Law*, 2nd edn (Hong Kong: Hong Kong University Press, 2010)

Guo, S., *Unemployment Insurance System and Reemployment in China (Zhongguo Shiye Baozhang Zhidu Yu Zaijiuye)* (Shanghai: Shanghai University of Finance and Economics Press, 2008)

Habisch, A., Jonker, J., Wegner, M. and Chidpeter, R. (eds), *Corporate Social Responsibility Across Europe* (Heidelberg: Springer, 2005)

Hancock, J., *Investing in Corporate Social Responsibility: A Guide to Best Practice, Business Planning and the UK's Leading Companies* (London: Kogan, 2005)

Hawkins, D.E., *Corporate Social Responsibility: Balancing Tomorrow's Sustainability and Today's Profitability* (Basingstoke: Palgrave MacMillan, 2006)

Head, J.W., *Global Business Law, Principles and Practice of International Commerce and Investment*, 2nd edn (Durham, NC: Carolina Academic Press, 2007)

Henriques, A. and Richardson, J., *The Triple Bottom Line, Does it All Add Up? Assessing the Sustainability of Business and CSR* (London: Earthscan, 2004)

Hong, W.L., *Securities Regulations: Theory and Practice (Zhengquan Jianguan: Lilun yu Shijian)*, (Shanghai: Shanghai University of Finance and Economics Press, 2000)

Horrigan, B., *Corporate Social Responsibility in the 21st Century: Debates, Models and Practices Across Government, Law and Business* (Cheltenham: Edward Elgar, 2010)

Huang, X., *Corporate Social Responsibility: Theory and Practice in China (Qiye Shehui Zeren: Lilun Yu Zhongguo Shijian)* (Beijing: Social Sciences Academic Press, 2010)

Huniche, M. and Padersen, E.R., *Corporate Citizenship in Developing Countries: New Partnership Perspectives* (Abingdon: Copenhagen Business School Press, 2006)

Hus, L.S., *The Political Philosophy of Confucianism: An Interpretation of the Social and Political Ideas of Confucius, His Forerunners, and His Early Disciples* (London: George Routledge & Son, 1932)

Jia, X. and Tomasic, R., *Corporate Governance and Resource Security in China: The Transformation of China's Global Resources Companies* (London: Routledge, 2010)

Jones, S., *BRICS and Beyond: Executive Lessons on Emerging Markets* (Chichester: Wiley, 2012)

Keay, A., *The Corporate Objective* (Cheltenham: Edward Elgar, 2011)

Keay, A., *The Enlightened Shareholder Value Principle and Corporate Governance* (Oxford: Routledge, 2013)

Keinert, C., *Corporate Social Responsibility as an International Strategy* (Heidelberg: Physica-Verlag, 2008)

Kiss, A. and Shelton, D., *International Environmental Law*, 2nd edn (New York: Transnational Publisher, 2000)

Lau, D.C., 'Introduction' in Confucius, *The Analects* (London: Penguin Books, 1979)

Learmount, S., *Corporate Governance: What Can be Learned from Japan?* (Oxford: Oxford University Press, 2002)

Li, P. and Zhang, Y., *Analysis on Social Cost of State-Owned Enterprises (Guoyou Qiye Shehui Chengben Fen'xi)* (Beijing: Social Sciences Academic Press, 2000)

Li, Y. and Liu, Y., *Bluebook of Corporate Social Responsibility in China 2011* (Beijing: People's Publishing House, 2011)

Li, Z., *A Research on Corporate Social Responsibility Information Disclosure (Qiye Shehui Zeren Xinxi Pilu Yanjiu)* (Beijing: Economic Science Press, 2008)

Liao, C., *The Governance Structure of Chinese Firms: Innovation, Competitiveness and Growth in a Dual Economy* (London: Springer, 2009)

Liu, J., *Corporate Social Responsibility (Gongsi Shehui Zeren)* (Beijing: Law Press, 1999)

Lu, X. and Enderle, G., *Developing Business Ethics in China* (Basingstoke: Palgrave Macmillan, 2006)

Lufrano, R., *Honourable Merchants: Commerce and Self-Cultivation in Late Imperial China* (Honolulu: University of Hawaii Press, 1997)

Mallin, C.A., *Corporate Governance*, 3rd edn (Oxford: Oxford University Press, 2010)

McBarnet, D., Voiculescu, A. and Campbell, T. (eds), *The New Corporate Accountability: Corporate Social Responsibility and the Law* (Cambridge: Cambridge University Press, 2007)

McDaniel, B.A., *Entrepreneurship and Innovation: An Economic Approach* (New York: M.E. Sharp, 2002)

McIntosh, M., Thomas, R., Leipziger, D. and Coleman, G., *Living Corporate Citizenship: Strategic Routes to Socially Responsible Business* (Harlow and London: Prentice-Hall/*Financial Times*, 2003)

Meadows, D.H., Meadows, D.L. and Behrens, W., *The Limits to Growth* (New York: Universe Books, 1972)

Mertha, A.C., *The Politics of Piracy: Intellectual Property in Contemporary China* (Ithaca, NY: Cornell University Press, 2007)

Milman, D., *National Corporate Law in a Globalised Market: The UK Experience in Perspective* (Cheltenham: Edward Elgar, 2009)

Mullerate, R. (ed.), *Corporate Social Responsibility: The Corporate Governance of the 21st Century* (London: Kluwer Law International, 2005)

Naughton, B., *The Chinese Economy: Transitions and Growth* (Cambridge, MA: MIT Press, 2007)

Parker, C., Scott, C., Lacey, N. and Braithwaite, J. (eds), *Regulating Law* (Oxford: Oxford University Press, 2004)

Parkinson, J., Gamble, A. and Kelly, G. (eds), *The Political Economy of the Company* (Oxford: Hart Publishing, 2000)

Parkinson, J.E., *Corporate Power and Responsibility: Issues in the Theory of Company Law* (Oxford: Clarendon Press, 1993)

Ping, J., *New Company Law Text Book (Xin Gongsi Fa Jiaocheng)* (Beijing: The Law Press, 1997)

Qu, Z., *The Historical Review and Current Reflections of Unemployment Insurance (Zhongguo Shiye Baoxian Lishi Huigu Jiqi Sikao)* (Shanghai: Shanghai Social Science Academy Press, 2009)

Sands, P., *Principles of International Environmental Law*, 2nd edn (Cambridge: Cambridge University Press, 2003)

Schmidt, H. and Drukarczyk, J., *Corporate Governance in Germany* (Baden-Baden: Nomos, 1997)

Selznick, P., *The Communitarian Persuasion* (Washington, DC: Woodrow Wilson Centre Press, 2002)

Sheikh, S., *Corporate Social Responsibilities: Law and Practice* (Abingdon and New York: Routledge, 1996)

Sheikh, S., *A Practical Approach to Corporate Governance* (London: LexisNexis UK, 2003)

Shi, C., *The Political Determinants of Corporate Governance in China* (London: Routledge, 2012)

Steiner, G., *Business, Government, and Society: A Managerial Perspective* (New York: Random House Business Division, 1985)

Steiner, J.F. and Steiner, G.A., *Business, Government, and Society: A Managerial Perspective, Text and Cases*, 13th edn (New York: McGraw-Hill, 2012)

Stone, C.D., *Where the Law Ends* (New York: Harper and Row, 1975)

Stout, L., *The Shareholder Value Myth: How Putting Shareholders First Harms Investors, Corporations, and the Public* (San Francisco: Berrett-Koehler, 2012)

Summers, J. and Hyman, J., *Employee Participation and Company Performance: A Review of the Literature* (York: Joseph Rowntree Foundation, 2005)

Sun, Y., *Complete Work of Sun Yat-sen, Volume 2* (Beijing: Zhonghua Book Company, 1982)

Tricker, B., *Corporate Governance: Principles, Policies, and Practices* (Oxford: Oxford University Press, 2009)

Tully, S. (ed.), *Research Handbook on Corporate Legal Responsibility* (Cheltenham: Edward Elgar, 2005)

Urip, S., *CSR Strategies: Corporate Social Responsibility for a Competitive Edge in Emerging Markets* (Chichester: John Wiley & Sons, 2010)

Visser, W., *The Age of Responsibility: CSR 2.0 and the New DNA of Business* (Chichester: John Wiley & Sons, 2011)

Werther, W.B. and Chandler, D., *Strategic Corporate Social Responsibility: Stakeholders in a Global Environment* (London: Sage, 2006)

Wu, C. and Jiang, T., *History of Chinese Enterprises: Modern History Volume (Zhongguo Qiye Shi: Jindai Juan)* (Beijing: Enterprise Management Publishing House, 2004)

Wu, G., *Zheng Guanying: Merchant Reformer of Late Qing China and His Influence on Economics, Politics, and Society* (New York: Cambria Press, 2010)

Yang, T. and Ge, D., *Corporations and Public Welfare* (*Gongsi Yu Shehui Gongyi II*) (Beijing: Social Sciences Academic Press, 2009)

Yang, Z., *A Chinese Model of Corporate Governance* (*Gongsi Zhide de Zhongguo Moshi*) (Beijing: Social Sciences Academic Press, 2009)

Yao, C., *Stock Market and Futures in the People's Republic of China* (New York: Oxford University Press, 1998)

Yao, X., *An Introduction to Confucianism* (Cambridge: Cambridge University Press, 2007)

Yeung, H.W.C., *Chinese Capitalism in a Global Era: Towards a Hybrid Model* (London: Routledge, 2004)

Zerk, J.A., *Multinationals and Corporate Social Responsibility: Limitations and Opportunities in International Law* (Cambridge: Cambridge University Press, 2006)

Zhang, W.B., *Confucianism and Modernization: Industrialization and Democratization of the Confucian Regions* (London: Macmillan Press, 1999)

Zhang, Z., *Difficult Transformation: Studies on the Contemporary Chinese Corporation* (*Jiannan de Bianqian: Jindai Zhongguo Gongsi Zhidu Yanjiu*) (Shanghai: Academy of Social Science Press, 2002)

Zhong, H., Sun, X., Zhang, C. and Zhang, T., *Corporate Social Responsibility (CSR) Report Preparation Guide 1.0* (*Zhongguo Qiye Shehuizeren Baogao Bianxie Zhinan 1.0)* (Beijing: Economy and Management Publishing House, 2009)

Zu, L., *Corporate Social Responsibility, Corporate Restructuring and Firm's Performance* (Berlin: Springer-Verlag, 2009)

Articles, Papers and Book Chapters

Aaronson, S.A., 'Corporate Responsibility in the Global Village: The British Role and the American Laggard' (2003) 108 *Business and Society Review* 309

Aaronson, S.A., 'A Match Made in the Corporate and Public Interest: Marry Voluntary CSR Initiatives and the WOT' (2007) 41 *Journal of World Trade* 629

Ackerman, R., 'How Companies Respond to Social Demands' (1973) 51 *Harvard Business Review* 88

Adams, C.A., 'The Ethical, Social and Environmental Reporting-Performance Portrayal Gap' (2004) 17 *Accounting, Auditing and Accountability Journal* 731

Adeyeye, A., 'Universal Standards in CSR: Are We Prepared?' (2011) 11 *Corporate Governance* 107

Aggarwal, R. and Chandra, A., 'Stakeholder Management: Opportunities and Challenges' (1990) 40 *Business* 48

Aguilera, R.V. and Jackson, G., 'The Cross-national Diversity of Corporate Governance: Dimensions and Determinants' (2003) 28 *Academy of Management Review* 447

Aguilera, R.V., Rupp, D., Williams, C. and Ganapathi, J., 'Putting the S Back in CSR: A Multi-level Theory of Social Change in Organizations' (2007) 32 *Academy of Management Review* 836

Aiyegbayo, O. and Villers, C., 'The Enhanced Business Review: Has it Made Corporate Governance More Effective?' (2011) *Journal of Business Law* 699

Albareda, L., Lozano, J.M., Tencati, A., Midttun, A. and Perrini, F., 'The Changing Role of Government in Corporate Social Responsibility: Drivers and Responses' (2008) 17 *Business Ethics: A European Review* 347

Anderson, C. and Guo, B., 'Corporate Governance under the New Company Law (Part 2): Shareholder Lawsuit and Enforcement' (2006) *China Law and Practice* (May) 15

Anthony, M., 'The New China: Big Brother, Brave New World or Harmonious Society?' (2007) 11 *Journal of Future Studies* 15

Aoi, J., 'To Whom Does the Company Belong? A New Management Mission for the Information Age' in D.H. Cew (ed.), *Studies in International Corporate Finance and Governance System: A Comparison of the U.S., Japan, and Europe* (Oxford: Oxford University Press, 1997)

Argandona, A., 'The Stakeholder Theory and the Common Good' (1998) 17 *Journal of Business Ethics* 1093

Armour, J., Deakin S. and Konzelmann S.J., 'Shareholder Primacy and the Trajectory of UK Corporate Governance' (2003) 41 *British Journal of Industrial Relations* 531

Arora, A., 'The Corporate Governance Failings in Financial Institutions and Directors' Legal Liability' (2011) 32 *Company Lawyer* 3

Arsalidou, D., 'The Withdrawal of the Operating and Financial Review in the Company Bill 2006: Progression or Regression?' (2007) 28 *Company Lawyer* 131

Association of Chartered Certified Accountants (ACCA), *Climbing Out of the Credit Crunch*, Policy Paper (September 2008)

Avgouleas, E., 'The Global Financial Crisis, Behavioural Finance and Financial Regulation: In Search of a New Orthodoxy' (2009) 9 *Journal of Corporate Law Studies* 23

Bainbridge, M., 'Independent Directors and the ALI Corporate Governance Project' (1993) 61 *George Washington Law Review* 1034

Bainbridge, S.M., 'In Defense of the Shareholder Wealth Maximization Norm: A Reply to Professor Green' (1993) 50 *Washington and Lee Law Review* 1423

Bainbridge, S.M., 'Director v. Shareholder Primacy in the Convergence Debate' (2002) 16 *Transnational Lawyer* 46

Bainbridge, S.M., 'The Creeping Federalization of Corporate Law' (2003) 26 *Regulation* 32

Bainbridge, S.M., 'Director Primacy: The Means and Ends of Corporate Governance' (2003) 97 *Northwestern University Law Review* 547

Balabanis, G., Phillips, H. and Lyall, J., 'Corporate Social Responsibility and Economic Performance in the Top British Companies: Are They Linked?' (1998) 98 *European Business Review* 25

Baxi, U., 'Market Fundamentalisms: Business Ethics at the Altar of Human Rights' (2005) 5 *Human Rights Law Review* 1

Baysinger, B.D. and Butler, H.N., 'Revolution Versus Evolution in Corporate Law: The ALI's Project and the Independent Director' (1984) 52 *George Washington Law Review* 563

Beattie, V. and McInnes, B., *Narrative Reporting in the UK and the US: Which System Works Best?* Institute of Chartered Accountants in England and Wales Briefing (London: Centre for Business Performance for ICAEW, 2006)

Bebchuk, L., 'The Case for Increasing Shareholder Power' (2005) 118 *Harvard Law Review* 833

Bebchuk, L.A., Cohen, A. and Ferrell, A., 'Does the Evidence Favor State Competition in Corporate Law' (2002) 90 *California Law Review* 1775

Bebchuk, L.A. and Roe, M., 'A Theory of Path Dependence in Corporate Governance' (1999) *Stanford Law Review* 127

Belal, A.R., 'A Study of Corporate Social Disclosures in Bangladesh' (2001) 16 *Managerial Auditing Journal* 274

Belal, A.R. and Lubinin, V., 'Corporate Social Disclosure (CSD) in Russia' in S.O. Idowu and W.L. Filho (eds), *Global Practice of Corporate Social Responsibility* (Berlin: Springer Verlag, 2008) p. 165

Berle, A.A., 'Corporate Powers as Power in Trust' (1931) 44 *Harvard Law Review* 1049

Berle, A.A., 'For Whom Corporate Managers are Trustees: A Note' (1932) 45 *Harvard Law Review* 1365

Bewley, K. and Li, Y., 'Disclosure of Environmental Information by Canadian Manufacturing Companies: A Voluntary Disclosure Perspective' (2000) 1 *Advances in Environmental Accounting and Management* 201

Blacconiere, W.G. and Northcut, W.D., 'Environmental Information and Market Reactions to Environmental Legislation' (1997) 12 *Journal of Accounting, Auditing and Finance* 149

Black, B., Cheffins, B. and Klausner, M., 'Outside Director Liability' (2006) 58 *Stanford Law Review* 1055

Blair, M.M. and Stout L.A., 'A Team Production Theory of Corporate Law' (1999) 85 *Virginia Law Review* 247

Blowfield, M., 'Corporate Social Responsibility: Reinventing the Meaning of Development' (2005) 81 *International Affairs* 515

Bogdanich, W., 'Toxic toothpaste made in China is found in U.S.', *New York Times*, 2 June 2007

Bouten, L., Everaet, P., Liedekerke, L.V., Moor, L.D. and Christiaens, J., 'Corporate Social Responsibility Reporting: A Comprehensive Picture' (2011) 35 *Accounting Forum* 187

Braendle, U., Casser, T. and Noll, J., 'Corporate Governance in China: Is Economic Growth Potential Hindered by *Guanxi*?' (2005) 16 *Business Strategy Review* 42

Braendle, U.C. and Noll, J., 'On the Convergence of National Corporate Governance Systems' (2006) 15 *Journal of Interdisciplinary Economics* 57

Brammer, S. and Parvelin, S., 'Building a Good Reputation' (2004) 19 *European Management Journal* 704

Bratspies, R.M., 'Sustainability: Can Law Meet the Challenge?' (2011) 34 *Suffolk Transitional Law Review* 283

Brenner, S.N. and Molander, E.A., 'Is the Ethics of Business Changing'(1977) 58 *Harvard Business Review* 54

Brunnermeier, M.K., 'Deciphering the 2007–2008 Liquidity and Credit Crunch' (2009) 23 *Journal of Economic Perspective* 77

Buhmann, K., 'Corporate Social Responsibility: What Role for Law? Some Aspects of Law and CSR' (2006) 6 *Corporate Governance: International Journal of Effective Board Performance* 188

Byerly, R.T., 'Seeking Global Solutions for the Common Good: A New World Order and Corporate Social Responsibilities' in I. Demirag, *CSR, Accountability and Governance: Global Perspectives* (Sheffield: Greenleaf Publishing, 2005) p. 122

Cadbury, A. and Millstein, I.M., *The New Agenda for ICGN*, Discussion Paper No. 1 for the ICGN Tenth Anniversary Conference, London, 13 July 2005

Campbell, D. and Beck, A.C., 'Answering Allegations: The Use of the Corporate Website for Restorative Ethical and Social Disclosure' (2004) 13 *Business Ethics: A European Review* 100

Campbell, J.L., 'Why Would Corporations Behave in a Socially Responsible Way? An Institutional Theory of Corporate Social Responsibility' (2007) 32 *Academy of Management Review* 946

Campbell, K. and Vick, D., 'Disclosures Law and the Market for Corporate Social Responsibility' in D. McBarnet, A. Voiculescu and T. Campbell, *The New Corporate Accountability: Corporate Social Responsibility and the Law* (Cambridge: Cambridge University Press, 2007) p. 241

Carroll, A.B., 'A Three-Dimensional Conceptual Model of Corporate Social Performance' (1979) 4 *Academy of Management Review* 497

Carroll, A.B., 'The Pyramid of Corporate Social Responsibility: Towards the Moral Management of Organizational Stakeholders' (1991) 38 *Business Horizons* 39

Carroll, A.B., 'Corporate Social Responsibility: Evolution of a Definitional Construct' (1999) 38 *Business and Society* 268

Carroll, A.B., 'A History of Corporate Social Responsibility: Concept and Practice' in A. Crane, A. McWilliams, D. Matten, J. Moon and D. Siegel (eds), *The Oxford Handbook of Corporate Social Responsibility* (Oxford: Oxford University Press, 2008) p. 20

Carroll, A.B. and Shabana, K.M., 'The Business Case for Corporate Social Responsibility: A Review of Concept, Research and Practice' (2010) 12 *International Journal of Management Reviews* 85

Cecil, L., 'Corporate Social Responsibility Reporting in the United States' (2008) 1 *McNair Scholars Research Journal* 43

Chan, A., 'Globalization, China's Free (Read Bonded) Labour Market and the Chinese Trade Unions' (2000) 6 *Asia Pacific Business Review* 260

Chan, K.M., 'Harmonious Society' in H.K. Anheier and S. Toepler (eds), *International Encyclopedia of Civil Society* (New York: Springer, 2009) p. 821

Cheffins, B., 'Did Corporate Governance "Fail" During the 2008 Stock Market Meltdown? The Case of the S&P 500' (2009) 65 *Business Lawyer* 1

Chen, C.H. and Al-Najjar, B., 'The Determinants of Board Size and Independence: Evidence from China' (2011) 21 *International Business Review* 831

Chen, G., Firth, M. and Xu, L., 'Does the Type of Ownership Control Matter? Evidence from China's Listed Companies' (2009) 33 *Journal of Banking and Finance* 171

Chen, H. and Zhang, H., 'Two-way Communication Strategy on CSR Information in China' (2009) 5 *Social Responsibility Journal* 440

Chen, J., 'Ownership Structure as Corporate Governance Mechanism: Evidence from Chinese Listed Companies' (2001) 34 *Economic of Planning* 53

Chen, S. and Bouvain, P., 'Is Corporate Responsibility Converging? A Comparison of Corporate Responsibility Reporting in the USA, UK, Australia and Germany' (2009) 87 *Journal of Business Ethics* 299

Cheung, T.S. and King, A.Y., 'Righteousness and Profitableness: The Moral Choices of Contemporary Confucian Entrepreneurs' (2004) 54 *Journal of Business Ethics* 245

Cheung, Y.L., Tan, W. and Zhang, Z., 'Does Corporate Social Responsibility Matter in Asian Emerging Markets?' (2010) 92 *Journal of Business Ethics* 401

Chivers, D., *The Companies Act 2006: Directors' Duties Guidance* (Corporate Responsibility Coalition, 2007)

Choudhury, B., 'Serving Two Masters: Incorporating Social Responsibility into the Corporate Paradigm' (2008) 11 *University of Pennsylvania Journal of Business Law* 631

Clark, D.C. and Howson, N.C., 'Pathway to Minority Shareholder Protection: Derivative Action in the People's Republic of China' in D. Puchniak, H. Baum and M. Ewing-Chow (eds), *The Derivative Action in Asia: A Comparative and Functional Approach* (Cambridge: Cambridge University Press, 2012) p. 243

Clark, R.C., 'Vote Buying and Corporate Law' (1979) 29 *Case Western Reserve Law Review* 776

Clarke, D.C., 'The Independent Director in Chinese Corporate Governance' (2006) 36 *Delaware Journal of Corporate Law* 125

Clarkson, M.B.E., Deck, M.C. and Shiner, N.J., 'The Stakeholder Management Model in Practice', paper presented at the annual meeting of the Academy of Management, Las Vegas, NV, 1992

Coffee, J.C., 'What Went Wrong? An Initial Inquiry into the Causes of the 2008 Financial Crisis' (2009) 9 *Journal of Corporate Law Studies* 1

Conley, J.M., 'An Emerging Third Way? The Erosion of the Anglo-American Shareholder Value Construct' (2005) 38 *Cornell International Law Journal* 493

Cooney, S., Biddulph, S., Li, K. and Zhu, Y., 'China's New Labour Contract Law: Responding to the Growing Complexity of Labour Relations in the PRC' (2007) 30 *UNSW Law Journal* 786

Cowe, R., *Developing Value: The Business Case for Sustainability in Emerging Markets* (London: Sustainability, International Finance Corporation and Ethos Institute, 2002)

Cowen, S.S., Ferreri, L.B. and Parker, L.D., 'The Impact of Corporate Characteristics on Social Responsibility Disclosure: A Typology and

Frequency-based Analysis' (1987) 12 *Accounting, Organizations and Society* 111

Cox, G., *Overcoming Short-termism within British Business: The Key to Sustained Economic Growth: An Independent Review by Sir George Cox commissioned by the Labour Party* (2013), available at Your Britain, Labour Party Policy Review website, www.yourbritain.org.uk/ uploads/.../Overcoming_Short-termism.pdf

Dahlsrud, A., 'How Corporate Social Responsibility is Defined: An Analysis of 37 Definitions' (2008) 15 *Corporate Social Responsibility and Environmental Management* 1

Daines, R., 'Does Delaware Law Improve Firm Value?' (2001) 62 *Journal of Financial Economics* 525

Dallas, L.L., 'Working Toward a New Paradigm' in L.E. Mitchell (ed.), *Progressive Corporate Law* (London: Kluwer, 1995) p. 35

Dalley, P.J., 'To Whom it May Concern: Fiduciary Duties and Business Associations' (2001) 26 *Delaware Journal of Corporate Law* 515

Dando, N. and Swift, T., 'Transparency and Assurance: Minding the Credibility Gap' (2003) 44 *Journal of Business Ethics* 195

Darigan, K.H. and Post, J.E., 'Corporate Citizenship in China: CSR Challenges in the "Harmonious Society"' (2009) 35 *Journal of Corporate Citizenship* 39

Davies, R., 'Corporate Citizenship and Socially Responsible Investment: Emerging Challenges and Opportunities in Asia', paper presented at the Association for Sustainable and Responsible Investment in Asia Conference, Hong Kong, 10 January 2005

Davis, K., 'The Case For and Against Business Assumption of Social Responsibilities' (1973) 16 *Academy of Management Journal* 312

de Bettignies, H.C., 'CSR "Fatigue" and China's Performance' (2011) *GRLI Partner Magazine* (January) 31

de Haan, A., 'The Financial Crisis and China's 'Harmonious Society''' (2010) 2 *Journal of Current Chinese Affairs* 69

Deakin, S., 'The Coming Transformation of Shareholder Value' (2005) 13 *Corporate Governance* 11

Dean, J., 'Stakeholding and Company Law' (2001) 22 *Company Lawyer* 66

Dean, J., 'The Future of U.K. Company Law' (2001) 22 *Company Lawyer* 104

DeBow, M.E. and Lee, D.R., 'Shareholders, Nonshareholders and Corporate Law: Communitarians and Resource Allocation' (1993) 18 *Delaware Journal of Corporate Law* 393

Debrox, P., 'Corporate Social Responsibility and Sustainable Development in Asia: A Growing Awareness' (2009) 8 *Asian Business and Management* 33

Deegan, C., 'The Legitimizing Effect of Social and Environmental Disclosure: A Theoretical Foundation' (2002) 15 *Accounting, Auditing and Accountability Journal* 282

Detomasi, D.A., 'The Multinational Corporation and Global Governance: Modelling Global Public Policy Network' (2007) 71 *Journal of Business Ethics* 321

Dodd, E.M., 'For Whom Corporate Managers are Trustees' (1932) 45 *Harvard Law Review* 1145

Donaldson, T., 'Three Ethical Roots of the Economic Crisis' (2012) 106 *Journal of Business Ethics* 5

Donaldson, T. and Preston, L.E., 'The Stakeholder Theory of the Corporation: Concept, Evidence, and Implications' (1995) 20 *Academy of Management Review* 65

Dowling, J. and Pfeffer, J., 'Organizational Legitimacy: Social Values and Organizational Behavior' (1975) 18 *Pacific Sociological Review* 122

Du, Z., 'Corporate Social Responsibility and Measures for Enforcement (*Qiye de Shehui Zeren Jiqi Shixian Fangshi*)' (2005) 4 *Journal of Renmin University of China* (*Zhongguo Renmin Daxue Xuebao*) 39

Dunfee, T.W. and Warrren, D.E., 'Is *Guanxi* Ethical? A Normative Analysis of Doing Business in China' (2004) 32 *Journal of Business Ethics* 191

Dyllick, T. and Hockerts, K., 'Beyond the Business Case for Corporate Sustainability' (2002) 11 *Business Strategy and the Environment* 130

Eberstadt, N.N., 'What History Tells Us about Corporate Responsibility' (1973) 66 *Business and Society Review* 76

Edwards, T., Marginson, P., Edwards, P., Ferner, A. and Tregaskis, O., *Corporate Social Responsibility in Multinational Companies: Management Initiatives or Negotiated Agreement?* (International Institute for Labour Studies, (2007)

Eisenberg, M.A., 'The Structure of Corporation Law' (1989) 89 *Columbia Law Review* 1461

Elbing, A., 'The Value Issue of Business: The Responsibility of the Businessman' (1970) 13 *Academy of Management Journal* 79

Elias, N. and Epstein, M., 'Dimensions of Corporate Social Reporting' (1975) 57 *Management Accounting* 36

Elkington, J., 'Towards the Sustainable Corporation: Win-Win-Win Business Strategies for Sustainable Development' (1994) 36 *California Management Review* 90

Elsayd, K., 'Re-examining the Expected Effect of Available Resources and Firm Size on Firm Environmental Orientation: An Empirical Study of UK Firms' (2006) 65 *Journal of Business Ethics* 297

Epstein, E., 'The Social Role of Business Enterprise in Britain: An American Perspective' (1977) 14 *Journal of Management Studies* 213

Estrin, S., 'State Ownership, Corporate Governance and Privatization' in *State-owned Enterprises and Privatization* (Paris: OECD, 1998)

Evan, M. and Freeman, R.E., 'A Stakeholder Theory of the Modern Corporation' in M. Snoeyenbos, R. Almeder and J. Humber (eds), *Business Ethics*, 3rd edn (New York: Prometheus Books, 2001)

Fan, D.K.K., Lau, C.M. and Young, M., 'Is China's Corporate Governance Beginning to Come of Age? The Case of CEO Turnover' (2007) 37 *Pacific-Basin Finance Journal* 105

Fan, R., 'Reconsidering Surrogate Decision Making: Aristotelianism and Confucianism on Ideal Human Relations' (2002) 52 *Philosophy East and West* 346

Fannon, I.L., 'The Corporate Social Responsibility Movement and Law's Empire: Is there a Conflict?' (2007) 58 *Northern Ireland Legal Quarterly* 1

Feinerman, J.V., 'New Hope for Corporate Governance in China?' (2007) 191 *China Quarterly* 590

Fields, T.D., Lys, T.Z. and Vincent, L., 'Empirical Research on Accounting Choice' (2001) 31 *Journal of Accounting and Economics* 301

Finch, V., 'Corporate Rescue in a World of Debt' (2008) *Journal of Business Law* 756

Firth, M., Fung, P.M.Y. and Rui, O.M., 'Corporate Performance and CEO Compensation in China' (2006) 12 *Journal of Corporate Finance* 693

Fisch, J.E., 'Measuring Efficiency in Corporate Law: The Role of Shareholder Primacy' (2006) *Journal of Corporation Law* 637

Fisch, J.E. 'Robert Clark's Corporate Law: Twenty Years of Change: Measuring Efficiency in Corporate Law: The Role of Shareholder Primacy' (2006) 31 *Iowa Journal of Corporate Law* 637

Fisk, C.L., 'Knowledge Work: New Metaphors for the New Economy' (2005) 80 *Chicago-Kent Law Review* 839

Fitchett, J.A., 'Consumers as Stakeholders: Prospects for Democracy in Marketing Theory' (2005) 14 *Business Ethics: A European Review* 14

Ford, T.L and Schipani, C.A., 'Corporate Governance, Stakeholder Accountability, and Sustainable Peace: A Symposium' (2002) 35 *Vanderbilt Journal of Transnational* Law 38

Forney, M., 'Pouring Cash', *Time*, 18 October 2004

Frederick, W.C., 'From CSR1 to CSR2: The Maturing of Business and Society Thought' (1994) 53 *Business and Society* 51

Frederick, W.C., 'Corporate Social Responsibility: Deep Roots, Flourishing Growth, Promising Future' in A. Crane, A. McWilliams, D. Matten, J. Moon and D. Siegel (eds), *The Oxford Handbook of Corporate Social Responsibility* (Oxford: Oxford University Press, 2008) p. 522

Freeman, E. and Moutchnik, A., 'Stakeholder Management and CSR: Questions and Answers' (2013) uwf Umwelt Wirtschafts Forum

Freeman, R.E., 'Stockholders and Stakeholders: A New Perspective on Corporate Governance' (1983) 3 *California Management Review* 88

Freeman, R.E., 'A Stakeholder Theory of the Modern Corporation' in T.L. Beauchamp and N.E. Bowie (eds), *Ethical Theory and Business*, 5th edn (Upper Saddle River, NJ: Prentice Hall, 1997) p. 69

Freeman, R.E., 'Divergent Stakeholder Theory' (1999) 24 *Academy of Management Review* 233

Freeman, R.E., Wicks A.C. and Parmar, B., 'Stakeholder Theory and "The Corporate Objective Revisited"' (2004) 15 *Organization Science* 364

French, H.W., 'Chinese success story chokes on its own growth', *New York Times*, 19 December 2006

French, P., 'China Briefing Part 1: Overview – Economic Revolution Brings Responsibility Rethink', *Ethical Corporation*, 2 February 2012

Friedman, M., 'The Social Responsibility of Business is to Increase Its Profits', *New York Times Sunday Magazine*, 13 September 1970

Friedman, M., 'Monopoly and the Social Responsibility of Business and Labor' in M. Friedman, *Capitalism and Freedom*, 40th anniversary edn (Chicago, IL: University of Chicago Press, 2002) p. 208

Gao, L. and Kling, G., 'Corporate Governance and Tunnelling: Empirical Evidence from China' (2008) 16 *Pacific-Basin Finance Journal* 591

Geis, J.P. and Holt, B., 'Harmonious Society: Rise of the New China' (2009) *Strategic Studies Quarterly* 75

German, J.D., 'The Social Utility of Wicked Self-Love: Calvinism, Capitalism, and Public Policy in Revolutionary New England' (1995) *Journal of American History* 965

Geva, A., 'Three Models of Corporate Social Responsibility: Inter-relationships between Theory, Research and Practice' (2008) 113 *Business and Society Review* 1

Gonella, C., Piling, A. and Zadek, S., *Making Values Count: Contemporary Experience in Social and Ethical Accounting* (London: ACCA, 1998)

Gray, R., Dey, C., Owen, D., Evans, R. and Zadek, S., 'Struggling with the Praxis of Social Accounting: Stakeholders, Accountability, Stakeholders, Accountability, Audits and Procedures' (1997) 10 *Accounting, Auditing and Accountability Journal* 325

Gray, R., Kouhy, R. and Lavers, S., 'Corporate Social and Environmental Reporting: A Review of the Literature and a Longitudinal Study of UK Disclosure' (1995) 8 *Accounting, Auditing and Accountability Journal* 47

Gu, M., '"Will an Independent Director Institution Perform Better than a Supervisor?" Comments on the Newly Created Independent System in the People's Republic of China' (2003) *Journal of Chinese and Comparative Law* 59

Guthrie, J.E. and Matthews, M.R., 'Corporate Social Accounting in Australia' (1985) 7 *Research in Corporate Social Performance and Policy* 251

Guthrie, J.E. and Parker, L.D., 'Corporate Social Reporting: A Rebuttal of Legitimacy Theory' (1989) 1 *Accounting and Business Research* 343

Hall, M.J.B., *The Sub-prime Crisis, the Credit Crunch and Bank "Failure": An Assessment of the UK Authorities' Response*, Discussion Paper Series, (London: Department of Economics, 2008)

Hart, O., 'Norms and the Theory of the Firm' (2001) 149 *University of Pennsylvania Law Review* 170

Hay, R. and Gray, E., 'Social Responsibilities of Business Management' (1974) 17 *Academy of Management Journal* 135

Healy, P.M. and Palepu, K.G., 'Information Asymmetry, Corporate Disclosure, and the Capital Markets: A Review of the Empirical Disclosure Literature' (2001) 31 *Journal of Accounting and Economics* 405

Hill, I., 'How Finance Can Help Move CSR up the Agenda' (2006) 16 *Cost and Management* 5

Hogner, R.H., 'Corporate Social Reporting: Eight Decades of Development at US Steel' (1982) 4 *Research in Corporate Performance and Policy* 243

Hoivik, H. von W., 'East Meets West: Tacit Messages about Business Ethics in Stories Told by Chinese Managers' (2007) 74 *Journal of Business Ethics* 457

Hooghiemstra, R., 'Corporate Communication and Impression Management: New Perspective Why Companies Engage in Corporate Social Reporting' (2000) 27 *Journal of Business Ethics* 55

Hopkins, M. and Crowe, R., 'Corporate Social Responsibility: Is there a Business Case?' (2003), available at www2.accaglobal.com/pdfs/members_pdfs/publications/csr03.pdf

Horrigan, B., '21st Century Corporate Social Responsibility Trend: An Emerging Comparative Body of Law and Regulation on Corporate Responsibility, Governance and Sustainability' (2007) 4 *Macquarie Journal of Business Law* 85

Horwitz, M., 'Santa Clara Revisited: The Development of Corporate Theory' (1985) 88 *West Virginia Law Review* 173

Hsu, H., 'A New Business Excellence Model with Business Integrity from Ancient Confucian Thinking' (2007) 18 *Total Quality Management and Business Excellence* 413

Hu, A., 'China in 2020: Comprehensive Well-off and the Goal of a Socialist Harmonious Society' in J. Zhou, A. Hu and S. Wang (eds),

Building a Harmonious Society: The Experiences of Europe and the Exploration of China (Beijing: Tsinghau University Press, 2007) p. 165

Hu, R., 'The Concept and Importance of Corporate Governance' in G. Tu and C. Zhu (eds), *Corporate Governance: International Experience and China Practice* (Beijing: People's Press, 2001)

Huang, D., Kong, Y. and Hua, Z., 'Symposium on China's Peaceful Development and International Law' (2006) 5 *Chinese Journal of International Law* 261

Huang, X., 'Modernising the Chinese Capital Market: Old Problems and New Legal Responses' (2010) 21 *International Commercial and Company Law Review* 223

Huchet, J.F. and Richer, X., *China in Search of an Efficient Corporate Governance System: International Comparison and Lessons*, Centre for Economic Reform and Transformation Discussion Paper No. 99/01 (Edinburgh: Herriot-Watt University, 11 February 1999)

Hulthausen, R.W. and Leftwich, R.W., 'The Economic Consequences of Accounting Choice' (1983) 5 *Journal of Accounting and Economics* 77

Huson, M.R., Parrino, R. and Starks, L.T., 'International Monitoring Mechanisms and CEO Turnover: A Long Term Perspective' (2001) 56 *Journal of Finance* 2265

Ioannou, I. and Serafeim, G., 'What Drives Corporate Social Performance: The Role of Nation-Level Institutions' (2012) 43 *Journal of International Business Studies* 834

Ip, P.K., 'The Challenge of Developing a Business Ethics in China' (2008) 88 *Journal of Business Ethics* 211

Jensen, M.C., 'Value Maximization, Stakeholder Theory, and the Corporate Objective Function' (2001) 14 *Journal of Applied Corporate Finance* 8

Jensen, M.H., *Serve the People! Corporate Social Responsibility (CSR) in China*, Asia Research Centre Copenhagen Discussion Paper 2006-6 (2006), available at http://openarchive.cbs.dk/bitstream/handle/10398/7405/cdp%202006-006.pdf

Johnson, A., 'After the OFR: Can UK Shareholder Value Still be Enlightened?' (2006) 7 *European Business Organization Law Review* 817

Jordan, C. and Jain, A., *Diversity and Resilience: Lessons from the Financial Crisis*, Centre for Corporate Law and Securities Regulation Research Paper, (Melbourne: University of Melbourne, 8 September 2009)

Kahn, J., 'Making trinkets in China and a deadly dust', *New York Times*, 18 June 2003

Kahn J. and Yardley, J., 'As China roars, pollution reaches deadly extremes', *New York Times*, 26 August 2007

Kaplan, S., 'Corporate Governance and Corporate Performance: A Comparison of Germany, Japan, and the U.S.' (1997) 9 *Journal of Applied Corporate Finance* 86

Karlsson, D., *Corporate Social Responsibility: A Tool for Creating a Harmonious Society in China* (Brussels: European Institute for Asian Studies, 2011)

Keay, A., 'Enlightened Shareholder Value, the Reform of the Duties of Company Directors and the Corporate Objective' (2006) *Lloyd's Maritime and Commercial Law Quarterly* 335

Keay, A., 'Section 172(1) of the Companies Act 2006: An Interpretation and Assessment' (2007) 28 *Company Lawyer* 106

Keay A., 'Tackling the Issues of the Corporate Objective: An Analysis of the United Kingdom's "Enlightened Shareholder Value Approach"' (2007) 29 *Sydney Law Review* 599

Keay, A., 'The Duty to Promote the Success of the Company: Is it Fit for Purpose?' in J. Loughrey, *Directors' Duties and Shareholder Litigation in the Wake of the Financial Crisis* (Cheltenham: Edward Elgar, 2013) p. 50

Kelly, D., 'Guest Editor's Introduction' (2006) 38 *Contemporary Chinese Thought* 3

Kelly, G. and Parkinson, J., 'The Conceptual Foundations of the Company: A Pluralist Approach' (1998) 2 *Company Financial and Insolvency Law Review* 174

Kerr, J.E., 'Sustainability Meets Profitability: The Convenient Truth of How the Business Judgement Rule Protects a Board's Decision to Engage in Social Entrepreneurship' (2007) 29 *Cardozo Law Review* 623

Kester, W.C., 'Governance, Contracting, and Investment Horizons: A Look at Japan and Germany' in D.H. Chew (ed.), *Studies in International Corporate Finance and Governance Systems* (Oxford: Oxford University Press, 1997) p. 227

Kirby, W.C., 'China Unincorporated: Company Law and Business Enterprise in Twentieth-Century China' (1995) 54 *Journal of Asian Studies* 43

Kirkpatrick, G., "The Corporate Governance Lessons from the Financial Crisis" (2009) 96 *Financial Market Trends* 1

Kolk, A., 'Environment Reporting by Multinationals from the Triad: Convergence or Divergence' (2005) 45 *Management International Review* 145

Kolk, A., 'Sustainability, Accountability and Corporate Governance: Exploring Multinationals' Reporting Practice' (2008) 18 *Business Strategy and Environment* 1

Konai, J., '"Hard" and "Soft" Budget Constraint' (1980) 25 *Acta Oeconomica* 231

Konai, J., 'Gomulka on the Soft Budget Constraint: A Reply' (1985) 19 *Economics of Planning* 49

Konai, J., 'The Soft Budget Constraint' (1986) *Kyklos* 3

Konai, J., 'Legal Obligation, Non-Compliance and Soft Budget Constraint', entry for P. Newman, *New Palgrave Dictionary of Economics and the Law* (New York: Macmillan, 1998) p. 533

Konai, J., 'The Concept of the Soft Budget Constraint Syndrome in Economic Theory' (1998) 26 *Journal of Comparative Economics* 11

Konai, J., Maskin, E. and Roland, G., 'Understanding the Soft Budget Constraint' (2003) 41 *Journal of Economic Literature* 1095

Konai, J. and Matits, A., 'Softness of the Budget Constraint: An Analysis Relying on Data of Firms' (1984) 32 *Acta Oeconomica* 223

Kong, J., 'What Virtues and Formalities Can Do for Corporate Social Responsibility and the Rule of Law in China' (2012) 14 *European Journal of Law Reform* 414

Kornhauser, M.E., 'Corporate Regulations and the Origin of the Corporate Income Tax' (1990) 66 *Indiana Law Journal* 53

Kruse, D., 'Economic Democracy or Just another Risk for Workers? Reviewing the Evidence on Employee Ownership and Profit Share', paper presented to Columbia University Conference on Democracy, Participation and Development, April 1999

La Porta, R., Lopez-de-Silanes, F. and Shleifer, A., 'Corporate Ownership around the World' (1999) 54 *Journal of Finance* 471

La Porta, R., Lopez-de-silanes, F., Shleifer, A. and Vishny, R.W., 'Legal Determinants of External Finance' (1997) 52 *Journal of Finance* 113

La Porta, R., 'The Quality of Government' (1999) 15 *Journal of Law, Economics and Organization* 222

Lan, T. and Pickles, J., *China's New Labour Contract Law: State Regulation and Worker Rights in Global Production Networks*, Economic and Social Upgrading in Global Production Network Working Paper 5 (2011), available at www.capturingthegains.org/pdf/ctg-wp-2011-05.pdf

Lane, C. 'Changes in Corporate Governance of German Corporations: Convergence to Anglo-American Model?' (2003) 7 *Competition and Change* 79

Lau, C., Fan, D.K.K., Young, M. and Wu, S., 'Corporate Governance Effectiveness during Institutional Transition' (2007) 16 *International Business Review* 425

Lee, H.Y., '*Xiagang*, The Chinese Style of Laying off Workers' (2000) 40 *Asian Survey* 914

Lee, J., *State Owned Enterprises in China: Reviewing the Evidence* (Organisation for Economic Cooperation and Development Working

Group on Privatisation and Corporate Governance of State Owned Assets, 2009)

Lee, S., *Implementing Corporate Social Responsibility in Health Sector*, EU-China Business Management Training Project Research Project No. 003 (2005)

Lee, T.A. and Tweedie, D.P., 'Accounting Information: An Investigation of Private Shareholder Understanding' (1975) 5 *Accounting and Business Research* 280

Lehman, C., *Stalemate in Corporate Social Responsibility Research*, American Accounting Association Public Interest Section Working Paper (1983)

Leisinger, K.M., 'The Corporate Social Responsibility of the Pharmaceutical Industry: Idealism without Illusion and Realism without Resignation' (2005) 15 *Business Ethics Quarterly* 577

Levitt, T., 'The Danger of Social Responsibility' (1958) 36 *Harvard Business Review* 41

Li, C., 'The *Kung-ssu-lü* of 1904 and the Modernization of Chinese Company Law' (1974) 10 *Zhengda Faxue Pinglun* (*Chengchi Law Review*) 171

Li, D.H., Moshirian, F., Nguyen, P. and Tan, L.W., 'Managerial Ownership and Firm Performance: Evidence from China's Privatizations' (2005) 21 *Research in International Business and Finance* 396

Li, D.H., 'Don't hate the rich, be one of them', *People's Daily*, 2 April 2009

Li, H., 'Capital Structure on Agency Cost in Chinese Listed Firms' (2011) 1 *International Journal of Governance* 295

Li, H., Meng, L., Wang, Q. and Zhou, L., 'Political Connections, Financing and Firm Performance: Evidence from Chinese Private Firms' (2008) 87 *Journal of Development Economics* 283

Li, P., 'Scholar Explores Harmonious Society Concept' (2005), available at www.china.org.cn/english/2005/Mar/121746.htm

Li, S., 'The Crisis Chain on Corporate Social Responsibility (*Qiye Shehuizeren Weiji Lian*)' (2011) 34 *Outlook Week* (*Liaowang*) 22

Li, S., Xia, J., Long, C.X. and Tan, J., 'Control Modes and Outcomes of Transformed State-Owned Enterprises in China: An Empirical Test' (2011) 8 *Management and Organization Review* 1

Li, W. and Zhang, R., 'Corporate Social Responsibility, Ownership Structure, and Political Interference: Evidence from China' (2010) 96 *Journal of Business Ethics* 631

Li, X., 'The Economic Character of the Enterprise Identified as a Unit (*Danweihua Qiye de Jingji Xingzhi*)' (2001) 7 *Economic Research Journal* (*Jingji Yanjiu*) 35

287

Li, Y., 'Comparative Studies on Supervision of Limited Corporations' in S. Shen (ed.), *Essays on International Commercial Law II* (Beijing: Law Publishing, 2002) p. 265

Li, Z., 'Lack of Corporate Social Responsibility Behind Recent China Accident', China Watch, World Institute Vision for a Sustainable World (12 December 2005), available at www.worldwatch.org/node/3859

Liang, Y., 'China's Short-Term and Long-Term Development After the 2007 Global Financial Crisis: Some Critical Reflection' (2012) 45 *The China Economy* 3

Lin, C., *Corporatisation and Corporate Governance in China's Economic Transition*, Department of Economics Discussion Paper Series (Oxford: Oxford University Press, 2000)

Lin, L.W., 'Corporate Social Responsibility in China: Window Dressing or Structural Change' (2010) *Berkeley Journal of International Law* 64

Lindblom, C.K., *The Concept of Organizational Legitimacy and its Implications for Corporate Social Responsibility Disclosure*, American Accounting Association Public Interests Section Working Paper (1983)

Liu, J.H., 'Some Thinking about Strengthening CSR' in Lou, J. and Gan, P., *Studies on Corporate Social Responsibility* (Beijing: Peking University Press, 2009) p. 199

Liu, M., 'Corporate Social Responsible Actions and Consumer Respondents' (2006) 25 *China Industry Economy* 64

Liu, M., 'Unsafe at any speed: the downside of China's manufacturing boom: deadly goods wreaking havoc at home and abroad', *Newsweek*, 16 July 2007

Liu, Q., 'Corporate Governance in China: Current Practices, Economic Effects and Institutional Determinants' (2006) 52 *Economic Studies* 415

Lockett, A., Moon, J. and Visser, W., 'Corporate Social Responsibility in Management Research: Focus, Nature, Salience and Influence' (2006) 43 *Journal of Management Studies* 115

Long, G., Zadek, S. and Wickerham, J., *Advancing Sustainable Competitiveness of China's Transnational Corporations* (London: AccountAbility, 2009)

Loughrey, J., Keay, A. and Cerioni, L., 'Legal Practitioners, Enlightened Shareholder Value and the Shaping of Corporate Governance' (2008) 8 *Journal of Corporate Law Studies* 79

Lu, H., 'Dirty Industry Migration in China: Lessons for Corporate Social Responsibility' (2005) 2 *US-China Law Review* 37

Lu, Z., von H. Hoivik, W. and Wang, L., 'Chinese Managers' Perception of Corporate Social Responsibility: What is the Status Quo in China?', paper presented at the World Business Ethics Forum, Hong Kong, 1–3 November 2006

Ma, J. and Zhai, F., 'Financing China's Pension Reform', paper prepared for conference on financial sector reform in China (2001)

Macalister, T., 'A change in the climate: credit crunch makes the bottom line the top issue', *The Guardian*, 6 March 2008

Machesani, D., 'The Concept of Autonomy and the Independent Directors of Public Corporations' (2005) 2 *Berkeley Business Law Journal* 315

Mackenzie, C., 'Boards, Incentives and Corporate Social Responsibility: The Case for a Change of Emphasis' (2007) 15 *Corporate Governance: An International Review* 935

Margolis, J.D. and Walsh, J.P., 'Misery Loves Companies: Rethinking Social Initiatives by Business' (2003) 48 *Administrative Science Quarterly* 268

Marinoff, L., 'What is Business Ethics? What are its Prospects in Asia?' in F.J. Richter and P.C.M. Mar (eds), *Asia's New Crisis: Renewal through Total Ethical Management* (Singapore: John Wiley & Son, 2004) p. 16

Martin, F., 'Corporate Social Responsibility and Public Policy' in R. Mullerate (ed.), *Corporate Social Responsibility: The Corporate Governance of the 21st Century* (London: Kluwer Law International, 2005) p. 77

Mathews, M.R., 'A Suggested Classification for Social Accounting Research' (1984) 3 *Journal of Accounting and Public Policy* 199

Matten, D. and Moon, J., 'Corporate Social Responsibility Education in Europe' (2004) 54 *Journal of Business Ethics* 323

Matten, D. and Moon, J., 'A Conceptual Framework for Understanding CSR' in A. Habisch, J. Jonker, M. Wegner and R. Chidpeter (eds), *Corporate Social Responsibility Across Europe* (Heidelberg: Springer, 2005) p. 335

McBarnet, D., 'Corporate Social Responsibility beyond Law, through Law, for Law: The New Corporate Accountability' in D. McBarnet, A. Voiculescu and T. Campbell, *The New Corporate Accountability: Corporate Social Responsibility and the Law* (Cambridge: Cambridge University Press, 2007) p. 9

McGuire, J., Sundgreen, A. and Schneeweis, T., 'Corporate Social Responsibility and Firm Financial Performance' (1988) 31 *Academy of Management Journal* 854

McKinsey & Co., 'The McKinsey Global Survey of Business Executives: Business and Society' (2006) 2 *McKinsey Quarterly* 33

McWilliams, A. and Siegel, D.S., 'Corporate Social Responsibility: A Theory of the Firm Perspective' (2001) 26 *Academy of Management Review* 117

Megginson, W.L. and Netter, J.M., 'From State to Market: A Survey of Empirical Studies on Privatization' (2001) 36 *Journal of Economic Literature* 321

Mei, S., 'The Corporate Governance of Listed Companies in China: Some Problems and Solutions' in R. Tomasic (ed.), *Corporate Governance: Challenges for China* (Beijing: Law Press China, 2005) p. 422

Mescher, B., 'The Law, Stakeholders and Ethics: Their Role in Corporate Governance' (2011) 8 *Macquarie Journal of Business Law* 37

Mickels, A., 'Beyond Corporate Social Responsibility: Reconciling the Ideals of a For-Benefit Corporate with Director Fiduciary Duties in the U.S. and Europe' (2009) 32 *Hastings International and Comparative Law Review* 271

Millon, D., 'Frontiers of Legal Thought: Theories of the Corporation' (1990) *Duke Law Journal* 201

Millon, D., 'Theories of the Corporation' (1990) 39 *Duke Law Journal* 201

Millon, D., 'Redefining Corporate Law' (1991) 24 *Industrial Law Review* 223

Milman, D., 'From Servant to Stakeholder: Protecting the Employee Interests in Company Law' in D. Feldman and F. Meisel (eds), *Corporate and Commercial Law: Modern Developments* (London: LLP, 1996) p. 147

Milman, D., 'Disqualification and Directors: An Evaluation of Current Law, Policy and Practice in the UK' (2013) 331 *Company Law Newsletter* 1

Milman, D., 'Ascertaining Shareholder Wishes in UK Company Law in the 21st Century' (2013) 331 *Company Law Newsletter* 1

Milne, M.J., 'Positive Accounting Theory, Political Costs and Social Disclosure Analysis: A Critical Look' (2002) 13 *Accountancy and Business Law* 369

Milne, M.J. and Gray, R., 'Future Prospectus for Corporate Sustainability Report' in J. Unerman, J. Bebbington and B. O'Dwyer (eds), *Sustainability Accounting and Accountability* (Abingdon: Routledge, 2007) p. 184

Mintzerberg, H., 'The Case for Corporate Social Responsibility' (1983) 4 *Journal of Business Strategy* 3

Mitchell, K., Agle, B.R. and Wood, D.J., 'Toward a Theory of Stakeholder Identification and Salience: Defining the Principle of Who and What Really Counts' (1997) 22 *Academy of Management Review* 853

Mitchell, L.E., 'The Board as a Path toward Corporate Social Responsibility' in D. McBarnet, A. Voiculescu and T. Campbell (eds), *The New Corporate Accountability: Corporate Social Responsibility and the Law* (Cambridge: Cambridge University Press, 2007) p. 279

Moon, J., 'The Firm as Citizen? Social Responsibility of Business in Australia' (1995) 30 *Australian Journal of Political Science* 1

Moon, J., 'Business Social Responsibility and New Governance' (2002) 37 *Government and Opposition* 385

Moon, J. and Shen, X., 'CSR in China Research: Salience, Focus and Nature' (2010) 94 *Journal of Business Ethics* 613

Moxey, P. and Berendt, A., *Corporate Governance and the Credit Crunch*, ACCA Discussion Paper (2008)

Mullich, J., 'Corporate Social Responsibility Emerges in China', (2010) *Wall Street Journal*, available at http://online.wsj.com/ad/article/chinaenergy-responsibility

Munllia, L.S. and Miles, M.P., 'The Corporate Social Responsibility Continuum as a Component of Stakeholder Theory' (2005) 110 *Business and Society Review* 371

Murdoch, H. and Gould, D., *Corporate Social Responsibility in China: Mapping the Environment* (Global Alliance for Workers and Communities, 2004)

Murray, E.A., 'The Social Response Process in Commercial Banks: An Empirical Investigation' (1976) 1 *Academy of Management Review* 5

Nakajima, C., 'The Importance of Legally Embedding Corporate Social Reasonability' (2011) 32 *Company Lawyer* 257

Nakajima, C. and Palmer, P., 'Anti-Corruption: Law and Practice' in A. Stachowicz-Stanusch (ed.), *Organizational Immunity to Corruption: Building Theoretical and Research Foundations* (Charlotte, NC: Information Age Publishing, 2010) p. 99

Neu, D., Warsame, H. and Pedwell, K., 'Managing Public Impressions: Environmental Disclosure in Annual Reports' (1998) 23 *Accounting, Organizations and Society* 265

Nicholas, D.C., China's Labour Enforcement Crisis: International Intervention and Corporate Social Responsibility (2009) 11 *Scholar* 155

Noronha, C., Tou, S., Cynthia, M.I. and Guan, J.J., 'Corporate Social Responsibility Reporting in China: An Overview and Comparison with Major Trends' (2012) 20 *Corporate Social Responsibility and Environmental Management* 29

Nussbaum, A.K., 'Ethical Corporate Social Responsibility and the Pharmaceutical Industry: A Happy Couple?' (2009) 9 *Journal of Medical Marketing* 67

O'Donovan, G., *Legitimacy Theory as an Explanation for Corporate Environmental Disclosure* (PhD thesis, Victoria University of Technology, 2000), available at http://vuir.vu.edu.au/15372/

Opper, S. and Schwaag-Serger, S., 'Institutional Analysis of Legal Change: The Case of Corporate Governance in China' (2008) 26 *Washington University Journal of Law and Policy* 245

Orlitzky, M., 'Corporate Social Performance and Financial Performance: A Research Synthesis' in A. Crane, A. McWilliams, D. Matten, J. Moon and D. Siegel (eds), *The Oxford Handbook of CSR* (Oxford: Oxford University Press, 2008) p. 113

Owen, D.L. and O'Dwyer, B., 'Corporate Social Responsibility: The Reporting and Assurance Dimension' in A. Crane, A. McWilliams, D. Matten, J. Moon and D. Siegel (eds), *The Oxford Handbook of CSR* (Oxford: Oxford University Press, 2008) p. 384

Owen, D.L., Swift, T.A., Humphrey, C. and Bowerman, M., 'The New Social Audit: Accountability, Managerial Capture or the Agenda of Social Champion' (2000) 9 *European Accounting Review* 81

Pannier, D., *Corporate Governance of Public Enterprise in Transitional Economies* (Washington, DC: World Bank, 1996)

Parker, C., 'Meta-regulation: Legal Accountability for Corporate Social Responsibility' in D. McBarnet, A. Voiculescu and T. Campbell (eds), *The New Corporate Accountability: Corporate Social Responsibility and the Law* (Cambridge: Cambridge University Press, 2007)

Patel, R.I., 'Facilitating Stakeholder-Interest Maximization: Accommodating Beneficial Corporations in the Model Business Corporation Act' (2010) 23 *St Thomas Law Review* 135

Patten, D.M., 'Media Exposure, Public Policy Pressure, and Environmental Disclosure: An Examination of the Impact of Tri Data Availability' (2002) 26 *Accounting Forum* 152

Payne, A., 'Corporate Governance in the USA and Europe: They are Closer Than You Might Think' (2006) 6 *Corporate Governance: International Journal of Effective Board Performance* **69**

Pearson, C., 'Corporate Social Responsibility Compliance for Foreign Invested Enterprises in China' (2009), available at www.dlapiper.com/foreign_enterprises_csr_compliance

Pedamon, C., 'Corporate Social Responsibility: A New Approach to Promoting Integrity and Responsibility' (2010) 31 *Company Lawyer* 172

Petkoski, D. and Herman, B., 'Summary Report' in D. Petkoski and B. Herman (eds), *Implementing the Monterrey Consensus: Governance Roles of Public, Private and Advocacy Stakeholders* (2003), available at http://info.worldbank.org/etools/docs/library/57431/monterrey_e conference.pdf

Pfeffer, J. and Veiga, J.F., 'Putting People First for Organisational Success' (1999) 13 *Academy of Management Executives* 37

Picciotto, S., 'Rights, Responsibilities and Regulation of International Business' (2003) 42 *Columbia Journal of Transnational Law* 131

Pinney, C.C., *Why China will Define the Future Corporate Citizenship* (Centre for Corporate Citizenship, Boston College, Carroll School of

Management, 2008), available at www.bcccc.net/index.cfm?fuse
action=Page.ViewPage&PageID=1905

Pinto, A., 'Globalization and the Study of Comparative Corporate Governance' (2005) 23 *Wisconsin International Law Journal* 477

Porter, M.E. and Kramer, M.R., 'Strategy and Society: The Link between Competition Advantage and Corporate Social Responsibility' (2006) 84 *Harvard Business Review* 78

Potter, P.B., 'Co-ordinating Corporate Governance and Corporate Social Responsibility' (2009) 39 *Hong Kong Law Journal* 675

Puri, P., 'The Future of Stakeholder Interests in Corporate Governance' (2010) 48 *Canadian Business Law Journal* 427

Reese, A., *Operating and Financial Review and the Business Review* (London: WSP Environmental, 2005)

Rhodes, M.J., 'Information Asymmetry and Socially Responsible Investment' (2010) 95 *Journal of Business Ethics* 145

Riley, T. and Cai, H., 'Unmasking Chinese Business Enterprises: Using Information Disclosure Law to Enhance Public Participation in Corporate Environmental Decision Making' (2009) 33 *Harvard Environmental Law Review* 177

Robinson, A.M. and Zhang, H., 'Employee Share Ownership: Safeguarding Investment in Human Capital' (2005) 43 *British Journal of Industrial Relations* 469

Roper, J. and Hu, H., 'Modern Chinese Confucianism: A Model for Western Human Capital Development?', paper presented at the European Academy of Business in Society Annual Colloquium, Warsaw, 2005

Roper, J. and Weymes, E., 'Reinstating the Collective: A Confucian Approach to Well-being and Social Capital Development in a Globalised Economy' (2007) 26 *Journal of Corporate Citizenship* 135

Rosoff, R.J., 'Beyond Codes of Conduct' (2004) 31 *China Business Review* 6

Roth, M., 'Employee Participation, Corporate Governance and the Firm: A Transatlantic View Focused on Occupational Pension and Co-Determination' (2011) 11 *European Business Organization Law Review* 51

Ruggie, J., 'Business and Human Rights: Together at Last: A Conversation with John Ruggie' (2011) 35 *Fletcher Forum of World Affairs* 117

Sahlman, W., *Management and the Financial Crisis (We have Met the Enemy and He is Us …)*, Harvard Business School Working Paper No. 10-033 (2009), available at www.hbs.edu/research/pdf/10-033.pdf

Sarkis, J., Li, N. and Zhu, Q., 'Winds of Change: Corporate Social Responsibility in China' (2011) *Ivey Business Journal* (January/February) 1

Sceats, S. and Breslin, S., *China and the International Human Rights System* (Royal Institute of International Affairs, 2012)

Schilling, M.A., 'Decades Ahead of Her Time: Advancing Stakeholder Theory through the Ideas of Mary Parker Follett' (2000) 6 *Journal of Management History* 224

Schwarcz, S.L., 'Rethinking a Corporations' Obligations to Creditors' (1996) 17 *Cardozo Law Review* 647

Schwarcz, S.L., 'Temporal Perspectives: Resolving the Conflict Between Current and Future Investors' (2005) 89 *Minnesota Law Review* 1044

Schwartz, M.S. and Carroll, A.B., 'CSR: A Three-domain Approach' (2003) 4 *Business Ethics* 503

Sealy, L.S., 'Fiduciary Relationships' (1962) 20 *Cambridge Law Review* 69

Sealy, L.S., 'Directors' Duties: An Unnecessary Gloss' (1988) 47 *Cambridge Law Journal* 175

See, G., 'Harmonious Society and Chinese CSR: Is there Really a Link?' (2008) 89 *Journal of Business Ethics* 1

Seki, T., 'Legal Reform and Shareholder Activism by Shareholder Investors in Japan' (2005) 13 *Corporate Governance* 377

Seligman, J., 'No one Can Serve Two Masters: Corporate Law and Security Law After Enron' (2002) 80 *Washing University Law Quarterly* 449

Sethi, S.P., 'Dimensions of Corporate Social Performance: An Analytic Framework' (1975) 17 *California Management Review* 58

Shankman, N.A., 'Reframing the Debate between Agency and Stakeholder Theories of the Firm' (1999) 19 *Journal of Business Ethics* 319

Shen, S. and Cheng, H., 'Economic Globalisation and the Construction of China's Corporate Social Responsibility' (2009) 51 *International Journal of Law and Management* 134

Shen, W. and Price, R., 'Confucianism, Labour Law and the Rise of Worker Activism' (2011), available at http://ssrn.com/abstract=1789966

Shen, X. and Fleming, G., *'Made in China' and the Drive to Include CSR*, GFC Working Paper 200803 (Centre for Global Finance, Nottingham University, 2008), available at www.nottingham.edu.cn/en/gfc/documents/research/gfcresearch/2008/gfcworkingpaper200803shenxim adeinchinaenglish.pdf

Shi, J. and Yang, W., 'Legal Reanalysis of CSR' in J. Lou and P. Gan, *Studies on Corporate Social Responsibility* (Beijing: Peking University Press, 2009) p. 243

Sims, G.K., 'The River Runs Black: The Environmental Challenge to China's Future' (2006) 65 *Journal of Asian Studies* 403

Souto, B.F., 'Crisis and Corporate Social Responsibility: Threat or Opportunity?' (2009) 2 *International Journal of Economic and Applied Research* 36

Spector, B., 'Business Responsibility in a Divided World: The Cold War Roots of the Corporate Social Responsibility Movement' (2008) 9 *Enterprise and Society: International Journal of Business History* 314

Stout, L.A., 'Bad and Not-So-Bad Arguments for Shareholder Primacy' (2002) 75 *South California Law Review* 1189

Stout, L.A., 'On the Proper Motives of Corporate Directors (or, Why You Don't Want to Invite Homo Economicus to Join Your Board)' (2003) 28 *Delaware Journal of Corporate Law* 1

Subramanian, G.., 'The Disappearing Delaware Effect' (2004) 46 *Journal of Law, Economics and Organisation* 525

Sulkowski, A.J., Parashar S.P. and Wei, L., 'Corporate Responsibility Reporting in China, India, Japan and the West: One Mantra Does not Fit All' (2008) 42 *New England Law Review* 787

Sundaram, A.K. and Inkpen A.C., 'The Corporate Objective Revisited' (2004) 15 *Organization Science* 350

Szabo, D.G., *Disclosure of Material CSR Information in the Periodic Report: Comparison of the Mandatory CSR Disclosure System for Listed Companies in the EU and the US*, Nordic and European Company Law LSN Research Paper Series No. 10-20 (2010)

Tai, H.C., 'The Oriental Alternative: An Hypothesis on Culture and Economy' in H.C. Tai (ed.), *Confucianism and Economic Development: An Oriental Alternative* (Washington DC: Washington Institute Press, 1989) p. 6

Tam, O.K., 'Ethical Issues in the Evolution of Corporate Governance in China' (2002) 37 *Journal of Business Ethics* 303

Tan, L.H. and Wang, J.Y., 'Modelling an Efficient Corporate Governance System for China's Listed State-owned Enterprises: Issues and Challenges in a Transitional Economy' (2007) 7 *Journal of Corporate Law Studies* 143

Tang, Y. and Chen, D., 'Analysis of Present Situation, Foundation and Content about Corporate Social Responsibility Information Disclosure in China' (2012) *M & D Forum* 96

Tao, S., 'Initial Studies on Sources of Shanghai Foundation in the Northern Warlords Time Period (*Beiyang Zhengfu Shiqi Shanghai Cishan Zijin Laiyuan Chutan*)' (2004) 1 *Files and History* (*Dang'an Yu Shixue*) 50

Tenev, S., Zhang, C. and Brefort, L., *Corporate Governance and Enterprise Reform in China: Building the Institutions of Modern Market* (Washington, DC: World Bank and the International Finance Corporation, 2002)

Testy, K., 'Convergence as Movement: Towards a Counter-Hegemonic Approach to Corporate Governance' (2002) 24 *Law and Policy* 433

Testy, K., 'Linking Progressive Corporate Law with Progressive Social Movements' (2002) 76 *Tulane Law Review* 1227

Tett, G., 'Should Atlas still shrug? The threat that lurks behind the growth of complex debt deals', *Financial Times*, 15 January 2007

Tomasic, R., 'Comparing Corporate Governance Principles: China, Australia and the OECD' in R. Tomasic (ed.), *Corporate Governance: Challenges for China* (Beijing: Law Press China, 2005) ch. 1, p. 3

Tomasic, R., 'Corporate Rescue, Governance and Risk-taking in Northern Rock' (Part I and II)' (2008) 29 *Company Lawyer* 297

Tong, Z., 'Thoughts on Protests Arising from Environmental Pollutions in China (*Dui Woguo Huanjing Wuran Yinfa Quntixing Shijian De Sikao*)' in D. Yang (ed.), *Crisis and Turning Point in Environmental Problems in China (Zhongguo Huanjing de Weiji yu Zhuanji)* (Beijing: Social Sciences Academic Press, 2008)

Trifiro, N., 'China's Financial Reporting Standards: Will Corporate Governance induce Compliance in Listed Companies?' (2007) 16 *Tulane Journal of International and Comparative Law* 271

Trotman, K.T. and Bradley, G.W., 'Association between Social Responsibility Disclosure and Characteristics of Companies' (1981) 6 *Accounting, Organizations and Society* 355

Tsui, M., 'Corporate Governance in China' (2010) *Corporate Governance eJournal* 1

Udell, G.F., 'Wall Street, Main Street and a Credit Crunch: Thoughts on the Current Financial Crisis' (2009) 52 *Business Horizons* 117

Ullmann, A.A., 'Data in Search of a Theory: A Critical Examination of the Relationship among Social Performance, Social Disclosure, and Economic Performance of U.S. Firms' (1985) 10 *Academy of Management Review* 540

Van der Weide, M., 'Against Fiduciary Duties to Corporate Stakeholders' (1996) 21 *Delaware Journal of Corporate Law* 27

Van Marrewijk, M., 'Concepts and Definitions of CSR and Corporate Sustainability: Between Agency and Communion' (2003) 44 *Journal of Business Ethics* 95

Van Rooij, B., 'The People's Regulation: Citizens and Implementation of Law in China' (2012) 25 *Columbia Journal of Asian Law* 116

Vandekerckhove, W. and Commers, M.S.R., 'Beyond Voluntary/ Mandatory Juxtaposition: Towards a European Framework on CSR as Network Governance' (2005) 1 *Social Responsibility Journal* 98

Villiers, C., 'Corporate Law, Corporate Power and Corporate Social Responsibility' in N. Boeger, R. Murray and C. Villiers, *Perspectives on Corporate Social Responsibility* (Cheltenham: Edward Elgar, 2010) p. 85

Vinten, G., 'Shareholder versus Stakeholders: Is there a Governance Dilemma' (2001) 9 *Corporate Governance* 36

Visser, W., 'Corporate Social Responsibility in Developing Countries' in A. Crane, A. McWilliams, D. Matten, J. Moon and D. Siegel (eds), *The Oxford Handbook of Corporate Social Responsibility* (Oxford: Oxford University Press, 2008) p. 473

Visser, W., 'Future Trends in CSR: The Next 10 Years' (2012) 11 *CSR International Inspiration Series* 1

Vob, S. and Xia, Y.W., 'Corporate Governance of Listed Companies in China', Track 8 of IFSAM VIIIth World Congress, Berlin, September 2006

Vodopivec, M. and Tong, M.H., *China: Improving Unemployment Insurance*, Social Protection and Labour of the World Bank Discussion Paper No. 0820 (2008)

Voss, S. and Xia, Y.W., 'Corporate Governance of Listed Companies in China', paper presented at Track 8 of IFSAM VIIIth World Congress, Berlin, September 2006, available at www.ctw-congress.de/ifsam/download/track_8/pap00750.pdf

Votaw, D., 'Genius Becomes Rare' in D. Votaw and S.P. Sethi (eds), *The Corporate Dilemma: Traditional Values versus Contemporary Problems* (Englewood Cliffs, NJ: Prentice Hall, 1973) p. 11

Waagstein, P.R., 'The Mandatory Corporate Social Responsibility: Problems and Implications' (2011) 98 *Journal of Business Ethics* 455

Wade, C.L., 'Commentary: Corporate Governance in Japan, Germany and Canada: What Can the U.S. Learn from Other Countries?' (2002) 24 *Law and Policy* 44

Walsh, B., 'Choking on Growth', *The New York Times*, 13 December 2004

Wang, J., Qin, S. and Cui, Y., 'Problems and Prospects of CSR System Development in China' (2010) 5 *International Journal of Business Management* 128

Wang, J.Y., 'Dancing with Wolves: Regulation and Deregulations of Foreign Investment in China's Stock Market' (2004) 5 *University of Hawaii Asian-Pacific Law and Policy Journal* 1

Wang, P., Wang, F., Zhang, J. and Yang, B., 'The Effect of Ultimate Owner and Regulation Policy on Corporate Social Responsibility Information Disclosure: Evidence from China' (2012) 6 *African Journal of Business Management* 6183

Wang, X., 'Government Function on Cultivating CSR: A Thinking on Loss of Truck Fence' (2010) 5 *International Journal of Business and Management* 162

Wang, Z., 'Major Issues to be Addressed in the Establishment and Development of China's Unemployment Insurance System', paper presented at EU-China Social Security Reform Co-operation Project, Unemployment Insurance Reform Seminar (2008)

Ward, H. and Smith, N.C., *Corporate Social Responsibility at a Crossroads: Future of CSR in the UK to 2015* (London: IIED, 2006)

Ward, H.E., Wilson, E., Zarsky, L. and Fox, T., *CSR and Developing Countries: What Scope for Government Action?* United Nations Sustainable Development Innovation Briefs, Issue 1, available at www.un.org/esa/sustdev/publications/innovationbriefs/no1.pdf

Warner, M. and Zhu, Y., 'Human Resource Management "with Chinese Characters": A Comparative Study of the People's Republic of China and Taiwan' (2002) 9 *Asia Pacific Business Review* 21

Watt, R.L. and Zimmermann, J.L., 'Towards a Positive Theory of the Determination of Accounting Standards' (1978) 53 *Accounting Review* 112

Wei, Y., 'Directors Duties under Chinese Law: A Comparative Review' (2006) 3 *University of New England Law Journal* 31

West, A. 'Corporate Governance Convergence and Moral Relativism' (2009) 17 *Corporate Governance: An International Review* 107

West, M., 'The Puzzling Divergence of Corporate Law: Evidence and Explanations from Japan and the United States' (2001) *University of Pennsylvania Law Review* 527

Whelan, G., 'Corporate Social Responsibility in Asia: A Confucian Context' in S. May, G. Cheney and J. Roper, *The Debate over Corporate Social Responsibility* (Oxford: Oxford University Press, 2008) p. 105

Wild, D., 'Accountants and the Crisis: CSR – Man Overboard' (2008) *Accountancy Age*, available at www.accountancyage.com/accountancy age/features/2222355/accountants-crisis-csr-man

Williams, C.A., 'The Securities and Exchange Commission and Corporate Social Transparency' (1999) 112 *Harvard Law Review* 1197

Winkler, A., 'Corporate Law or the Law of Business? Stakeholders and Corporate Governance at the End of History' (2004) 67 *Law and Contemporary Problems* 109

Woetzel, J.R., 'Reassessing China's State-owned Enterprises' (2008) *McKinsey Quarterly* 1

Wong, C., 'Rebuilding Government for the 21st Century: Can China Incrementally Reform the Public Sector?' (2009) 200 *China Quarterly* 929

Wong, L., 'Corporate Governance in China: A Lack of Critical Reflexivity?' in C.R. Lehman, T. Tinker, B. Merino and M. Neimark (eds), *Corporate Governance: Does Any Size Fit?* (Oxford: Elsevier, 2005) p. 117

Woo, W.T., *Reframing China Policy: The Carnegie Debates; Debate 2: China's Economy – Arguing for the Motion* (Carnegie Endowment for International Peace, Central University of Finance and Economics, Beijing, Brookings Institution, Washington, DC and University of California, Davis, CA, 2006)

Woodbine, G.F., 'Moral Choice and the Declining Influence of Traditional Value Orientation within the Financial Sector of a Rapidly Developing Region of the People's Republic of China' (2004) 55 *Journal of Business Ethics* 43

Wright, P.C., Szeto, W.F. and Lee, S.K., 'Ethical Perceptions in China: The Reality of Business Ethics in an International Context' (2004) 41 *Management Decision* 180

Wu, B. and Zheng, Y., *A Long March to Improve Labour Standards in China: Chinese Debates on the New Labour Contract Law*, University of Nottingham China Policy Institute Briefing Series, Issue 39 (2008)

Wu, J.L., '"Market Socialism" and Chinese Economic Reform', paper submitted to the IES's Round Table on Market and Socialism Reconsidered (2004), available at bm.ust.hk

Xu, Z. and Liu, N., *Research on Win-Win Management Control Mode of CSR Based on Society Harmony and Corporate Sustainable Development*, proceedings of International Conference on Management Science and Engineering (2008), available at www.bmtfi.com/upload/product/200910/2008glhy02a19.pdf

Yamagami, T. and Kokubu, K., 'A Note on Corporate Social Disclosure in Japan' (1991) 4 *Auditing and Accountability Journal* 32

Yan, M., 'Obstacles in China's Corporate Governance' (2011) 31 *Company Lawyer* 311

Yan, Y., 'An Exploratory Analysis about the Rendering Government: A Special Distribution System of Enterprises' Profits during the Late Qing Dynasty' (2005) 4 *Journal of Anhui TV University* 101

Yang, J., 'The Shareholder Meeting and Voting Rights in China: Some Empirical Evidence' (2007) 18 *International Company and Commercial Law Review* 4

Yang, J., Chi, J. and Young, M., 'A Review of Corporate Governance in China' (2011) 25 *Asian-Pacific Economic Literature* 15

Yeoh, P., 'Corporate Governance Models: Is there a Right One for Transition Economies in Central and Eastern Europe?' (2007) 49 *Managerial Law* 57

Yeung, H.W., 'International/Transnational Entrepreneurship and Chinese Business Research' in L.P. Dana (ed.), *The Handbook of Research on International Entrepreneurship* (Cheltenham: Edward Elgar, 2004) p. 73

Yi, X., 'Improving Corporate Responsibility Competitiveness to Promote Harmonious Society' (2005), available at www.wtoguide.net/html/2005 Sino-European/14_36_14_633.html

Yip, A., 'Risk Governance as Part of Corporate Governance' (2008) 23 *Journal of International Banking Law and Regulation* 493

Yip, E., van Saden C. and Cahan, S., 'Corporate Social Responsibility Reporting and Earnings Management: The Role of Political Costs' (2011) 5 *Australasian Accounting Business and Finance Journal* 17

Young, A., 'Conceptualising a Chinese Corporate Governance Framework: Tensions between Traditions, Ideologies and Modernity' (2009) 19 *International Company and Commercial Law Review* 235

Young, A., Li, G. and Lau, A., 'Corporate Governance in China: The Role of the State and Ideology in Shaping Reform' (2007) 28 *Company Lawyer* 204

Young, N., 'Three C's: Civil Society, Corporate Social Responsibility and China' (2002) 29 *China Business Review* 34

Yu, J., 'Social Conflict in Rural China' (2007) 3 *China Security* 2

Yuan, J., 'Formal Convergence or Substantial Divergence? Evidence from Adoption of the Independent Director System in China' (2007) 9 *Asian-Pacific Law and Policy Journal* 71

Zadek, S., Forstater, M. and Yu, K., *Corporate Responsibility and Sustainable Economic Development in China: Implications for Business* (US Chamber of Commerce, National Chamber Foundation and Asia Department, 2012)

Zambon S. and Del Bello, A., 'Towards a Stakeholder Responsible Approach: The Constructive Role of Reporting' (2005) 5 *Corporate Governance: International Journal of Business in Society* 130

Zapalska, A.M. and Edwards, W., 'Chinese Entrepreneurship in a Cultural and Economic Perspective' (2001) 39 *Journal of Small Business Management* 286

Zeghal, D. and Ahmed, S.A., 'Comparison of Social Responsibility Information Disclosure Media Used by Canadian Firms' (1990) 3 *Accounting, Auditing and Accountability Journal* 38

Zhang, X. and Xu, C., 'The Late Qing Dynasty Diplomatic Transformation: Analysis from an Ideational Perspective' (2007) 1 *Chinese Journal of International Politics* 405

Zhao, J., 'Modernising Corporate Objective Debate towards a Hybrid Model' (2011) 62 *Northern Ireland Legal Quarterly* 361

Zhao, J., 'Promoting More Socially Responsible Corporations through UK Company Law after the 2008 Financial Crisis: Turning of the Crisis Compass' (2011) 22 *International Company and Commercial Law Review* 275

Zhao, J. and Wen, S., 'Gift Giving, *Guanxi* and Confucianism in a Harmonious Society: What Chinese Law Could Learn from English Law on Aspects of Directors' Duties' (2013) 34 *Company Lawyer* 381

Zhao, L., 'The Transformation and Trend in Corporate Social Responsibility in China' (2005) 2 *Management Research* 7

Zhao, L. and Roper, J., 'A Confucian Approach to Well-being and Social Capital Development' (2011) 30 *Journal of Management Development* 740

Zhao, S., 'The Proposal on Patented Management by *Zheng Guanying* and Practice from Shanghai Machine Weaving Bureau' (2005) 4 *Journal of Shijiazhuang Teachers College* 22

Zhe, Z., 'Toward Harmonious Society through Rule of Law', *China Daily*, 10 March 2008

Zhou, H., 'Directors' Duty of Good Faith' in P. Jiang and Z. Yang (eds), *Civil Law and Commercial Law Forum* (Beijing: China University of Political Science and Law Press, 2004) p. 434

Zhou, W., *Will CSR Work in China?* Business for Social Responsibility Working Paper (2006)

Zhu, W. and Yao, Y., 'On the Value of Traditional Confucian Culture and the Value of Modern Corporate Social Responsibility' (2008) 3 *International Journal of Business and Management* 58

Zingales, L., 'Corporate Governance' in P. Newman, *The New Palgrave Dictionary of Economics and Law* (Basingstoke: MacMillan, 1998) p. 501

Index

CSR guidelines 81–2, 197, 200–201
international ranking 89
state-owned shares 93
Siegel, D.S. 10
Sinopec Group 212
Skiye Jiugo 56–61
Social Accountability International 75
social security reforms
    healthcare systems 164–6
    lay-offs and redundancies 161–4
    pension systems 166–7
    unemployment insurance 162–4
social welfare
    CSR role in 25–6, 28
*The Socialist System of Law with
    Chinese Characteristics (2011)*
    128–9
SOE *see* state-owned enterprises
Spector, B. 28
stakeholder theory 6–7, 26–7, 121–2,
    125, 228–30
stakeholders
    and competitiveness, relationship
        between 7–8
    Confucian heirarchy influences on
        44–5
    CSR responsibilities towards 7–8,
        84–5
    definition 6–8
    directors' decisions, influences on
        38–9
    and Harmonious Society 226–31,
        234–9
    legal protection, need for 114–15
    stakeholder interest protection
        advantages 123–5
        as approach to CSR 7–8
        and competitiveness 123–4
        and convergence corporate
            governance model 157–8
        and Corporate Governance Code
            (2002) 126–7, 200
        influences on 122–3
        trends 118–25
State Asset Management Committees
    160–61
State Environmental Protection
    Administration (SEPA) 80, 195–7

State Ocean Administration
    on Bohai Bay oil spill 245–6
State-Owned Assets Supervision and
    Administrative Commission
    on CSR
        definitions 11
        Guidelines 82, 195, 214
    role of 20, 94
state-owned enterprises
    characteristics 20–21, 94
    concentrated shareholdings 94–6
    corporate governance 93–4, 108–9
        challenges 159
        incentives 159–60
        influence on 107–8
    CSR in
        government interference 213–15,
            254, 258–9
        influence on 16, 65–9
        and responsibilities to stakeholders
            84–5
    decline in 66–7, 252
    dual track system stage 66
    enterprises running social activities
        (qiye ban shehui) 62
    healthcare responsibilities 164–5
    primacy of 20
    redundancies in 162
    reforms
        purpose 160–61
        stages 65–9
    during Republic of China 60–64
    role of 19–20
    shareholdings, types of 93–5
    soft budget constraints 63
    state share ownership 93
    supervisory boards, role of 97–9,
        101–2
    Tie Fan Wan policy 62, 66
    works units *(Danwei)* 61–2, 252
Stout, L. 261
structure development theories 27
Sun, Y. 56–7
surveys, of CSR developments 184–5,
    253–4
sustainability
    concept development 28, 31–6
    definition 32–3